The Investment Assets Handbook

The Investment Assets Handbook

A definitive practical guide to asset classes

Yoram Lustig

HARRIMAN HOUSE LTD

18 College Street
Petersfield
Hampshire
GU31 4AD
GREAT BRITAIN

Tel: +44 (0)1730 233870
Email: enquiries@harriman-house.com
Website: www.harriman-house.com

First published in Great Britain in 2014

Copyright © Harriman House

The right of Yoram Lustig to be identified as the Author has been asserted in accordance with the Copyright, Design and Patents Act 1988.

ISBN: 9780857194015

British Library Cataloguing in Publication Data
A CIP catalogue record for this book can be obtained from the British Library.

 Harriman House

To Yoav & Yael

Free eBook edition

As a buyer of the print edition of *The Investment Assets Handbook* you can now download the eBook edition free of charge to read on an eBook reader, smartphone or computer. Simply go to:

http://ebooks.harriman-house.com/investmentassets

or point your smartphone at the QRC below.

You can then register and download your eBook copy of the book.

www.harriman-house.com

@harrimanhouse

www.facebook.com/harrimanhouse

www.linkedin.com/company/harriman-house

Contents

About the Author

Yoram Lustig is a multi-asset portfolio manager and author. He has been professionally managing assets since 2002 and writing since 2012.

In 2013 he joined AXA Investment Managers as Head of Multi-Asset Investments (MAI) UK and Deputy Global Head of MAI and has been the lead fund manager of AXA IM Smart Diversified Growth Fund since its launch in April 2014.

From 2009 to 2012, he was Head of Multi-Asset Funds at Aviva Investors, leading the multi-asset team and managing a range of multi-billion pound, multi-asset portfolios, focusing on institutional investors. From 2002 to 2009 he was head of portfolio construction at Merrill Lynch, managing multi-asset discretionary portfolios, focusing on wealthy individuals. He began his career in 1998 as a lawyer, specialising in corporate, financial and commercial law.

Yoram's previous book, *Multi-Asset Investing: A practical guide to modern portfolio management*, was published by Harriman House in 2013,

He was awarded the Chartered Advisor in Philanthropy (CAP) designation in 2007; the Professional Risk Manager (PRM) certification in 2005; the Chartered Financial Analyst (CFA) designation in 2004; an MBA from London Business School in 2002; and a law degree from Tel Aviv University in 1997. He is admitted to both the Israel and New York State Bars. Yoram studied Electrical Engineering for two years in the Technion – Israel Institute of Technology – prior to his military service.

He lives in London, he is married and is a father of two young children.

Disclaimer

The views and opinions expressed in this book are those of the author in his private capacity and do not necessarily reflect those of any organisation or other person.

Acknowledgements

I wish to thank many people. I sincerely thank all the people who were acknowledged in my first book, namely Peter Stanyer, Ben Guyatt, Andrew Keegan, Steve Fedor, Ricardo Fakiera, Roger Matloff, Justin Onuekwusi, Nick Samouilhan, Gavin Counsell, Andrew Ridgers, Jonathan Abrahams, Mirko Cardinale, Adrian Jarvis and Jason Josefs.

The list of dear colleagues from AXA Investment Managers to whom my gratitude is due is too long. Nevertheless, I want to mention a number of people, in no particular order: Serge Pizem, Julien Fourtou, Nigel Richardson, Jaspal Sian, Gaurav Bamania, Fiona Hu, Michele Tursi, Ernst Dolce, Tara Botche, Christoph Metz, Kyra Tilquin, Matthieu Tonneau, Stephane Castillo-Soler, Andrew Etherington, Anne Gagliardini, Brenda Clarke, Daniel Leon, Lionel Gitzinger, Mathieu Maronet, Marc Irvine, Thibaut Ferret, Martin Deux, Christian Borth, Francisco Arcilla, Shane Curran, Ouajnat Karim, Stephanie Condra, Cecile-Agathe Bouchet, Jayne Adair, Christophe Coquema, Tim Gardener, Irshaad Ahmad, Lisa O'Connor, Manisha Patel, Herschel Pant, Sam Berman, Sally Blackney, Martin Powis, Tracey Milner, Mark Yeates, Elodie Laugel, Craig Beach, Mikifumi Watanabe, Chris Iggo, Richard Peirson, Aarnout Snouk Hurgronje, Francois Holleaux, Othmane Laghzaouni, Shiblee Alam, Katharine Dymoke, Erwan Boscher, Jonathan Crowther, Shaj Alam, Fiona Southall, Franz Wenzel, Mathieu L'Hoir, Maxime Alimi and David Page. I could have added even more names, and I have probably forgotten some.

I thank a number of colleagues with whom I had the privilege of working, including Lauren Seyer, Maddi Forester, Andrew Richards, Hugh Ferry, Ashvin Chhabra, Gary Dugan, Dennis Geelan, Paul Sarosy, Robert Belinky, Nick Bartlett, Tony Hubbard and Michael Regy.

I thank the team at Harriman House for their support and partnership, and in particular to Craig Pearce for his editing, creativity and ideas.

I thank again my wife Mika whose endless patience and support enabled me to write a second book. I want to thank my children, Yoav and Yael, and also ask for their forgiveness as I have spent less time with them while working on the books, mainly over weekends and nights.

Before this begins to sound like an acceptance speech at the Oscars, last but certainly not least I thank my readers. They are the reason for writing this book. As J.K. Rowling puts it "no story lives unless someone wants to listen." An author is nothing without his readers.

Preface

The single most critical ability for successful investing is forecasting the future. Alas, most of us cannot forecast the future. The trick then becomes understanding the drivers of investment returns and the distribution of potential outcomes (risk). With this understanding comes the ability to invest in a sensible way, which should deliver a reasonable performance even when the future is unknown.

In my first book, *Multi-Asset Investing: A practical guide to modern portfolio management*,[1] I described the key ingredients for constructing and managing multi-asset portfolios. The book covered top-down asset allocation, bottom-up investment selection and the portfolio construction process of combining assets. The result is a multi-asset portfolio.

However, a sound portfolio is comprised of solid building blocks. The building blocks of a multi-asset portfolio are the single asset classes – not only securities or equities but also different combinations of bonds, cash and alternative investments, and different markets. It is essential for multi-asset investors to understand each single asset class, its interactions with other asset classes, its potential rewards and risks, and its role within a multi-asset portfolio. Without this understanding, they cannot properly construct and manage multi-asset portfolios.

This book describes the underlying single asset classes – the basic building blocks of multi-asset portfolios. The aim is to cover the full spectrum of different asset classes and investment types available today.

The focus of this book

The main objectives of this book are to delve deep into each asset class and describe its main characteristics. This is not to say that what I have done is exhaustive, as a number of books could be written about each single asset class on its own. In this book you will find a thorough background to each asset class and references to additional sources of information.

After all, multi-asset investors should know enough about each asset class to enable them to invest effectively, but they cannot be an expert on each asset.

---

[1] Lustig, Yoram, *Multi-Asset Investing: A practical guide to modern portfolio management* (Harriman House, 2013).

A note on my first book

This volume is independent of my first book, *Multi-Asset Investing*, and can be read on its own. However, the two books complement each other. The first book covers many topics and subjects that are useful in understanding and analysing different asset classes and these are not repeated in this book.

For example, the first book described how to consider the asymmetry of return distributions of some asset classes or adjust their smoothed reported returns due to appraisal-based valuations (relevant particularly to real estate, private equity and some hedge fund strategies). These techniques are important to truly understand the risk and characteristics of some asset classes.

It is recommended, therefore, to read the two books. Readers who are broadly familiar with the mechanics and characteristics of each asset class should start with the first book. Readers who need more background about each asset class are recommended to start with this book. Together the two books should offer a comprehensive background for multi-asset investing, covering the underlying single asset classes and different investment types and techniques.

Book structure

This book is divided into four parts. Part I starts with an introduction and a general discussion about the definition of an asset class, the main features that can be used to characterise an asset class and the roles that different assets fulfil within a multi-asset portfolio.

Part II covers *traditional asset classes*: global equities, fixed income and cash. These classic asset classes are the most well-known, researched and commonly used across portfolios. Reliable data and long histories of returns are normally available for these asset classes. It is relatively easy to pinpoint their roles in portfolios and establish their expected return, risk and correlations with other investments.

Global equities are divided into developed market, emerging market, small capitalisation and frontier market equity. While each equity group has different risk and return characteristics, equities share similar characteristics across the different groups since they all have the same legal structure and features.

Fixed income, on the other hand, is a diverse asset class, having securities with markedly different characteristics and features. Fixed income can also be subdivided into different asset classes, including government bonds, inflation-linked bonds, corporate bonds, high-yield (junk) bonds, global developed bonds and emerging market debt. The second part also looks at two types of hybrid asset classes, convertible bonds and preferred stocks, which share similarities with both equities and fixed income.

Part III covers the four groups of mainstream *alternative investments*: real estate, commodities, private equity and hedge funds. The popularity of these investments has increased over the last two decades. While they are not as well-known and widely used across portfolios as traditional asset classes, there is plenty of data and research covering them.

Most portfolios typically should include alternative investments to improve diversification, expand the investment opportunity set and take advantage of alpha opportunities. Using these investments in portfolios should be the norm, not the exception. While two decades ago these investments were perhaps new, unfamiliar and difficult to access, today there are no such reasons to exclude them from portfolios when they are appropriate for inclusion (e.g. bearing in mind liquidity or price considerations). The days when these types of alternative investments were considered exotic are gone.

Part IV ventures into *new alternative investments*. These investments include currency, infrastructure, structured finance, leveraged loans, structured products, alternative or smart betas, volatility, art, insurance-linked securities and timber. These investments have gained a growing reputation over the last decade because of their development, increasing accessibility and/or investors' continued quest for new and uncorrelated investments.

Most of the new alternative investments are still uncommon in most portfolios and they are not as familiar as the investments covered in the previous three parts. It is challenging to model them because they lack reliable data and long historic track records. However, these investments offer investment opportunities that should not be readily passed up when appropriate. You may find this exploration of less known asset classes and investment types to be the most interesting part of the book.

Each part or chapter of the book can be read on a standalone basis. Readers who are interested only in alternative investments, for example, can focus their attention on this section.

Each asset chapter covers a description of the asset and its characteristics, its historic performance, some ways to model its future long-term performance, why to invest in it (what roles it performs in a multi-asset portfolio), its risks, how to access it and other relevant topics. Some long-term investment themes that may have a material impact on the future behaviour of assets and the nature of investing are also highlighted and discussed.

PART I

INTRODUCTION

What is an asset class?

A simple way to define an asset class is to break it into two single words and examine the definition of each. In the Oxford Dictionary, *asset* is defined as a "useful or valuable thing, person or quality" or "property owned by a person or company, regarded as having value and available to meet debts, commitments or legacies". *Class* is defined as "a set or category of things having some property or attribute in common and differentiated from each other by kind, type or quality".

As per the dictionary, an asset class is a category of valuable things that share common attributes and can be differentiated from other asset classes. Using more financial language, an asset class is defined as a broad group of securities or investments that exhibit similar characteristics, tend to behave similarly during different market conditions and are subject to the same laws, regulations and legal definitions. Each asset class is expected to reflect different risk and return investment characteristics and to perform differently during different market conditions.

A distinction should be made between *assets* and *investment assets*. Assets can be a range of valuable things, such as a smartphone, a car or a dishwasher. Each of these delivers utility to its owner.

Investment assets also deliver utility, but it is a financial or monetary utility. Equities, bonds and cash deposits, for instance, provide dividends, interest and potential capital appreciation. Some investment assets provide more than just monetary utility. Owners can live in their residential property while enjoying possible price appreciation. The focus in this book, of course, is on *investment assets*.

Asset classes can be distinguished in various ways and classified using different classification frameworks. *Traditional asset classes*, typically the most commonly used assets in portfolios, include equities (stocks), bonds (fixed income securities) and cash (including cash equivalents and money market vehicles).

Alternative investments are best classified as non-traditional assets. They include asset classes or investment types such as real estate (often classified as a traditional asset class) and commodities. Private equity is an alternative asset class but is sometimes considered a sub-asset class of equities, which is comprised of publicly traded equities and privately owned equities.

Hedge funds fall under alternative investments, but are not an asset class. Rather, hedge funds have different exposures to different asset classes. They are best described as a series of characteristics, including usually flexible actively managed investment vehicles that use derivatives and investment techniques such as leverage and short selling. Hedge funds are not a separate asset class per se.

Other more esoteric, less common and more ambiguously classified alternative investments include currency, infrastructure, securitised investments (e.g. asset-backed securities (ABS) and mortgage-backed securities (MBS), which can potentially be classified as fixed income), leveraged loans, volatility, art (including different collectibles such as stamps and wine), insurance-linked securities, timber and alternative or smart beta.

Asset class in its broadest definition can include intellectual property (i.e. intangible assets), such as patents, trademarks, copyrights and goodwill. Human capital can be considered an asset as well, since it can be a source of income and it can be valuable. These assets can be included on the balance sheets of corporations or individuals. However, they are not considered investment assets and are therefore out of this book's scope.

Asset classes with a low correlation to the investment opportunity set of traditional or common assets provide the largest diversification benefits within portfolios, and this is one of the drivers in the ongoing quest to find such assets. Financial innovation, such as derivatives and securitisation, technological developments, such as the internet, and falling expected returns and increasing risks of traditional asset classes have resulted in continued expansion of the asset universe. More and more assets and investment types are becoming accessible to investors.

Real and capital assets

Asset classes fall into two broad categories of real assets and financial or capital assets. *Real assets* are things that you can touch; they are tangible. Real estate (i.e. buildings), commodities and art are real assets. *Financial* or *capital assets* are intangible assets, deriving their value because of contractual claims.

These days, financial or capital assets are no longer represented by a piece of paper (e.g. a stock certificate), but rather by information held on computers. Examples include equities, bonds and cash. Capital assets are normally much more liquid than real assets and they are commonly traded on financial markets. Derivatives on commodities and real estate are a transformation of rights on real assets into financial assets.

The economic function of capital assets, such as equities (ownership in companies) and corporate bonds (liabilities of companies), is to raise external resources or financing for companies. Investors in these securities are either the company's shareholders or debt holders, bearing the risk that the future cash flows generated by the company may be lower than expected and may cease to occur during bad times, such as recessions. Investors expect to be compensated for taking such risks. These assets represent the discounted value of future cash flows. Their value depends on the decisions of corporate managers and the commercial fortunes of the issuing company.

Real assets, such as property and commodities, are different; they do not raise financial resources for companies. Rather, property and commodities are the basic resources allowing companies to operate and influence the future value of their outputs (or inputs). Investors in property and commodities receive compensation for bearing the risk of short and long-term property and commodity price fluctuations.

No matter which type the asset is, the common attribute of capital and real assets is that investors in these assets assume risks and expect to be compensated for taking these risks. The types of risks and their levels are different and hence the expected and realised rewards are different. As the distribution of potential outcomes is wider, the risk is higher. According to basic financial theory, when the risk is higher the required potential reward must also be higher to attract investors to assume the risk.

Super asset classes

Robert Greer proposes a classification framework based on three super asset classes: capital assets, consumable/transformable assets and store of value assets:[2]

- *Capital assets*, such as equities, bonds and real estate, generate a stream of cash flows and their value can be measured by calculating the present value of these cash flows.[3]

- *Consumable/transformable assets*, such as commodities, do not generate a stream of future cash flows, but rather a single cash flow when they are sold or utility when they are consumed.

- *Store of value assets*, such as currency and art, do not generate cash flows and cannot be consumed, but still they have a monetary value.

The borders separating super asset classes may sometimes be blurry. For example, precious metals, such as gold, are both consumable/transformable and store of value assets.

Income and price appreciation

The reason for investing in assets or investments is to generate returns. Total returns are made up of two components: *income* and *price appreciation*. Some

[2] Greer, Robert, 'What is an Asset Class Anyway?', *The Journal of Portfolio Management* (1997).
[3] Present value models calculate today's value of future cash flows. The model requires the value and timing of future cash flows and the appropriate interest rate or discount factor to calculate their present value. The discount factor reflects the risk of the assets or cash flows and the time value of money.

assets are more focused on generating income, such as fixed income investments. Other assets do not generate any income and their return is solely dependent on potential price appreciation. Commodities and art are examples of investments that do not generate income. Most assets, such as equities, deliver a combination of income (e.g. dividends) and potential price or capital appreciation.

Income is usually more reliable and predictable than price appreciation. For some assets, such as government or corporate bonds, income payments are mandatory contractual obligations and will be paid as long as the issuer can make the payments.

Potential price appreciation, as it says, is only a *potential*. It depends on the prevailing price of the asset as determined by market forces (supply and demand) at the time that the asset is sold.

Income is a positive *nominal* return, albeit it can fall to zero; for example, if a company stops paying dividends on its stock or defaults on its debt obligations. *Real* income can be negative due to inflation. Price appreciation can be negative (i.e. price depreciation).

Where price appreciation is a larger component in the total return of an asset, the larger is the risk of a negative total return, all else being equal. Because of the relatively lower risk of income compared to price appreciation, as income becomes a larger component in the total return of an asset, the lower becomes the total expected return, all else being equal.

Income is a significant component of total returns and as the investment horizon becomes longer, income becomes a more dominant component of total return over capital appreciation.[4] Gold, for example, as a non-income producing asset, typically falls short of equities and real estate in the long term primarily because of its lack of income.

Income can provide an element of a lower-risk return compared to capital appreciation and income-producing assets can offer more stable returns over time. This means income can be regarded as a buffer or a safety net. Capital appreciation, on the other hand, can offer material potential returns – capital appreciation is a potential growth engine. Assets can be distinguished, therefore, by their income and price appreciation characteristics.

Risk and conservative assets

A helpful framework for classifying assets is by *risk assets* (growth assets) and *conservative assets* (safe assets). Risk assets, as their name implies, have a higher level of risk compared to conservative assets. The challenge is how to define risk and how to measure risk.

---

[4] The present value of the terminal value (selling price) is lower as the investment horizon is longer.

Different assets entail different types and levels of risk. Risk is a multifaceted concept and includes different factors and measures. The three main risk categories are market risk, credit risk and operational risk.

Investment risk is usually measured by volatility of returns. Volatility measures the dispersion of returns without differentiating between unwanted returns below the mean and wanted returns above the mean. Downside risk measures, such as Value at Risk (VaR), focus on the negative, bad returns. When returns are symmetric, volatility is typically strongly associated with downside risk.

Liquidity risk is yet another dimension of risk that is not necessarily captured by volatility. Some illiquid assets, such as real estate, appear to have low volatility because their returns are smoothed due to appraisal-based valuations that are anchored to the last known prices. However, considering only the volatility of real estate's past returns, without considering liquidity risk and transaction costs, may be very deceiving and can conceal the real risks of real estate investing.

Using *volatility* as a measure of risk, the obvious risk assets include equities, high-yield bonds, emerging market debt (EMD), commodities, private equity and aggressive hedge fund strategies. The obvious conservative assets include government bonds of selected safe-haven countries, investment grade corporate bonds of established corporations, cash and conservative hedge fund strategies.

Ambiguous assets whose definition is not clear-cut or can change with time include government bonds of governments whose credit rating has deteriorated (e.g. Portugal, Ireland, Italy, Greece and Spain), corporate bonds of corporations falling from grace (e.g. Lehman Brothers), real estate, and hedge fund strategies whose style may drift. Foreign government bonds whose currency risk is not hedged can be a risk asset because of the volatility of exchange rates, while they can be a conservative asset for investors whose base currency is that of the bonds.

Using *liquidity* as a measure of risk the classification of assets as risky or conservative may dramatically change. Real estate is clearly a risk asset. Equities, in particular large capitalisation[5] stocks within developed countries, are a conservative asset. Government bonds, one of the most liquid assets, remain conservative. However, corporate bonds may turn into risk assets, depending on liquidity of specific issuers and market conditions. As we can see, asset classification is fluid and can change based on the risk metric and market conditions.

The presence of *liabilities* or investment objectives can also change the classification of assets. When investors have a stream of liabilities with a long duration, cash may be a risk asset because of its mismatch with liabilities. Government bonds or inflation-linked bonds with a matching duration to that of liabilities are the conservative assets.

---

[5] Market capitalisation is calculated by multiplying the market price per share by the number of outstanding shares.

When the investment objective is maintaining the purchasing power of assets over the long term (i.e. keeping pace with inflation), cash and government bonds are risk assets. Inflation-linked bonds are the conservative assets.

The overall point here is that asset classification is typically not general and applicable to all situations and circumstances. Classification is circumstance-dependent. Investors should consider the specific situation when thinking about how to classify assets.

Alpha and beta

Another type of asset or investment includes *strategies* that aim to benefit from *skilful active management*, or alpha. For example, hedge funds are classic skill-based investments whose attractiveness relies on manager skill. The reason that hedge funds command high fees is that investors pay for talent.

Another example is private equity. This asset heavily depends on the manager's skill to select and invest in private companies that turn out to be successful. Skill, expertise and intuition are needed to identify infant companies that will mature into success stories as opposed to those that are doomed to fail. Lacking skill, there is no point investing in hedge funds and private equity.

Not all assets require manager skill. Assets can be classified by their risk factor or *beta* exposures. Beta exposure delivers a natural return; it does not require skill (alpha) and can be accessed through paying relatively low fees and typically at a low cost. Beta exposures are market or systematic exposures and can be measured by the sensitivity of assets to equity markets, interest rates, inflation, credit spreads, volatilities, currencies and other systematic risk factors. Multi-factor models can measure the exposures of assets to different betas, and assets can be classified according to these sensitivities.

Taking it one step further, different betas can be considered as different assets. Assets such as equities, bonds and cash can be considered as conduits to gain exposure to different bundles of betas.[6] Under this classification framework the role of asset allocation is to diversify the portfolio across betas (risk factors) and determine the exposure to each beta. Multi-asset portfolios are turned into multi-beta portfolios.

Asset classes should have an inherent non-skill based return (beta), which distinguishes them from investment strategies like hedge funds that are not considered separate asset classes. This implies that asset classes are only those that can be accessed through passive investments. However, there are some assets in the alternative space, such as real estate and infrastructure, that are still considered asset classes but cannot be passively accessed.

---

[6] If the same risk factors are priced identically in two assets then they are integrated.

Smart beta strategies fall between alpha and beta. They alter the normal beta exposure of traditional assets by applying systematic construction methodologies (e.g. equally weighting equities instead of market-cap weighting), and include systematic, rule-based investment tilts, or benefit from persistent market anomalies (e.g. underweight high-beta stocks) that should deliver superior returns over time. Smart beta strategies are often designed to harvest risks that are rewarded by risk premiums. Smart beta aims to outperform passive investments at lower fees than those of actively managed investments.

Sub-asset classes

Asset classes can be further divided into sub-asset classes. Equities can be sliced and diced by market capitalisation (small, mid, large cap) and investment style (value and growth). Each combination (e.g. large cap value, large cap growth, small cap value, small cap growth) may be regarded as a separate sub-asset class.

Global equities can be divided into regions: North America, United Kingdom, Europe excluding UK, Pacific excluding Japan, Japan, emerging market equities and so on. Global equities or equities within each region can then be divided into sectors.[7] These sub-asset classes, while sharing some similarities, can be differentiated to justify different categorisations.

Taking another asset example, global bonds can be divided by type of issuer (sovereigns of developed country, sovereigns of developing country, corporates), features (nominal, inflation-linked, fixed rate, floating rate, non-callable, callable), credit ranking (investment grade, below investment grade, high-yield or junk) and maturity (short, intermediate, long). With ten to 20 asset classes, each divided into sub-asset classes, the number of choices investors face is enormous.

Criteria for asset classes

Not each type or group of investments can be classified as an asset class. To be an asset class a group of investments needs to meet six criteria:[8]

1. *Same type*. The investments need to be the same type of securities. The investments within the group should be relatively homogenous and share similar attributes.

2. *High correlation*. The correlation among the different investments needs to be high.

---

[7] The Global Classification Standard (GICS) was developed by MSCI and Standard & Poor's and classifies public equities by ten sectors: energy, materials, industrials, consumer discretionary, consumer staples, health care, financials, information technology, telecommunications services and utilities.

[8] Partially based on Maginn, John, Tuttle, Donald, McLeavey, Dennis and Pinto, Jerald, *Managing Investment Portfolios: A Dynamic Process*, 3rd ed. (John Wiley & Sons, 2007).

3. *Material size.* The size of the group of investments needs to be material. That is, an asset class as a group of investments should make up a preponderance of the world's investable wealth.

4. *Reliable data.* The group of investments needs to have a reliable set of data.

5. *Accessible passively.* The group of investments needs to be accessed passively (i.e. the performance of the group can be indexed).

6. *Exclusive.* The group of investments needs to be exclusive. Different asset classes should be mutually exclusive and not overlapping.

According to these criteria, hedge funds, for instance, are clearly not an asset class. They invest in different types of securities, the correlation between different hedge fund strategies can be low or even negative, available data is lacking, passive access to hedge funds is limited and hedge funds as a group are not exclusive since some provide exposure to other asset classes or combinations of other asset classes. The only criterion that hedge funds meet is that their share of the global investable universe is material. Passing a single criterion out of six is insufficient to be classified as an asset class.

Global equities, on the other hand, are clearly an asset class. They include the same type of securities (common stocks). While the correlation among single equities may diverge, when grouped together equity markets have a relatively high correlation. The size of global equities is huge, they have one of the most reliable sets of data, they can be easily accessible passively and they are exclusive. Global equities meet all six criteria.

Classification of assets

There are different ways to classify asset classes (income or price appreciation generator, risk or conservative asset, alpha or beta return provider). The classification of assets is often subjective and depends on the specific circumstances and overall portfolio to which the asset belongs. The classification helps investors to better understand each asset. Whatever classification is used, the important aspect is to understand the role that each asset or investment plays in the overall portfolio. As Peter Lynch put it, "Know what you own, and know why you own it."

Investing in portfolio context

Multi-asset investing is about combining less than perfectly correlated sources of beta with sources of alpha to increase the likelihood of meeting the portfolio's investment objectives. As described earlier, *beta* refers to returns driven by systematic market risks, such as equity, credit and maturity risks, or fundamental macroeconomic factors such as GDP growth, interest rates and inflation. These returns correspond to the returns of major asset classes, such as equities, bonds and commodities.

Each asset class should provide exposure to betas that are less than perfectly correlated with the betas offered by other asset classes. Therefore, combining as many asset classes with different beta exposures as possible delivers the widest investment opportunity set and risk reduction through diversification.

Alpha refers to skill-based returns. These returns are generated by investment managers' active decisions of market timing and security selection. Skill-based investments are commonly called strategies.

Since each investment manager generates a unique alpha, investors can choose from a virtually infinite number of alphas. Unlike beta, alpha is a zero-sum game. The excess returns that one investor generates through successful investment decisions come at the expense of another investor. Opposite every winning side there is a losing side.

Strategic asset allocation (SAA), or beta allocation, determines the long-term exposures to the various assets in the investment opportunity set. The objective of SAA is to harvest beta returns. The SAA decision is separate from the investment selection decision or alpha decision. Once the SAA is set, the investment selection decision fills each asset class with products or specific investments to implement the SAA.

In addition to beta and alpha sources of return, a third source of return is *liquidity premium*. Liquidity premium compensates investors for investing in investments that are not frequently traded. The magnitude of the liquidity premium depends on the holding horizon (i.e. the longer the lock-up, the longer the expected compensation) and on the volatility of the underlying asset. For example, the liquidity premium of private equity is expected to be higher than that of real estate.

Different assets combine beta, alpha and liquidity sources of risk and return. For example, an exchange traded fund (ETF) on liquid US large cap stocks generates beta return. An actively managed fund investing in US large cap stocks generates a combination of beta and alpha returns. A US private equity fund generates a combination of beta (exposure to the US public equity market), alpha (manager skill) and liquidity premium returns.

The returns and risks of each asset are therefore different. Investing in illiquid assets entails significant downside risk since these assets can quickly lose value during liquidity shocks. Investing in alpha entails manager or selection risk (i.e. negative alpha) and forecasting risk since forecasting short-term alpha return is less certain than forecasting long-term beta return. Investing in beta entails market risk since markets can fall and without active management the investments will fall with markets (investments can fall more than markets with unsuccessful active management).

Investors need to understand the beta, alpha and liquidity risk and return drivers of each asset to be able to construct portfolios that instead of allocating across assets, allocate across imperfectly correlated underlying sources of risk and return. This is the key to constructing truly diversified portfolios as opposed to portfolios that are merely varied and not diversified. Varied portfolios invest in different investments that are highly correlated and therefore may seem diversified but are not truly so.

The global market portfolio

The investment opportunity set should include as many assets as possible that make up the unobservable global *market portfolio*,[9] which is included in modern portfolio theory's capital asset pricing model (CAPM). The market portfolio is a portfolio consisting of a weighted sum of every asset in the market, with weights in the proportions in which they exist in the market.

According to modern portfolio theory (MPT), the market portfolio has the most efficient or optimal risk and return trade-off of any possible portfolio. The market portfolio consists of the entire investment opportunity set. The investment opportunity set should include all assets that are non-overlapping and mutually exclusive.

The global market portfolio is not investable in practice. It is only a theoretical concept, as a true global market portfolio needs to include every single possible available asset, including real estate, precious metals, stamp collections, jewellery, intellectual property and anything with any worth (as per *Roll's Critique*).[10] While not achievable in practice, investors can aim to include as many assets as possible to get as close as possible to the global market portfolio. The first step in combining all possible assets is to really understand them.

To understand the characteristics of each asset investors need to get to know them, get familiar with them, understand their return behaviours and risks, and grasp the unique beta exposures that they provide, as well as their potential alpha and liquidity premium. Then, assets can be smartly combined into portfolios with the widest possible investment opportunity set and proper risk-reducing diversification. The result is a portfolio sitting on the highest possible, most efficient point on the efficient frontier. According to financial theory, this is what each rational investor should strive to do.

Investing in portfolio context is treating each investment as part of a collection of different investments. Each investment is not held on its own on a standalone

---

[9] The global market portfolio is a theoretical portfolio consisting of every asset in the market, with each asset weighted in proportion to its total value in the market. The expected return of the market portfolio is identical to the expected return of the market as a whole. Because a market portfolio is completely diversified, it is exposed only to systematic risk (market risk) and not to unsystematic risk (idiosyncratic risk).

[10] Roll, Richard, 'A Critique of the Asset Pricing Theory's Tests', *Journal of Financial Economics* 4 (1977).

basis, but it is part of a combination of different investments. The risk and return characteristics of each asset, therefore, should be considered in isolation, to understand the asset, and as part of an overall portfolio combining a number of assets, to understand how each asset interacts and works together with the others. The key to understanding assets in a portfolio context is to know how they behave as a group, how to combine them, how they impact on the portfolio's risk and return, and which role each asset fulfils.

The important risk metric in portfolio context is marginal contribution to risk and the important return metric is return contribution. Investors need to assess how each investment impacts the return and risk of the entire portfolio.

While equities are a risk asset on a standalone basis, when adding a small equity allocation to a fixed income portfolio the risk of the portfolio can actually decrease because of diversification. The marginal contribution to risk of equities can be negative. This example highlights the importance of assessing assets in portfolio context.

Asset allocation

Long-term capital market assumptions (CMAs) have the strongest predictive power. SAA can relatively accurately predict expected return and risk over the next five to ten years, compared to tactical asset allocation (TAA) and security selection which aim to predict market and security returns over the short term. SAA, therefore, should normally set the long-term asset allocation or investment policy as this has the highest likelihood of meeting the portfolio's investment objective with minimum risk.

Since SAA looks at least five years ahead and does not consider the potential circumstances over the next year or few months, tactical views should adjust the long-term SAA to short-term risks and opportunities. If the United States and China were about to begin World War III, for example, SAA may still expect equities to generate 8% per year, but TAA may say sell equities now. TAA looks at what SAA does not see.

However, generating TAA views is more inaccurate than doing so for those of SAA. Accurately generating tactical views is challenging. There are many incorrect investment decisions. However, one or two right decisions at the right time when the market begins to plunge or when scarce opportunities present themselves may be all it takes to make the difference. This is the importance of TAA. Dynamic asset allocation is the key and dynamic asset allocation is all about shifting the allocation of the portfolio across different assets at the right time and magnitude. Successful dynamic asset allocation depends on understanding the dynamism of assets. Through asset allocation assets are managed in portfolio context.

The roles of assets in portfolios

Every asset in a portfolio should have a clear role. There must be a valid reason for investing in each investment. If the investor does not know the reason for holding an asset it should not be included in the portfolio.

The six valid roles for including investments in portfolios are:

1. Generating returns.

2. Generating income.

3. Matching liabilities.

4. Hedging.

5. Protecting.

6. Diversifying.

The objective of generating returns is the reason for investing – making money. Investments can generate returns through exposure to a risk premium (beta) and/or through skill-based return generation (alpha). Most assets can play a role of generating returns.

The objective of generating income is a subset of generating total returns. Portfolios' investment objectives can include an income element and some investments generate a stream of income in the form of interest payments (e.g. bonds), dividends (e.g. equities), or other forms of income (e.g. rental income from real estate).

The objective of matching liabilities is to reduce the risk that cash is unavailable for meeting obligations as they fall due. Liability matching is dominated by fixed income investments (e.g. government bonds) and derivatives that synthetically replicate the characteristics of fixed income investments (e.g. interest rate and inflation swaps) because liabilities behave like short positions in fixed income. When buying a bond, investors receive cash inflows in the form of interest payments and repayment of the principal at maturity. A liability is the opposite; the debtor pays interest and the principal at maturity to the creditor. In this sense, a liability is equivalent to a loan of a bond issuer. Hence, liabilities can be modelled as short bond positions.

The objective of hedging is to reduce or eliminate a certain risk in a portfolio. Hedging is most commonly achieved through derivatives. For example, equity risk can be mitigated through a short futures position on the equity index with similar characteristics to those of the holdings whose risk is mitigated. Often, hedging does not entail the transaction costs as does selling the underlying holdings.

The objective of protecting is to generate a return during certain scenarios when other assets in the portfolio are expected to perform poorly. For example, government bonds are expected to perform well when risk assets fall because of a flight to quality. Protective assets include government bonds, gold, managed futures, safe haven currencies, such as US dollar and Japanese yen, and tail hedging strategies.

The objective of diversification is to reduce the portfolio's risk. The fundamental reason behind multi-asset investing is that different assets have different exposure to beta risks and their alphas, if they have any, are normally less than perfectly correlated with each other and with the other betas. Therefore, combining different assets reduces idiosyncratic risk. Alternative investments usually offer betas that are different to those of traditional assets, as well as alpha and liquidity premiums. They expand the universe of sources of returns and enhance diversification.

There may be other roles for investments in portfolios that are not valid from an investment perspective. Seeding new products, investing in products to support the relationship with their sponsor (e.g. personal favour), investing for emotional utility (e.g. an antique car collection), or including investments because of their marketing appeal, are a few examples of non-investment reasons. Such investments may be valid from a commercial or personal perspective but they may not have a valid investment rationale.

Before making any investment, investors should ask themselves, "What is the role of the investment in the portfolio?" If there is no clear answer, perhaps the investment should be avoided. Adding unnecessary investments may increase complexity and costs without adding benefits.

Summary

- This book focuses on single asset classes and different investment types. Multi-asset investors must understand these asset classes and investments since they are the basic foundations or building blocks of multi-asset portfolios.

- An asset class is defined as a broad group of securities or investments that exhibit similar characteristics, tend to behave similarly during different market conditions, are subject to the same laws, regulations and legal definitions, and are expected to reflect different risk and return investment characteristics.

- Assets can be classified as traditional investments (equities, fixed income and cash) and alternative investments (real estate, commodities, private equity, hedge funds and so on).

- Assets with a low correlation to the investment opportunity set of traditional assets provide the largest diversification benefits within portfolios.

- Assets can be classified as real assets and financial or capital assets. Capital assets are used by corporations for financing (e.g. stocks are the company's shareholder equity and bonds are the company's liabilities). Real assets are tangible and typically used as resources in the operations of corporations.

- The three super asset classes are capital assets, consumable/transformable assets and store of value assets.

- Total return is made of income and price appreciation. Different assets deliver different combinations of income and potential price appreciation.

- The classification of assets into risk and conservative assets is a helpful framework and depends on the risk metric (e.g. volatility, liquidity), presence of liabilities and investment objectives.

- Another type of asset includes strategies that aim to benefit from skilful active management (alpha), such as hedge funds and private equity.

- Assets can be classified by their risk factor or beta exposures. Each asset provides an exposure to a bundle of different betas or risk factors.

- Asset classes can be further divided into sub-asset classes (cap size, investment style, regions).

- The six criteria for an investment group to meet for it to be considered an asset class are: same type of securities; high correlation among investments; material size of investment group; reliable data; can be passively accessed; and exclusive.

- Multi-asset investing is all about combining less than perfectly correlated sources of beta with sources of alpha to increase the likelihood of meeting the portfolio's investment objectives.

- Different assets combine beta, alpha and liquidity premium sources of risk and return.

- Investors need to understand the beta, alpha and liquidity risk and return drivers of each asset to be able to construct portfolios that allocate across the underlying sources of risk and return instead of allocating across assets.

- The investment opportunity set should include as many assets as possible that make up the unobservable global market portfolio, which is included in Modern Portfolio Theory's capital asset pricing model (CAPM). While the global market portfolio is not achievable in practice, investors can aim to include as many assets as possible to get as close as possible to it.

- The key to understanding assets in portfolio context is to know how they behave as a group, how to combine them, how they impact the portfolio's risk and which role each asset fulfils.

- The important risk metric in portfolio context is marginal contribution to risk and the important return metric is return contribution. Investors need to assess how each investment impacts the return and risk of the entire portfolio.

- The reasons for including investments in portfolios include: generating returns; generating income; matching liabilities; hedging; protecting; and diversifying.

PART II

TRADITIONAL ASSET CLASSES

INTRODUCTION

Traditional assets are long-established investments, including equities (stocks), fixed income (bonds) and cash. Old-fashioned balanced funds mainly invest in these traditional assets, while modern multi-asset portfolios go beyond traditional assets and add alternative investments (e.g. real estate, hedge funds, private equity and commodities). Yet, traditional assets still commonly make up the core exposure of modern portfolios.

Traditional assets are relatively easy to model for strategic asset allocation and they are the most readily accessible assets. These assets are represented by established, published and typically investable indices, such as the S&P 500, MSCI World and FTSE 100 indices for equities, Barclays, FTSE and iBoxx[11] indices for fixed income and LIBOR for cash.

When an index representing an asset is available, it is easy to use historic returns and forward-looking matrices, such as yields (i.e. dividend yield and bond yield to maturity), to model the asset for asset allocation purposes. Passive vehicles that track the indices (beta exposure) or active portfolios that try to beat them (beta plus alpha exposure) are normally available, so accessing these assets is straightforward. All of this means traditional assets are readily included in portfolios.

Unbundling traditional asset classes

Traditional assets are not only the most basic building blocks of portfolios, but they also enable investors to expose their portfolios to most systematic beta exposures or risk factors. Equity market risk, interest rate risk, credit risk, inflation risk and currency risk can all be accessed through traditional assets and their combinations. Through sub-asset classes it is possible to gain exposure to the next level of risk factors, such as equity small cap, equity value, emerging market equity, frontier equity and below investment grade credit.

An intuitive analogy describing the relationship between risk factors and investments is that "factor risk is reflected in different assets just as nutrients are obtained by eating different foods. Peas, wheat, and rice all have fibre. Similarly, certain sovereign bonds, corporate bonds, equities and credit default swap

---

[11] www.markit.com.

derivatives all have exposure to credit risk. Assets are bundles of different types of factors just as foods contain different combinations of nutrients".[12]

Four or five underlying risk factors can explain approximately 70% of the variation of returns of most liquid assets.[13] By unbundling assets into their risk factors investors can really control the exposures and asset allocation of their portfolios. Because traditional assets are represented by published indices with an established track record, a multi-factor model can easily be used for risk factor analysis to identify the underlying investment risks that explain the return variation of each asset class or a portfolio. In this sense, traditional assets can be considered as conduits to gain access to risk factors.

According to finance theory, certain systematic risks should be compensated by the market with long-term rewards or risk premiums. Equity risk premium, maturity premium, credit premium and liquidity premium are the most basic examples. These beta exposures attract returns to compensate investors for assuming the systematic risks without the need for manager alpha or payments of high fees. Hence, constructing portfolios of diversified systematic risk exposures can deliver long-term, finely-tuned, risk controlled returns. Investors should harvest the long-term returns that risk premiums deliver.

Traditional asset classes

This part of the book covers traditional assets. We will start with global equities, which can be divided into developed, emerging market and frontier market equities. Next, fixed income will be reviewed. The fixed income universe is heterogeneous and includes government bonds, inflation-linked bonds, corporate bonds, high-yield bonds, global developed bonds and emerging market debt.

Part II continues with reviewing two hybrid asset classes: convertible bonds and preferred stocks. These two classes sit on the border between equities and fixed income. Finally, Part II ends with a review of cash and cash-equivalents.

Summary

- Traditional asset classes include equities, fixed income and cash.

- Old fashioned balanced funds mainly invest in traditional assets while modern multi-asset portfolios invest in alternative investments as well. Nevertheless, traditional assets still normally make up the lion's share of all portfolios.

---

[12] Ang, Andrew, 'The Four Benchmarks of Sovereign Wealth Funds', Columbia Business School and NBER (September 2010).

[13] Bhansali, Vineer, 'Beyond Risk Parity', *The Journal of Investing* 20 (2011).

- It is relatively easy to model traditional assets for asset allocation purposes since they have reliable, published indices with long track records. It is also relatively easy to access traditional assets either via actively managed or passive vehicles.

- Through traditional assets investors can access most systematic beta exposures or risk factors.

- Traditional assets can be considered as conduits to gain access to risk factors. Each asset is a basket of different risk factors.

- Assets can be unbundled to their risk factors through multi-factor models and investors can control the exposure of their portfolios to risk factors that should be compensated by long-term risk premiums.

- Equity risk premium, maturity premium, credit premium and liquidity premium are the most basic examples for traditional risk premiums.

CHAPTER 1: GLOBAL EQUITIES

Global equities are the core investment in most portfolios. Equities are the basic fundamental risk or growth asset, exposing portfolios to the equity risk factor and consequently to the equity risk premium (ERP). Equities are therefore the most common risk asset in portfolios and as the risk level of portfolios increases, so does the allocation to equities. The main role of equities in portfolios is delivering long-term growth (i.e. capital appreciation).

What are equities?

Equity, or stock, represents ownership of shares in publicly[14] traded companies and offers participation in the commercial and financial fortunes of businesses, including their profits (earnings), dividends and the potential growth in the value of their tangible and intangible (intellectual property) assets. Equity holders own part of the company and its business.

The management of companies is tasked, in theory, to increase shareholder value by acting in the best interest of equity holders (shareholders) through undertaking projects with a positive Net Present Value (NPV).[15] The holders of common stock have voting rights to select the company's Board of Directors, which oversees and governs the activity of the company and selects its Chief Executive Officer (CEO), and vote at shareholder general meetings, including Annual General Meetings (AGMs) and Extraordinary General Meetings (EGMs).

Through their voting rights, shareholders nominate management and can influence the way the company is managed. However, to make a material impact on the company's management a shareholder needs to own a material proportion of the company's stocks, unless many shareholders vote in concert.

Equity holders have a residual ownership claim to the assets of a company upon liquidation, after it satisfies obligations to its debt holders. That is, shareholders reside at the bottom of the company's capital structure. If a company is liquidated (i.e. it ceases to exist) its assets are sold and the proceeds are used to satisfy claims according to the legal priority of claims. The order of claims is usually the company's creditors

---

[14] Private equity, in contrast to public equity, is not traded publicly on stock exchanges.

[15] NPV is the sum of the present values of the individual cash inflows (earnings) minus outflows (expenses).

with a fixed charge over assets, employees, creditors with a floating charge over assets and unsecured creditors. If any proceeds are left after satisfying the claims of all senior claimants, then they are paid to the company's shareholders. Holders of preferred shares have a priority over holders of common stocks.

Investing in one stock is investing in one company or one business. Investing in an equity index, such as the S&P 500 or FTSE 100, is respectively an investment in the 500 or 100 largest businesses in a country. Since these businesses reflect the wide economy, investing in the index is like investing in the economy.

Equities are like a large discounting machine that discounts the market views on the future prospects of each company and the general economy. In the short term the prices of equities are greatly affected by sentiment. Over the long term they are more affected by fundamentals. Benjamin Graham described this situation as follows: "In the short run the market is a voting machine but in the long run it is a weighing machine."

Drivers of equity returns

The returns delivered by equities consist of two elements: changes in the price of equity (i.e. the difference between the purchasing price and the selling price), and the dividends that equities may pay to shareholders. Equity prices and returns of equity are influenced by a number of factors.

Company fundamentals

Equity holders are exposed to the commercial achievements or failures of the company as they are reflected in the fundamentals of the company's commercial and business results.

Company fundamentals include earnings (after-tax net profits) and the cash flows that are paid to shareholders in the form of dividends. When the company does well and it is profitable, earnings are positive. The earnings can be either reinvested in the business to support and grow it (retained earnings) or distributed to shareholders. The two ways to distribute earnings are either share repurchase (reducing the number of shares so each remaining shareholder holds a larger stake in the company) or dividends.

Fundamental analysis looks at the economics of the company's business, the balance sheet, the income statement (profit & loss (P&L)), cash flows, quality of management, industry analysis and business strategy[16] to try to determine

---

[16] One example for a framework for industry analysis and business strategy is Porter's five forces analysis: Threat of new competition, threat of substitute products or services, bargaining power of customers, bargaining power of suppliers and intensity of competitive rivalry. Porter, Michael, 'The Five Competitive Forces that Shape Strategy', *Harvard Business Review* (2008).

whether the company is likely to do better or worse in the future. The challenge is to correctly forecast the future situation of the company since this will drive its equity returns. The current situation and the past are already reflected, or priced into, the current equity price.

Commonly, equity prices are driven by the results of companies relative to expectations. If, for example, the expectations were for a company to generate a certain profit and the results are still a positive profit but below expectations, equity prices may fall. The reason is that the expectations are priced into equity prices and disappointing results revise prices downward. Results above expectations, even if the company announces a loss, may result in its equity price rising.

Since equity prices reflect forward-looking, expected company fundamentals, a good company does not necessarily mean a good stock. A company's past success is already reflected in its share price. If the fundamentals deteriorate or disappoint relative to expectations and the share price is already high, it may drop. Also, a high share price means less room for high future returns. For an expensive stock to become even more expensive the company needs to do well. The stock price increases only if the expected commercial fortunes of the issuing company improve.

Peter Lynch summarised this as follows: "I think you have to learn that there's a company behind every stock, and that there's only one real reason why stocks go up. Companies go from doing poorly to doing well or small companies grow to large companies."

Valuation

Valuations come in the form of multiples (price to earnings (P/E), cash flows, sales or book value (P/B)) that investors are willing to pay for the company's equity. For example, a P/E of 10 means that the equity price reflects ten years of annual earnings per share (EPS). Valuation reflects the price that the market currently assigns to the equity; not necessarily the true or intrinsic value of the equity. Valuations focus on the price of equities relative to that of other companies at the same time or relative to the historic price of the company's equity, while fundamentals focus on the equity's intrinsic value (i.e. the worth of the business divided by the number of shares). While price is available and visible on a daily basis, intrinsic value needs to be calculated or estimated.

Market exposure

Market exposure is the name for the general macro-economic factors that affect equity prices across the market (e.g. interest rates and economic growth). Investing in each stock is like making two investments: one in the company that issues the stock and a second in the general equity market. While company-specific risk (idiosyncratic risk) can be diversified away through proper diversification, the equity market risk (systematic or undiversifiable risk) cannot be diversified away by investing only in equities. It is recommended to hold at least 30 stocks to diversify idiosyncratic risk.

Market exposure is often measured by the beta of the stock with respect to the general market. According to finance theory (Modern Portfolio Theory and CAPM) investors are rewarded only for assuming market risk, not stock-specific risk, since the latter can be easily removed through diversification. According to theory, markets do not compensate investors for taking unnecessary risks.

The link between economic conditions and equity returns is not always straightforward. While many investors focus on forecasting the GDP growth rate with the aim of predicting equity returns, higher economic growth does not necessarily mean higher equity returns, especially in the long run. High wealth generation as measured by real per capita GDP growth does not necessarily mean higher real equity returns. A country becoming richer does not always translate into higher equity returns.[17]

The first reason is that stock prices reflect anticipated business conditions. So it is future economic growth, not past economic growth, that drives equity prices. A second reason is that equities of growing countries are becoming less risky and hence their returns are lower. Distressed economies turning around should come with bigger rewards as compensation for larger risks. The third reason is that the price of equities in growing economies has been bid up. The last reason is luck. Countries with strong GDP growth rates have limited upside. Countries with a weak GDP growth rate have limited downside and remarkable upside.

Inflation

Equities offer some degree of purchasing power protection. Equities represent claims against real assets, such as factories, equipment and inventories, whose value is expected to keep pace with inflation. Normally, companies increase the prices of the goods and services that they sell in line with rising costs of raw materials used in production to keep their profit margin in line with inflation. Therefore, in theory, rising prices of goods and services should be reflected in equity prices over the long term. However, companies have contracts with suppliers of inputs, labour and capital that are usually fixed in nominal terms. Therefore, these contracts act much like nominal bonds (i.e. they are not adjusted for inflation). In addition, unexpected inflation is associated with negative shocks to aggregate output, which is generally bad news for equities.[18] Hence, stocks do not necessarily provide a good hedge against inflation, in particular unexpected inflation.

---

[17] Dimson, Elroy, Marsh, Paul and Staunton, Mike, 'The growth puzzle', *Credit Suisse Global Investment Returns Yearbook 2014*.

[18] Fama, Eugene, 'Stock Returns, Real Activities, Inflation and Money', *American Economic Review* 71 (1981).

Sentiment

Psychological factors in the form of investors' views on macro- and micro-economic prospects are likely to affect equity prices. These influence the expected market return (beta) imbedded in each equity return and the equity risk premium (ERP) that compensates investors for taking equity market risk over lower risk assets, such as government bonds or cash.

Fear and greed are powerful forces in the equity market. When fear is high, the ERP is high (fearful investors demand higher compensation for taking risk) and equity prices drop to adjust for the higher expected returns (a lower price means potential higher future returns as the starting point is lower). The opposite occurs when greed takes over and investors are willing to assume more risk: they accept lower compensation for assuming risk, the ERP is lower and stock prices can go higher. When equity prices go too high, far above valuations, it usually ends with a crash or a correction. Sentiment is volatile and greed can quickly turn into fear.

John Maynard Keynes used the term *animal spirits* back in 1936[19] to describe emotions that influence human behaviour and which can be measured in terms of consumer confidence. As Keynes described it:

> "Even apart from the instability due to speculation, there is the instability due to the characteristic of human nature that a large proportion of our positive activities depend on spontaneous optimism rather than mathematical expectations, whether moral or hedonistic or economic. Most, probably, of our decisions to do something positive, the full consequences of which will be drawn out over many days to come, can only be taken as the result of animal spirits – a spontaneous urge to action rather than inaction, and not as the outcome of a weighted average of quantitative benefits multiplied by quantitative probabilities."

In August 2007 investment bank State Street Global Markets said, "Market participants don't know whether to buy on the rumour and sell on the news, do the opposite, do both, or do nothing, depending on which way the wind is blowing." This is a perfect explanation of what sentiment is. Supply and demand, which set equity prices, are driven by emotional human beings, whose actions can be driven by irrational exuberance and panic.

Liquidity

The level of liquidity in the economy can affect equity prices. Policy makers (e.g. central banks) set monetary and fiscal policies that define general liquidity. When interest rates are low and money is cheap, investors have more to invest, including in equities. Typically liquidity is high when policy makers aim to stimulate the

---

[19] Keynes, John Maynard, *The General Theory of Employment, Interest and Money* (1936).

economy to overcome a slowdown or to help it get out of recession, so coincidently liquidity is high at the best time to invest in equities (i.e. near the end of a recession).

Technical factors

Technical factors are based on technical analysis and aim to decide whether markets are overbought or oversold, when markets reach support or resistance levels, and how seasonal factors may affect equity prices (e.g. January effect). While according to theory technical analysis is fruitless because efficient equity prices reflect all past information, if a sufficient number of investors follow technical analysis it may create supply and demand. This in turn may move equity prices. Technical factors may therefore be helpful. They should not be solely relied upon, but can complement other factors, in particular to help the timing of trades.

* * *

In summary, equity prices are affected by:

1. nominal growth in earnings per share (EPS) or dividends (dividends = EPS * payout ratio);

2. changes in the price/earnings ratio; and

3. dividend yields.

Those factors are affected by the fortunes of the specific company as well as those of the economy (the state of the economy impacts the profitability of companies and the interest rate used to discount cash flows to calculate their present value). In the long term, dividend yield and growth in earnings or dividends have a much larger impact on equity returns than changes in valuations. In the short term, valuations have a much larger impact.

Equity valuation

The price of any financial instrument is the present value of its future cash flows. The challenge is estimating the amount and timing of cash flows and the appropriate interest rate (discount factor) to discount the cash flows to calculate their present value. It is important to ensure that if the cash flows are real, the discount factor is real (i.e. excluding inflation) and if the cash flows are nominal, the discount factor is nominal (i.e. including inflation).

In theory, equity price represents the present value of future cash flows in the form of dividends and terminal value (the equity's selling price). The discount factor in the present value calculations should represent the required rate of return to compensate investors for equity risk. Therefore:

$$P_0 = \sum D_t/(1+r)^t + P_N/(1+r)^N$$

where P_0 is the present value (the security's price); D_t is the dividend (or cash flow) at time t; r is the interest rate used to discount each cash flow; P_N is the terminal value (the security's selling price); and N is the length of time to when the security is sold (holding period). When N is long the present value of the terminal value is small and may even be negligible (if the holding period is perpetual the present value of the terminal value is zero). The conclusion is that, in theory, the dividends and discount rate are the major factors determining the equity price.

The Gordon growth model[20] for equity valuation uses three variables to calculate the price of equity (P_0): next year's dividend (D_1 or the dividend at t=1); the company's cost of equity or required rate of return (r); and the rate of perpetual growth of dividends (g). Note that r must be larger than g (r > g).

$$P_0 = D_1/(r-g)$$

In practice, the two most common equity valuation methods are *discounted cash flows* and *relative valuation*. A less common valuation method is *contingent claim valuation*.

Discounted cash flows (DCF)

The required inputs for the valuation are: discount rates; expected cash flow growth; expected cash flows; and timing of cash flows. In the strictest sense, the only cash flow that equity holders receive out of a publicly traded firm is dividends. Models that use the dividends as cash flows are called dividend discount models.

A broader definition of cash flows to equity is the cash flows that are left over after claims of non-equity holders have been met (interest and principal payments to debt holders and preferred dividends) and after enough of these cash flows has been reinvested into the firm to sustain the projected growth in cash flows. This is called *free cash flow* (FCF) and models that use these cash flows are called FCF discount models. The challenge with FCF models is that the evaluator needs to project FCFs into the future and hence the models rely on numerous assumptions (model risk).

DCF models aim to calculate the stock's fair-value or intrinsic value without considering the current market sentiment with respect to the stock.

---

[20] Gordon, Myron, 'Dividends, Earnings and Stock Prices', *Review of Economics and Statistics,* The MIT Press (1959).

Relative valuation

While the focus in academia and business schools is on discounted cash flow valuations, the reality is that most assets are valued on a relative basis. In relative valuation, assets are valued by looking at how the market prices similar assets. For example, when determining the price of a house, investors often look at the price for which similar houses in the neighbourhood are sold rather than relying on an intrinsic valuation. Extending this analogy to stocks, investors often decide whether a stock is cheap or expensive by comparing its price to that of similar stocks (usually in its peer group).

Commonly, multiples, such as price to earnings, sales or book value are used. The premise is that equities of companies with comparable businesses should have similar multiples. If, for example, the average P/E ratio of shares of pharmaceuticals in the United States is 10 and the P/E ratio of the shares of one company is 8, then it is traded at a cheaper price relative to its peers. If the EPS of this company is $1 then its equity price should be $10 rather than $8.

Importantly, investors need to understand why the company is undervalued by the market. Is the company undergoing difficulties? Are there good reasons for its low relative share price, such as dropping sales, incompetent management or severe competition? Is it a value trap (i.e. it is cheap because it should be cheap)? If the answer to these questions is no, then the company's share may be a buying opportunity.

One shortcoming of relative valuation is that when a company is a conglomerate or made up of different distinct business units, each business unit may require a separate comparative valuation. The equity price is an aggregation of the prices of the different units. Evaluators need to consider whether the company benefits from synergies and therefore the total is larger than the sum of the parts.

Another shortcoming of relative valuation is that multiples are highly affected by current market sentiment and may be disconnected from fair-value. The premise of comparative valuation is that the market correctly prices other securities. However, this may not occur at all times.

Another challenge with relative valuation is that the timing of convergence to the relative valuation is unknown. A company's stock traded at a P/E of 8, while the average is 10, may keep trading at 8 for a long time.

Contingent claim valuations

This method uses option-pricing models, developed to value listed options, assets, businesses and equity stakes in businesses. These applications are often categorised as *real options*. The method recognises that the value of assets depends on cash flows that are contingent on a future event occurring. Real option valuations tend to value underlying options as a set of managerial rights to wait, grow, expand, use flexible operating processes or abandon a project, or the use of the asset even after the investment has been made. This method is not commonly used in practice, except when needing to evaluate intangible assets, such as brands or copyrights, or assets without known cash flows, such as development of a pharmaceutical drug or a new product, innovation or service.

Valuation in the primary and secondary markets

A stock price's valuation in the *primary market* and *secondary market* is different. The first price of a stock is set for its initial public offering (IPO) by the investment banks involved in the IPO. The banks use valuation models to price the stock. Valuation models are based on numerous assumptions and usually changing the assumptions can justify a range of prices. You can start with the price and change the assumptions to justify it (i.e. reverse engineering).

Once the company is floated on the primary market and its stocks begin trading in the secondary market, market forces determine the share price. It is not uncommon that after the IPO the share price can change considerably, moving from the price as valued by the banks to the price valued by the market.

Banks have an interest in a high stock price since their fees are a function of the capital raised through the IPO. Therefore, the share price may fall after an IPO. A good example is the flotation of Facebook, whose share price dropped after its IPO in May 2012 (it did recover and exceeded its initial flotation price in 2013).

Equity categorisation

Equities are offered in many different variations, including:

- Company size (large capitalisation, mid capitalisation, small capitalisation and SMID, which is small and mid capitalisation).

- Industry or sector (Financials, Information Technology, Consumer Discretionary, Industrials, Healthcare, Consumer Staples, Energy, Materials, Telecommunications and Utilities).

- Style (value, growth, core and GARP, which is growth at a reasonable price; value can be broken into deep value and relative value).

- Regions or countries.

Different combinations of these categorisations can create different sub-asset classes. For example, in the United States commonly classifying equities by size (small, mid and large) and style (value and growth) creates a 2x3 matrix with six different US equity sub-asset classes (e.g. large cap value, small cap growth). However, the correlations among these sub-asset classes may be high and they may have large overlaps, meaning they are not exclusive separate sub-asset classes.

Investors using these sub-asset classes for diversification purposes may overestimate their risk-reducing benefits.

Geographical sub-classes

Another of the ways to create sub-asset classes is to categorise equities around the world by *regions*. The six main regions include:

1. United States or North America (including Canada);

2. United Kingdom;

3. Europe excluding UK (Europe ex UK);

4. Japan;

5. Pacific excluding Japan (Pacific or Asia ex Japan can include all countries in the region or just the developed ones: Australia, New Zealand, Hong Kong and Singapore); and

6. emerging market equity (EME or GEM, Global Emerging Markets).

The first five categories are developed equities (when Pacific ex Japan includes only developed Asia). EME is sometimes classified as a different asset class because of its higher risk, different characteristics and economic backdrop relative to other regional equities. EME includes the developing countries in Asia, so in portfolios that include both regions, developed Asia should be used to avoid the partial overlap between Asia and EME (e.g. China, India, Indonesia, Malaysia, Thailand, Philippines, Taiwan and South Korea).

Taiwan and South Korea are still classified as emerging countries by MSCI. However, they are under review to be potentially reclassified as developed countries. The two countries meet many (Taiwan) or most (South Korea) developed market criteria, such as economic development, market size and liquidity. However, accessibility issues (e.g. currency convertibility and operational issues related to efficient processing of equity trading) have prevented these countries from being classified as developed up until now.

In the United States the commonly used equity regions are:

1. United States;

2. EAFE (Europe, Australasia and the Far East, or developed equities outside the United States); and

3. emerging market equities.

International equities commonly refer to equities outside the United States, while global equities refer to equities around the globe, including the United States.

Global portfolios can invest in equities using a regional breakdown or a global equity portfolio (i.e. a portfolio invested in equities of companies across the globe), or a combination of both. A combination can include a look-through into the holdings within the global equity portfolio and supplementing them as required. For example, if the global equity portfolio holds 50% North American and 50% European equities, separate investments in Japanese, Pacific and emerging market equities can complement the global equity portfolio based on the portfolio's objectives.

When equity regions are used the allocation to different equities is determined by the portfolio's top-down asset allocation. When a global equity portfolio is used the allocation to different regional equities is determined by the bottom-up security selection of the global equity portfolio manager. The look-through into the global equity portfolio can be used to adjust the bottom-up regional allocation to the requirements of the top-down asset allocation of the entire multi-asset portfolio.

Global sectors

Allocation across *global sectors* (i.e. diversifying the equity investments by sectors, such as financials, technology and so on, instead of by regions) is another approach, but it is less common. The risk-reduction benefits of globally diversified portfolios are due to low cross-country correlations. However, with the lowering of trade barriers and the emergence of large trading blocs (e.g. the North American Free Trade Agreement (NAFTA) and the European Union), world markets have become increasingly integrated. Thus in recent years rising correlations among regional equity market returns have diminished the benefits of global country diversification, inciting investors to consider the merits of global sector diversification instead.

The rising correlation of country index returns has prompted research on global sectors and industries. Richard Roll[21] has argued that "industrial composition is important in explaining the correlation structure of country index returns." Although the findings of more recent research are not unanimous, at least for the developed countries, country effects no longer dominate sector and industry effects in explaining the variation in security returns.[22]

The relative importance of country versus sector depends on a number of considerations. Country generally matters more than sector for emerging markets and the Pacific Rim, while sector is generally more important for North American and European firms. However, other distinctions exist, even within those geographic regions and among sectors.

---

[21] Roll, Richard, 'Industrial Structure and the Comparative Behavior of International Stock Market Indices', *Journal of Finance* 47 (1992).

[22] Baca, Sean, Garbe, Brian and Weiss, Richard, 'The Rise of Sector Effects in Major Equity Markets', *Financial Analysts Journal* 56:5 (2000); and Cavaglia, Stefano, Brightman, Christopher and Akek, Michael, 'The Increasing Importance of Industry Factors', *Financial Analysts Journal* 56:5 (2000).

For example, the global pricing of commodities, such as oil, affects energy stocks more than country of domicile. Thus, although globalisation will likely be an ever more important consideration, its effects are uneven. Therefore, investors should consider diversifying their portfolios broadly across both country and sector lines to gain the full benefits of a global portfolio.

Global equity country and sector breakdown

Table 2.1 shows the country and sector breakdown of the MSCI World Index,[23] covering only developed countries. The table shows that when investing in global developed equities following the market-capitalisation weighted MSCI World Index, over 50% of the portfolio holds US equities and over 20% of the portfolio holds financials. Investors need to understand the breakdown of indices to avoid unwanted concentrated exposures in countries or sectors.

Table 2.1: MSCI World Index country and sector breakdown by market capitalisation, March 2014

Country	Weight %	Sector	Weight %
United States	53.8	Financials	20.8
United Kingdom	8.4	Information Technology	12.4
Japan	7.9	Consumer Discretionary	12.1
Canada	4.1	Health Care	12.0
France	3.9	Industrials	11.0
Germany	3.8	Consumer Staples	9.7
Switzerland	4.2	Energy	9.3
Australia	3.2	Materials	5.8
Spain	1.5	Telecommunications	3.5
Netherlands	1.5	Utilities	3.2
Others	7.6	Other	0.3

Source: MSCI World Index.

Table 2.2 shows the country and regional breakdown of MSCI All Country World Index,[24] covering both developed and developing countries. While the market capitalisation of emerging markets has increased over recent years, they still make up a relatively small portion of the global equity market. However, this is likely

---

[23] The MSCI World Index is a free float-adjusted market capitalisation weighted index that is designed to measure the equity market performance of developed markets. www.msci.com.

[24] The MSCI AC World Index or MSCI ACWI is a free float-adjusted market capitalisation weighted index that is designed to measure the equity market performance of developed and emerging markets. www.msci.com.

to change in the future, with the continued increase of developing economies' share in global equities.

Table 2.2: MSCI AC World Index country and regional breakdown by market capitalisation, March 2014

Country	Weight %	Sector	Weight %
United States	48.4	Financials	21.0
United Kingdom	7.6	Information Technology	12.7
Japan	7.2	Consumer Discretionary	11.9
Canada	3.7	Health Care	11.0
Switzerland	3.7	Industrials	10.9
France	3.5	Consumer Staples	9.6
Germany	3.5	Energy	9.6
Australia	2.8	Materials	5.8
China	1.8	Telecommunications	3.9
South Korea	1.6	Utilities	3.2
Others	16.2	Other	0.4

Source: MSCI AC (All Country) World Index.

The country weights in MSCI All Country World Index have dramatically changed over the last 20 years,[25] as detailed in Table 2.3. Most notably, the weights of emerging market equities increased dramatically from below 1% in 1987 to over 12% in 2012. The weight of Japan fell from nearly 40% in 1987 to below 7% in 2012.

Investors should monitor this dynamism. Blindly following indices may mean that the characteristics of investments change over time, resulting in risk and return that are different than expected. This highlights the point that investing is not a static, 'shoot and forget' exercise, but it needs ongoing monitoring and maintenance.

---

[25] 'Emerging Markets: A 20-year Perspective', MSCI/Barra.

Table 2.3: MSCI AC World Index regional breakdown by market capitalisation over time, October 2012. Latam is Latin America; EMEA is Europe, Middle East and Africa

Region	1987	1992	1997	2002	2007	2012
Emerging Asia	0.4	3.0	2.5	2.2	6.2	7.6
Emerging Latam	0.3	2.2	2.6	0.7	2.3	2.7
Emerging EMEA	0.0	0.1	1.7	1.1	2.8	1.7
EME	0.7	5.3	6.8	4.0	11.3	12.1
North America	34.7	42.4	48.6	56.2	45.5	51.5
Europe	22.5	26.0	30.2	28.5	30.2	24.4
Japan	39.4	22.3	11.3	8.4	8.6	6.9
Asia/Pacific ex Japan	2.8	4.0	3.1	2.9	4.4	4.9
Developed	99.3	94.7	93.2	96.0	88.7	87.9

Source: MSCI AC (All Country) World Index.

Access

Equity is one of the oldest and most common assets and this, combined with ongoing developments and financial innovation, means the number of ways to invest in equities is virtually infinite.

Investors can access equities through individual stocks; exchange traded funds (ETFs) and passive funds tracking equity indices; derivatives, such as futures and options on individual stocks or equity indices; enhanced indexing funds tracking equity indices and aiming to add some alpha with a limited tracking error; actively managed long-only funds aiming to beat equity indices to add alpha; structured products offering different exposures to equity markets; smart beta equity strategies; and hedge funds, such as equity long-short, offering equity exposure that may deviate substantially from equity indices and rely more on manager skill.

The different ways of access differ by beta, alpha and liquidity. Passive trackers and derivatives focus on beta. Actively managed funds combine beta and alpha. Hedge funds may focus on alpha with low beta (market neutral funds aim to have a beta of zero or close to zero). Individual large cap stocks and ETFs are very liquid. Structured products and hedge funds with lock-in periods may be illiquid.

Each investment option can focus on a different equity sub-category (e.g. an ETF tracking a US large cap index, an actively managed fund focusing on UK small caps or a hedge fund specialising in the global technology sector). Actively managed funds can follow fundamental analysis, quantitative models, technical analysis or a combination thereof. Each manager has a different philosophy and process to try to add value (alpha).

Each investment has different fees and costs. Passive tracking funds and futures contracts are relatively inexpensive (a few basis points per annum). Hedge funds may be relatively expensive (e.g. 2% per annum asset-based fee plus 20% performance fee). Different investment styles have different turnovers with different levels of transaction costs. Fees and costs come out of net performance, impacting the investor's returns, and are a major consideration when selecting investments. Investors should remember, however, that the cheap option is not always the best option. Sometimes it is worthwhile to pay more for quality and skill that can translate into superior returns.

Past and future equity returns

Taking a look at past equity returns, let's begin with a look back to the market of the 1990s.

Equity markets enjoyed a strong performance during the 1990s due to several factors. As part of the digital and information technology revolution, the internet started to amass a large number of users in 1997. However, while the internet has contributed to the way businesses are operating (e.g. e-mails, access to information, online systems), most internet-related companies were not successful in the 1990s. The internet was more a public perception than underlying economic reality. Nevertheless, public perception is sometimes all that is required to drive equity returns, and the hype around the internet's potential pushed equity prices upward.

The collapse of communism in the Soviet Union and Eastern Europe during the 1990s was another factor that perhaps increased the demand for US equities, as the United States was perceived as victorious in the Cold War. A cultural shift in the United States during the 1990s towards materialism may have been another factor pushing equity prices upwards. Successful business ventures and entrepreneurs received more publicity and demand for stock increased.

The trend of compensating executives with stock options encouraged managers to engage in share price inflating activities. The US Congress shifted from a Democrat to Republican majority during the 1990s and passed favourable tax legislation for businesses. Increased coverage of stock markets in the media made information on stocks readily available and motivated more people to invest in the stock market. Stories about people amassing wealth in the stock market created a herd mentality and an increasing number of people wanted to join the bandwagon.

Figure 2.1 shows the cumulative performance of US equities since January 1900. The equity rally during the 1990s is similar to the rally of the 1920s or the *Roaring Twenties*. During the 1920s equity markets roared upwards until the stock market collapse on 29 October 1929, marking the beginning of the Great Depression. It took World War II to end for equities to resume their rise.

Similarly, since 2000 the secular rise in equity markets has paused and equities have been moving sideways for a decade with two bear markets (the internet bubble burst in 2000 and the credit crunch in 2008). While in 2013 equity markets reached new all-time highs, the long and strong equity performance of the 1990s is unlikely to repeat itself.

Figure 2.1: Cumulative return S&P 500 Index, January 1900 to December 2013

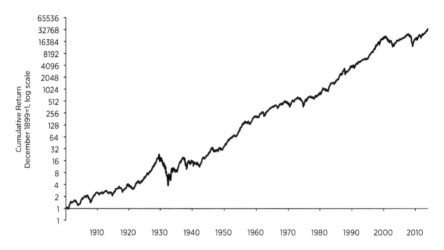

Source: Global Financial Data, S&P 500 Index.

Figure 2.2 shows the rolling ten-year annualised returns of the S&P 500 Index since January 1910. Equity markets seem to move in long cycles in which ten-year returns touch or surpass 20% per annum and then touch or go below 0% per annum. The stock market pendulum swings from highs to lows, from peak to trough, from rich to cheap, from greed to fear.

The figure also demonstrates the benefit of investing in equities over the long term. Most ten-year holding periods generated positive equity returns (with three exceptions during the Great Depression, World War II and the 2008 crisis). All three exceptions were followed by a strong recovery. Patience, not panicking and a long investment horizon are invaluable virtues for successful equity investing.

Our world has changed over the last two decades. Emerging markets are a much more dominant global force, in particular China. The West is burdened with unprecedented levels of public debt. Growing global population, global warming, global geopolitical tensions and depleting global resources are all trends that will continue to affect our lives and the returns of equities, as equities are like a mirror reflecting the global economy.

The aging baby boomers reaching retirement is a long-term investment theme and a global trend that may change the returns from equities over the coming decades. Baby boomers are the people who were born after World War II (in the late 1940s and early 1950s). This generation is now at retirement age and this may create a large demand for equities in specific sectors, such as healthcare. Companies that need to pay the retirement benefits of the baby boomers are going to face difficulties, as well as the work force. The world is facing a pensions crisis.

Figure 2.2: Rolling ten-year annualised return S&P 500 Index, January 1910 to December 2013

Source: Global Financial Data, S&P 500 Index.

Another significant change is that baby boomers have been investing in equities until retirement. Now, as they reach retirement, they can be expected to shift their portfolios to more conservative investments, such as bonds, and sell equities. This puts a selling pressure on equity prices and reduces the demand for equities.

Also applying downward pressure to future equity returns is the equity risk premium (ERP). The ERP is measured against cash or government bond yields. Interest rates and yields at such low levels mean that equity returns are expected to be low as well, assuming the ERP is constant. However, a positive force supporting equity returns is that the relative unattractiveness of cash and bonds increases the demand for equities as investors seek sources of yield and return.

While equities are unlikely to deliver returns as high as those in the 1990s, they are still expected to deliver reasonable returns over the long term. The big question is what these future returns are going to be. One thing for sure is that they are going to be different to the historic ones. Nevertheless, there are still plenty of reasons for investing in equities.

The reasons for investing in equities

It is not surprising that equities make up the core of many portfolios. There are many good reasons for investing in them, including:

High expected return

The expected return of equities is usually higher than that of other types of assets. The expected return of equities is mainly derived from the exposure to equity market risk (beta exposure). This systematic return can be achieved cost effectively through passive investments.

Additional return can be generated by security selection through active management. This alpha usually demands a fee, without a guarantee that it is going to be positive (i.e. active managers can outperform or underperform their benchmark). Nevertheless, the skill-free equity beta expected return is still higher than the expected return of most other investments even without adding any alpha.

Income

Most equities pay regular income in the form of dividends. Dividends are paid out of companies' profits and are not contractually obligatory, as are coupon payments on bonds. Loss-making companies may stop paying dividends and companies on a growth path may retain dividends (retained earnings) to support growth. However, most established companies pay regular dividends. When yields on cash and bonds are at low levels, equity dividends are regarded as an alternative source of income.

Accessibility

The abundance of choices for investing in equities makes them one of the most readily accessible investments. Equities are offered on both a passive and active basis, with different choices of regions, sizes, styles, sectors and so on. Equity is an asset that has been actively managed for decades, both on a long-only basis and more recently via hedge funds focusing on equities.

The derivative market on equities is well developed, offering numerous choices. Exchange traded derivatives (ETD) on single equities and equity indices in the form of futures contracts and options, as well as over-the-counter (OTC) derivatives, are abundant. Because equities are liquid, can be shorted and are easily accessible, banks can hedge their market exposure when offering equity OTC derivatives and structured products.

Liquidity

Large cap developed equities are one of the most liquid asset classes. Public equities are traded on stock exchanges around the globe. Liquidity is good for investors since they can quickly and cost-efficiently invest in equities and disinvest from equities. The flip side of ample liquidity is that it does not generate a liquidity premium.

The equity derivative market further enhances liquidity and enables investors to quickly and cost efficiently change the exposure to equity markets. Tactical Asset Allocation (TAA) decisions, for example, can be implemented using futures contracts to increase and decrease the exposure to equity markets without the need to buy and sell underlying securities. Trading underlyings is both costly (i.e. transaction costs) and disruptive to equity fund managers, who need to change their portfolios to meet cash inflows (they must invest or spend the cash) and outflows (they must sell holdings to raise cash).

Long-term growth

Equities normally play a role as the growth engine of portfolios. Equities are expected to increase in value over time because of inflation, population growth and economic growth. Successful businesses are expected to grow with time and so the prices of their equities should appreciate. Through equity investing, investors can participate in the economy's long-term growth and buy a share in businesses, some of which are successful and expected to increase their profitability over time.

Diversification

Equities have an imperfect correlation with other types of assets. Portfolios can benefit from risk reduction by including equities alongside other investments, such as bonds. Most non-equity investments in portfolios are held to diversify the equity exposure and reduce some of the equity risk.

Low minimum investment

Investing in equities requires a relatively low capital investment compared to other asset classes and investments, such as bonds and real estate. Investors do not need huge amounts of cash to buy a diversified portfolio of equities.

Shorting

Equities are the most common type of security in the security lending industry, making them available for borrowing for shorting. Equities can be synthetically shorted via derivatives (e.g. short futures contracts or long put options). Hence, investors can benefit from falling equity prices. However, shorting should be done with caution. As the upside potential for equity price is limitless, so is the downside risk for short equity positions.

Hedgeable

Due to their liquidity, ability to be shorted and the ample choice of derivatives, equities are one of the easiest assets to hedge. When investors want to adjust their equity exposure they can do so quickly and relatively cheaply by hedging. For example, instead of selling equities to reduce exposure – which would incur transaction costs – investors can short equity futures contracts.

While transaction costs are minimised, basis risk means that if the performance of the futures contract does not exactly match that of the equities held within the portfolio the hedge is imperfect.

Data

There are numerous equity indices with long records of daily historic returns. For current pricing, equities are priced on a daily basis. The plentiful data enables investors to model equities and analyse them. No other asset class offers such robust data.

Alpha

Many equity markets are efficient most of the time. The average active equity manager does not beat the passive index net of fees and costs. However, talented equity managers do exist. Only a number consistently and skilfully beat their benchmark, but those who do can be a source for precious alpha. Outperforming managers do not make solely correct decisions – rather, they need to make more correct than incorrect decisions, the right correct decisions and avoid stupid decisions. As Charlie Munger, the Vice Chairman of Berkshire Hathaway, put it, "It is remarkable how much long-term advantage people like us have gotten by trying to be consistently not stupid, instead of trying to be very intelligent."

* * *

It should be noted that most of the advantages of equity investing are mostly applicable to large cap developed equities. Small caps and emerging market equities are less liquid, have lower accessibility and fewer choices. They should, however, offer higher returns, in theory, since their risks are higher.

Risks

Equities are the archetypal risk asset. Mark Twain described the risk of equity markets as follows: "October. This is one of the peculiarly dangerous months to speculate in stocks. The others are July, January, September, April, November, May, March, June, December, August and February."

Investors investing in equities expect rewards higher than those offered by conservative assets, such as most fixed income investments and cash. This expectation is reflected in the equity risk premium. However, with high expectations investors should also expect and accept high risks. Equity investing can experience severe drawdowns and prolonged periods of negative returns. Equity investors must be able and willing to live with the risk of equities. If you can't stand the heat, get out of the kitchen.

The main risks of investing in equities include:

Volatility

The volatility of equity returns is normally higher than that of other asset classes, such as government bonds and cash. Since the forward looking views and expectations for both the economy and the issuing company are priced into an equity, its price can swing materially, depending on the discounting of the future fortunes of the company and the economy, or just optimism and pessimism or euphoria and panic. Investors' sentiment can drive equity performance and equity markets can diverge from fundamentals during times of fear or greed. Because most equity markets are efficient and traded continuously, news is priced in quickly and equity prices react quickly. Rapid adjustments to volatile news increase volatility.

Investors should differentiate between bad and good volatility. Volatility is bad when it results in an unrecoverable loss. For example, if investors are forced to sell their holdings after a loss or they sell them due to panic, volatility is bad. Volatility is good, however, since high volatility should attract high returns. Also, volatility creates opportunities since it means that prices diverge from intrinsic value, creating buying or shorting opportunities.

Drawdowns

Equities may experience severe drawdowns. Investors tend to overreact to good and bad news, with overreaction on the upside creating bubbles and overreaction on the downside creating drawdowns.

Drawdowns occur much more frequently and severely than predicted statistically by the normal distribution. Typically, if investors remain invested in the market after a drawdown then with time losses can be recouped – albeit 'with time' can mean a few years. However, many investors panic after a drawdown and exit the market, missing the recovery. These investors crystallise the loss and may never recoup it. For the brave or smart, drawdowns usually mean a buying opportunity. Patience, self-control and a clear head are crucial for successful equity investing.

One way to control the magnitude of drawdowns is through diversification and indeed one reason for a multi-asset investing approach is to control downside equity risk. In a portfolio equity risk can be mitigated by lowering the allocation to equities when there are concerns and increasing the allocation to diversifying, risk reducing, defensive investments, such as government bonds or cash.

Deflation

Equities tend to underperform in deflationary periods. During an economic environment when inflation turns negative, companies normally experience lower profit margins or losses. Stocks of highly leveraged companies are particularly vulnerable since such companies face insolvency risk (there is no inflation to help reduce their debt and their cash flows are muted). However, *high quality stocks* could be a potentially dim light in an otherwise dark scenario.

High quality stocks are issued by companies with low leverage, high profitability and low earnings volatility. While the majority of companies will lose pricing power and succumb to weak margins in an environment of negative inflation, large cap high quality companies that dominate their industries may be able to maintain pricing power. Many of these stocks will also pay dividends, which will provide valuable cash during deflation. Companies with pristine balance sheets may be the answer for investors who hold equities in a deflationary period.

Place in capital structure

In bankruptcy or liquidation equity holders may lose their entire investment because of their low place in the pecking order of the company's capital structure. They only get the leftovers from the company's assets after all other stakeholders are satisfied. Diversification is therefore important to reduce idiosyncratic risk. Holding a portfolio of 50 stocks, for example, mitigates the impact of one company failing.

Overstated past performance

Due to biases in indices, such as survivorship bias, past performance of markets may be overstated. Past performance based on indices does not account for transaction costs, management fees and taxes, which means the actual performance as experienced by investors will be lower.

Disappointing returns

Equities can deliver negative or flat returns over long time periods. Over a decade from 2000 to the end of 2012, most equity markets moved largely sideways because of two bear markets (2000 high-tech bubble burst and 2008 global financial crisis). While over the very long term equity returns do turn positive, not all investors have the luxury of a long investment horizon. For many investors performance is measured over short time periods, so surviving over the long term is not guaranteed (i.e. equity managers may be fired due to poor short-term performance).

Changing correlation

The correlation of equities across regions and with other asset classes tends not to be stable over time and therefore equity diversification benefits may be overstated. At times of financial stress correlations across risk assets (e.g. equities, corporate bonds and commodities) tend to move towards 1.00, as investors sell all risk assets. This means diversification benefits diminish just when most needed.

Currency risk

Global equity investing includes currency risk. Currency risk is a source of both risks and returns. Currency risk is a manageable risk and can be hedged easily using forward and futures currency contracts. However, currency hedging is more expensive for illiquid currencies (e.g. emerging country currencies); it may be more expensive when there are large short-term interest rate differentials between the investor's base currency and foreign currencies (i.e. when the interest rate on the foreign currency is higher than that of the base currency);[26] and hedging a currency when the currency of the benchmark is unhedged introduces relative risk (although absolute risk may be lower).

Manager risk

It is challenging for active management to add value in efficient equity markets. Alpha from active investment decisions can be negative. On average, after accounting for fees and transaction costs, average active managers are expected to underperform their index.[27] Security selection skill and/or manager selection skill are required to add value from active equity management over time.

* * *

Most of these risks assume holding a diversified portfolio of equities with the stock specific risk diversified away. Investing in equities is particularly risky when the investment horizon is short. Only investors with a long-term investment horizon should invest in equities.

Figure 2.3 shows the rolling ten-year annualised volatility of the S&P 500 Index since 1910. The Great Depression saw volatility of equities reach extreme highs, not seen before and not seen since (and hopefully not to be repeated again). It should be noted that very low volatility is not necessarily good for investors. First, low volatility means fewer opportunities for active management in both asset allocation and security selection. Second, as per finance theory, expected return is a function of volatility, so low volatility may mean low returns.

---

[26] Hedging a long position in foreign currency is like borrowing in the foreign currency (shorting the foreign currency) and making a deposit in the base currency (going long the base currency). The hedger pays an interest rate on the foreign currency and receives an interest rate on the base currency.

[27] Sharpe, William, 'The Arithmetic of Active Management', *The Financial Analysts Journal* 47 (1991).

Figure 2.3: Rolling ten-year annualised volatility S&P 500 Index, January 1910 to December 2013

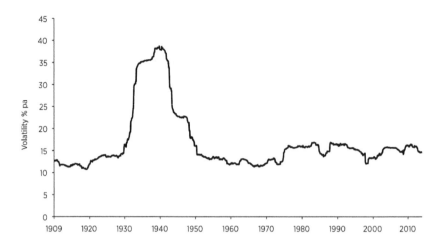

Source: Global Financial Data, S&P 500 Index.

Figure 2.4 shows the drawdowns of the S&P 500 Index since 1900. This chart vividly demonstrates the risk of investing in equities. Drawdowns of over 40% have occurred four times since 1900 (1930s Great Depression, 1970s bear market, 2000 internet bubble burst and 2008 global financial crisis).

Figure 2.4: S&P 500 Index drawdowns, January 1900 to December 2013

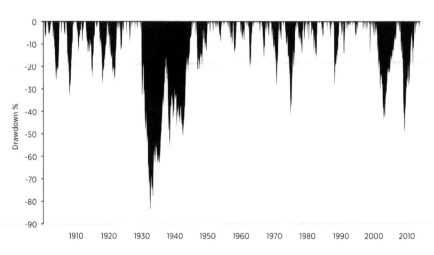

Source: Global Financial Data, S&P 500 Index.

Investment principles of Benjamin Graham

Benjamin Graham is considered the father of fundamental equity security analysis and value investing. He wrote, together with David Dodd, the famous book *Security Analysis*[28] and he also wrote the book *The Intelligent Investor*[29] on the subject of value investing. Graham's most famous pupil was Warren Buffett. Graham advocated three principles on investing in equities:

1. Always invest with a margin of safety. The smart investor buys securities at a significant discount to their intrinsic value.

2. Expect volatility and profit from it. Volatility is part of equity investing. Instead of exiting the markets during times of stress, the smart investor welcomes downturns as times to find investment opportunities. John Maynard Keynes also recognised the opportunities that volatility brings in equity investing, saying, "It is largely the fluctuations which throw up the bargains and the uncertainty due to fluctuations which prevents other people from taking advantage of them."

3. Know what kind of investor you are. Investors should know their investor selves. If an investor is willing to make a serious commitment in time and energy to become a good investor who equates the quality and amount of research with expected return then the investor should be active or an enterprising investor. Otherwise, the investor should invest passively and be a defensive investor. Another distinction between types of investors is between investor and speculator. An investor looks at a stock as part of a business and a stockholder is an owner of a business. A speculator plays with expensive pieces of paper with no intrinsic value.

Graham's principles are timeless. He introduced the idea that buying stocks is buying ownership of a business with a value and not just a piece of paper with a value. He summarised the way to invest as follows:

> "The individual investor should act consistently as an investor and not as a speculator. This means that he should be able to justify every purchase he makes and each price he pays by impersonal, objective reasoning that satisfies him that he is getting more than his money's worth for his purchase."

Global equity return and risk characteristics

One of the best ways to get to know an asset class is to download its monthly total returns to Microsoft Excel and crunch the numbers. Calculating and charting historical returns, risks and correlations with other asset classes can teach us about the behaviour of the asset class and the way it interacts with other assets.

---

[28] Graham, Benjamin and Dodd, David, *Security Analysis* (1934).
[29] Graham, Benjamin, *The Intelligent Investor* (1949).

Table 2.4 uses the monthly returns of MSCI global equity indices to show the historical return and risk characteristics of regional equities. The MSCI World Index represents developed countries.[30] The six regions are the United Kingdom, North America (United States and Canada), Europe excluding United Kingdom (Europe ex UK), Japan, Pacific ex Japan and emerging markets equities (EME).

Calculations are done in local currencies. The MSCI World Index, MSCI North America Index, MSCI Pacific ex Japan Index[31] and MSCI Emerging Markets Index[32] are all denominated in US dollars ($). The MSCI UK Index is measured in sterling (£), the MSCI Europe ex UK Index[33] is measured in euro (€) and MSCI Japan Index is measured in Japanese yen (¥).

All calculations are based on monthly total returns (including dividends and reinvestment of dividends) over the same time period to enable like to be compared with like. Over the particular time period, equity markets delivered on average between 6% and 8% per year (with the exception of Japan, whose equity market has been disappointing). The performance of equities is dependent on the measuring time and it will vary. However, an average return within this range is a reasonable expectation from equity investing over the long term. Equity-like returns are often defined as being 4% to 5% above the return of cash.

Volatility measures the dispersion of returns. It is the most commonly used metric for investment risk. High volatility means a wider dispersion and therefore higher probability for material negative, as well as positive, returns. Notice the materially higher volatility of Pacific ex Japan and emerging markets relative to the more developed equity regions. While similar to returns, volatility varies over time – over long time periods it is more stable than returns. Volatility from 14% to 18% is a reasonable expectation for developed market equities.

Skewness measures the symmetry of the distribution of returns relative to the normal distribution. Negative skewness means that the distribution is skewed to the left – more returns lie on the left side of the average return. Equity markets typically have negative skewness, but not overly negative (other assets may have skewness below -1).

Kurtosis, or more precisely excess kurtosis, measures whether the distribution of returns has a higher kurtosis coefficient relative to 3, that of a normal distribution.

---

[30] The MSCI World Index includes Australia, Austria, Belgium, Canada, Denmark, Finland, Germany, Hong Kong, Ireland, Israel, Italy, Japan, Netherlands, New Zealand, Norway, Portugal, Singapore, Spain, Sweden, Switzerland, the United Kingdom and the United States. The MSCI AC World index or MSCI All Country World Index includes both developed and emerging markets.

[31] The MSCI Pacific ex Japan Index includes Australia, Hong Kong, New Zealand and Singapore.

[32] The MSCI Emerging Markets Index includes Brazil, Chile, China, Colombia, Czech Republic, Egypt, Hungary, India, Indonesia, Korea, Malaysia, Mexico, Morocco, Peru, Philippines, Poland, Russia, South Africa, Taiwan, Thailand and Turkey.

[33] The MSCI Europe ex UK Index includes Austria, Belgium, Denmark, Finland, France, Germany, Greece, Ireland, Italy, the Netherlands, Norway, Portugal, Spain, Sweden and Switzerland.

Positive kurtosis indicates a higher probability of extreme returns than predicted under normality (i.e. fat tails, meaning more returns in the tails of the distribution than normal distribution).

A combination of negative skewness and high kurtosis indicates high fat-tail risk. This means that extreme negative returns in terms of both higher frequency and magnitude should be expected compared with a normal distribution. Equity markets do have negative skewness and positive kurtosis. This indicates that crashes occur more frequently and severely than predicted under the normal distribution. Other assets, however, may have worse characteristics than do equities in terms of downside risk, as will be reviewed in later sections.

The Sharpe ratio is a common measure of risk-adjusted returns. Developed by William Sharpe, the ratio divides the assets' excess return over the risk free return (cash or government bond return) by risk as measured by standard deviation (volatility). The Sharpe ratio of global developed markets is around 0.25 (during the particular time period). This is relatively low compared to other assets, such as most bonds. Typically, assets with lower volatilities have a higher Sharpe ratio, albeit they should deliver lower returns than assets with a higher volatility.

Max drawdown measures the maximum drop from peak to trough over a particular time period. It is a common measure of downside risk and illustrates the potential loss from an investment. The max drawdown of equities shows that investors can expect a drop of over 50% in equity investments. However, investors who do not sell their holdings after such a loss, due to either panic or being forced to sell, can recoup the losses over time. Equity investing requires calm, patience and a long time horizon – it is not for everyone.

Table 2.4: Global and regional equity return and risk characteristics, January 1996 to December 2013. Sharpe ratio calculated using $ cash returns

	World	UK	North America	Europe ex UK	Japan	Pacific ex Japan	EME
Start month	Jan-96	Jan-96	Jan-96	Jan-96	Jan-96	Jan-96	Jan-96
Performance (% pa)	6.7	6.4	7.9	7.7	0.0	7.3	6.2
Volatility (% pa)	15.8	14.1	16.0	17.9	18.3	22.2	24.4
Skewness	-0.77	-0.64	-0.67	-0.62	-0.24	-0.53	-0.77
Kurtosis	1.52	0.66	1.02	0.99	0.79	1.76	1.95
Sharpe ratio	0.26	0.27	0.33	0.28	-0.14	0.21	0.14
Max drawdown (%)	-53.6	-41.7	-51.0	-56.4	-70.6	-60.1	-61.4

Source: Bloomberg, MSCI World Index, MSCI UK Index, MSCI North America Index, MSCI Europe ex UK Index, MSCI Japan Index, MSCI Pacific ex Japan Index, MSCI Emerging Markets Index.

Table 2.5 shows the correlations across the different regional equity markets. Correlation measures how two assets move in relation to each other. Correlation ranges from -1 (perfect negative correlation) to 1 (perfect positive correlation). Correlation measures the degree of co-movement, not its magnitude. So you can have two assets with high correlation but one with low volatility and another with high volatility.

In portfolio context, imperfect correlation is the key for diversification benefits. Investors should seek to combine imperfectly correlated assets to reduce portfolio risk. The correlations among different regional equities are usually quite high, above 0.70. However, there are still diversification benefits in mixing global equities.

The Japanese equity market has the lowest average correlation with the other regions. However, the performance of Japanese equities has been disappointing and the market has been moving sideways since the middle 1980s, which explains the relatively low correlation with other equity markets.

Table 2.5: Global and regional equity correlation matrix, January 1996 to December 2013

Correlation matrix	World	UK	North America	Europe ex UK	Japan	Pacific ex Japan	EME
World	1.00	0.86	0.96	0.86	0.66	0.83	0.83
UK	0.86	1.00	0.82	0.85	0.54	0.70	0.70
North America	0.96	0.82	1.00	0.83	0.57	0.75	0.77
Europe ex UK	0.86	0.85	0.83	1.00	0.59	0.65	0.72
Japan	0.66	0.54	0.57	0.59	1.00	0.57	0.60
Pacific ex Japan	0.83	0.70	0.75	0.65	0.57	1.00	0.89
EME	0.83	0.70	0.77	0.72	0.60	0.89	1.00

Source: Bloomberg, MSCI World Index, MSCI UK Index, MSCI North America Index, MSCI Europe ex UK Index, MSCI Japan Index, MSCI Pacific ex Japan Index, MSCI Emerging Markets Index.

Figure 2.5 shows the cumulative performance of the MSCI World Index since January 1970. The chart shows how $1 invested in the index would have grown in nominal terms (without adjusting the returns for inflation) and in real terms (adjusted for US inflation). It is important to adjust for inflation in this way, as inflation can have a material impact on performance, especially over long horizons. Note how inflation caused equity investing to generate negative real returns during the 1970s, when inflation was high.

One observation from the chart is that equity investing can generate remarkable returns over time. Another observation is that equity investing is risky – there are material drops in equity markets, such as those in 1973 (oil crisis), 2000 (high-tech bubble burst) and 2008 (global financial crisis).

Figure 2.5: Cumulative return of the MSCI World Index in nominal and real terms (adjusted to US inflation), January 1970 to December 2013

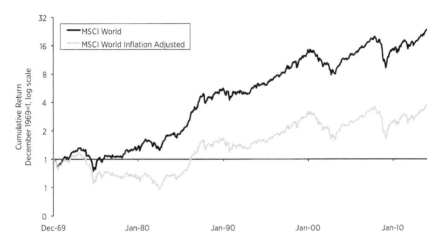

Source: Bloomberg, MSCI World Index, US inflation.

Figure 2.6 compares the cumulative performance of the equity markets of three countries: the United Kingdom, United States[34] and Japan. Each performance is measured in local currency (£, $ and ¥ respectively). From the perspective of a US-based investor, for example, measuring the returns of foreign equities in their local currency assumes a perfect currency hedge.

Figure 2.6: Cumulative return of UK, North America and Japan equities, January 1970 to December 2013

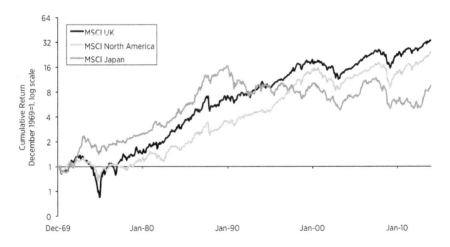

Source: Bloomberg, MSCI UK Index, MSCI North America Index, MSCI Japan Index.

[34] MSCI North America is used to represent the United States and includes the performance of Canadian stocks.

The equity markets of the United Kingdom and United States have performed similarly over the last four decades. The Japanese equity market was the best performing market out of the three until the end of the 1980s – then at this point it began to move sideways and it has continued in this vein for two "lost" decades.

Investors should aim to pick up structural changes in the behaviour of assets as past performance is not necessarily indicative of future performance and yesterday's winners can be tomorrow's losers. While equity markets may be correlated, tactically or dynamically switching exposure can add value if done correctly. Investors need to be dynamic with their investments. Buy and hold strategies for asset allocation can be costly as investors should not expect the performance of the 1990s, for instance, to be repeated.

Small caps

Small capitalisation stocks (small caps) are shares of relatively small publicly traded corporations with a total market capitalisation of less than approximately $2 billion.[35] Shares of companies with a market cap below $250 million are considered micro-caps.

Small cap stocks, which are tracked for instance by the Russell 2000 Index[36] in the United States, and the FTSE 250 Index[37] or FTSE SmallCap Index[38] in the United Kingdom, tend to be issued by young, potentially fast-growing companies. Small cap companies are typically less affected by the global economy and more by the local economy since they are usually less export oriented. Over the long term (though not in every period) small cap stocks as a group have produced stronger returns than any other investment category.

A number of studies show that a difference in return behaviour between small and large capitalisation stocks exists.[39] Based on standard portfolio theory, if small cap returns do not perfectly correlate with large cap returns, investors can gain from *size diversification*.

---

[35] The $2 billion threshold is not used uniformly and small caps may have different definitions.

[36] The Russell 1000 Index measures the performance of the large cap segment of the US equity universe. It is a subset of the Russell 3000 Index and includes approximately 1,000 of the largest securities based on a combination of their market cap and current index membership. The Russell 1000 Index represents approximately 92% of the US market. The Russell 2000 Index measures the performance of the small cap segment of the US equity universe. It is a subset of the Russell 3000 Index representing approximately 10% of the total market capitalisation of that index. www.russell.com.

[37] The FTSE 250 Index is a market capitalisation index consisting of the 101st to the 350th largest companies listed on the London Stock Exchange.

[38] The FTSE SmallCap Index consists of the 351st to the 619th largest companies listed on the London Stock Exchange.

[39] Banz, Rolf, 'The Relationship Between Return and Market Value of Common Stocks', *Journal of Financial Economics* 9 (1981); and Chan, K.C., and Chen, Nai-Fu, 'Structural and Return Characteristics of Small and Large Firms', *Journal of Finance* 46 (1991).

As a group these stocks represent a non-negligible portion of the overall stock market – for the US market, considering a long-term average, small capitalisation stocks account for about 12% of the total market capitalisation.[40] This suggests that small caps can be classified as a separate sub-asset class.

According to the Fama-French three factor model,[41] three systematic risks – namely equity market risk, value risk (over growth) and size risk (small capitalisation stocks) – are rewarded by risk premiums. Small capitalisation stocks should therefore attract a beta return beyond that of large cap equity investing.

Figure 2.7 compares the cumulative performance of US small caps (Russell 2000 Index) and large caps (Russell 1000 Index). Over the specific time period used below, small and large caps have had broadly the same return. However, small caps were more volatile and therefore an inferior investment compared to large caps on a risk-adjusted basis. As this shows, there is no guarantee that small caps always generate higher returns than large caps.

Figure 2.7: Cumulative return of US large and small capitalisation stocks, January 1979 to December 2013

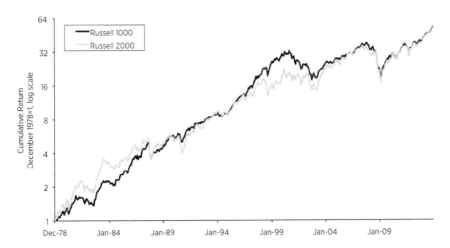

Source: Bloomberg, Russell 1000 Index, Russell 2000 Index.

Table 2.6 shows the return and risk of the different Russell indices, representing large and small caps, as well as value and growth investment styles. Over the measuring period small cap value stocks (Russell 2000 Value Index) delivered the highest returns and the highest risk-adjusted performance (Sharpe ratio). This is in line with the Fama-French theory. Small size and value investing has

---

[40] Pradhuman, Satya Dev, *Small-Cap Dynamics: Insights, Analysis and Models* (Bloomberg Press, 2000).

[41] Fama, Eugene and French, Kenneth, 'Common risk factors in the returns of stocks and bonds', *Journal of Financial Economics* 33 (1993).

been rewarded over the period. The choices between small and large and between value and growth can have an impact on results. This demonstrates that a range of different asset classes offers a choice and correctly choosing among them offers opportunities to enhance returns and reduce risks.

Table 2.6: US small, large, value and growth equity return and risk characteristics, January 1979 to December 2013. Sharpe ratio calculated using $ cash returns

	Russell 1000	Russell 1000 Value	Russell 1000 Growth	Russell 2000	Russell 2000 Value	Russell 2000 Growth
Start month	Jan-1979	Jan-1979	Jan-1979	Jan-1979	Jan-1979	Jan-1979
Performance % pa	12.0	12.5	11.4	12.1	13.7	10.0
Volatility % pa	15.5	21.0	17.4	19.8	17.5	23.0
Skewness	-0.70	0.52	-0.64	-0.82	-1.04	-0.61
Kurtosis	2.22	10.39	1.87	2.73	3.79	1.96
Sharpe ratio	0.45	0.35	0.36	0.36	0.49	0.22

Source: Bloomberg, Russell 1000 Index, Russell 1000 Value Index, Russell 1000 Growth Index, Russell 2000 Index, Russell 2000 Value Index, Russell 2000 Growth Index.

Equity investment styles

Commonly, in particular in the United States, equity portfolios follow a particular style category, purchasing stocks with either growth or value characteristics. A range of different style categories are as follows:

- *Core style.* The philosophy behind a core investment style is to have no intended bias towards growth or value. Typically, a core portfolio manager seeks to buy shares in companies that the manager believes will perform well in all market environments. The portfolio tends to contain a mixture of both growth and value shares.

- *Value style.* Value investing seeks to buy companies that offer the best value for money. Value managers look for stocks with prices that are believed to be undervalued relative to other similar stocks on the market or relative to the stock's fair-value. Undiscovered companies or stocks that have price movements that do not correspond to the company's long-term fundamentals are generally considered to be value investments.

- *Relative value style* employs a value-oriented strategy that is diluted compared with *true value style*. Relative value managers tend to outperform deep value managers during periods when growth is outperforming value; however, they tend to trail during market conditions that favour deep value. Relative value managers have a definite value emphasis, but often have some growth overlays in security selection.

- *True value style* exhibits characteristics similar to those of the Russell 1000 Value Index. *Deep value* investing is the extreme of the value-oriented styles. A deep value strategy typically avoids stocks that are the latest market fad and typically invests in companies or industries that are out of favour, with the anticipation that the tide will turn and the investment will pay off. Deep value managers tend to demonstrate performance volatility, as they usually outperform their less value-biased peers during periods when value is outperforming growth. The reverse occurs when growth is outperforming – at these times deeper value styles generally underperform their relative and true value peers.

- *Growth style*. Portfolio managers following a growth style search for companies with earnings that grow, or which are expected to grow, at a rapid pace. The companies are expected to grow faster than the stock market's average. A growth investor tends to aim for big gains over the long term and must be willing to withstand the ups and downs of the growth-oriented market.

- *Growth at a Reasonable Price* (GARP) investing combines the search for sustainable earnings growth with an emphasis on valuation. GARP investing reflects the desire to find companies that could be undervalued but have solid sustainable growth potential. A GARP investment has historically been favoured when the economy begins to slow because the consistent earnings of high-quality companies become increasingly attractive. The philosophy of GARP portfolio managers is that over long periods of time stocks go up because of earnings growth.

- A *true growth* portfolio typically displays characteristics similar to those of the Russell 1000 Growth Index. True growth portfolio managers typically seek to purchase only companies that remain faithful to the category of a growth investment style. Portfolio managers who seek the highest earnings growth, regardless of valuation, are considered *aggressive growth* managers. They seek aggressive and sometimes emerging growth stocks, and these are often in dramatically overweight traditional growth-oriented sectors like technology.

Emerging market equity

Emerging markets are countries experiencing rapid economic growth. Some emerging countries own large quantities of important natural resources and commodities, some are experiencing rapid building of infrastructure, and some are experiencing massive industrialisation and expansion of their service industries. Emerging countries are expected to account for a meaningful and rising share of global economic activity and growth.

Emerging countries are located in Asia, Latin America (Latam), Eastern Europe and Africa (most countries in Africa are often referred to as *frontier countries*, since they are not yet emerging). BRIC is an acronym used to refer to the four largest emerging countries: Brazil, Russia, India and China. BRICS is another version of this, which includes South Africa. Another acronym for a group of more recently emerging countries is MINT; this refers to Mexico, Indonesia, Nigeria and Turkey. Each emerging region has unique dynamics and may be treated as a separate sub-asset class for asset allocation purposes.

Emerging market countries should be differentiated between commodity exporters (e.g. Russia) and commodity importers (e.g. China), since the commodity market has a material impact on the performance of their equity markets. Countries can also be distinguished based on those with a current account deficit and those with a current account surplus. This has a substantial influence on the policy of their central banks, and on inflation and their currencies.

One of the most important global economic trends of the last few decades is the rise of China. China has been transitioning to its version of a market economy, with rapid urbanisation, industrialisation and economic growth, overtaking other economies, such as Japan, Germany, France and the United Kingdom, in terms of its GDP. China is expected to overtake the United States as well before too long.

This shift has changed the global economy as well as the manufacturing in many industrialised countries as they have moved their operations to China. 'Made in China' appears on more and more products. Even on an iPhone it says, 'Developed by Apple in California. Assembled in China'. This is one of the trends that is going to impact the future of investing.

China now faces the challenges of maintaining its impressive economic expansion, developing its own consumer base and dealing with political issues. It is yet to be seen how the internal dynamics of China are going to affect the global economy.

China is not the only trend involving emerging markets. Once attractive only for their natural resources or as a source of cheap labour and low-cost manufacturing, emerging markets are increasingly seen as promising markets in their own right. Rapid population growth, sustained economic development and a growing middle class are factors that combine to drive forward the development of emerging economies.

The International Monetary Fund (IMF) forecasts that by 2020, the BRICs are expected to account for nearly 50% of all global GDP growth. Leading companies of emerging markets will become a disruptive force in the global competitive landscape as they continue to be competitive in their countries while expanding into other emerging and developed countries.

Rising population and prosperity drive new consumer growth and urbanisation. Up to 2050 the world's population is expected to grow by 2.3 billion people, eventually reaching 9.1 billion. The combined purchasing power of the global middle classes is estimated to more than double by 2030 to $56 trillion. Over 80% of this demand will come from Asia. Most of the world's new middle class will live in the emerging world.

As the global influence of emerging markets continues to grow, inevitably this leads to greater influence on world economic policy. These changes in the dominance of emerging economies are a long-term investment theme and a structural shift that investors should consider when formulating investment strategies.

As emerging markets continue to emerge, their equity markets are going to behave more like those of developed markets. Global equities in general are going to increasingly be driven by economic developments in emerging countries. The roles of emerging market equities within portfolios – and their risk and return characteristics – may change forever.

The reasons for investing in emerging market equity

Investing in emerging market equity (EME) offers a number of opportunities, including:

- *High growth prospects.* Emerging market equities present the chance to participate in the relatively high growth prospects for companies in emerging markets. High growth prospects should translate into high returns. Some emerging markets start from a relatively low base and hence have a large potential for growth.

- *Active management opportunities.* Since emerging market equities are less researched and the markets are less efficient, they may offer more opportunities for active managers to add value. This depends, however, on accessing skilful active managers who are able to add value in a heterogeneous, global market that requires significant resources to be covered properly.

- *Diversification.* Emerging market equities are less correlated with developed market equities than other developed market equities. Therefore they may offer more diversification benefits.

- *Reduced exposure to the woes of the West.* Emerging economies are less affected by some of the challenges of Western economies in the form of high levels of debt, low yields on public debt and limited monetary and fiscal tools to support economic growth. Western economies have borrowed for decades to support their high standard of living and growth and now face the challenge of paying this debt. Emerging economies have much lower levels of debt and their organic economic growth may have changed the balance of power between the developed world and the developing world.

- *EME risk premium.* Investing in EME exposes portfolios to an EME risk premium. This risk premium is different to that of developed equities.

Risks in emerging market equity investing

EME has higher expected returns compared to developed equities. Higher expected returns come with higher risks. In addition to the general risks of equities, the main risks of EME include:

- *Risks related to emerging countries.* Companies in emerging countries are exposed to issues such as protectionism, lack of transparency, corruption, unstable governments and geopolitical risks.

- *Trading costs.* The costs of trading and holding EME are usually higher than those for developed equities.

- *Regulatory risk.* Emerging market stock exchanges may have restrictions or may experience sudden changes to regulations affecting investors.

- *Taxes.* Tax consequences of investing in emerging market equities can be material. For example, it is usually much more difficult to reclaim dividend withholding tax of EME compared to developed equities. Withholding tax reclaims arise because the rate permitted under the terms of double taxation treaties is less than the default rate applied by most foreign governments. When comparing EME funds with indices it is usually recommended to use a net total return index (e.g. the MSCI Emerging Market Net Index)[42] to capture the impact of withholding taxes.

- *Volatility.* Emerging market equities tend to have a much higher volatility than that of developed market equities. The higher volatility of EME means a risk of material drawdowns.

Emerging markets have come a long way over recent decades. Governments are more stable, inflation is more under control, government accounts are more balanced and public debt defaults are more uncommon.

All these developments mean that EME are not as risky as they used to be. The downside is that the expected returns of EME are not as high as they used to be

---

[42] Net total return indices reinvest dividends after the deduction of withholding taxes, using (for international indices) a tax rate applicable to non-resident institutional investors who do not benefit from double taxation treaties. www.msci.com.

and the correlation of EME with developed equities is not as low as it used to be, losing some diversification benefits. Lower risk has advantages and disadvantages.

Emerging market equity return and risk characteristics

Figure 2.8 shows the cumulative performance of the MSCI Emerging Market Equity Index since January 1998 (compared to the performance of global developed equities as measured by the MSCI World Index). As you can see, EME has experienced stronger rallies and falls compared to developed equities, which is what we would expect based upon the factors discussed above.

Figure 2.8: Cumulative return of emerging market and global developed equities, January 1988 to December 2013

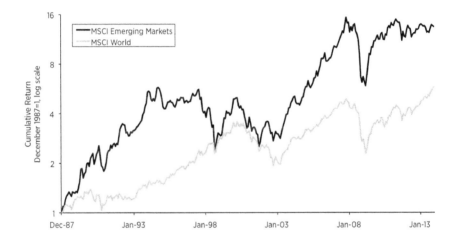

Source: Bloomberg, MSCI Emerging Markets Index, MSCI World Index.

Figure 2.9 shows the rolling 36-month correlation between EME and developed global equities (MSCI World Index). The correlation has been increasing, indicating that returns of equities of companies in emerging markets are becoming more similar to those of developed markets, globalisation increases the integration of companies across the globe; and diversification benefits of global equity investing are diminishing.

Figure 2.9: Rolling 36-month correlation of emerging market and global developed equities, January 1991 to December 2013

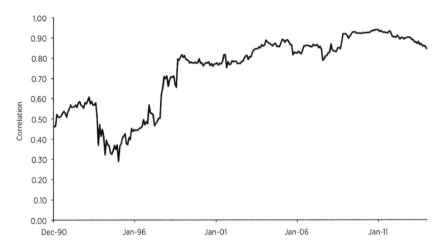

Source: Bloomberg, MSCI Emerging Markets Index, MSCI World Index.

Figure 2.10 compares the rolling 36-month annualised volatility of EME and developed global equities (MSCI World Index). Volatility of EME has been constantly higher than that of developed equities. At times of financial stress (for instance the 1998 Russian debt crisis and 2008 global financial crisis) the volatility of EME has spiked from below 20% to over 30%.

Figure 2.10: Rolling 36-month volatility of emerging market and global developed equities, January 1991 to December 2013

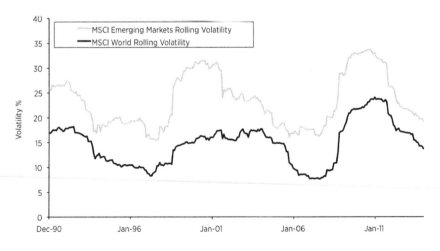

Source: Bloomberg, MSCI Emerging Markets Index, MSCI World Index.

Frontier markets

Frontier markets are an investable subset of emerging markets with lower market capitalisations and liquidity than the more developed emerging markets. These markets have restrictions, making them unsuitable for inclusion in the indices of larger emerging markets, but they demonstrate accessibility to foreign investors and are not subject to extreme economic and political instability. These are markets that are yet to emerge; they are less developed than are emerging markets.

Frontier markets can be divided into three groups:

1. small countries with a relatively high development level that are too small to be considered emerging markets (e.g. Estonia);

2. countries with investment restrictions that have begun to loosen as of the mid-2000s (e.g. the countries of the Gulf Cooperation Council); and

3. countries at a lower development level than the existing mainstream emerging markets (e.g. Kenya and Vietnam).

The frontier equity markets are typically pursued by investors seeking high, long-term returns and low correlations with other equity markets. Investors in frontier markets must accept higher risks compared to emerging and certainly developed equity markets. The implication of a country being labelled as frontier is that, over time, the market will become more liquid and exhibit similar risk and return characteristics to the larger, more liquid developed emerging markets.

Frontier markets return and risk characteristics

Figure 2.11 compares the cumulative performance of frontier markets (MSCI Frontier Emerging Markets Index),[43] emerging markets and global developed markets. All three exhibited severe losses in the 2008 equity market crash. While developed and emerging markets recovered from their lows, frontier markets are as yet far below their previous peak. Frontier markets offer opportunities and risks. Hence careful selection and a dynamic approach are recommended when investing in these markets.

Table 2.7 shows the historical return and risk characteristics of frontier markets, EME and selected developed regional equities.

---

[43] The MSCI Frontier Markets Index includes Argentina, Bahrain, Bangladesh, Bulgaria, Croatia, Estonia, Jordan, Kenya, Kuwait, Lebanon, Lithuania, Kazakhstan, Mauritius, Nigeria, Oman, Pakistan, Qatar, Romania, Serbia, Slovenia, Sri Lanka, Tunisia, Ukraine, United Arab Emirates and Vietnam.

Figure 2.11: Cumulative return of frontier market, emerging market and global developed equities, January 2003 to December 2013

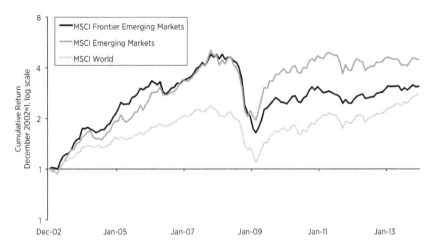

Source: Bloomberg, MSCI Frontier Emerging Markets Index, MSCI Emerging Markets Index, MSCI World Index.

Table 2.7: Frontier, emerging, developed and regional equity return and risk characteristics, January 2003 to December 2013. Sharpe ratio calculated using $ cash returns

	Frontier	Emerging	Developed	Pacific ex Japan	North America	UK	Europe ex UK
Start month	Jan-2003	Jan-2003	Jan-2003	Jan-2003	Jan-2003	Jan-2003	Jan-2003
Performance (% pa)	10.8	14.6	9.8	15.7	9.6	9.3	8.3
Volatility (% pa)	20.3	23.3	15.7	21.3	14.7	13.7	15.8
Skewness	-1.26	-0.71	-0.94	-0.86	-0.89	-0.67	-0.55
Kurtosis	5.56	2.06	2.65	2.64	2.62	1.01	1.67
Sharpe ratio	0.46	0.56	0.52	0.66	0.55	0.57	0.43
Max drawdown (%)	-65.8	-61.4	-53.6	-60.1	-51.0	-40.0	-53.9

Source: Bloomberg, MSCI Frontier Emerging Markets Index, MSCI Emerging Markets Index, MSCI World Index, MSCI Pacific ex Japan Index, MSCI North America Index, MSCI UK Index, MSCI Europe ex UK Index.

Figure 2.11 and Table 2.7 show that over the last decade (since January 2003) emerging markets (frontier, global emerging and Pacific ex Japan) outperformed developed markets (North America, United Kingdom and Europe ex UK). This performance was accompanied by higher risk (volatility and maximum drawdowns). However, the higher risk was compensated by the higher reward, as indicated by the Sharpe ratios.

Figure 2.12 shows the distribution of monthly returns of frontier, emerging and global developed equities with a normal distribution superimposed on the histogram. Frontier markets exhibit negative skewness with fat-tails (high excess kurtosis), indicating that they are more sensitive to downside risk than global emerging and developed equity markets. When they crash they really crash and it happens more often than statistically expected under a normal distribution.

Figure 2.12: Distribution of monthly returns for frontier, emerging and global developed equities, January 2003 to December 2013

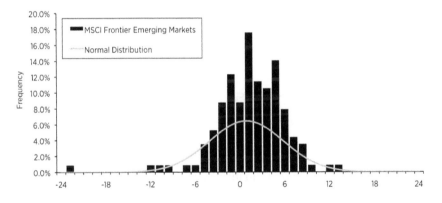

Source: Bloomberg, MSCI Frontier Emerging Markets Index, MSCI Emerging Markets Index, MSCI World Index.

Conclusions

Equities are the growth locomotive in portfolios. They offer the highest expected returns compared to almost all other asset classes and can be accessed relatively easily and cheaply. Riding the beta of equities is all that it takes to generate equity returns. Alpha can be a bonus, but it is not a necessity.

Equities allow almost everyone to be a partial owner of the most successful businesses in the world. However, never forget that equities are a risk asset. Equity investors must accept the risk of a loss. Investing in equities requires patience, a long investment horizon and an appetite for risk.

Benchmarked portfolios must stay invested. Not investing is a relative risk. The allocation to equities in the benchmark determines the typical portfolio's risk level (not considering active management). Investors should think carefully about the exposure to equities. On the one hand, it is risky. On the other hand, risk pays off. The challenge is to know when to take risk and when to avoid it.

Summary

- The main role of equities in portfolios is delivering long-term growth. Equities are the most common risk or growth assets in portfolios. As the portfolio's risk level increases, so does the allocation to equities.

- Equity represents partial ownership in a company. Shareholders are owners of the company and participate in its future commercial fortunes.

- Equity prices and returns are affected by several factors, including: company fundamentals; valuation (e.g. P/E ratio); market exposure (beta); inflation; sentiment; liquidity; and technical factors.

- The three methods for evaluating equities are: discounted cash flows; relative valuation (e.g. comparable P/E ratios); and contingent claim valuations (real options).

- Equities can be categorised by regions and/or global sectors.

- The ways to access equities are numerous, with different degrees of beta (index tracking versus market neutral hedge funds), alpha (passive versus active) and liquidity (large cap developed stocks versus structured products).

- Only investors with a long-term investment horizon should invest in equities.

- The reasons for investing in equities include: high expected returns; income from dividends; accessibility; liquidity; long-term growth; diversification benefits; low minimum investment requirement; easy to short; hedgeable; data; and alpha.

- The main risks of investing in equities include: relatively high volatility; drawdowns; underperformance during deflation; high losses during bankruptcy or liquidation; index biases overstate past returns; negative or flat returns over long time periods; unstable correlation with other investments; currency risk; and active management is hard in efficient markets.

- Small capitalisation stocks should be considered as a separate sub-asset class. Historically, they have generated higher returns than most other assets and are expected to generate higher returns in the future (with corresponding higher risk).

- Emerging market equity (EME) is typically considered a separate asset class to developed market equity.

- The opportunities that come from investing in EME compared to developed equities include: participation in relatively high-growth prospects; alpha from active management due to lower market efficiency; diversification benefits due to lower correlation; emerging economies do not face the sovereign debt challenges of Western economies; and EME investing exposes the portfolio to the EME risk premium.

- The risks of EME investing include: political risk; relatively high trading costs; regulatory risk; taxation; and high volatility and potential material drawdowns.

- Frontier markets are a subset of EME offering higher potential returns, higher risks and lower correlation with other asset classes.

- The key to success in portfolio management is to take risk and to know when to reduce it.

CHAPTER 2: FIXED INCOME

Introduction – bond basics

Fixed income (also referred to as fixed interest or bonds) in its narrowest definition refers to debt investments that provide a return in the form of fixed periodic payments (interest) and the eventual return of principal at maturity. Unlike variable-income securities, where payments change based on some underlying measure such as short-term interest rates (e.g. Libor), the payments of fixed-income securities are known in advance.

The broader definition of fixed income is any type of investment that is not equity and where the borrower or issuer is contractually obliged to make payments on a fixed schedule, even if the number and size of payments may be variable. Under this definition fixed income refers to all securities representing a promise from issuers to make contractual payments to investors, typically in the form of a series of coupons and a principal repayment due at final maturity. Floating rate notes (FRNs), from which income is not fixed, also fall under the broader definition of fixed income.

The bond market is by far the largest securities market in the world; a $90 trillion global marketplace with virtually limitless investment options. By comparison, the size of the world's equity market is estimated to be about $36 trillion. As the number of new fixed income products grows even bond experts are challenged to keep pace with their development.

Traditionally, bonds were a means of earning interest while preserving capital. However, bonds have evolved into investments that can offer many potential benefits to portfolios, including attractive capital appreciation.

What is a bond?

A bond is a loan that the bond purchaser or bondholder (i.e. creditor) lends to the bond issuer (i.e. borrower). Governments, corporations and municipalities issue bonds to raise capital (public and private debt). Investors buying government bonds lend money to the government and investors buying corporate bonds lend money to the corporation. Like a loan, a bond promises to pay interest (or coupons) periodically and repay the principal at a stated time or maturity.

To set the coupon, the issuer considers the prevailing interest rate environment to ensure that the coupon is competitive with those on comparable bonds and attractive for investors. The coupons are also determined by the maturity of the bond and issuer's creditworthiness. As the maturity of the bond gets longer, more factors can have a negative impact on the issuer's ability to pay bondholders, and more market forces may negatively affect the return on the bond (e.g. changes in interest rates and inflation). The additional risk incurred by a longer maturity bond has a direct relation to the coupon that the issuer must pay. In other words, an issuer has to pay a higher interest rate for a longer-term bond. Investors will potentially earn greater returns on longer-term bonds to compensate them for the risk. This compensation is called *maturity premium* or *term premium*.

Every bond also carries some credit risk that the issuer will default or fail to pay the promised interest and fully repay the loan. Issuers with higher credit risk must compensate investors by paying higher coupons. Investors purchasing bonds with higher credit risk can potentially earn higher returns to compensate them for the risk. This compensation is called *credit premium*.

Relationship between bond price and yield

A bond's price is the present value of its future cash flows. Future cash flows are the coupon payments (commonly paid semi-annually) and the payment of the principal at maturity. *Yield to maturity (YTM)* is the rate of interest used to discount all the coupons and principal to get to the current bond price. Therefore:

$$P_0 = C_t/(1+YTM)^t + P_T/(1+YTM)^T$$

where P_0 is the current bond's market price; C_t is the coupon at time t; P_T is the principal or par value; T is the time to maturity; and YTM is the yield to maturity.

The bond price is the prevailing market price that investors need to pay to purchase the bond. The bond price can be higher or lower than its nominal value (i.e. face value), which remains constant throughout the life of the bond. For example, a bond's nominal value can be $1,000, while the bond price can be $998 or $1,005.

The yield is the return that investors realise by holding the bond. While there are several types of yields (e.g. nominal yield is the interest rate divided by face value and current yield is the interest rate divided by current bond price), yield to maturity (YTM) is the discount rate that equates future cash flows (including repayment of principal at maturity) with current bond price.

There is an inverse relationship between bond price and yield. As the bond price is lower, the yield is higher and vice versa. When interest rates in the market increase, for example, the coupons of a bond become less competitive. The bond price needs to decrease so its yield increases and it becomes competitive.

YTM assumes that there is no default and the bond is held to maturity. While some investment textbooks and investment education literature claim that another assumption is that all coupons are reinvested at the YTM (i.e. when receiving the coupon cash payments the investor can invest them and earn on them an interest rate equal to the YTM), this is a common misconception.[44] The reinvestment of coupons is needed to realise a compound yield, not a simple yield, which equals to the YTM. YTM is the promised yield on the bond based on its current market price.

If the bond is held to its maturity, the realised return of the bondholder is the YTM. If the bond is sold before its maturity, the realised total return differs from the YTM since instead of getting back the face value of the bond, the investor gets the prevailing bond price. The total return of a bond is a function of coupon payments (interest), capital gains or losses realised by investors and the effect of defaults. The net asset value of an active bond portfolio or fund, or the price of a bond index, is marked to market and can fluctuate on a daily basis. So the total return of bonds depends not only on the interest rate, but also on capital gains or losses due to trading bonds at their bond price.

Fixed income categorisation

Fixed income securities can be categorised by different dimensions. One dimension is the *issuer*, which is the entity borrowing the money, issuing the bond, paying the interest (coupons) and hopefully returning the principal at maturity. Issuers include governments of developed countries (sovereign bonds) and developing countries (emerging market debt), corporations (corporate bonds), municipalities (municipal bonds, mostly relevant to the United States), government agencies (agency bonds issued by entities such as Fannie Mae, Freddie Mac, Sallie Mae and the Federal Home Loan Banks) and other organisations (e.g. supranational bonds issued by organisations whose members transcend national boundaries).

A second dimension is *credit quality*, which can be divided into investment grade and below investment grade (high-yield), as well as the full spectrum of credit ratings (e.g. AAA, AA, A, BBB, BB, B, CCC) as assigned by credit rating agencies (e.g. Moody's, Standard & Poor's).

A third dimension is *maturity*. Maturities can range from days (Treasury Bills and money market or cash equivalents, short maturity), through a couple of years (intermediate bonds, medium maturity), up to 30 years and even more (long maturity). US Treasury securities, which are issued by the United States Department of the Treasury through the Bureau of Public Debt, are divided into

---

[44] Forbes, Shawn, Hatem, John and Paul, Chris, 'Yield-to-Maturity and the Reinvestment of Coupon Payments', *Journal of Economics and Finance Education* 7 (2008); and Rosen, Lawrence, *The McGraw-Hill Handbook of Interest, Yields, and Returns* (McGraw-Hill, 1995).

Treasury Bills (T-Bills) with a maturity below one year, Treasury Notes with maturities between two and ten years and Treasury Bonds with maturities between 20 and 30 years.

A fourth dimension is *bond features*. Bonds can have a fixed interest (nominal or standard bonds), interest linked to inflation (inflation-linked bonds), convertibility to stocks (convertible bonds) or variable interest (floating rate notes). They may be callable by the issuer before their maturity (callable bonds) or have other different features. Different combinations of the different dimensions described here mean there are endless types of fixed income instruments.

The fixed income derivative market offers a wide range of interest rate, credit and inflation derivatives. The most common fixed income derivatives are credit default swaps (CDS), interest rate swaps, inflation swaps, bond futures, interest rate futures and forward rate agreements (FRAs).

The universe of fixed income is much wider than that of equities. Some reasons for this are that some issuers issue bonds but do not issue equities (e.g. governments and municipalities borrow money but do not share their ownership with the public), each issuer may issue many types of fixed income instruments while typically there is only a single type of common stock per issuer, and fixed income instruments come with many different features. Entities are always on the lookout for innovative ways to borrow money, which helps to explain the many different varieties of bonds.

The reasons to invest in fixed income

Fixed income is a heterogeneous group of assets and as such there are different reasons to invest in the different fixed income investments.

As the name of fixed income implies, income (or yield) is one of the main reasons for fixed income investing. However, in many instances the income is not fixed or safe as the word fixed may imply. Bonds issued by governments or corporates with a high credit rating are likely to be a more stable source of income than those issued by governments of emerging countries or corporates with a below investment grade rating. The level of yield is a function of risk, so safe-haven or low-risk government bonds normally offer a much lower yield than riskier high-yield bonds.

A second main reason to invest in fixed income is capital appreciation. Some fixed income investments are growth assets, such as emerging market debt and high-yield bonds. When rates are high and expected to decline, government and corporate bonds may also be a source of growth. Through fixed income investing portfolios are exposed to maturity risk and credit risk, which are sources of risk premiums and hence systematic returns.

A third main reason for fixed income investing is diversification, in particular for portfolios that include other asset classes, such as equities. Here again the correlation between different fixed income investments and equities can vary. Government bonds should have a low correlation with equities, while high-yield bonds should have a much higher correlation with equities.

There are other reasons to invest in fixed income and these will be covered under each specific fixed income asset class.

Risks of fixed income investing

As the roles for investing in fixed income vary depending on each type of fixed income investment, so do the risks. Different fixed income investments come with different risks.

Generally, the three main risks in fixed income investing are interest rate risk, inflation risk and credit risk. Interest risk is the risk that increasing rates reduce the price of a bond and its yield becomes less competitive. Some fixed income investments, such as FRNs, eliminate the interest rate risk. However, when a risk is reduced or eliminated it usually comes at the expense of reward. Therefore, the yield of FRNs is normally lower than that of standard bonds as investors expect to be compensated for assuming risks. If rates are rising, however, the total return of an FRN can be higher than that of a standard bond.

The second main risk of fixed income investing is inflation risk. Fixed income pays investors cash flows in the future. The real value of these cash flows is affected by the rate of inflation. Increasing inflation is therefore a risk. Inflation-linked bonds eliminate this risk. However, they will underperform standard bonds if realised inflation is below expectations. Interest rate risk and inflation risk together form the real interest rate risk.

The third main risk of fixed income investing is credit risk. Fixed income is a contractual obligation of the issuer to pay interest and return of capital to the investor. If the issuer defaults on its obligation, the investors may not get all the interest, may not get paid on time and may not get back the principal.

Other risks of fixed income investing will be covered under each specific fixed income asset class.

Inflation

Investors ultimately care about the *real* purchasing power of their returns, so inflation is a concern for investors. Bond yields and prices are driven by changes in real interest rates and changes in inflation expectations. Those two drivers affect the shape of the yield curve (positive, flat or negative slope) and bond prices.

Standard bonds (i.e. those that are not inflation linked) are nominally denominated assets and their yields are set to compensate investors for expected inflation over the bond's life. When inflation is unexpectedly higher than the level reflected in the bond price when purchased (and hence reflected in the bond yield), the real purchasing power of the bond's cash flows falls short of expectations. If unexpected inflation leads to revisions of future expected inflation, this loss of real purchasing power can be significant. The longer the life of the bond, the higher the inflation risk.

Inflation hurts bond investors for three main reasons, beyond the drop in price and the drop in purchasing power of future cash flows:

1. higher inflation means that bonds are less attractive as a safe-haven due to heightened uncertainty;

2. when inflation is high it is more volatile; and

3. high inflation hurts companies and consequently the correlation between equities and bonds may increase.

At times of higher inflation bonds lose some of their safe-haven attributes. Their beta should be higher to compensate investors for the risk and the yield curve slopes higher, with higher long-term yields compensating investors for the duration risk of longer maturities.

As inflation over the last couple of decades is not as high as it was for the majority of the 20th century and central banks are now more effective at controlling inflation, bond expected returns should be lower than in the past.

However, the future inflation rate is uncertain. Central banks in Europe and the United States have taken unprecedented measures to stimulate the economies following the 2008 financial crisis and 2011 European sovereign debt crisis. Quantitative easing and inflating the balance sheets of central banks on both sides of the Atlantic are like a huge money printing machine. As central banks focus more on supporting economic growth and less on combating inflation, inflation may rise again in the future.

The yield curve

The yield curve or *term structure of interest rates* is a curve showing several yields or interest rates across different contract lengths (e.g. three months, two years, 30 years) for a similar debt contract. The curve shows the relationship between the interest rate and the time to maturity (the "term") of the debt for a given borrower in a given currency.

The yield curve is important for fixed income analysis since investors can build bond portfolios with different maturities and durations, as well as making use of derivatives, in line with their expectations on the changes in the shape of the yield curve (yield curve positioning). For example, if an investor expects a curve steepener (long-term yields are expected to rise quicker than short-term yields) a trading strategy may be to buy 5-year bonds and short 10-year bonds. This relative trade can make a profit if the investor's view materialises.

The shape of the yield curve indicates the cumulative priorities of all lenders relative to a particular borrower (such as the US Treasury, the Treasury of Japan, the Treasury of Greece and so on). Usually, lenders are concerned about a potential default, rising interest rates or inflation, so they offer long-term loans for higher interest rates than they do for shorter-term loans.

Uncommonly, when demand for long-term debt contracts is higher than for short-term debt contracts, the yield curve inverts, with higher interest rates at the short end of the curve than for those in its long end (this is known as an *inverted yield curve*). An inverted yield curve often indicates a risk of an economic recession looming or at least an expectation for it by the market. Historically, inversion of the yield curve has preceded many economic recessions. The yield curve inverted in 2000, for example, just before the US equity market collapsed.

Three main theories attempt to explain the shape of the yield curve:

1. market expectation hypothesis,

2. liquidity premium theory, and

3. market segmentation theory.

The *market expectation hypothesis* assumes that the various maturities are perfect substitutes and the shape of the yield curve depends on market participants' expectations of future interest rates plus a constant risk premium. These expected rates, along with an assumption that arbitrage opportunities are traded away, is enough information to construct a complete yield curve.

Rates on a long-term instrument are equal to the geometric mean of the yield on a series of short-term instruments. This theory perfectly explains the observation that yields usually move together. However, it fails to explain the persistence in the shape of the yield curve. The shortcoming of the expectation theory is that it neglects the interest rate risk and reinvestment risks inherent in investing in bonds (because forward rates are not perfect predictors of future rates).

The *liquidity premium theory* asserts that long-term interest rates not only reflect investors' assumptions about future interest rates but also include a premium for holding long-term bonds (investors prefer short-term bonds to long-term bonds), called the *term premium* or the *liquidity premium*. This premium compensates investors for the added risk of having their money tied up for a longer time period, including the greater price uncertainty.

Due to the term premium, long-term bond yields tend to be higher than short-term yields, and the yield curve normally slopes upward. Long-term yields are also higher not just because of the liquidity premium, but also because of the risk premium added by the risk of default from holding a security over the long term.

According to the *market segmentation theory*, financial instruments of different terms are not substitutable. As a result, the supply and demand in the markets for short-term and long-term instruments are determined largely independently. Prospective investors decide in advance whether they need short-term or long-term instruments. If investors prefer their portfolio to be liquid, they will prefer short-term instruments to long-term instruments. Therefore, the market for short-term instruments will receive a higher demand. Higher demand for the instrument implies higher prices and lower yields. This explains the stylised fact that short-term yields are usually lower than long-term yields.

This theory explains the predominance of the normal yield curve shape. However, because the supply and demand of the two markets are independent, this theory fails to explain the observed phenomenon that yields tend to move together (i.e. upward and downward shifts in the curve).

The *preferred habitat theory*, which is another version of the market segmentation theory, states that in addition to interest rate expectations, investors have distinct investment horizons and require a meaningful premium to buy bonds with maturities outside their preferred maturity or habitat. Proponents of this theory believe that short-term investors are more prevalent in the fixed-income market and therefore longer-term rates tend for the most part to be higher than short-term rates, but short-term rates can be higher than long-term rates occasionally. This theory is consistent with both the persistence of the normal yield curve shape and the tendency of the yield curve to shift up and down while retaining its shape.

Fixed income in portfolios

Bonds and equities are the two most common assets in most portfolios. Equities provide the risk element and bonds provide the conservative element. Traditionally the main investment decision of asset allocation was the balance between equities and bonds. When investors wanted to increase risk, the allocation to equities was increased at the expense of the allocation to bonds. Conversely, reducing risk was achieved through increasing the allocation to bonds and cash and reducing the allocation to equities.

Today, the decision is no longer solely the equity/bond split in most portfolios as more asset classes are included in the asset allocation mix and other techniques are used to control risk (e.g. hedging, insurance). Nevertheless, fixed income – with all its different variations – still makes up the bulk of portfolios together with equities.

Fixed income portfolio management

The broad and deep fixed income market offers investors plenty of levers to pull as they aim to maximise income and capital appreciation from fixed income portfolios. One widely used active approach to fixed income portfolio management is known as *total return* investing, which uses a variety of strategies to maximise capital appreciation in addition to the return from interest payments. The common techniques for adding this value in fixed income portfolios include:

- *Credit analysis.* Using fundamental, bottom-up credit analysis, managers attempt to identify individual bonds that may rise in price due to an improvement in the issuer's creditworthiness. Bond prices may increase, for example, when a company appoints new and better management. The other side of credit analysis is to avoid issuers that might default. Credit analysis is similar to equity analysis in many aspects. Basically, both credit and equity analysis is an attempt to predict companies' cash flow generation prospects.

- *Macroeconomic analysis.* Top-down macro analysis aims to identify bonds that may rise in price due to economic conditions, a favourable interest rate environment or global growth patterns. For example, as emerging markets have become greater drivers of global growth in recent years, many bonds from governments and corporate issuers in these countries have risen in price.

- *Sector rotation.* Based on their economic outlook, managers invest in certain sectors that should increase in price during a particular phase in the economic cycle and avoid those that are expected to underperform.

- *Market analysis.* Portfolio managers can buy and sell bonds to take advantage of changes in supply and demand that cause price movements. Large institutional investors, such as pension funds and insurance companies, hold large amounts of bonds. Monitoring their trading patterns can help with estimating the direction of bond prices. Issuance of new bonds by governments and corporates may impact bond prices as it generates supply and the demand in issuances is a gauge for the appetite for purchasing bonds.

- *Duration management.* To express a view on expected changes in interest rates and manage interest rate risk, portfolio managers can adjust the duration of portfolios. Managers anticipating a rise in interest rates can attempt to protect bond portfolios from a negative price impact by shortening duration. Conversely, to maximise the positive impact of an expected drop in interest rates, active managers can lengthen duration.

- *Yield curve positioning.* Bond managers can adjust the maturity structure of portfolios based on expected changes in the relationship between bonds with different maturities as reflected by the yield curve. While yields normally rise with maturity, this relationship can change, creating opportunities for managers to position a portfolio in the area of the yield curve that is likely to perform the best in a given economic environment.

- *Roll down.* When short-term interest rates are lower than longer-term rates a bond is valued at successively lower yields and higher prices as it approaches maturity – this is known as 'rolling down the yield curve'. Managers can hold a bond for a period of time as it appreciates in price and sell it before maturity to realise the gain. This strategy has the potential to continually add to total return in a normal interest rate environment.

- *Derivatives.* Managers can use futures, options and derivatives to express a wide range of views, from the creditworthiness of a particular issuer to the direction of interest rates. Derivatives can also be used to hedge unwanted risks and indeed assume wanted risks.

- *Relative value.* Relative value trades aim to capture anomalies in the pricing of different fixed income securities and derivatives.

The bear and bull camps

While equities appreciate on good news (e.g. GDP growth above expectations),[45] fixed income, in particular government bonds, appreciates on bad news (e.g. GDP growth below expectations). Weakening economic growth, for example, implies lower interest rates and inflation – this is good news for bonds and bad news for equities.

Equity investors are part of the bull camp; they hope for good news and they normally see the glass half full. Fixed income investors are part of the bear camp; they hope for bad news and they normally see the glass half empty.

Multi-asset investors must be in the middle camp to objectively weigh the bear and bull views and they then tilt their portfolio more to equities or bonds depending on which asset they believe is likely to perform better.

Outstanding debt in the United States

The outstanding debt in the United States as of the end of 2013 was over $39 trillion.[46] The US debt market is divided into Treasuries (30%), corporate bonds (23%), MBS/CMOs[47] (i.e. mortgages) (22%), municipal bonds (9%), the money market (6%), agencies (5%) and asset backed securities (ABS) (3%).

Figure 2.13 shows the current breakdown of the US debt market. Figure 2.14 shows the amount of outstanding debt of treasuries and corporates, and the overall total, since 1980. The United States has a massive and growing mountain of debt.

The significance of this is that it not only shows the huge amounts of debt in the United States, but it is also another long-term investment theme that investors should consider – the *debt mountain*. Is the amount of debt of the United States sustainable? What are the long-term implications of the unprecedented and growing levels of borrowing across the Western world (most Western developed economies are sitting on growing debt mountains)?

---

[45] GDP growth above expectations can result in falling equity prices in the short term. For example, if the market expects central bank intervention growth is weak, strong GDP growth reduces the likelihood of the intervention and can cause equity prices to drop.

[46] SIFMA, Securities Industry and Financial Markets Association. www.sifma.org.

[47] MBS are mortgage-backed securities and CMOs are Collateralised Mortgage Obligations.

Figure 2.13: US outstanding debt breakdown, 2013

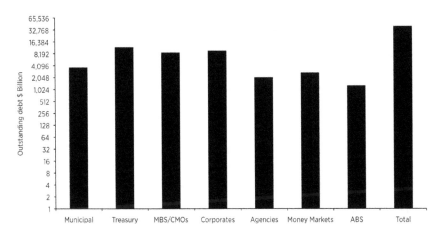

Source: SIFMA.

Figure 2.14: US outstanding Treasuries, corporate debt and total debt, 1980 to 2013

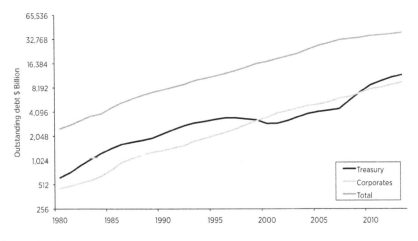

Source: SIFMA.

Two long-term implications are that economies must continue to grow so they can generate enough cash to service their debt and economies must generate inflation to shrink the real value of their debt. In that sense, the debt mountain provides a strong incentive for governments to reflate their economies.

One result of the growing debt mountain for fixed income investors is that the creditworthiness of safe-haven bonds, like those issued by the US government, may be under pressure in the future. At some point the credit rating of the US government might deteriorate if credit agencies believe that the debt level is unsustainable. The US government may need to offer higher yields on its bonds to compensate investors for the higher risk. This will also impact the shape of the yield curve and hence fixed income investment strategies.

Another potential implication is that equity-investing can benefit from the growing debt mountain as the risk of bonds increases while governments are forced to take reflationary measures that support equities.

Summary

- Fixed income is any type of investment that is not equity. The borrower or issuer is contractually obliged to make payments on a fixed schedule, even if the number and size of payments may be variable.

- The fixed income market can be categorised by issuer, credit quality, maturity and bond features.

- With a wide range of fixed income derivatives and an expanding universe of issuers, the fixed income universe is much wider than that of equities.

- The price of a bond is the present value of its future cash flows in the form of coupon payments and principal payment at maturity. Yield to maturity is the discount rate equating the present value of all cash flows to current price.

- The main reasons to invest in fixed income as a general asset class include: income, capital gains and diversification.

- The main risks of investing in fixed income as a general asset class include: interest rate risk, inflation risk and credit risk.

- Inflation hurts bond investors for three main reasons beyond the drop in bond price and the purchasing power of future cash flows: higher inflation means that bonds are less attractive as a safe-haven due to heightened uncertainty; when inflation is high it is more volatile; and high inflation hurts companies and so the correlation between equities and bonds may increase.

- The common fixed income portfolio management techniques are credit analysis, macroeconomic analysis, sector rotation, market analysis, duration management, yield curve positioning, roll down, derivatives and relative value.

- Equity investors are part of the bull camp and fixed income investors are part of the bear camp. The optimists versus the pessimists.

- Fixed income investments and equities are the two most common assets in most portfolios.

Government bonds

Government or sovereign bonds (colloquially *govis*) represent debt taken by governments of developed countries and a promise to pay the bond holders (lenders) money in the form of a series of coupons (interest) and principal repayment at the bond's maturity. Sovereign debt of countries such as the United States, United Kingdom, Germany, Japan and Switzerland is considered one of the safest investments. When these countries take a loan and promise to pay it back, it is extremely unlikely that they are going to disappoint their creditors.

When investing in government bonds, investors have a number of investment choices, including country of issuance, maturity and coupon configuration (e.g. fixed, floating and zero coupon bonds, which as their name implies pay no coupons). However, the choices are narrower than other fixed income markets (i.e. the market breadth is lower). For example, when investing in UK government bonds (gilts) there is a single choice of issuer (the UK government), while when investing in the UK corporate bond market the number of issuers is numerous.

The sovereign market is often called the rates market since interest rates are the prominent factor affecting the price of government bonds. The main factors influencing sovereign debt's returns are fiscal and monetary policy, the outlook for the economy, inflation or deflation, flows, issuance volume and the shape of the yield curve.

Defaults of developed, investment grade government bonds should be carefully considered, in particular following the lessons of the 2008 financial crisis and the 2011 European sovereign debt crisis, when investment grade sovereign debt of some countries was quickly downgraded to below investment grade. Sovereign debt of countries like Portugal, Italy, Ireland, Greece and Spain (PIIGS) quickly turned from safe haven to junk (high-yield). Investors with an appetite for risk were able to realise attractive gains by investing in the bonds of countries such as Italy and Spain.

Table 2.8 shows selected countries that have a high amount of public debt and their credit ratings.

Table 2.8: Top 20 countries ranked by public debt as a percentage of GDP, 2012

Country	Public debt ($ billions)	% GDP	S&P credit rating
Japan	134	214	AA-
Zimbabwe	129	202	Not rated
Greece	158	161	B-
Lebanon	131	128	B
Jamaica	135	127	CCC+
Italy	115	126	BBB
Portugal	116	124	BB
Ireland	110	118	A-
France	87	90	AA
United Kingdom	90	90	AAA
Spain	79	85	BBB
Canada	59	84	AAA
Germany	69	80	AAA
United States	107	73	AA+
Netherlands	51	69	AA+
Brazil	45	55	BBB-
India	59	50	BBB-
Turkey	34	36	BB+
Mexico	37	35	BBB+
China	26	32	AA-

Source: CIA World Factbook, International Monetary Fund (IMF), Standard & Poor's.

It is important to look at the absolute amount of a country's public debt in the context of its GDP. The *debt-to-GDP ratio* is one of the indicators of the health of an economy.[48] It is the amount of national debt of a country as a percentage of its Gross Domestic Product (GDP).

A low debt-to-GDP ratio indicates an economy that probably produces enough goods and services to generate taxes to pay back its debt. Governments aim for low debt-to-GDP ratios and can stand up to the risks involved in increasing debt as their economies have a higher GDP and profit margin. When analysing the

---

[48] The debt-to-GDP ratio is similar to the interest coverage ratio for companies. This ratio is used to determine how easily a company can pay interest on its outstanding debt. The interest coverage ratio is calculated by dividing a company's earnings before interest and taxes (EBIT) of one period by the company's interest expenses of the same period. A higher ratio indicates better ability to pay interest on debt.

creditworthiness of a government the debt-to-GDP ratio is the relevant metric. So based on the data in Table 2.8, the creditworthiness of the United States is better than that of the United Kingdom, even if the former has more debt than the latter.

The debt-to-GDP ratio of the United States is about 73%. The level of public debt in Japan is 214% of GDP. Almost a third of US public debt is held by foreign countries, particularly China and Japan. Conversely, less than 5% of Japanese public debt is held by foreign countries. All these factors should be considered when assessing the creditworthiness of a government. As more debt is held by foreigners, it may be more difficult for the government to pay it back without defaulting or reaching an agreement on debt restructuring, if this should be needed.

Government bond valuation

The government bond markets of developed countries[49] are efficient. The issues are traded in high volumes, they are normally liquid and many sophisticated market players participate in their trading. The market forces of supply and demand set the prices of government bonds and their YTM. The YTMs of government bonds are widely used as the benchmark for valuation and pricing of other fixed income instruments. Corporate bonds, for example, are valued using the spread between their YTM and the YTM of corresponding government bonds.

The reasons to invest in government bonds

Government bonds have been commonly the second most popular asset class in multi-asset portfolios after equities (though it should be noted there is the prospect of corporate bonds overtaking government bonds in coming years). The reasons for investing in government bonds and their roles in portfolios include:[50]

- *Expected stable cash flows or capital preservation.* Government bonds should have low default risk. Governments of countries such as the United States, Japan, Germany and the United Kingdom are not expected to default on their contractual obligations. The cash flows of bonds with fixed coupons are known in terms of amounts and timing.

- *Income generation.* The coupon payments are a source of regular and stable income. In that sense government bonds are similar to a time deposit (i.e. interest-bearing bank deposit with a specific date of maturity). The main difference is that a bond is a transferable security, so the investor can sell it at the prevailing bond price.

---

[49] The top ten developed countries with the largest amounts of public debt are Greece, Japan, Portugal, Italy, Ireland, Singapore, the United States, Iceland, Belgium and the United Kingdom.

[50] The list of reasons for investing in government bonds is applicable to bonds issued by governments of countries that have not been materially impacted by the 2011 sovereign debt crisis.

- *Easy to model.* When held to maturity the expected return of government bonds is close to their YTM. Historic data on government bonds is readily available and therefore they are easily modelled for asset allocation purposes.

- *Immunise or hedge liabilities.* Government bonds can be used to hedge liabilities. A simple, crude way to immunise liabilities is to match their duration with that of a portfolio of bonds or to match the cash outflows with those of a portfolio of bonds. The advantage of using government bonds to hedge liabilities is that credit risk is normally low. This is also a disadvantage since the yield is low relative to bonds that have higher credit risk.

- *Low return volatility.* Government bonds have relatively low standard deviation (compared to equities and other risk assets).

- *Interest rate and inflation risks.* Government bonds expose portfolios to interest rate and inflation risk factors and are therefore a source of systematic risks and returns. Some risks are valuable resources because they are expected to be compensated by the market. Through government bonds investors can specifically get exposure to interest rate and inflation risks while limiting exposure to credit risk.

- *Maturity risk premium.* Long-term government bonds offer a maturity risk premium and their returns tend to outperform cash and short-term bonds over long-term investment horizons.

- *Diversification benefits.* Government bonds tend to have low correlation with equities and other risk assets. For example, government bonds should perform better than other assets during an economic contraction and recession (since interest rates and inflation are dropping) and during deflation (long-maturity government bonds are one of the best assets to hold during periods of deflation).

- *Protection.* Govis tend to perform positively in slowing economic conditions and when there is a flight to quality. Therefore, govis offer some protection in portfolios against negative equity markets. To provide the protection, the government bonds must have a long duration so their price changes sufficiently to partly offset potentially significant drops in equity markets. The price of a bond with duration of five years, for example, will increase by about 5% for every 1% drop in YTM.

- *Source for liquidity and collateral.* Government bonds of countries with large economies (such as the United States, United Kingdom and Germany) are liquid and can be used as a source of liquidity and collateral.

- *Safety deposit box.* The real yield of government bonds can turn negative when the rate of inflation is above the nominal yield. Even when the yield on bonds is negative, investors sometimes still invest in government bonds of countries with a safe-haven reputation (such as Switzerland). Investors prefer to lend their money to governments that are very likely to keep it safe and pay it back, even at a loss, than to deposit it with banks that may fail. This is akin to putting the money under a large mattress. Return on capital has been replaced by return of capital. As Will Rogers said, "People should be more concerned with the return of their principal than the return on their principal."

It is useful to look at long-term data on how government bonds have performed, as this will provide further evidence for why they are a popular investment asset. Figures 2.15 to 2.18 show US equities and US Treasuries (10-year government bonds) over a 110-year period (since January 1900).

Figure 2.15 compares the cumulative performance of equities and bonds. Over the long term, investing in US equities was rewarded much more than investing in US government bonds. The equity ride was much bumpier – the line representing equity investing is not as smooth as that representing the investment in government bonds. This shows the higher risk of equity investing compared to government bond investing.

Figure 2.15: Cumulative performance of the S&P 500 Index and US 10-year Treasuries, January 1900 to December 2013

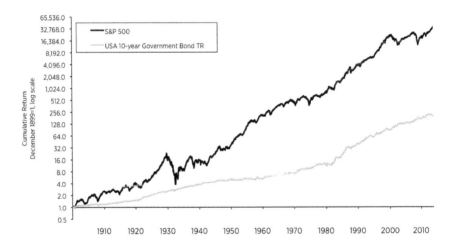

Source: Global Financial Data, S&P 500 Index, USA 10-year Government Bond TR Index.

Figure 2.16 compares the rolling annualised performance over 10-year periods. Over most 10-year periods equity investing generated higher returns than government bond investing. However, there are periods of equity market crashes, during which government bonds can provide a source of positive returns. There was no 10-year period during which US government bonds delivered negative *nominal* returns.

Figure 2.16: Rolling 10-year annualised return of the S&P 500 Index and US 10-year Treasuries, January 1910 to December 2013

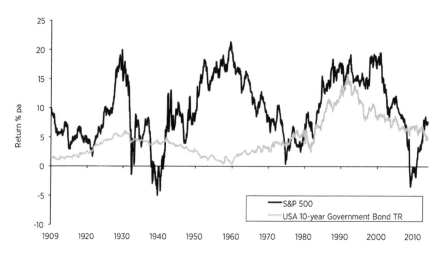

Source: Global Financial Data, S&P 500 Index, USA 10-year Government Bond TR Index.

Figure 2.17 shows the 10-year rolling correlation. While intuitively the correlation between equities and government bonds should be negative, it can turn positive. Correlations between asset classes are not stationary – they change, sometimes markedly. Once again this highlights the requirement to be dynamic when investing. Investors need always to adapt to changing circumstances.

Figure 2.17: Rolling 10-year correlation between the S&P 500 Index and US 10-year Treasuries, January 1910 to December 2013

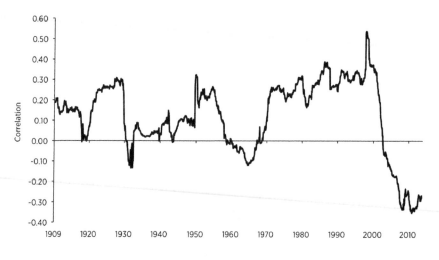

Source: Global Financial Data, S&P 500 Index, USA 10-year Government Bond TR Index.

Figure 2.18 compares the 10-year rolling annualised standard deviation of the two asset classes. The risk of equities, as measured by standard deviation, is higher than that of government bonds. High risk should be compensated over time by higher return. However, it can mean periods of severe underperformance of the riskier asset.

Figure 2.18: Rolling 10-year annualised volatility of the S&P 500 Index and US 10-year Treasuries, January 1910 to December 2013

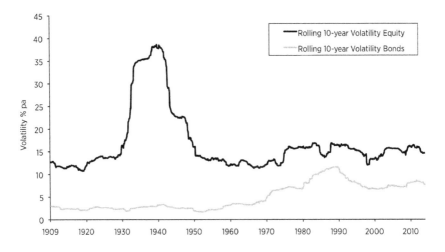

Source: Global Financial Data, S&P 500 Index, USA 10-year Government Bond TR Index.

Equities tend to outperform government bonds over the long term. However, government bonds have relatively low correlation with equities and they are affected differently by some economic developments. For example, slowing economic growth is bad news for equities but good news for government bonds, all else being equal, since it means lower expected interest rates and lower inflation.

Government bonds also tend to perform well when equity markets crash because a flight to quality means that investors are rushing out of equity and other risk assets to the safe havens of conservative assets, such as government bonds as well as gold, US dollar, Japanese yen and Swiss franc (e.g. the 1930s Great Depression and the 2008 crisis). Government bonds, therefore, offer diversification for equities and also some portfolio protection in stressful times.

The roles of government bonds in portfolios are to deliver relatively stable returns, diversify the equity and other risk assets and provide protection against stress in risk assets. In particular, long duration government bonds hedge against weak consumer activity and provide a payoff during economic downturn. When liabilities are present, bonds may have a role in hedging liabilities.

According to Dimson, Marsh and Staunton,[51] from 1980 to the end of 2010 government bonds returned 6% per annum in real terms in the United States. During the preceding 80 years the return was only 0.2%. In the United Kingdom the return in real terms was 6.3% since 1980 and -0.5% during the preceding 80 years.

Risks of government bonds

Government bonds of certain countries are a conservative asset and should have lower risks than risk assets, such as equities. Nevertheless, as with any asset, there are plenty of risks that must be well understood. The main risks of investing in government bonds include:

- *Interest rate risk.* Bond prices decrease when interest rates increase. A bond offering a certain coupon rate becomes less competitive when interest rates increase since other investments offer higher interest rates. Therefore, the price of the bond adjusts downward as interest rates rise so that its yield becomes competitive again. The longer the duration of the bond, the larger the impact on its price due to interest rate changes.

- *Credit risk.* Credit risk is the risk of a loss of principal, interest payments or financial reward stemming from a borrower's failure to repay a loan or to meet a contractual obligation. Default risk falls under credit risk and means an event in which the borrower is unable to make the required payments on the debt obligations. Credit events include, beyond the failure to pay, bankruptcy of the borrower, debt restructuring[52] (e.g. haircut), repudiation,[53] moratorium,[54] obligation acceleration or obligation default. While a sovereign default of a developed economy should be very rare in modern times, it is still a risk (e.g. 2011 European debt crisis and the credit-rating downgrade of the United States in August 2011).

- *Reinvestment risk.* Reinvestment risk is the possibility of coupons invested at lower interest rates than expected (because prevailing interest rates have decreased) and hence realising a lower total compounded return than expected.

---

[51] Dimson, Elroy, Marsh, Paul and Staunton, Mike, 'Fear of falling', *Credit Suisse Global Investment Returns Yearbook 2011.*

[52] Debt restructuring is a process that allows a borrower facing cash flow problems and financial distress to reduce and renegotiate its delinquent debts in order to improve or restore liquidity and rehabilitate itself so that it can continue its operations.

[53] Anticipatory repudiation (anticipatory breach) is a term in the law of contracts describing a declaration by the promising party to a contract that it does not intend to fulfil its contractual obligations.

[54] A debt moratorium is a delay in the payment of debts or obligations. The term is generally used to refer to acts by national governments. A moratory law is usually passed in a period of particular political or commercial stress.

- *Inflation risk.* The coupons and principal of nominal bonds are not adjusted to inflation, which can erode the value of cash flows. As the duration of the bond is longer the risk of inflation is higher. High levels of inflation can seriously affect the realised real returns from bonds.

- *Yield curve risk.* When the yield curve shifts, a bond price, which was priced based on the initial yield curve, changes. If the yield curve flattens (steepens), then the yield spread between long and short-term interest rates narrows (widens). A bear flattener means that short-term interest rates are increasing at a faster pace than long-term rates. This causes the yield-curve to flatten and hurts bond prices. A bear steepener, on the other hand, means that the long end of the curve is rising at a faster pace than the short end and, again, bond prices fall. The rate at the short end of the yield curve is influenced by short-term interest rates as set by central banks and is much more volatile than the long end of the curve. The rates at the long end of the curve are set by market forces (i.e. prevailing prices of bonds), not by policy.

- *Currency risk.* When investing in unhedged foreign bonds, currency exposure is a risk that can materially amplify the volatility of bonds – in fact it can dominate the risk of investing in government bonds. This risk can be easily managed by hedging the currency exposure, in particular for currencies of developed countries.

- *Manager risk.* Most government bond markets are efficient and liquid. The universe of issues in each country is usually small (e.g. 30 to 40 bonds in the index), making it more challenging for managers because of limited opportunities for breadth of investment decisions. The opportunities for active management to add value are therefore limited. Some active managers tend to invest in corporate bonds, invest off-benchmark and take other risks within government bond portfolios to try to beat the benchmark. When investing in government bond funds, investors should conduct due diligence to understand exactly what the fund manager can and cannot do. If the fund manager has flexibility to invest in other assets or other currencies and investors are not aware of this, they may be surprised when they find out later that the fund does not represent pure exposure to government bonds. This does not imply that manager flexibility is negative per se, just that investors need to be aware of what they are investing in.

Historically, government bond market drawdowns have been larger and/or longer than those of equity markets and in real terms bonds can be a risk asset. Figure 2.19 shows the drawdown of real returns of 10-year US Treasuries since January 1926. When inflation is considered, government bonds experienced a long drawdown from the beginning of the 1940s (the Great Depression) to the middle of the 1980s (when yields reached an all-time high). This is a 40-year drawdown. Equities have never experienced such a long drawdown.

Figure 2.19: US 10-year Treasuries real return drawdown, January 1926 to December 2013

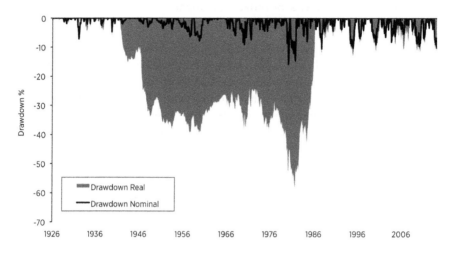

Source: Global Financial Data, USA 10-year Government Bond TR Index, US inflation.

Risk measures

There are two important risk measures for bonds:

1. *Duration* is a measure of the sensitivity of bond prices to changes in interest rates (this is the first derivative of price with respect of interest rates). Duration can be used to estimate the bond price fluctuations due to interest rate risk. If interest rates move up by 1%, for example, the price of a bond with duration of five years moves down by 5%. The duration is only an estimate of the change in price since it assumes that the entire interest rate yield curve moves in parallel (i.e. all rates along the yield curve move by the same amount, which is 1% in the example just given). This is an unrealistic assumption but good enough for an estimate. Duration is a function of the maturity and coupons. Longer maturity means longer duration. Higher coupons mean shorter duration, since a higher proportion of the cash flows from the bond are due sooner.

2. *Convexity* is a measure of the sensitivity of bond duration to changes in interest rates (this is the second derivative of price with respect of interest rates). Duration and convexity are helpful in quantifying the interest rate risk of bonds.

Government bonds and the yield curve

Figure 2.20 shows the yield curves of US Treasury bonds on January 2008 and March 2014. Back in January 2008 the slope of the yield curve was much flatter compared with that in March 2013.

The short end of the curve, representing short maturity bonds, is much more volatile than the long end of the curve. Central banks control short-term interest rates, while market forces set long-term interest rates. The yield curve at the beginning of 2008 was more 'normal' than the one in 2013. Short-term interest rates were at a level of about 3% and 10-year rates at a level of close to 4%. Then, the global financial crisis struck. Central banks lowered short-term yields to flush the economy with liquidity and the short end of the yield curve collapsed. The good news is that the steepness of the yield curve in March 2013 indicates that the market expects yields to move back toward 'normal' levels from close to all-time lows at the depth of the crisis.

Figure 2.20: US Treasury bond yield curve, November 2000, January 2008 and March 2013

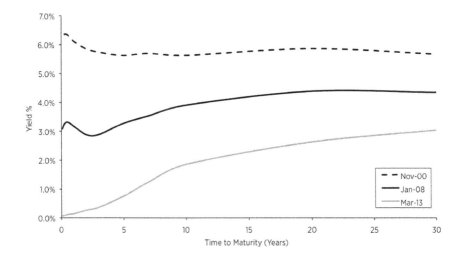

Source: U.S. Department of the Treasury.

Normal level of yields

The 'normal' 10-year government bond yield has historically been connected to the nominal GDP growth rate. When the economy is strong, central banks hike rates and bond yields rise. Similarly, when inflation (one of the components of nominal GDP) is rising, so is the inflation expectation component of the bond market. Economic growth and inflation are therefore two variables that influence bond yields.

This makes sense from a microeconomic perspective. Bond yields naturally settle at a level where supply equals demand. If the level of yields is materially lower than the rate of GDP growth, investors will not buy bonds as they would rather invest in assets directly connected to the economy, such as equities. Bond prices will therefore decrease, pushing yields upward.

If yields are materially higher than growth, borrowers will not borrow as they cannot earn a sufficient return on their projects to justify the loan. Weak supply of bonds will push their price up and their yield down.

The equilibrium 10-year bond yield is hence the rate of economic growth, including inflation, or nominal GDP growth rate. If the trend of real growth of the economy is 3% and the inflation rate is 2%, the 'normal' 10-year bond yield is about 5%.

Today, in a world in which central banks have quantitative easing and unconventional monetary measures in place, the question remains when bond yields will reach such a 'normal' level, as they are still at a much lower level than that. The actions of central banks may artificially set a low level for yields. Also, the future trend real GDP growth rate may be different to the historical one and the future inflation rate may be different than that of the past. The future role of central banks and their set of monetary tools may have changed following the events since 2008. Under these circumstances it is hard to estimate what is 'normal' any more. The global financial system may be undergoing a structural shift and investors will need time to adapt to a new set of rules.

2011 sovereign debt crisis

Government bonds should provide an element of safety and stability. However, with the unprecedented levels of public debt of Western developed countries, unprecedented low yields of bonds of some governments (e.g. United States, Japan, Germany and United Kingdom) and unprecedented default risks of other governments (e.g. Portugal and Greece) that have come to the fore since the 2008 financial crisis, the role and safety of government bonds may have changed forever.

During the 2011 European sovereign debt crisis some sovereigns, such as Italy and Spain, saw the yields on their 10-year government bonds surpassing 7%. These countries were considered top credit quality before the crisis.

The key to the safe-haven status of sovereign debt is credibility. The credibility is that the government is going to stand behind its contractual obligations and pay the coupons and return the principal on time to its lenders. Once this credibility is dented lenders lose faith in the government. They will demand a much higher yield to lend to the government to compensate them for the risk. The higher yields make it more difficult for the government to tap capital markets for financing since the interest payments are much higher. With higher interest payments it becomes more difficult for the government to repay its debt and lenders continue to lose even more confidence in the government. This is a vicious circle with potentially devastating results.

Governments in this situation may be required to ask for help from other countries or entities, as did the governments of some European countries during the 2011 and 2012 European debt crisis, for example, Greece required a bailout from the European Central Bank and the European Union. Such a bailout can come in the form of a commitment to buy the sovereign debt of the beleaguered government, keeping the yield of its debt at acceptable low levels with the aim of returning confidence.

During the 2011 European sovereign debt crisis it emerged that the default risk of many governments with a credit rating of A and above was much higher than equivalently-rated corporate bonds. Investing in sovereign bonds of developed countries has become much more akin to investing in corporate bonds and requires closer analysis of governments' creditworthiness.

Long-term perspective on government bonds

US government bonds have enjoyed a secular bull run, in particular since the beginning of the 1980s. Figure 2.21 shows the cumulative performance of US 10-year Treasuries in nominal and real terms since January 1926. US government bonds have taken off as inflation was brought under control at the beginning of the 1980s.

Figure 2.21: Cumulative performance of US 10-year Treasuries, January 1926 to December 2013

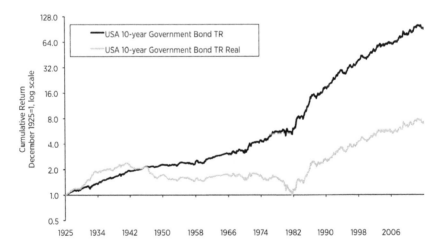

Source: Global Financial Data, USA 10-year Government Bond TR Index, US Inflation.

As Figure 2.22 shows, the 10-year government bond yield in the US reached almost an all-time low at the end of 2012. This means that 10-year government bonds are offering a low yield, likely to be lower than inflation, hence offering negative real yields. This also means that the yield has one secular direction (upwards) and the price of Treasuries have one secular opposite direction (downwards).

Figure 2.22: US 10-year government bond yield, January 1926 to December 2013

Source: Global Financial Data, USA 10-year Bond Constant Maturity Yield.

Since 1926 yields have ranged from a little less than 1.5% to a little bit above 15.8% with an average rate of 5.0%. However, the left-hand side of Figure 2.22 clearly represents a different world from the right-hand side. Somewhere between the mid-1950s and the mid-1970s rates have become much more volatile.

From 1926 through 1959, interest rates ranged from the all-time low of a little more than 1.5% in 1945 to a high of 4.7% in 1959. The range from low to high was only 3.1%; the average rate was 3.1%. Since then, the range has been from the 2012 European sovereign crisis panic low of 1.6% to the September 1981 all-time high of 15.8%. The range was over 14%; the average rate during that period was 6.5%.

Past and future government bond returns

Since the beginning of the 1980s, 10-year US government bonds have returned 8.5% per annum. This return was driven by high yields at the beginning of the 1980s and their continuous reduction (so the total returns of bonds were made of high carry and price appreciation). At the beginning of the 1980s inflation was brought under control by central banks and has been kept at low rates. The time period of decreasing yields and inflation may have been the golden age for government bonds.

The starting point today is different. Yields are close to all-time lows. This means that over the next decade the expected return on 10-year Treasuries is about 3%[55] (when bonds are held to maturity). Investors in US Treasuries should expect slightly

---

[55] Based on yield as of the end of 2013.

positive real returns, assuming that the inflation rate will be about 2%. At present government bonds are not an attractive investment from a return perspective.

Figure 2.23 shows the US Consumer Price Index (CPI) since January 1913.[56] The chart shows that the 1970s were a period of high inflation, while since 1982 the pace of inflation has been much more subdued (as can be seen by the slope of the line). It is difficult to predict how inflation is going to look going forward. It is yet to be seen how the end of quantitative easing and the potential changing roles of central banks (e.g. focusing on economic growth and the labour market instead of on inflation) will impact inflation.

Figure 2.23: US CPI, January 1913 to December 2013

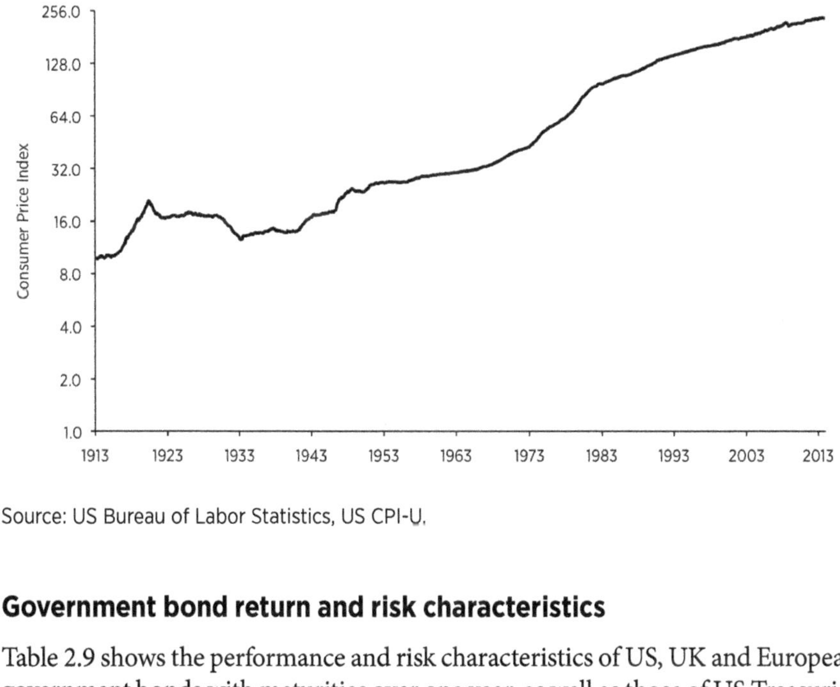

Source: US Bureau of Labor Statistics, US CPI-U.

Government bond return and risk characteristics

Table 2.9 shows the performance and risk characteristics of US, UK and European government bonds with maturities over one year, as well as those of US Treasuries in real terms (US Tr. Real) and US inflation-linked bonds. The performance and risk characteristics of US 10-year constant maturity government bonds and US equities are included as well. Table 2.10 is a correlation matrix of the different government bond indices and equities.

The average annual total return of 10-year government bonds was around 5% to 6%. This is 1% to 2% below the return of US equities over the same time period. The return of government bonds was generated at a much lower risk level than

---

[56] US Department of Labor, Bureau of Labor Statistics, www.bls.gov. All Urban Consumers CPI-U.

that of equities, as the volatility, Sharpe ratio and max drawdown clearly show. Government bonds have lower downside risk than that of equities, and are less susceptible to crashes, as indicated by their skewness. However, the performance of the past should not be expected to continue in the years ahead as 10-year yields move back to 'normal' levels, putting downward pressure on the total return of government bonds.

The impact of inflation on return can be material, effectively cutting it in half from around 6% to 3%. Investing in inflation-linked bonds may be a solution for long-term investors who wish to protect their wealth from inflationary erosion. However, the choice between nominal and inflation-linked bonds depends on investors' expectations about future inflation.

The correlation matrix shows that government bonds not only have diversification benefits when mixed with equities, but also when bonds issued by different governments are mixed together. The correlations across different govis is imperfect. Investors should, however, carefully manage the currency exposure when investing in overseas bonds.

Table 2.9: Government bond return and risk characteristics, March 1997 to December 2013. Sharpe ratio calculated using $ cash returns

	US Treasuries	UK gilts	European govis	US linkers	US Tr. Real	US 10-Yr	US equities
Start month	Mar-1997	Mar-1997	Mar-1997	Mar-1997	Mar-1997	Mar-1997	Mar-1997
Performance (% pa)	5.5	6.3	5.2	6.1	3.1	6.0	7.1
Volatility (% pa)	4.6	5.3	3.6	5.9	5.0	7.7	16.0
Skewness	-0.14	0.18	-0.01	-0.84	0.33	0.08	-0.64
Kurtosis	1.37	0.68	-0.16	4.34	2.96	1.36	0.84
Sharpe ratio	0.66	0.72	0.75	0.61	0.13	0.45	0.29
Max drawdown (%)	-5.0	-5.9	-6.0	-11.9	-7.1	-10.1	-50.9

Source: Bloomberg, Global Financial Data, Citigroup United States WGBI TR Index, Citigroup United Kingdom WGBI TR Index, Citigroup European WGBI TR Index, Barclays Capital US Inflation Linked Bonds TR Index, USA 10-year Government Bond TR Index, S&P 500 Index, US inflation.

Table 2.10: Correlation matrix, March 1997 to December 2013

Correlation matrix	US Treasuries	UK gilts	European govis	US linkers	US Tr. Real	US 10-Yr	US equities
US Treasuries	1.00	0.73	0.65	0.67	0.97	0.98	-0.26
UK gilts	0.73	1.00	0.68	0.48	0.74	0.75	-0.14
European govis	0.65	0.68	1.00	0.40	0.65	0.67	-0.17
US linkers	0.67	0.48	0.40	1.00	0.59	0.66	0.02
US Tr. Real	0.97	0.74	0.65	0.59	1.00	0.94	-0.24
US 10-Yr	0.98	0.75	0.67	0.66	0.94	1.00	-0.26
US equities	-0.26	-0.14	-0.17	0.02	-0.24	-0.26	1.00

Source: Bloomberg, Global Financial Data, Citigroup United States WGBI TR Index, Citigroup United Kingdom WGBI TR Index, Citigroup European WGBI TR Index, Barclays Capital US Inflation Linked Bonds TR Index, USA 10-year Government Bond TR Index, S&P 500 Index, US inflation.

Figure 2.24 shows the cumulative performance of US, UK and European government bonds with maturities above one year since October 1992. While correlated, bonds issued by different sovereigns do offer different return and risk profiles. Note the underperformance of European govis following the 2010 European sovereign debt crisis, and the following rebound in 2012.

Investors can benefit by diversifying across different bonds. If skill for active management exists, investors can add value by dynamically allocating across different government bond markets. While the breadth of each government bond market is narrow, by expanding the universe to include several countries the breadth can be increased.

Figure 2.25 shows the cumulative performance of US Treasuries and US linkers (TIPS or Treasury Inflation-Protected Securities) since March 1997. Nominal government bonds and inflation-linked government bonds are two distinct asset classes. Each can outperform or underperform depending on the expected and unexpected inflation rate. Once again, skilled investors can benefit by changing the allocations across the two asset classes, depending on expectations on inflation rates.

Figure 2.24: Cumulative performance of US, UK and European government bonds, October 1992 to December 2013

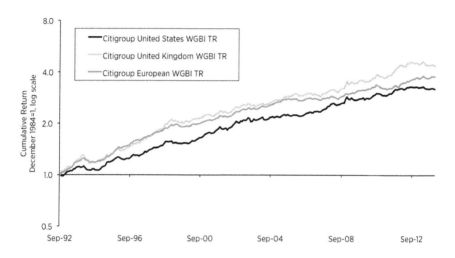

Source: Citigroup United States WBGI TR Index, Citigroup United Kingdom WBGI TR Index, Citigroup European WGBI TR Index.

Figure 2.25: Cumulative performance of US Treasury and inflation-linked bonds, March 1997 to December 2013

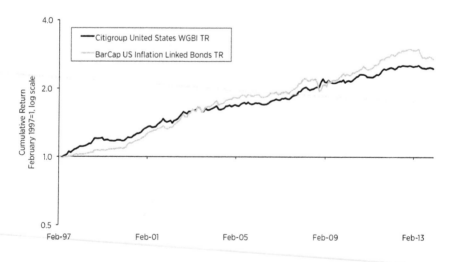

Source: Citigroup United States WGBI TR Index, Barclays Capital US Inflation Linked Bonds TR Index.

Figure 2.26 shows the cumulative performance of US Treasuries using nominal and real returns since January 1985. The impact of inflation on the return of government bonds over long investment horizons can be devastating. One of the most important considerations for long-term investors and savers is to protect their assets against inflation.

Figure 2.26: Cumulative performance of US Treasury bonds using nominal and real returns adjusted to US inflation, January 1985 to December 2013

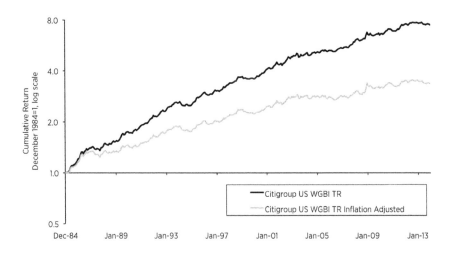

Source: Citigroup United States WGBI TR Index, US inflation.

Figure 2.27 shows the rolling 36-month correlation between US Treasury bonds and US equities. Until the equity market crash following the high-tech bubble burst in 2000, the correlation was positive. It has turned negative just when needed as equities fell. During this time government bonds received a boost from the aggressive monetary action of the Federal Reserve when interest rates were cut and the expectations were for rates to remain low. The correlation has remained negative since then (although this does not mean that the correlation will remain negative going forward).

Figure 2.28 shows the rolling 36-month annualised volatility of US Treasury bonds with maturities over one year and US Treasury bonds with 10-year maturity. Longer duration means higher sensitivity to changes in interest rates and higher volatility. The higher risk of longer maturities should be compensated by attracting a maturity risk premium.

Figure 2.27: Rolling 36-month correlation between US Treasury bonds and US equities, January 1973 to December 2013

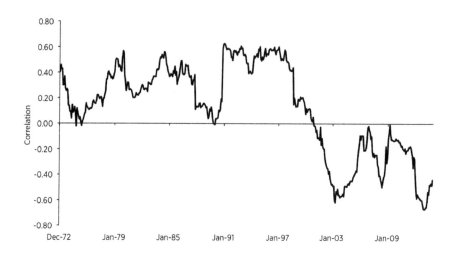

Source: Citigroup United States WGBI TR Index, S&P 500 Index.

Figure 2.28: Rolling 36-month volatility of US Treasury bonds with > 1-year maturity and with 10-year maturity, January 1988 to December 2013

Source: Global Financial Data, Citigroup United States WGBI TR Index, USD 10-year Government Bond TR Index.

Figure 2.29 shows the cumulative performance of US Treasury bonds with maturities over one year and US Treasury bonds with 10-year maturity. Over the measurement period the maturity premium has indeed paid off. Taking higher risk was rewarded. However, in periods of increasing interest rates, longer maturities are expected to underperform shorter maturities. Duration management is one of the ways to control such risk.

Figure 2.29: Cumulative performance of US Treasury bonds with > 1-year maturity and with 10-year maturity, January 1985 to December 2013

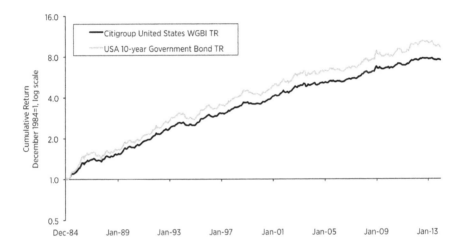

Source: Global Financial Data, Citigroup United States WGBI TR Index, USD 10-year Government Bond TR Index.

Figure 2.30 shows the average performance of US Treasuries with maturities over one year ranked by deciles of average US equity performance. The chart demonstrates the protective features of government bonds, which tend to perform well when equity markets perform poorly.

Figure 2.30: Average performance of US equities and Treasury bonds ranked by performance deciles of US equities, January 1985 to December 2013

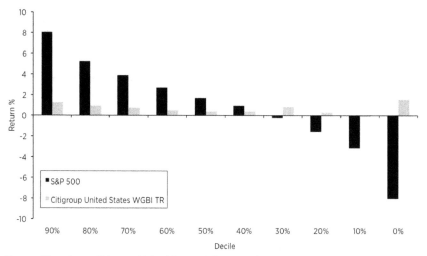

Source: Bloomberg, Citigroup United States WGBI TR Index, S&P 500 Index.

Expected return

The long-term expected return of nominal bonds is their yield minus an adjustment for the expected cost of default, assuming bonds are held to maturity. Relaxing the assumption of holding the bond to maturity, a duration adjustment is needed, assuming that the yield is going to move back to the 'normal' level (nominal GDP growth rate). Investors should apply discretion on whether they believe that the yield is going to normalise and at what time. Assuming government bonds of core countries are not expected to default, the bond's yield-to-maturity is a good indicator of expected return over an investment horizon matching the bond's maturity.

Access

Investors have three main ways to purchase government bonds:

1. The first way is to buy individual bonds. In the United States government bonds can be purchased directly from the treasury or via a broker, as they are traded on the stock exchange. The yield on new issuances is set in an auction. US bonds are sold in increments of $1,000. In the United Kingdom gilts can be bought from the Debt Management Office (DMO) or via a broker. They are sold in small increments, so investors can easily build a diversified portfolio, perhaps following a ladder strategy with bonds maturing at different times.

2. The second way is to buy a fund investing in government bonds. There is a choice between actively managed funds or passive funds and exchange traded funds (ETFs), passively tracking a bond index. Funds are available for bonds ranging across different countries and regions, as well as across different maturity ranges (e.g. 1-3, 0-5, 1-10, 7-10, 10-15, 15-30 years). If investors believe that active management for this asset class may struggle to add value due to its efficiency and shallow breadth, passive funds are offered relatively cheaply (e.g. TER of up to 20 basis points for retail investors and much lower for large institutional investors).

3. The third way to buy govis is through the derivative market. For example, futures contracts on 10-year government bonds for major countries, such as the United States, United Kingdom and Germany, are liquid and readily available. Buying or selling futures contracts is cheap (transaction costs are negligible) and quick. Futures can be shorted allowing investors to express a negative view on govis. The main shortcoming is that the contract size is normally large (e.g. over £200,000), making it difficult to trade for small investors.

Conclusions

Govis are the ultimate conservative asset. The United States, United Kingdom and Germany are not going to default on their debt obligations. This means that government bonds play a key role in portfolios, offering an anchor of stability and protection. When all hell breaks loose, government bonds should be an island of safety.

However, with yields of core countries near all-time lows, the roles of govis are questionable until yields reach a 'normal' level once again. Government bonds of most core countries are expected to generate a low single digit real return over the next decade and are not an attractive investment from a return perspective.

We might question whether this is the end for government bonds in portfolios. Without returns and protection power, government bonds are losing their main roles. However, over time yields will normalise and the 10-year yield of the bonds of the core countries will get back to a 4% or 5% level. Then the role of protection will be back and government bonds will regain their role in portfolios.

Summary

- Government or sovereign bonds are issued by governments. Issuing bonds is one of the primary ways for governments to borrow money (i.e. raise public debt).

- The debt-to-GBP ratio indicates a country's ability to repay its public debt.

- The prices of developed government bonds, whose markets are efficient, are set by market forces of supply and demand.

- The reasons to invest in government bonds include: stable cash flows; income source; easy to model; hedge liabilities; relatively low return volatility; exposure to interest rate and inflation risk factors; maturity risk premium; low correlation with other asset classes; protection; source for liquidity and collateral; and as a safety deposit box.

- The risks of investing in government bonds include: interest rate risk; credit risk; reinvestment risk; inflation risk; yield curve risk; currency risk; and manager risk.

- The 'normal' 10-year government bond yield is connected to nominal GDP growth.

- Government bonds of most core countries are expected to generate low single digit real returns over the next decade and are not an attractive investment from a return perspective.

- The long-term expected return of a government bond is yield-to-maturity, minus the expected cost of default, plus an adjustment for mean-reversion of yield back to a 'normal' level (nominal GDP growth rate). The third variable can be dropped if the bond is held to maturity.

- Govis can be accessed through individual bonds, active and passive funds or the derivative market.

Inflation-linked bonds

Inflation-linked bonds (ILBs), inflation indexed bonds, or colloquially *linkers*, are fixed income securities primarily issued by sovereign governments (e.g. United States, United Kingdom and France) with their coupons and/or principal adjusted for inflation as measured by a recognised inflation index (e.g. Consumer Price Index (CPI) in the United States or Retail Price Index (RPI) in the United Kingdom).

For example, the US government issues Treasury Inflation-Protected Securities (TIPS) that pay semi-annual coupons. The coupon rate is multiplied by the principal which is adjusted for inflation. The interest on TIPS is therefore adjusted for inflation, as well as the principal, and the bonds pay real interest, rather than nominal interest as do standard bonds.

Table 2.11 shows the country and maturity breakdown of global inflation-linked bonds in the Barclays World Government Inflation-Linked Bond Index. Not all governments issue linkers. The United States, United Kingdom and France issue the majority of the global linker market. However, as the tables show, linkers come with a range of currencies and maturities. This allows investors to diversify their linker portfolio and use it to hedge a range of liabilities with different currencies and horizons.

Table 2.11: Global inflation-linked bond country and maturity breakdown in Barclays World Government Inflation-Linked Bond Index, March 2014

Country	% of Index
United States	45.6
United Kingdom	31.1
France	12.7
Germany	4.1
Canada	2.6
Japan	1.8
Sweden	1.6
Australia	1.3
New Zealand	0.3

Maturity (Years)	% of Index
0-3	13.3
3-5	13.1
5-7	12.8
7-10	16.0
10-15	14.6
15-20	8.8
20+	21.4

Source: Barclays World Government Inflation-Linked Bond Index.

The earliest recorded inflation-linked bonds were issued by the Commonwealth of Massachusetts in 1780 during the American Revolutionary War. Much later, emerging market countries, which were affected by high inflation, began issuing ILBs in the 1950s. In the 1980s, the United Kingdom was the first developed country to issue linkers. Several other countries followed, including Australia, Canada, Mexico and Sweden. In January 1997 the United States issued TIPS, now the largest component of the global ILB market.

Today, inflation-linked bonds are typically sold by governments aiming to reduce borrowing costs (lenders demand a lower interest on ILBs because of lower inflation risk) and broaden their investor base (e.g. investors who seek inflation protection or to hedge liabilities). Corporations occasionally issue inflation-linked bonds for the same reasons, but the total amount of outstanding corporate linkers is relatively small.

The *breakeven inflation rate*, which is the spread between the yields on conventional or nominal government bonds and equivalent (i.e. similar maturity, credit risk and liquidity) inflation-linked bonds, indicates the expected inflation rate that is priced into the market. It is the rate differential at which the expected returns of ILBs and nominal bonds are equal. If investors expect inflation to be higher than the breakeven inflation rate then inflation-linked bonds are expected to outperform nominal bonds, and vice versa.

For example, if the 10-year gilt yield is 5% and that on 10-year UK indexed-linked gilts is 3%, then the breakeven inflation rate is 2%. The market expects an annual inflation rate of 2% in the UK over the next ten years. If the investor thinks that the inflation rate is actually going to be 3%, then linkers are the preferred asset. If the investor thinks that the inflation rate is actually going to be 1%, then nominal gilts are the preferred asset.

Linkers are a real asset class, together with real estate and commodities, because they provide a hedge against inflation. They are a conservative asset since they offer the stability of government bonds plus an additional reduction of inflation risk.

The reasons for investing in inflation-linked bonds

Linkers are mostly government bonds and the reasons for investing in them are similar to those for investing in govis. The reasons for investing in linkers and their roles in portfolios include:

- *Inflation hedge*. Linkers offer a hedge against inflation. They provide a real income stream and their principal should keep pace with general inflation.

- *Diversification benefits*. Their positive correlation with unanticipated increases in inflation (linkers' prices increase, while the prices of equities and conventional bonds decrease) offers diversification against other assets and protection for portfolios against unexpected inflation hikes. They play a risk-reducing role through diversification and a protective role. As with standard bonds, linkers need to have a long duration to have sufficient fire power to provide protection when it is needed.

- *Low return volatility*. The standard deviation of linkers tends to be lower than that of nominal bonds because of the relative stability of real interest rates.

- *Risk-free investment*. Inflation-linked bonds should be considered as the closest thing to a risk-free asset for investors with a stream of liabilities whose duration matches that of the linkers. Investors with a long investment horizon and a concern about inflation should consider linkers as the ultimate risk-free asset.

- *Hedging liabilities*. Linkers can be used to hedge both the duration and inflation risk of liabilities.

Risks

Most of the risks of government bonds apply to linkers as well. The difference between nominal govis and linkers is inflation risk. While inflation risk for nominal bonds is an increase in inflation, the inflation risk for linkers is a decrease in inflation or deflation. The main risks of investing in linkers include:

- *Tax treatment*. Some linkers (such as TIPS) whose principal is adjusted for inflation but where the adjustments are paid only at maturity are still taxed each year (*phantom income*). This may result in negative cash flows for investors at high tax brackets. Therefore, those investors should hold linkers in tax efficient wrappers (e.g. pension schemes or ISAs in the UK).

- *Real interest rate risk.* Increases in real interest rates can cause capital losses on linkers.

- *Changing correlation.* The correlation between linkers and nominal bonds can increase over the short term due to factors affecting the prices of both in a similar way (such as changes to real and nominal interest rates or a flight to quality). When this occurs portfolios can lose some of their risk reduction from diversification.

- *Falling inflation risk.* During time periods of declining inflation expectations, falling inflation rates or deflation, linkers tend to underperform nominal bonds.

- *Reference index change.* Issuers may have various index contingencies in the event that the applicable index (e.g. CPI) is discontinued or fundamentally altered in a manner materially adverse to investors. This creates risk when there is a mismatch between the inflation applicable to the investor and the inflation measured by the linker's inflation index.

Just like nominal bonds, whose prices move in response to nominal interest rate changes, ILB prices increase when real yields decline and decrease when real yields rise. Should an economy undergo a period of deflation (a sustained decline in price levels), the inflation-adjusted principal could decline below its par value. Subsequently, coupon payments may be based on this deflation-adjusted amount.

However, many ILB-issuing countries, such as the United States, Australia, France and Germany, offer deflation floors at maturity. This means that if deflation drives the principal amount below par, an investor would still receive the full par amount at maturity. While coupon payments are paid on a principal adjusted for inflation or deflation, investors receive the greater of the inflation-adjusted principal or the initial par amount at maturity.

Linkers and nominal government bonds are in many ways substitutable assets. The question that investors should ask themselves when deciding between linkers and govis is whether realised inflation is going to be above or below the breakeven rate. If investors think that it is going to be above, then linkers will outperform govis. If investors think that inflation is going to be below, then linkers will underperform govis.

Emerging market linkers

Inflation-linked bonds are commonly issued by governments of developing or emerging markets. Over the past decade emerging market governments have issued more debt denominated in their local currencies in order to be less dependent on their exchange rates versus the US dollar. Part of this local currency debt has been issued in inflation-linked bonds. Since South Africa was the first emerging market to issue linkers in 2000 the emerging market debt (EMD) linker market has grown materially. At the end of 2010 the total amount of inflation-linked debt outstanding in emerging markets was $82 billion, which is about 14% of the global supply of inflation-linked bonds.[57]

The common benchmark for EMD linkers is the Barclays Emerging Market Government Inflation-Linked Bond Index. The EME linker market is dominated by a few issuing countries,[58] with Latin America, and in particular Brazil, accounting for half the market capitalisation. From an investment perspective, EMD linkers should outperform nominal EMD when real interest rates are expected to come down.

Several studies have empirically investigated the value added by inflation-linked bonds in portfolios. These studies have found that the added value was hampered by relatively low, stable inflation in developed markets. Thus, the studies have found little evidence that inflation-linked bonds of developed economies add value to a portfolio of nominal bonds and stocks.[59] However, emerging market linkers do expand the efficient frontier of portfolios consisting of nominal bonds and stocks.

Taxation is one of the risks of investing in emerging markets. The finance ministry of Brazil tried to slow the appreciation of the Brazilian real by implementing the *Imposto sobre Operações Financeiras (IOF)* tax on financial transactions. The 6% tax was paid up front by foreign investors in Brazil's fixed income securities. While this high level may seem daunting in many ways, after-tax yields on Brazilian debt could still be attractive relative to other bonds. The tax was cancelled in 2013, but it demonstrated the tax risk of the EMD market.

Expected return

The expected return of inflation-linked bonds is their yield plus realised inflation. Realised inflation is unknown and therefore it is more difficult to forecast the expected return of linkers than that of nominal govis. If the breakeven inflation rate is used as expected inflation, then the expected return of linkers is similar to equivalent government bonds with adjustments for liquidity.

Figure 2.31 shows the yield on 10-year Treasury and 10-year inflation indexed bonds. As can be seen in the chart, nominal bonds normally have a higher yield

[57] Swinkels, Laurens, 'Emerging Market Inflation-Linked Bonds', *Financial Analysts Journal* 68 (2012).

[58] The main developing countries issuing ILBs are Turkey, Brazil, Mexico, South Africa, Israel, Chile, Poland and Thailand. (Israel was in fact declared a developed country by MSCI in May 2009.)

[59] Hunter, Delroy and Simon, David, 'Are TIPS the "Real" Deal? A Conditional Assessment of Their Role in a Nominal Portfolio', *Journal of Banking & Finance* 29 (2005); and Brière, Marie and Signori, Ombretta 'Do Inflation-Linked Bonds Still Diversify?', *European Financial Management* 15 (2009).

than that of linkers since the return of nominal bonds does not include inflation (i.e. nominal bonds need to offer a higher yield to compensate investors for inflation risk).

Figure 2.31: 10-year Treasury yield and 10-year inflation indexed bond yield, January 1997 to December 2013

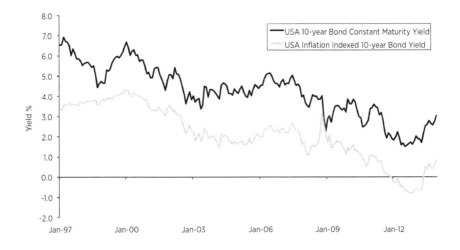

Source: Global Financial Data, USA 10-year Bond Constant Maturity Yield, USD Inflation Indexed 10-year Bond Yield.

Inflation-linked bond return and risk characteristics

Figure 2.32 shows the cumulative performance of US inflation-linked bonds since March 1997, as well as the performance of US nominal government bonds and UK inflation-linked bonds. The return patterns of the three asset classes are different. As the inflation rates in the United States and United Kingdom differ, as well as their yield curves, investors should consider diversifying their portfolios across linkers issued by different issuers (preferably hedging currency risk). Global diversification allows investors to express their views on inflation rates in different countries.

Figure 2.33 shows the rolling 36-month correlation between US inflation-linked bonds and US government bonds. Notice the drop in correlation that occurred in 2008. With the recession hitting the global economy, expected inflation dropped and linkers generated negative returns, while nominal government bonds rallied due to a flight to quality and dropping interest rates. The correlation has been increasing since 2011. Unlike linkers, nominal government bonds have protective power when expected inflation suddenly falls during a recession or a systemic shock to the financial system.

Figure 2.32: Cumulative performance of US and UK inflation-linked bonds and nominal US government bonds, March 1997 to March 2013

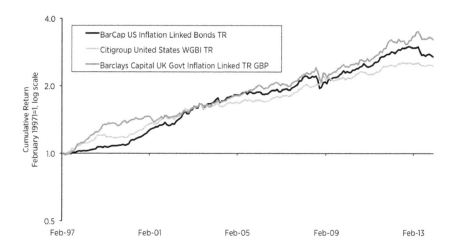

Source: Barclays Capital US Inflation Linked Bonds TR Index, Citigroup United States WGBI TR Index, Barclays Capital UK Govt Inflation Linked TR GBP Index.

Figure 2.33: Rolling 36-month correlation between US Treasury bonds and US inflation-linked bonds, March 2000 to March 2013

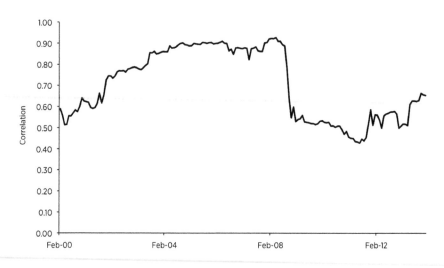

Source: Citibank United States WGBI TR Index, Barclays Capital US Inflation Linked Bonds TR Index.

Figure 2.34 shows the average performance of US linkers ranked by deciles of average US inflation. As expected, linkers perform at their strongest when inflation is high.

Figure 2.34: Average performance of US inflation-linked bonds and US inflation rate, ranked by inflation rate, March 1997 to December 2013

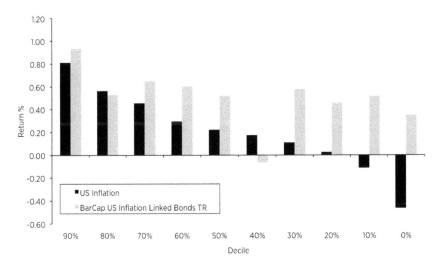

Source: Barclays Capital US Inflation Linked Bonds TR Index, US inflation.

Figure 2.35 shows the average excess performance of US linkers above US nominal government bonds ranked by deciles of average US inflation. Linkers outperform nominal government bonds on average when inflation is high. More precisely, linkers will outperform nominal bonds when realised inflation is above the breakeven inflation.

Figure 2.35: Average excess performance of US inflation-linked bonds above US nominal government bonds and US inflation rate, ranked by inflation rate, March 1997 to December 2013

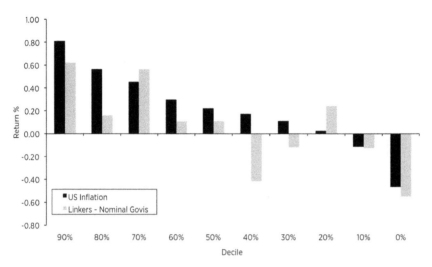

Source: Barclays Capital US Inflation Linked Bonds TR Index, Citigroup United States WGBI TR Index, US inflation.

Access

Similar to government bonds, linkers can be bought as individual bonds or via active and passive funds. The choice of linker funds is not as broad as that of govis (in fact it is much more limited), since the linker market is smaller and the demand for linkers is not as large as that of govis. Also, the derivate market for linkers is not as developed as that of govis. Listed futures contracts on linkers are not available as they are for govis.

Conclusions

For investors with a long investment horizon, inflation is a serious concern. Linkers with a matching duration to that of liabilities are the ultimate risk-free assets. Investors without any insight into investing should hold linkers matching the duration of their liabilities. Linkers offer investment opportunities within portfolios, in particular when investors expect realised inflation to be higher than breakeven inflation. Linkers are also a source for the collective market expectations on inflation through the breakeven inflation rate.

Linkers add another layer of stability to nominal government bonds because inflation risk – the most fundamental risk for long-term investors – is addressed. Addressing inflation risk allows for long-term stability in the face of inflation.

Summary

- Inflation-linked bonds (ILBs) are designed to protect investors from inflation. The principal of ILBs is adjusted for inflation and the coupon rate is applied to the inflation-adjusted principal.

- The breakeven inflation rate (the yield spread between ILBs and nominal bonds) indicates the inflation expectations priced into the market.

- The reasons for investing in ILBs are: inflation hedge; diversification benefits and a protective role; low return volatility; as close to risk free as it gets for investors with liabilities matching duration; and liability hedging for both duration and inflation risks.

- The risks of investing in ILBs include: tax treatment; real interest rate risk; changing correlation; falling inflation; and a change to reference index.

- The expected return of ILBs is their yield plus expected realised inflation (when held to maturity).

- While more limited than that of government bonds, access to linkers is available through individual bonds or active and passive funds.

Corporate bonds

Corporate bonds are debt issued by corporations to raise money (borrow money) to support their operations. Corporate bonds are one of the most common asset classes in portfolios, alongside equities and government bonds. Corporate bonds typically have a maturity of more than one year, while corporate debt with shorter maturities is called *commercial paper*. The corporate bond asset class is commonly called *credit, or more specifically investment grade credit*.

The two main components of a corporation's capital structure are equity (invested by shareholders who share the corporation's ownership) and corporate bonds (invested by debt holders who lend money to the corporation). Investors in corporate bonds are creditors of the company that issued the debt.

Compared to government bonds, corporate bonds generally have a higher risk of default. This risk depends on the financial situation of the corporation issuing the bond, the current market conditions, the situation of the government to which the bond issuer is compared and the corporation's credit rating. Corporate bond holders are compensated for this risk by the higher yield of corporate bonds compared to equivalent government bonds (*credit risk premium*).

The difference between the yield of a corporate bond and that of an equivalent government bond is called the yield spread or *credit spread*. Corporate bonds are a *spread product* because their price is a function of the difference of their interest rates to those of government bonds. Government bonds are often more liquid than corporate bonds and hence the credit spread also includes a *liquidity premium*.

Governments issuing bonds can print more money to repay their debt as long as the bonds are denominated in the country's currency and the government has control over its fiscal and monetary policies (e.g. countries in the European Monetary Union have lost exclusive control over these policies). The risk of printing money is inflation. Conversely, corporations cannot print money and must generate cash flows or raise capital to repay their debt. Otherwise, they need to default or declare themselves bankrupt. This difference between countries and corporations is one of the distinguishing aspects of government and corporate debt.

Corporate bonds are often listed on major exchanges. However, despite being listed on exchanges, the lion's share of trading volume in corporate bonds in most developed markets takes place in decentralised, dealer-based, over-the-counter (OTC) markets.

Some corporate bonds have an embedded call option (*callable bonds*) that allows the issuer to redeem the debt before its maturity date. Callable bonds offer higher interest or are sold at a lower price than equivalent non-callable bonds to reflect the value of the call option that is held by the issuing company.

The analysis of corporate bonds to assess whether they are a good investment, what the risks are, and so on, is called *credit analysis*. This has many similarities with equity analysis as both need to assess the financial health and future prospects of the issuing corporation. Expected profitability, for example, determines whether the corporation will generate sufficient cash flows to cover its interest payments on its debt and whether its share price will appreciate. Equity and credit analysts therefore often jointly research companies.

Like government bonds, inflation adversely affects corporate bonds. Like equities, worsening company fortunes adversely affect corporate bonds because of worsening creditworthiness. Corporate bonds, therefore, share some characteristics with government bonds and some with equities. The lower the credit rating, the closer the behaviour of the corporate bond will be to that of equity.

Agency theory

Unlike shareholders, debt holders prefer that the company is managed prudently so it is able to pay back its debt. Equity holders, on the other hand, prefer the company to grow and expand, activities that sometimes require more risk taking than prudent management. Debt holders and equity holders, therefore, may have different perspectives on the way that they prefer companies to be managed.

Agency theory looks at the conflict of interests between stakeholders with different interests in the same assets. The two main examples are the conflicts between shareholders and managers and between shareholders and debt holders. Following a riskier, higher-return strategy benefits shareholders to the potential detriment of debt holders. A riskier strategy increases the risk of default on debt. However, since debt holders are only entitled to a fixed return they will not benefit from higher returns. That is, they do not participate in the upside of risky activities. Shareholders, on the other hand, benefit from the higher returns due to successful risk taking. However, if the risk does not pay off, shareholders share only a limited loss with debt holders because of their limited liability.

This conflict can be addressed by the use of debt covenants (clauses in the indenture or debt agreement limiting the borrower from certain activities, such as additional borrowing, to protect creditors from potential default of the borrower), or by providing debt holders with a hedge against such risk taking activities by shareholders by issuing convertible debt or debt bundled with warrants.

Corporate bond categories

The universe of corporate bonds includes many types of issues with different features and characteristics. One of the main divisions of corporate bonds is into secured and unsecured debt.

In a *secured loan* the borrower pledges some asset (e.g. a car or property) as collateral for the loan. In the event of default the creditor takes possession of the asset used as collateral and may sell it to regain some or all of the loan amount (e.g. foreclosure of a home). From the creditor's perspective, this is a category of debt in which a lender has been granted a portion of the bundle of rights to specified property. If the sale of the collateral does not raise enough money to pay off the debt, the creditor can often obtain a deficiency judgment against the borrower for the remaining amount. A mortgage is a type of a secured loan that is secured by the collateral of a specific piece of real estate.

Unsecured debt, on the other hand, refers to debt or a general obligation that is not collateralised by a lien on the borrower's specific assets. In the event of the borrower's default or bankruptcy, the unsecured creditors will have a general claim on the borrower's assets after the specific pledged assets have been assigned to the secured creditors. However, the unsecured creditors will usually realise a smaller proportion of their claims than the secured creditors. The yield on unsecured debt is higher than on comparable secured debt to compensate investors for the higher risk.

Corporate bonds can also be divided into senior and junior or subordinated debt. *Senior debt* takes priority over unsecured or otherwise more *junior debt* owed by the issuer. Senior debt has greater seniority in the issuer's capital structure than subordinated debt. In the event the issuer defaults or goes bankrupt, senior debt theoretically must be repaid before other creditors receive any payment. As always, higher risk demands a higher potential return and therefore the yield on subordinated debt is higher than that of comparable senior debt.

The reasons for investing in corporate bonds

Corporate bonds have similar advantages to those of government bonds, such as fixed coupons and the ability to hedge liabilities. However, credit risk is much more dominant and must be taken into account.

The reasons for investing in corporate bonds and their roles in portfolios include:

- *Credit risk premium.* Credit risk is one of the systematic risks that should be compensated by the market. However, credit risk accounts for only a fraction of the credit spread,[60] which includes other factors such as a liquidity premium.

- *Yield pickup relative to government bonds.* Corporate bonds normally offer a higher yield than comparable government bonds to compensate investors for the higher credit risk. This means that credit offers higher income and higher long-term expected total returns (YTM adjusted for expected default loss) than government bonds.

- *Potential capital gain.* When yields on comparable government bonds fall and/or the spread between the corporate bond and comparable government bond tightens, the corporate bond's price rises. If the bond is held to maturity this does not affect the investor. However, selling the bond before its maturity can allow the investor to bank a capital gain.

- *Stable income and capital preservation.* Similarly to government bonds, investment grade corporate bonds should provide a steady stream of interest payments.

- *Conservative asset.* Bonds issued by large, stable companies may be considered a conservative asset. In August 2011 Standard & Poor's lowered the credit rating of the United States from a perfect AAA to AA-. Also, most American companies that had a triple A rating have lost it. However, four American companies have retained the perfect AAA credit rating even following the US downgrade: ADP (Automatic Data Processing), Johnson & Johnson, Microsoft and Exxon Mobil. In theory, as per their credit ratings, the debt of these companies is less risky than that of the US government, and going by their credit rating their debt should be a conservative asset.

- *Diversification.* Credit has a less than perfect correlation with other asset classes and offers diversification benefits for portfolios. Diversification benefits can be further improved by including debt of foreign corporations (potentially hedging their currency risk so currency risk does not dominate the return and risk profile of the foreign credit investing).

- *Diversity.* The corporate bond market is diverse, offering investors many choices.

---

[60] Huang, Jing-Zhi, and Huang, Ming, 2003, 'How Much of Corporate-Treasury Yield Spread Is Due to Credit Risk?: A New Calibration Approach', 14th Annual Conference on Financial Economics and Accounting (FEA), Texas Finance Festival (2003).

- *Opportunities for active management.* Its diversity and wealth of different choices and options mean the corporate bond market offers opportunities for active management to add value. The efficiency of the credit market is not as high as that of other assets, such as government bonds, because of lower frequency of trading, a larger number of non-researched issuers, deeper breadth and so on. Lower efficiency offers more opportunities for active management.

- *Hedge liabilities.* Similarly to government bonds and linkers, corporate bonds can be used to hedge liabilities. However, credit risk must be considered.

- *Easily modelled.* Corporate bonds have established indices and it is relatively easy to model their expected returns for asset allocation purposes.

Figure 2.36 shows the rolling 10-year annualised returns of US corporate bonds, US equities and 10-year Treasury bonds. Since January 1992 a diversified portfolio of US credit has generated similar returns to those of long-term Treasuries. It can also be seen that the credit premium did not generate superior results compared to the maturity premium over most 10-year periods.

Figure 2.36: Rolling 10-year annualised returns of US credit, Treasuries and equities, January 1992 to December 2013

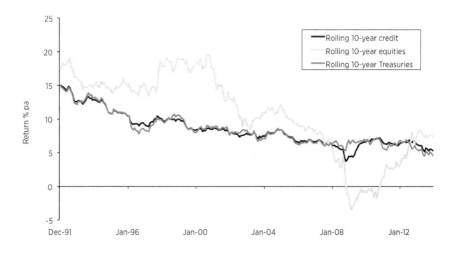

Source: Bloomberg, Citigroup United States WGBI TR Index, BofA Merrill Lynch U.S. Corporate Master TR Index, S&P 500 Index.

Figure 2.37 shows the yield of US corporate bonds compared to the 10-year yield of Treasuries. As can be seen, corporate bonds offer a higher yield than Treasuries to compensate investors for the higher credit risk.

Figure 2.37: Average yield of US investment grade corporate bonds and 10-year Treasuries, October 2002 to December 2013

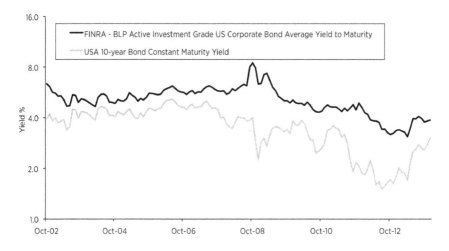

Source: Bloomberg, Global Financial Data, FINRA – BLP Active Investment Grade US Corporate Bond Average Yield to Maturity, USA 10-year Bond Constant Maturity Yield.

Risks

Corporate bonds share some similar risks with other fixed-income instruments, such as government bonds. The risks of investing in corporate bonds include:

- *Credit spread risk.* A widening credit spread is a risk that may result in a drop of a corporate bond's price. The bond's credit spread may be insufficient to compensate for the default risk if the credit rating of the issuer deteriorates. As the coupon and principal are fixed, the bond's market price falls and consequently the yield widens to a level that offers an appropriate credit spread to reflect the credit rating. If the investor sells the bond before maturity a capital loss can materialise.

- *Interest rate risk.* The general level of yields in a bond market, as expressed by government bond yields, can change and thus affect the prices of corporate bonds as the YTM of fixed coupon bonds adjusts to appropriate levels. The price of corporate bonds is determined by the government bond yield plus the credit spread. Changes to government bond yields affect the yield on corporate bonds and therefore their price. Short duration bonds can be used to limit interest rate risk.

- *Default risk.* Issuers of corporate bonds may default on their contractual obligations and pay less than promised and/or not at the time promised. Consequently, investors in corporate bonds may realise a lower return than expected.

- *Liquidity risk.* A thin secondary market may raise liquidity risk for corporate bonds. This risk is more severe in developing countries than developed ones and depends on the general demand for corporate bonds as well as the demand for specific issues. During the 2008 credit crunch, for example, liquidity for corporate bonds almost completely dried up.

- *Increased issuance.* Heavy issuance of new bonds similar to the one held may depress its price (excess supply may reduce the price).

- *Inflation risk.* Inflation reduces the real value of future fixed cash flows and increased inflation or expected inflation may reduce the bond price.

- *Taxation risk.* Unanticipated changes in taxation may adversely impact the value of a bond to investors and consequently its immediate market value.

- *Changing correlation.* Worsening economic conditions adversely affect companies. Equity prices and corporate creditworthiness depend on the commercial prospects of companies, as well as other similar factors, so the correlation between equities and corporate bonds may increase at times of stress. The 2008 financial crisis was an example of increasing correlation and price drop of both equities and corporate bonds. At times of stress, when diversification is needed the most, corporate bonds may stop providing diversification with equities. This is an important distinction between corporate bonds and government bonds. Government bonds may provide protection at times of stress because of a flight to safety into government bonds and accommodative monetary policy. Credit spreads may widen and corporate bonds may disappoint at times of stress.

- *Construction of market-cap credit indices.* Most bond indices follow a market-capitalisation weighting. The result is that issuers with large amounts of outstanding debt (i.e. highly leveraged corporations) constitute a larger weight in the index than issuers with lower amounts of debt. That is, less creditworthy issuers take a larger proportion of the index than more creditworthy issuers. This is the opposite of what most investors seek. Another issue of the index is that falling angels, or issuers that lose their investment grade rating, are automatically dropped from the index. This means that the fall in their price is crystallised without benefiting from the potential rebound, which often follows. Therefore, passively tracking a corporate index has material limitations. Two ways to overcome them are through active management or smart beta strategies.

The risks to bond prices are particularly relevant when bonds are not held to maturity and portfolios are marked to market on a regular basis. If bonds are held to maturity, the holder receives the coupons and principal at maturity, unless there is a credit event. If the holder does not hold the bonds until maturity, changes to their prices affect the total return (interest and capital gains or losses). Most actively traded bond portfolios buy and sell bonds and do not hold them to maturity. Hence, capital gains and losses normally comprise a large portion of the performance of such portfolios.

Corporate bonds are a risk asset because they are affected by many similar factors that affect equities. Unlike government bonds, which benefit from worsening economic growth, corporate bonds may be adversely affected by slowing growth due to widening credit spreads. However, the result depends on the balance between the positive affect due to falling interest rates on the benchmark government bonds, on the one hand, and the widening spread between government bond yields and corporate bond yields on the other hand.

Credit rating

Credit rating agencies play an important role for corporate bonds (and increasingly for government bonds). A credit agency's rating estimates an issue's minimum creditworthiness. Many investors rely on the credit rating to decide on the suitability of bonds for portfolios, as portfolios may have restrictions on holding below investment grade bonds or may target specific average credit ratings. Capital adequacy requirements of banks and insurance companies, for example, require holding bonds with a minimum credit rating.

Two risks related to this are default and deterioration of creditworthiness. A downgrade of rating by an agency can cause losses because the price of corporate bonds depends on the spread, which is linked to creditworthiness and expected *recovery rate* at default. The price also depends on liquidity and investors' herding.

In 2008, criticism of credit rating agencies was intense, with claims that ratings were based on backward-looking information. The fall of Lehman Brothers, to which the three main credit rating agencies gave at least an A rating until 15 September 2008, the day that Lehman filed for bankruptcy, triggered the criticism. Investors can conduct their own credit analysis to assess changes to creditworthiness to protect themselves from credit agencies being slow to change ratings.

In 2011 Standard & Poor's (S&P) controversially downgraded the credit rating of the United States a notch from a perfect AAA to AA-. The 2011 European sovereign debt crisis and accompanying ratings changes for the affected countries meant that sovereign debt of some governments came to be treated as credit.

The potential for credit rating change is asymmetric. High-rated bonds are unlikely to have their rating increased, hence their upside is limited. Lower-rated bonds have more potential for an upgrade, and with it an upside potential.

Credit rating is linked to maturity. The longer the maturity the higher the risk of a downgrade and the higher the spread to compensate investors for a downgrade risk.

Table 2.12 shows the historic default rates for corporate bonds under the different credit ratings of Moody's and S&P. The historic default rates are not the probability of default of each category since the probabilities vary from year to year depending on market conditions (i.e. they are higher during contraction and recession, lower during recovery and expansion). The historic default rates for AAA bonds are less than 1%, while nearly 70% of CCC bonds have defaulted.

Table 2.12: Historic corporate bond default rates

	Credit rating	Historic default rate of bonds rated at this level by Moody's (%)	Historic default rate of bonds rated at this level by S&P (%)
Investment grade	Aaa/AAA	0.5	0.6
	Aa/AA	0.5	1.5
	A/A	1.3	2.9
	Baa/BBB	4.6	10.3
Below investment grade	Ba/BB	19.1	29.9
	B/B	43.3	53.7
	Caa-C/CCC-C	69.2	69.2
Total	Investment grade	2.1	4.1
	Non-investment grade	31.4	42.4
	All	9.7	13.0

Source: Moody's, Standard & Poor's.

Floating rate notes (FRNs)

Floating rate notes (FRNs) or *floaters* are bonds that have a variable coupon, equal to a money market reference rate, like LIBOR or the federal funds rate, plus a quoted spread (quoted margin). The spread is a rate that remains constant. The majority of FRNs have quarterly coupons (i.e. they pay out interest every three months). At the beginning of each coupon period, the coupon is calculated by taking the fixing of the reference rate for that day and adding the spread. A typical coupon may look like: 3-month dollar LIBOR +0.20% (20 basis points).

In the United States, government sponsored enterprises (GSEs) such as the Federal Home Loan Banks,[61] the Federal National Mortgage Association (Fannie

---

[61] The Federal Home Loan Banks (FHLBanks) are 12 US government-sponsored banks that provide stable, on-demand, low-cost funding to American financial institutions (not individuals) for home mortgage loans, small business, rural, agricultural, and economic development lending. With their members, the FHLBanks represents the largest collective source of home mortgage and community credit in the United States.

Mae) and the Federal Home Loan Mortgage Corporation (Freddie Mac) are important issuers of FRNs. In Europe the main issuers are banks.

FRNs carry little interest rate risk. An FRN has a duration close to zero (the duration is maximum three months at the beginning of each coupon period), and its price shows low sensitivity to changes in market rates. When market rates rise, the expected coupons of the FRN increase in line with the increase in forward rates, meaning that its price remains constant. Thus, FRNs differ from fixed rate bonds, whose prices decline when market rates rise.

As FRNs are almost immune to interest rate risk, they are considered conservative investments for investors who believe that market rates will increase. The risk that remains is credit risk.

Floaters usually pay a lower yield than comparable fixed rate bonds because of lower interest rate risk. When interest rates are declining, floaters will underperform fixed rate bonds since the floaters' price does not appreciate and their yield declines. Floaters offer no maturity premium and they offer no protective power in portfolios since their yield is linked to that of cash.

Credit default swaps (CDS)

Characteristics of CDS

A credit default swap (CDS) is a financial swap agreement according to which the seller of the CDS will compensate the buyer in the event of a loan default or other stipulated credit event. The buyer of the CDS makes a series of payments (the CDS fee or *spread*) to the seller and in exchange receives a payoff if the loan defaults.

A CDS is linked to a *reference entity* or reference obligor, usually a corporation or government. The reference entity is not a party to the CDS contract. The buyer makes regular premium payments to the seller and the premium amounts constitute the spread charged by the seller to insure against a credit event. The spread is expressed as a percentage of the notional amount of the CDS.

For example, if the CDS spread is 50 basis points, then an investor buying $10 million worth of protection must pay the issuing bank $50,000 per annum. These payments continue until either the CDS contract expires or the reference entity defaults. If the reference entity defaults, the protection seller (the bank) pays the buyer the par value of the bond in exchange for physical delivery of the bond, although settlement may also be by cash or auction.

The trader selling the CDS is viewed as being long on the CDS and the credit, as if the trader owned the bond. In contrast, the trader who bought protection is short on the CDS and the underlying credit. In either case the speculator does not own the bond, so the position is said to be a *synthetic* long or short position.

Therefore, CDS have opened up important new avenues to speculators. Traders can go long on a bond without any upfront cost of buying a bond; all the trader needs to do is promise to pay in the event of default. Also, shorting a bond faces difficult practical problems, such that shorting is often not feasible, but CDS have made shorting credit possible and popular.

A default is often referred to as a *credit event* and includes such events as failure to pay, restructuring and bankruptcy or a drop in the borrower's credit rating. CDS contracts on sovereign obligations usually include as credit events repudiation, moratorium and acceleration. Most CDS are in the $10 million to $20 million range with maturities between one and ten years. Five years is the most common maturity.

The differences between a CDS and insurance

Investors may buy protection to hedge the default risk on a bond or other debt instrument, regardless of whether they hold an interest in or bear any risk of loss relating to such bond or debt instrument. In this way, a CDS is similar to credit insurance.

CDS are *not insurance policies* and they are not subject to regulations governing traditional insurance. The most important difference between CDS and insurance is that an insurance contract provides an indemnity against the losses actually suffered by the policy holder, whereas the CDS provides an equal pay-out to all holders, calculated using an agreed, market-wide method, regardless of whether the holder suffered any loss because of the credit event.

Unlike an insurance policy, investors can buy and sell protection without owning the debt of the reference entity. These *naked CDS* allow traders to speculate on the creditworthiness of reference entities. CDS can be used to create synthetic long and short positions in the reference entity. Naked CDS constitute most of the market in CDS.

CDS and FRNs

The parties of a CDS are not exposed to *interest rate risk*. A CDS behaves in many respects as a leveraged corporate floating rate note (FRN) without the FRN's LIBOR payments. The CDS buyer pays fixed payments to the seller and the seller agrees to pay the buyer a lump sum upon a credit event of the underlying. The seller's risk exposure is the same as the risk of owning an FRN issued by the underlying's issuer, while the risk exposure of the buyer is the same as the risk of shorting the FRN.

The exposure to credit spreads is the same as that of an FRN whether the investor buys the FRN or sells a CDS. When credit spreads move up upon a credit event, the investor can lose up to the notional amount of the CDS in the same way as buying an FRN with the same worth, maturity and underlying credit as the CDS.

The opposite is true when selling an FRN or buying a CDS. Because the parties do not exchange the notional, the CDS is equivalent to a leveraged FRN.

CDS risks

CDS contracts come with a few risks. When entering into a CDS, both the buyer and seller of credit protection take on *counterparty risk*. The buyer takes the risk that the seller may default. If the CDS seller (usually a bank) and the reference entity default simultaneously (double default), the buyer loses the protection against default by the reference entity. If the seller defaults but the reference entity does not, the buyer may need to replace the defaulted CDS at a higher cost.

The CDS seller takes the risk that the buyer may default on the contract, depriving the seller of the expected revenue stream. More importantly, a CDS seller normally limits its risk by buying offsetting protection from another party. That is, it hedges its exposure. If the original buyer drops out, the seller squares its position by either unwinding the hedge transaction or by selling a new CDS to a third party. Depending on market conditions, that may be at a lower price than the original CDS and may therefore involve a loss to the seller.

In the future, in the event that regulatory reforms require that CDS are traded and settled via a central exchange and clearing house, there will no longer be counterparty risk, as the risk of the counterparty will be held with the central exchange and clearing house.

As is true with other forms of over-the-counter (OTC) derivative, CDS may involve *liquidity risk*. If one or both parties to a CDS contract must post collateral, margin calls can require the posting of additional collateral. The required collateral is agreed by the parties when the CDS is first issued. This margin amount may vary over the life of the CDS contract, if its market price changes or the credit rating of one of the parties changes. Many CDS contracts even require paying an upfront margin at the beginning (initial margin).

Roles of CDS

CDS can be used for speculation, hedging, arbitrage and synthetically gaining credit exposure. CDS allow *speculation* on changes in CDS spreads of single names or of market indices such as the Markit CDX North American indices and Markit iTraxx European and Asian indices.[62]

A trader may believe that an entity's CDS spreads are too high or too low relative to the entity's bond yields and attempt to profit from that view by entering into a trade (known as a basis trade) that combines a CDS with a cash bond and an interest rate swap. Traders may speculate on an entity's credit quality, since

---

[62] www.markit.com.

generally CDS spreads increase as creditworthiness declines, and decline as creditworthiness increases. The trader may therefore buy CDS protection on a company to speculate that it is about to default. Alternatively, the trader may sell protection if the view is that the company's creditworthiness may improve.

CDS are often used to manage the risk of default that arises from holding debt. A bank, for example, may *hedge* its risk that a borrower may default on a loan by entering into a CDS contract as the buyer of protection. If the loan defaults, the proceeds from the CDS contract cancel out the losses on the underlying debt.

Capital structure arbitrage is an example of an *arbitrage* strategy that utilises CDS transactions. This technique relies on the principle that a company's stock price and its CDS spread should exhibit negative correlation. If the outlook for a company improves then its share price should go up while its CDS spread should tighten, since it is less likely to default on its debt. However, if its outlook worsens then its CDS spread should widen while its stock price should fall.

Techniques reliant on this are known as capital structure arbitrage because they exploit market inefficiencies between different parts of the same company's capital structure (i.e. mispricing between a company's debt and equity). An arbitrageur may attempt to exploit the spread between a company's CDS and its equity in certain situations.

CDS can be used to *synthetically gain credit exposure*, instead of buying or selling physical corporate bonds. This is helpful when investors wish to implement a multi-asset derivative overlay (i.e. expressing asset allocation views through futures, options and other derivatives without trading the underlying positions), or change the exposure to corporate bonds without selling or buying bonds (and hence reducing transaction costs). The challenge is that CDS are OTC derivatives and not everyone can trade them. This may improve as listed CDS or listed futures contracts on CDS are introduced into the market. Another challenge is the basis risk between the CDS and the bond portfolio held by the investor.

Corporate bond return and risk characteristics

Table 2.13 shows the performance and risk characteristics of US, UK and European corporate bonds, US government bonds with maturities over one year, global high-yield bonds, emerging market debt and global equities. Table 2.14 is a correlation matrix of the different indices.

A few observations can be made from the tables. First, US investment grade credit has generated a strong performance over the measuring period. Trailing US equities by 1% per annum on return, but with about a third of equity's volatility, the risk-adjusted performance of US credit has been impressive (note the high Sharpe ratio). Today, however, with underlying low rates expected to rise and tight credit spreads, investment grade credit may be in a bubble situation. Caution is warranted when investing in credit going forward.

A second observation is that credit markets in different regions behave differently. This is evident from the different realised returns and correlation matrix. The European investment grade credit market, for example, has not done as well as that of the United Kingdom, which in turn trailed that of the United States. The different asset classes within fixed income provide diversification opportunities, as well as opportunities for successful active investors to add value through dynamic asset allocation. Credit markets in different countries perform differently due to differing macroeconomic factors, including policy, which affects rates, and the health of the corporate sector, which affects spreads.

Table 2.13: US corporate bond return and risk characteristics, October 1998 to December 2013. Sharpe ratio calculated using $ cash returns

	US credit	UK credit	European credit	US Treasuries	High-yield	EMD	US equities
Start month	Oct-1998	Oct-1998	Oct-1998	Oct-1998	Oct-1998	Oct-1998	Oct-1998
Performance (% pa)	9.3	6.2	4.8	7.2	7.4	9.8	10.4
Volatility (%)	5.9	4.9	3.5	4.8	10.4	14.0	15.5
Skewness	-0.27	-0.18	-0.51	0.04	-1.14	-2.08	-0.45
Kurtosis	2.90	0.77	1.92	0.73	7.66	12.61	1.87
Sharpe ratio	0.83	0.78	0.74	0.70	0.24	0.50	0.33
Max drawdown (%)	-16.1	-8.7	-6.8	-5.3	-34.2	-32.7	-50.9

Source: Bloomberg, Global Financial Data, BofA Merrill Lynch US Corporate Bond Master TR Index, iBoxx £ Non-Gilts Overall TR Index, BofA Merrill Lynch EMU Corporate Bond TR Index, Citigroup United States WBGI TR Index, BofA Merrill Lynch Global High Yield Index, JPM Emerging Markets Bond Index Plus EMBI+ Composite, S&P 500 Index.

Table 2.14: Correlation matrix, October 1998 to December 2013

Correlation matrix	US credit	UK credit	European credit	US Treasuries	High-yield	EMD	US equities
US credit	1.00	0.72	0.80	0.58	0.57	0.59	0.20
UK credit	0.72	1.00	0.78	0.46	0.35	0.38	0.14
European credit	0.80	0.78	1.00	0.36	0.49	0.42	0.18
US Treasuries	0.58	0.46	0.36	1.00	-0.17	0.20	-0.32
High-yield	0.57	0.35	0.49	-0.17	1.00	0.61	0.65
EMD	0.59	0.38	0.42	0.20	0.61	1.00	0.50
US equities	0.20	0.14	0.18	-0.32	0.65	0.50	1.00

Source: Bloomberg, Global Financial Data, BofA Merrill Lynch US Corporate Bond Master TR Index, iBoxx £ Non-Gilts Overall TR Index, BofA Merrill Lynch EMU Corporate Bond TR Index, Citigroup United States WBGI TR Index, BofA Merrill Lynch Global High Yield Index, JPM Emerging Markets Bond Index Plus EMBI+ Composite, S&P 500 Index.

As the correlation matrix indicates, corporate bonds have a relatively low correlation with equities (albeit the correlation is positive, unlike the negative correlation of government bonds with equities). Adding global corporate bonds to the mix can further enhance the diversification benefits.

Figure 2.38 shows the cumulative performance of US credit, Treasury bonds and equities since January 1985. The performance of credit tracks that of government bonds but is also positively correlated with the expected fortunes of the economy as reflected in equity prices.

Figure 2.39 shows the rolling 36-month correlation between US credit and Treasuries and between US credit and US equities. During the 2008 crisis the correlation between credit and equities spiked up from below zero to over 0.60 as both asset classes fell. A risk factor analysis reveals that the returns of credit are affected by the equity market risk factor. During the 2008 crisis a much larger proportion of credit returns were driven by the equity risk factor, explaining the increased correlation.

Figure 2.38: Cumulative performance of US credit, Treasuries and equities, January 1985 to December 2013

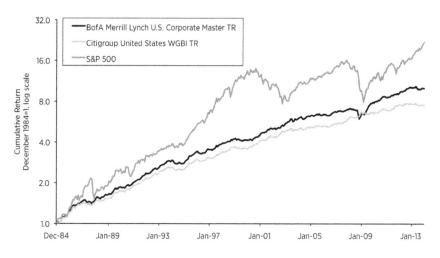

Source: Citigroup United States WGBI TR Index, BofA Merrill Lynch U.S. Corporate Master TR Index, S&P 500 Index.

Figure 2.39: Rolling 36-month correlation between US credit and Treasuries and between US credit and US equities, January 1988 to December 2013

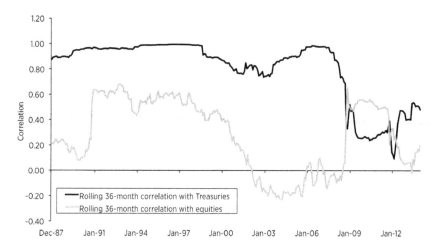

Source: Citigroup United States WGBI TR Index, BofA Merrill Lynch U.S. Corporate Master TR Index, S&P 500 Index.

Figure 2.40 shows the rolling 36-month volatility of US credit, Treasuries and equities. The 2008 crisis was an outlier over the time period since 1988. Investment grade credit and Treasuries have similar volatility, however, when the confidence in corporate bonds fell through the floor in 2008, their volatility jumped. When the situation calmed down, the volatility returned to normal levels.

Figure 2.40: Rolling 36-month volatility of US credit, Treasuries and equities, January 1988 to December 2013

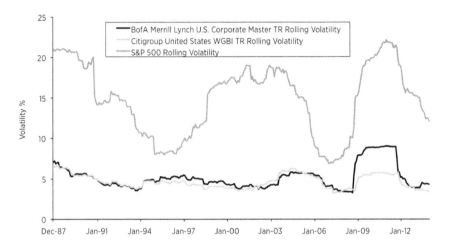

Source: Citigroup United States WGBI TR Index, BofA Merrill Lynch U.S. Corporate Master TR Index, S&P 500 Index.

Figure 2.41 shows the average performance of US credit ranked by the average decile performance of US equities. Credit does not provide the protection that Treasuries do, as it does not perform strongly when equity falls. Credit is much more positively correlated with equities than govis are.

Figure 2.41: Average performance of US credit and US equities ranked by performance of US equities, January 1982 to December 2013

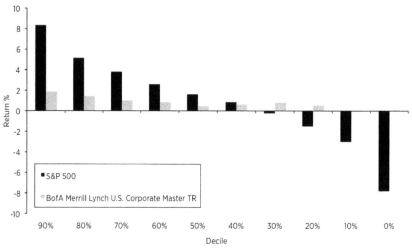

Source: Bloomberg, S&P 500 Index, BofA Merrill Lynch U.S. Corporate Master TR Index.

Access

Accessing the credit market via purchasing individual bonds is becoming easier. For example, in the United Kingdom the London Stock Exchange launched a retail bond market in 2010, called the Order Book for Retail Bonds. The minimum investment is low in this market, allowing firms to tap the retail market for borrowing and for small investors to access the corporate bond market directly. All that investors need to do is to contact their bank, broker or investment platform. The internet contains abundant information on the subject.

Corporate bond funds are plentiful, either actively or passively managed. The credit market is relatively inefficient and careful credit analysis can add value. Therefore, investors should consider active management or smart beta strategies that can deliver superior results to those of passive trackers. Funds offer diversification, sharing of costs and professional management. They do come, however, with a fee. Unlike individual bonds that allow investors to customise their holdings and hold the bonds to maturity (if so they wish), fund's prices fluctuate as they are marked to market on a daily basis.

While the listed derivative market for credit is still developing, the OTC market offers ways to access credit, for example via CDS.

Conclusions

Corporate bonds are a double act: they depend on the rate of the underlying government bonds and the credit spread between the yield of corporate bonds and that of government bonds. The rate of government bonds reacts differently to the credit spread. Strengthening economic conditions, for instance, may mean increasing rates and tightening credit spreads. Financial stress may mean dropping rates and widening credit spreads. Two opposite forces are at play. The performance of corporate bonds is a function of which of the two forces has the upper hand. Credit lies on the border between conservative government bonds and risky equities. It exposes portfolios to the credit risk premium.

Equity is investing in businesses and corporate bonds are lending to businesses. The return on the equity and bonds depends on the company's commercial fortunes. If a company is successful its equity should appreciate and its credit rating may improve. The price of its debt will increase as well. So we can say that corporate bonds and equities are on the same page, while government bonds and equities are on different pages.

Corporate bonds sit between the equity bull camp and the government bond bear camp. They are spread investments. Good news for the economy means that the spread narrows but the rate increases. Bad news for the economy means that the spread may expand but the rate eases.

Summary

- Corporate bonds (credit) are issued by corporations to raise debt capital (i.e. borrow).

- While sovereigns can print money to repay their debt, corporations cannot and must stay solvent. The credit risk of corporate bonds should come with a credit premium to compensate investors for the risk. The credit spread also includes a liquidity premium, since credit is not as liquid as government bonds.

- The main reasons for investing in credit include: credit risk premium; yield pickup relative to government bonds; potential capital gain; stable income and capital preservation; diversification; diversity; opportunities for active management; hedging liabilities; and easily modelled.

- Corporate bonds are a risk asset since they are affected by many factors that affect equities in a similar way. The main risks of investing in corporate bonds include: credit spread risk; interest rate risk; default risk; liquidity risk; increased issuance; inflation risk; taxation risk; changing correlation.

- Capital gains and losses are realised only if bonds are not held to maturity.

- Credit rating and credit rating agencies play an important role in corporate bond investing – a deterioration in credit rating can cause a drop in bond price. A criticism often levelled at credit rating agencies is that their analysis is backward looking.

- Floating rate notes (FRNs) are bonds that have a variable coupon, equal to a money market reference rate, like LIBOR, plus a quoted spread (quoted margin). An FRN's duration equals the time of the next coupon reset date (e.g. three months).

- A credit default swap (CDS) is a financial swap agreement that the seller of the CDS will compensate the buyer in the event of a loan default or other credit event. The buyer of the CDS makes a series of payments (the CDS fee or spread) to the seller and in exchange receives a payoff if the loan defaults.

- CDS behave in many respects as a leveraged corporate floating rate note (FRN), since the parties are not exposed to interest rate risk.

- CDS can be used to speculate on the credit spread of the reference entity, hedge credit risk, exploit arbitrage opportunities and synthetically gain credit exposure.

- Corporate bonds can be accessed through individual bonds, active and passive funds and derivatives (e.g. CDS).

High-yield bonds

High-yield bonds or *junk bonds* are corporate bonds with a credit rating below investment grade (speculative grade, rated below BBB by Standard & Poor's and Fitch or rated below Baa by Moody's). As such they have a higher level of credit risk compared with investment grade corporate and government bonds. Different ratings of high-yield bonds have different levels of credit risk, as shown in Table 2.15.

Until the 1980s, high-yield bonds were mostly the outstanding bonds of *fallen angels*, former investment grade companies that had been downgraded below investment grade.[63] Then investment banks, led by Drexel Burnham Lambert,[64] launched the modern high-yield bond market in the 1980s. It sold new bonds issued by companies with below-investment grade ratings, mainly to finance mergers and acquisitions or leveraged buyouts (LBOs) in which an acquirer issues speculative grade bonds to help pay for an acquisition of a target company's equity and then use the target's cash flows to help pay the debt over time.

The high-yield bond market has since evolved and today much high-yield debt is used for general corporate purposes, such as financing capital needs or consolidating and paying down bank lines of credit. Mainly focused in the United States through the 1980s and 1990s, the high-yield sector has since grown significantly around the globe in terms of issuance, outstanding securities and investor interest.

---

[63] The opposite of fallen angels are rising stars, companies whose credit rating has been upgraded.

[64] Drexel Burnham Lambert was a Wall Street investment banking firm which first rose to prominence and then was forced into bankruptcy in February 1990 by its involvement in illegal activities in the junk bond market, driven by Drexel employee Michael Milken. At its height, it was the fifth-largest investment bank in the United States.

New high-yield issuance can vary greatly from year to year depending on economic and market conditions, typically expanding along with economic growth when investors' appetite for risk often increases, and waning in recessions or market environments when investors are more cautious.

The high-yield bond market includes both originally-issued high-yield bonds and the outstanding bonds of fallen angels, which can have a significant impact on the overall size of the market if large or numerous companies are downgraded to high-yield status. Conversely, the sector can shrink when companies are upgraded out of the speculative grade market into the investment grade sector.

Table 2.15: Bond credit quality ratings

	Credit risk	Moody's	S&P	Fitch
Investment grade	Highest quality	Aaa	AAA	AAA
	High quality (very strong)	Aa	AA	AA
	Upper medium grade (strong)	A	A	A
	Medium grade	Baa	BBB	BBB
Below investment grade	Lower medium grade (somewhat speculative)	Ba	BB	BB
	Low grade (speculative)	B	B	B
	Poor quality (may default)	Caa	CCC	CCC
	Most speculative	Ca	CC	CC
	No interest being paid or bankruptcy petition filed	C	C	C
	In default	C	D	D

Source: Moody's, Standard & Poor's, Fitch.

Table 2.16 shows how the global high-yield bond market (as represented by the Markit iBoxx Global Developed Markets High Yield Index) is broken down into sectors, countries and maturities. Table 2.17 shows the breakdown by credit ratings. While the issuers of the high-yield market are well diversified across sectors, geographically the market is still dominated by US issuers. The US high-yield market is the deepest. In terms of maturities, most issues are within the five to ten year range.

Table 2.16: Global high-yield bond market breakdown into sectors, countries and maturities, October 2012

Sector	%
Consumer Services	14.6
Industrials	14.0
Financials	12.8
Oil & Gas	9.8
Consumer Goods	9.8
Telecommunications	9.0
Health Care	7.9
Basic Materials	5.9
Utilities	5.9
Technology	5.8
Other/Undefined	4.5

Country	%
United States	65.0
United Kingdom	5.2
France	4.1
Luxembourg	4.0
Canada	3.4
Netherlands	2.9
Germany	2.9
Bermuda	1.4
Ireland	1.3
Cayman Islands	1.1
Total	91.2

Maturity (years)	%
0-1	0.0
1-5	27.5
5-10	67.5
10-15	1.0
15-20	0.0
20-25	0.0
25+	0.5
Average (years)	4.3

Source: Markit iBoxx Global Developed Markets High Yield Index.

Table 2.17: Global high-yield market credit rating breakdown, October 2012

S&P/Moody's	S&P	Moody's
AAA/Aaa	0.0%	1.3%
AA+/Aa1	0.0%	0.0%
AA/Aa2	1.3%	0.0%
AA-/Aa3	0.0%	0.0%
A+/A1	0.0%	0.0%
A/A2	0.0%	0.0%
A-/A3	0.0%	0.0%
BBB+/Baa1	0.2%	0.0%
BBB/Baa2	0.0%	0.2%
BBB-/Baa3	4.2%	0.8%
BB+/Ba1	11.6%	7.2%
BB/Ba2	13.7%	16.4%
BB-/Ba3	18.8%	18.1%
B+/B1	13.9%	18.9%
B/B2	13.0%	7.2%
B-/B3	9.4%	13.9%
CCC+/Caa1	5.0%	7.3%
CCC/Caa2	3.7%	2.6%
CCC-/Caa3	0.3%	1.2%
CC/Ca	0.2%	0.1%
C/C	0.0%	0.0%
Not Rated	2.7%	2.7%

Source: Markit IBoxx Global Developed Markets High Yield Index.

The reasons for investing in high-yield bonds

As a risk asset, high-yield bonds offer high yields (income) and relatively high potential returns. The reasons for investing in high-yield bonds and their roles in portfolios include:

- *Speculative credit risk premium.* Similar to investment grade corporate bonds, which expose portfolios to the credit risk premium, high-yield bonds expose portfolios to a below investment grade credit risk premium or speculative credit risk premium. Making an analogy from small cap equities, which expose portfolios to a small cap risk factor that has been historically compensated by markets, the speculative credit risk factor may be a source of long-term attractive rewards.

- *Yield pickup relative to investment grade bonds.* High-yield bonds offer yields with positive spreads relative to equivalent investment grade bonds. During certain market conditions (i.e. low turbulence with low default rates) they offer attractive returns compared to investment grade bonds and may even be competitive with equity returns.

- *Income.* High-yield bonds can be used in portfolios that aim to deliver high income, in particular during time periods of low interest rates when yield is scarce and generating yield requires taking risk. Average yields in the high-yield bond sector vary depending on the economic climate, generally rising during downturns when default risk also rises (high-yield companies may be more negatively affected by adverse market conditions than investment grade companies). For example, for much of the 1980s and 1990s, US high-yield bonds typically offered 300 to 400 basis points of additional yield relative to US Treasury securities of comparable maturity. Following the 2008 crisis, the spread between high-yield and government bonds was even greater.

- *Growth.* An economic upturn or improved performance at the issuing company can have a significant impact on the price of a high-yield bond. This capital appreciation is an important component of a total return investment approach. Events that can push up the price of a bond include ratings upgrades, improved earnings reports, mergers and acquisitions, management changes, positive product developments or market-related events (similar to events that support equity prices). On the opposite side, if an issuer's financial health deteriorates, rating agencies may downgrade the bonds and this can reduce their value.

- *Lower volatility than equities.* While the returns of high-yield bonds may have high levels of standard deviation, during appropriate market conditions they offer lower volatility than equities. High-yield bonds can be used as a substitute for equities since they offer growth with lower downside risk relative to equities.

- *Opportunities for active management.* The high-yield bond market is less efficient and less analysed than the investment grade bond market so it offers opportunities for value through active management, focusing on analysing bottom-up creditworthiness, capital structure, leverage, cash flows, liquidity, covenants, asset quality and corporate balance sheets. The risks of high-yield bonds mean an active approach is recommended so a professional portfolio manager can aim to avoid investing in companies that are likely to default.

- *Rights upon liquidation.* High-yield bonds are higher in the pecking order of a company's capital structure (the right to company assets at liquidation) than equities and preferred shares.

- *Portfolio tactical positioning.* High-yield bonds can be an attractive asset class during periods of monetary easing and steepening yield curves. Tactical allocation to high-yield bonds during appropriate time periods can add value.

- *Diversification.* High-yield bonds offer diversification benefits in portfolio context due to their imperfect correlation with other asset classes.

Figure 2.42 compares the yields of US high-yield bonds, investment grade corporate bonds and 10-year Treasuries. High-yield bonds consistently offer higher yields than investment grade corporates and Treasuries (hence the name high-yield). During the 2008 crisis the yields on high-yield bonds spiked. High-yield bond investors who did not sell their holdings recouped losses. Investors who saw the spike in yields as a buying opportunity have made a good profit.

Figure 2.42: Average yield of US high-yield bonds, investment grade corporate bonds and 10-year Treasuries, October 2002 to December 2013

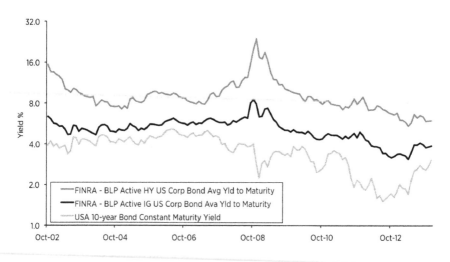

Source: Bloomberg, Global Financial Data, FINRA – BLP Active HY US Corporate Bond Index Average Yield to Maturity, FINRA – BLP Active Investment Grade US Corporate Bond Average Yield to Maturity, USA 10-year Bond Constant Maturity Yield.

Note how the investment grade and high-yield spreads over Treasury yields materially contracted in 2013. The market was expecting lower defaults as the economic conditions and sentiment improved markedly from their position in the depths of the crisis. Also, the low yields on offer by government bonds pushed investors to seek yields in the corporate sector, including the high-yield market. This demand pushed prices up and yields down.

Risks

High-yield bonds are a risk asset as well as a fixed income asset. In addition to the risks of government and investment grade corporate bonds, the specific risks of investing in junk bonds include:

- *Downside risk.* High-yield bonds can suffer substantial impairments to their value as a result of credit deterioration and default.

- *Liquidity risk.* During certain times the high-yield bond market can suffer from illiquidity and wide bid-ask spreads. When liquidity is dry, transaction costs of trading high-yield bonds can balloon.

- *Volatility.* High-yield bonds are volatile relative to government and investment grade corporate bonds. Volatility per se is, however, not a concerning risk. The concern is downside risk in the form of losses that cannot be recovered or take a long time to recover. Volatility without unrecovered losses may cause sleepless nights, but should not be feared by investors with appropriately long investment horizons.

- *Increased issuance.* Due to a relatively concentrated and opportunistically minded population of issuers and investors, and the emergence of credit derivatives that allow traders to short corporate debt, high-yield bonds may experience feast-or-famine new issue volume and significant intra-year or year-to-year swings in prices and yields, followed by extensive periods of relative quietude.

- *Challenging modelling.* Some high-yield bond features relating to callability, claw back terms and other indenture provisions may be arcane, difficult to model under various economic scenarios and ignored or poorly understood by issuers, investors and intermediaries, leading to unforeseen and possibly unfavourable consequences.

- *Bubble conditions.* The performance of the high-yield market has been very strong over the last few years, seeing valuations soaring and spreads contracting. One of the causes of the 2008 crisis was subprime lending – banks extended mortgage lending to individuals with questionable financial ability to repay their loans. The situation in the high-yield market has some similarities. Banks are lending to corporations with below investment grade credit ratings at decreasing interest rates. Default risk might be under-priced.

This may be a corporate subprime bubble developing. Investors should closely monitor the high-yield market because deteriorating economic conditions, a drop in liquidity provided by central banks or increasing rates can have a devastating impact on the asset class.

High-yield bond portfolios should be well diversified and professionally managed. This may reduce the risks of high-yield bonds compared to a concentrated portfolio with only a few issues, where a default of one may materially affect the entire portfolio's performance. Comprehensive research into the financials of the issuing companies may help mitigate the risk of default. Investors should also monitor the overall market and the general economic situation to gauge whether tactical allocation into or out of the high-yield market is warranted.

Short duration high-yield bonds

Like most fixed income securities, high-yield bonds include duration risk. As rates have been approaching multi-year lows following the 2008 crisis, short-duration high-yield bond investing has gained popularity.

Focusing on high-yield bonds with short maturities, investors can still enjoy higher yields compared to equivalent investment grade bonds, but with controlled duration risk. Short duration investing has also gained popularity for investment grade credit. While the investors must compromise on lower yields compared to longer dated bonds, total returns may be superior if rates move upwards as capital losses are mitigated.

Access

While a few years ago accessing high-yield bonds was restricted to active funds or individual bonds, today exchange traded funds (ETFs) are available on high-yield bond indices. The typical Total Expense Ratio (TER) of a high-yield bond ETF is around 40 basis points. The trading costs of buying or selling a high-yield bond fund or ETF may be 50 basis points (depending on the size of the investment, the fund's AUM and the market's liquidity). When buying or selling holdings in a collective invested in high-yield bonds this cost may be represented in the collective's dilution levy or swing price.

Short duration high-yield bond indices are available and investors can get exposure to these indices via funds or ETFs. Short duration high-yield bonds may still offer an attractive yield with a lower duration risk (e.g. average duration of two years) than regular high-yield bond indices (e.g. average duration closer to four years).

Asset class classification

The answer to the question of whether high-yield bonds are closer to investment grade bonds or equities in terms of volatility, correlations and returns depends on the market conditions and type of high-yield bonds. While legally high-yield bonds are debt instruments, they exhibit a higher correlation with equities and their volatility levels are much closer to that of equities than to that of investment grade corporate bonds or government bonds.

High-yield bonds can be a substitute for equities as they are risk assets that can offer attractive returns during certain time periods. High-yield bonds have lower downside risk compared to that of equities because a large portion of their total return is driven by income. Using them as an equity substitute can still generate long-term returns but with a lower risk.

The equity substitution strategy was popular at the beginning of 2003. After the bear market that followed the burst of the high-tech bubble in 2000, corporations restructured their balance sheets by deleveraging them. Healthier balance sheets and accommodative monetary policy meant a supportive environment for high-yield bonds. The fortunes for equities were more uncertain since it was unclear at the beginning of 2003 whether equities would end their bear market. Substituting some of the allocation to equities with high-yield bonds was a reasonable strategy. However, in the event equities rallied sharply in March 2003, outpacing the returns of high-yield bonds – the high-yield bonds delivered handsome returns, but not as high as those of equities.

Then 2008 saw a golden opportunity for high-yield bonds, as well as for investment grade corporate bonds. After the fall of Lehman Brothers and the emergence of the credit crunch and financial crisis the prices of high-yield bonds and credit fell sharply. The yields on these investments skyrocketed, implying unprecedented and unrealistic default rates. The market panicked and bond prices reflected panic rather than fair values.

Applying normal costs of expected defaults to extreme high yields meant that the expected returns of high-yield bonds and corporate bonds were unusually attractive. High-yield bonds offered higher expected returns than those of equities with a lower expected volatility. Such investment opportunities are rare (perhaps once in a lifetime) and when they appear investors should grab them with both hands.

Expected return

The long-term, sustainable (i.e. ignoring short-term noise) expected return of investment grade corporate bonds is their yield adjusted to the expected loss due to defaults. The expected return of high-yield bonds is derived in the same way. The difference between investment grade and high-yield bonds is that the yield of high-yield bonds is higher, as well as the expected loss from defaults. Under normal market conditions, taking into account these two opposing factors, high-yield bonds have a higher expected return than investment grade bonds.

High-yield bond return and risk characteristics

Figure 2.43 shows the cumulative performance of global high-yield since January 1998, as well as the performance of US equities. Clearly, high-yield bonds are a risk asset with similar characteristics to those of equities. The strong performance of the asset class over recent years may mean that the valuations of high-yield bonds are stretched, perhaps to the extent of being in bubble territory. Investing in the asset going forward should be done with caution as rising rates and compressed spreads may mean that future returns may be disappointing.

Figure 2.43: Cumulative performance of global high-yield bonds and US equities, January 1998 to December 2013

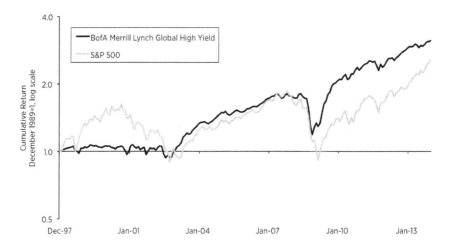

Source: Bloomberg, BofA Merrill Lynch Global High Yield Index, S&P 500 Index.

Figure 2.44 compares the rolling 36-month correlation between global high-yield bonds and US Treasuries and between global high-yield bonds and US equities. Most of the time high-yield bonds have a higher correlation with equities than with Treasuries. While contractually and legally high-yield bonds are bonds, they behave more like equities than investment grade bonds.

Figure 2.45 shows the rolling 36-month volatility of global high-yield bonds, Treasuries and US equities. The volatility of high-yield bonds is between that of Treasuries and that of equities. At times of market stress high-yield bond volatility is closer to that of equities than to that of Treasuries, most notably during the 2008 global financial crisis. Based on the correlation and volatility of high-yield bonds, clearly they are a risk asset and not a conservative asset.

Figure 2.44: Rolling 36-month correlation between global high-yield bonds and US Treasuries and US equities, January 2001 to December 2013

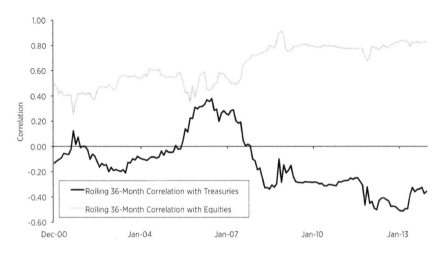

Source: Bloomberg, BofA Merrill Lynch Global High Yield Index, Citibank United States WGBI TR Index, S&P 500 Index.

Figure 2.45: Rolling 36-month volatility of global high-yield bonds, US Treasuries and US equities, January 2001 to December 2013

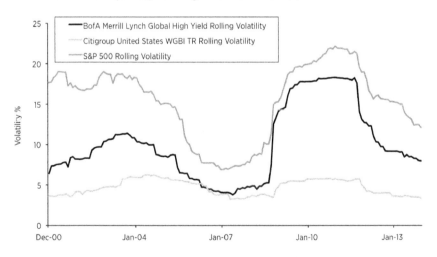

Source: Bloomberg, BofA Merrill Lynch Global High Yield Index, Citibank United States WGBI TR Index, S&P 500 Index.

Figure 2.46 compares the drawdowns of global high-yield bonds and US equities. It can be seen that during the high-tech bubble burst, high-yield bonds did not experience a severe drawdown as equities did. During the 2008 crisis, high-yield bonds did have a major drawdown but they recovered much quicker than equities. High-yield bonds are a risk asset but with lower downside risk compared to equities.

Figure 2.46: Drawdowns global high-yield bonds and US equities, January 1998 to June 2013

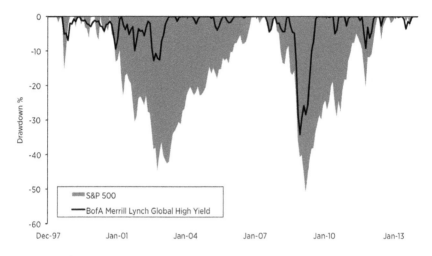

Source: Bloomberg, BofA Merrill Lynch Global High Yield Index, S&P 500 Index.

Conclusions

Undoubtedly a risk asset, high-yield bonds allow investors to dial up the risk level within fixed income to generate high yields and capital appreciation.

High-yield investing involves risks and should be done professionally and in a risk controlled way. However, the high-yield bond market presents attractive opportunities that should not be passed by lightly. High-yield bonds can play a role as an equity substitute in portfolios, providing a long-term growth engine.

High-yield bonds are a step away from corporate bonds and are closer to equities. Companies issuing high-yield bonds are below investment grade. If they stay below investment grade and do not default, investors get an attractive yield, above that of investment grade corporates. If they improve their credit rating (rising stars), there is upside potential, similar to the upside potential of equities. High-yield bonds offer both high yield and upside potential as their price may increase.

Summary

High-yield bonds have a credit rating below investment grade. They offer higher yields than equivalent investment grade bonds with higher default risk.

- The reasons to invest in high-yield bonds include: speculative credit risk premium; yield pickup relative to investment grade bonds; income; potential growth; lower volatility than equities; opportunities for active management; preferred rights upon liquidation compared to equity; portfolio tactical positioning; and diversification.

- The risks of investing in high-yield bonds include: downside risk; liquidity risk; volatility; increased issuance; challenging modelling; and potential bubble conditions.

- High-yield portfolios should be well diversified and professionally managed to mitigate some of the risks of high-yield bond investing.

- High-yield bonds are a risk asset and may be a substitute for equities since they offer long-term potential growth with lower downside risk compared to that of equities.

- The long-term, sustainable expected return of high-yield bonds is their yield adjusted for the expected loss due to defaults.

Global developed bonds

Global developed bonds (commonly known as overseas bonds) include bonds issued by governments of developed countries and corporations operating in such countries around the world. This is a large and diverse asset class with issuers across many countries, currencies, sectors, quality ratings, maturities, structures and types of issue. Issuers include sovereigns, government agencies, supranational bodies, corporates and others. As opposed to emerging market debt, global developed bonds are issued by entities operating in developed countries. The three main sub-sectors within global developed bonds include investment grade sovereign, corporate bonds and inflation-linked bonds.

Investing in global developed bonds is based on the same principles as investing in local government bonds, corporate bonds and inflation-linked bonds. However, currency risk should be considered and investors should consider that the diversification benefits of investing in these bonds are affected by different regional factors (e.g. interest rates, policies of central banks, yield curves and inflation).

The reasons for investing in global developed bonds

Global developed bonds have similar opportunities to those of local bonds, with some differences. The specific reasons for investing in global developed bonds and their roles in portfolios include:

- *Expanded investment opportunity set.* Global bonds expose portfolios to local and global monetary, fiscal and currency policies. The asset class provides many and diverse investment opportunities.

- *Diversification.* The economic and inflation cycles and yield curves of countries and regions may be different, providing diversification.

- *Protection.* Similar to local government bonds, global sovereign bonds may provide some protection to portfolios at times of stress in risk assets and flight to quality. When the yields of local bonds are low and hence their protection is limited (i.e. the scope for a drop in yields is limited), overseas bonds with higher yields can instead provide protection, in particular when currency risk is hedged. As countries and regions are more connected due to globalisation, stress in major economies such as the United States or Europe can spill over and drag more countries into stress, resulting in a drop in yields of their government bonds. Investors should make the distinction between safe-haven countries, such as the United States, United Kingdom, Germany and Japan, and others, such as peripheral European countries (e.g. Italy, Spain). The yields of the former normally fall during economic stress due to a flight to quality and increased demand for their government bonds. The yields of the latter may rise during economic stress, reflecting their increased default risk (increased borrowing costs) and a sell-off of their government bonds.

- *Active management.* The global bond market is heterogeneous and includes opportunities to capitalise on inefficiencies among international capital markets. These features provide opportunities for active management to deliver excess returns. In a similar way to global equities, global bonds provide a wide spectrum of choices for active managers. Skilled managers can translate this wealth of choices into wealth generation. Local bond mandates that allow some exposure to foreign bonds can use the latter to try to generate excess returns. Global bonds also provide opportunities for pair trading. Investors can short bonds whose yield is low and go long bonds whose yield is high with the view that the yields will converge (e.g. long high-yielding Italian government bonds and short low-yielding German bunds), enabling them to benefit from the two legs of the trade.

Risks

Global developed bonds include all the risks of local bonds. The additional risks of investing in this asset class include:

- *Currency risk.* Currency risk can double or triple the volatility of unhedged foreign bonds – this exposure can dominate returns. The risk of developed countries' currencies can be hedged relatively easily using currency forward and futures contracts and other derivatives, and as a rule of thumb the currency risk of overseas developed bonds should be hedged.

- *Changing correlations.* Increasing globalisation and international cooperation may cause the correlation between local and foreign bonds to increase, diminishing the diversification benefits.

European debt crisis

Global developed bonds have become a potential replacement for euro zone government bonds following the 2011 European sovereign debt crisis. As the government bonds of countries such as Spain, Italy and even Germany have become increasingly risky, these bonds have lost their safe-haven status and investors have lost confidence in them. Replacing euro zone sovereign debt with global developed bonds from countries such as the United States, United Kingdom, Switzerland and Australia, while hedging the currency risk if necessary, has become a solution for safe-haven investments for euro-based investors.

Figure 2.47 compares the yield on emerging market debt with that on 10-year Italian government bonds. It shows how Italian government bonds lost their safe-haven status. In 2011, during the European sovereign debt crisis, the Italian bond yield surpassed that of emerging markets. The market assigned a higher risk of default to Italy than to emerging market economies. With hindsight, Italian bonds were a lucrative investment opportunity as their yields fell during 2013 and 2014. Investors benefited both from high yield (carry) and capital gains.

Figure 2.47: Yield on emerging market debt and Italian 10-year government bonds, January 1998 to January 2013

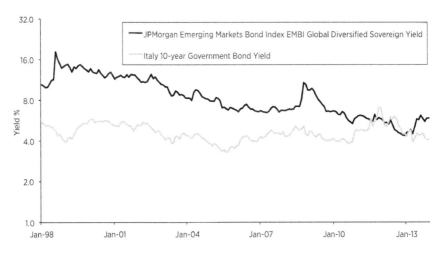

Source: Bloomberg, Global Financial Data, JPMorgan Emerging Markets Bond Index EMBI Global Diversified Sovereign Yield, Italy 10-year Government Bond Yield.

Expected return and cost of currency hedging

Similar to local bonds, the expected long-term, sustainable return of foreign bonds is their yield adjusted for expected loss due to defaults (assuming bonds are held to maturity). Dissimilar to local bonds, the additional element of investing in foreign bonds is currency risk. If the currency risk is unhedged, which is not recommended, the expected return should be adjusted for expected currency return, which is difficult to estimate.

If the currency risk is hedged, which is recommended, the expected return should be adjusted for the cost of hedging. The theoretical cost of hedging is the differences in short-term interest rates between the foreign and base currencies. Therefore, the expected return of foreign bonds on a currency hedged basis is yield adjusted for expected loss due to defaults, minus the short-term interest rate on the foreign bond's currency, plus the short-term interest rate on the base currency.

Global developed bond return and risk characteristics

Figure 2.48 shows the cumulative performance of global developed bonds (as represented by the BofA Merrill Lynch Global Broad Market Index) and US Treasuries from December 1996. Figure 2.49 shows the rolling 36-month correlation between the two asset classes. As can be seen, global developed bonds are a distinct asset class to local government bonds, with a different return profile and imperfect correlation. Adding global developed bonds to a multi-asset portfolio adds diversification benefits and expands the investment opportunity set. The correlation between US Treasuries and global developed bonds dropped during the European sovereign debt crisis of 2011 as the performance of US government bonds and that of European bonds diverged.

Figure 2.48: Cumulative performance of global aggregate and US Treasuries, December 1996 to December 2012

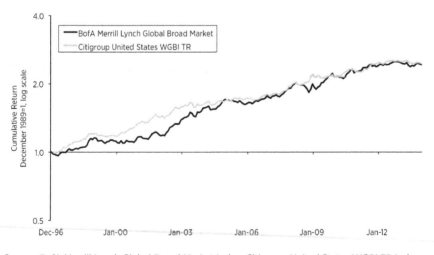

Source: BofA Merrill Lynch Global Broad Market Index, Citigroup United States WGBI TR Index.

Figure 2.49: Rolling 36-month correlation between global aggregated and US Treasuries, December 1999 to December 2013

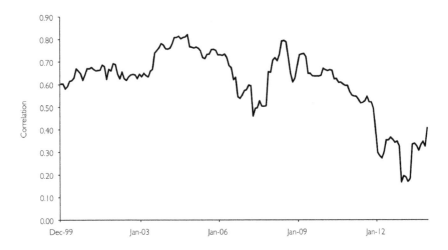

Source: BofA Merrill Lynch Global Broad Market Index, Citigroup United States WGBI TR Index.

Global developed bond index

The most common index representing global developed bonds is the Barclays Capital Global Aggregate Bond Index. The index used to be called the Lehman Global Aggregate Bond Index before the demise of Lehman Brothers. The index is made up of approximately 50% government bonds, 15% government-related bonds, 15% corporate bonds and 20% securitised bonds. This composition fluctuates over time. More than 50% of the index is made of Aaa bonds, then there are 30% Aa bonds, 10% A bonds and less than 10% Baa bonds.

The approximate country weights of the index are listed in Table 2.18. The high exposure of the index to Japanese Government Bonds (JGBs), which are unattractive due to their low yields, and to euro zone government bonds, which have become riskier following the European sovereign crisis, has made the index unattractive for investors seeking safe-haven investment grade bonds. Portfolios that track the index or maintain a low tracking error with it may offer investors different characteristics to those which are expected.

Table 2.18: Approximated country weights in Barclays Global Aggregate Bond index

Country	Weight (%)
Australia/New Zealand	1.5
Canada	2.5
Denmark/Norway/Sweden	1.0
Eurozone	25.0
Japan	20.5
United Kingdom	5.5
United States	40.5
Others	3.5

Source: Barclays Capital Global Aggregate Bond Index.

A potential solution to address the unattractive composition of the global aggregate index is to customise it. Bonds of each region can be modelled and the mix of regional bonds can be optimised to create an optimal benchmark. For example, the exposure to JGBs can be removed and the mix between sovereign bonds, corporate bonds and inflation-linked bonds can be optimised.

Access

Like with other fixed income investments, investors can directly purchase individual global developed bonds. However, it is more challenging to purchase global developed bonds than local bonds since the bonds are listed on different exchanges around the world and currency risk needs to be managed.

Collective investment schemes (CIS), either actively managed or passively tracking indices, are available for the asset class. However, the choice is narrower than that of local bonds.

Strategic bond funds have gained popularity over recent years. These funds have flexibility to tap different global fixed income markets, not only global developed bonds, but also below investment grade markets. These funds can also use derivatives to control risks, such as duration and credit risk. Strategic bond funds can add value if managed by a skilled fund manager. However, investors must pay attention to the style of the fund to understand which asset classes it is exposed to.

Conclusions

Investing in global developed bonds is another weapon in the arsenal of investors. When the 10-year yield on local bonds is low (e.g. 1.5%) and that of foreign developed bonds is higher (e.g. 4% on Australian govis), foreign bonds can play a protective role in a portfolio, providing a source of income and an opportunity for a profit. Similarly, if you are domiciled in the United States and the 10-year Treasury yields less than 2%, you can buy an Australian govi yielding 4%. You buy the Aussie and hedge the Australian dollar and you have yourself a deal as long as the Australian government does not default on its debt and the currency hedging costs do not consume all the yield pick-up.

As long as the currency risk is managed, the costs of currency hedging are acceptable and investors have the resources to understand the investment, investing in overseas bonds may present attractive opportunities.

Summary

- Global developed bonds include fixed income securities issued by governments and entities across the world covering sovereign, corporate and inflation-linked bonds.

- The main reasons for investing in global developed bonds include: expanded investment opportunity set; diversification; protection; and opportunities for active management.

- The risks of global developed bonds include all the risks of local bonds and in addition include currency risk and changing correlation risk.

- The expected return of foreign bonds on a currency hedged basis is yield adjusted for expected loss due to defaults, minus the short-term interest rate on the foreign bond's currency, plus the short-term interest rate on the base currency.

Emerging market debt

Emerging market debt (EMD) refers to bonds issued by governments of developing countries or by corporations operating in developing countries. However, corporations in developing countries generally tend to borrow from banks and other sources as public debt issuance requires both sufficiently developed capital markets and large borrowing needs. Therefore, the corporate EMD market is much smaller than the sovereign EMD market.

Sovereign EMD has historically been primarily issued in foreign currencies, mainly in either dollar or euro (*hard currency*), as opposed to the local currency of the issuing country (local or *soft currency*). Governments issuing debt in local currency can print money to pay off their debt, increase inflation and potentially devalue the currency. However, when the debt is issued in foreign currency, the sovereign has no flexibility of printing money to pay it off. The development of pension systems in certain countries has led to increasing issuance in local currencies, as pension schemes create demand for local currency denominated bonds since their liabilities are denominated in local currencies and they use bonds for liability hedging.

EMD tends to have a lower credit rating than sovereign debt of developed countries because of the increased economic and political risks. While most developed countries have a credit rating above A, most EMD is rated below investment grade, though a few developing countries enjoy credit ratings of A+ (such as Chile and China).

Following the 2008 credit crisis and the 2011 European sovereign debt crisis, certain emerging market countries have emerged as possibly less prone to default than Western developed markets. The governments of some developing countries have not accumulated unsustainable amounts of debt, as have those of Western countries.

History

During the 1970s, US and European multinational banks lent capital to governments of developing countries, particularly in Latin America. In the late 1970s and early 1980s the global economy faced difficulties because of increasing oil prices, double-digit inflation rates and high interest rates. These factors caused developing countries to fall behind on their external debt servicing obligations and culminated in the 1982 *Mexican debt crisis*, when the Mexican government declared a moratorium on servicing interest payments on its debt. Other countries followed suit and the multinational banks found themselves sitting on a pile of nonperforming assets.

Following this crisis US and European banks began exchanging their nonperforming loans into tradable instruments and by the late 1980s this practice had grown into a reasonably systematic market with the 1989 *Brady Plan* (named after then US Treasury Secretary Nicholas Brady).

The *Brady bond* market was an early instance of securitisation, by which tradable securities backed by specific assets and cash flows were created. Banks were able to convert their outstanding loans to governments of developing countries into Brady bonds. They were tradable instruments, denominated in US dollars and usually collateralised by 30-year US Treasury zero-coupon bonds purchased by the issuing country using funds from the IMF, World Bank and the country's foreign currency reserves. This allowed the banks to systematically write down the nonperforming loans on their balance sheets. Mexico issued the first Brady bond in 1990 and the market grew to $190 billion, representing 13 countries,[65] in its first six years.

Around the time of the Brady Plan, the global economy was undergoing seismic changes. The Berlin Wall collapsed and the economies of Eastern Europe and the former Soviet Union joined the global free economy. China, India and the markets of Southeast Asia were rapidly evolving into high-growth, affluent

---

[65] Argentina, Brazil, Bulgaria, Costa Rica, Dominican Republic, Ecuador, Mexico, Morocco, Nigeria, Philippines, Poland, Uruguay and Venezuela.

economies. As these countries grew in size and their creditworthiness strengthened, their debt and equity markets developed. Capital flowed freely from the developed markets of North America, Europe and Japan into emerging markets. Much of these flows were speculative and included hedge funds and other market players seeking to benefit from the attractive potential returns offered by these rapidly changing markets.

However, in many instances market growth outpaced the implementation of a sound legal and economic infrastructure. Weak banking systems and current account deficits made these countries vulnerable to external shocks. An external shock indeed occurred in the summer of 1997 when Thailand's currency, the baht, depreciated by more than half and the Korean won followed shortly thereafter with a 70% plunge.

The Asian currency shocks led to a massive capital flight from the region, causing local bond and stock markets to plunge. Unfortunately, the crisis did not stop at Asia. Investors considered emerging markets as a single block or asset class and massively sold their holdings in Asia, Eastern Europe and Latin America in a flight to quality. In August 1998, Russia defaulted on its $72 billion outstanding debt obligations. This created a global financial dislocation including the infamous failure of the hedge fund *Long-Term Capital Management (LTCM)* in the autumn of 1998.

The contagion of the 1990s rattled the financial markets. In November 2001 Argentina defaulted on $82 billion of its debt obligations. The country restructured its debt obligations and continued to receive funds from the IMF to aid in its recovery. However, emerging debt markets did not collapse. On the contrary, many enjoyed solid growth after 2002 with perennially strong stock markets, strengthening sovereign debt ratings and economic growth. Many of the countries that ran current account deficits in the 1990s (deficits accompanied by high inflation and weak domestic financial positions) moved into trade surpluses during this time and built up sizable foreign exchange reserves. Countries such as Brazil, which allowed its currency to float, have seen their local currencies appreciate dramatically against the US dollar.

One of the trends of the last two decades is the enhanced growth of developing countries. The reforms in developing countries include: improved fiscal discipline and responsiveness, financial-market liberalisation, deregulation and privatisation, more flexible exchange-rate adjustment and external borrowing initiatives, closer integration with the global economy, increased receptivity to external practices, technology and ways of thinking, and higher levels of communication and disclosure.

While ten years ago the volatility of EMD was in line with or even higher than that of equities, it has come down materially over the last decade. This is an example of a structural economic shift that changes the volatility and nature of an asset class.

The reasons for investing in EMD

EMD is a risk asset and should deliver long-term growth and diversification in portfolio context. Investors should not expect EMD to deliver the protective and safe-haven qualities of developed bonds. At times of stress investors are likely to rush out of EMD and into the safety of developed government bonds.

The main reasons for investing in EMD include:

- *Growth*. EMD has historically generated returns comparable to equities. The total returns of EMD include a large income component because of the relatively high yields that developing countries need to pay on their debt to attract investors and compensate them for risks.

- *Income*. EMD can be a source for relatively high income in portfolios. When bond yields of developed countries are low, generating high income is challenging and investors need to explore investments such as EMD, high-yield bonds and real estate to generate income.

- *Diversification*. EMD tends to have low correlation with other assets. The main drivers affecting the performance of EMD are related to the economic situation of the issuing developing countries and their expected capacity to repay their debt obligations. These factors can be independent from factors that affect other asset classes, in particular those which are offered by developed countries or corporations operating in developed countries. While EMD has a positive correlation with equities, this correlation is far from perfect. EMD still provides diversification benefits in multi-asset portfolios that are dominated by equities.

- *Increased confidence*. With the development and progress of emerging economies over the last two decades, the volatility of EMD seems to have decreased and investors have higher confidence in the ability of developing countries to stand behind their contractual debt obligations.

- *Opportunities for active management*. EMD is a heterogeneous asset class, many issues are not heavily researched and many of the markets are not efficient. Markets that are not heavily researched, with thin trading volumes and underdeveloped derivative markets, may offer opportunities for arbitrage and generating excess returns. These features open the door for active managers to add value.

Figure 2.50 compares the yields on EMD and 10-year US Treasuries. It can be seen that EMD offers attractive yields relative to Treasuries as a compensation for their higher risk.

Figure 2.50: Yield of EMD and 10-year US Treasuries, January 1998 to December 2013

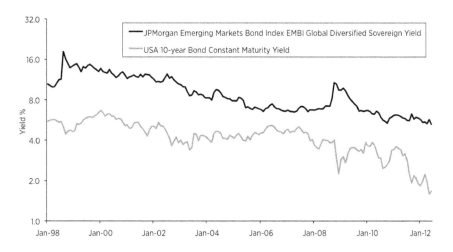

Source: Global Financial Data, JPMorgan Emerging Markets Bond Index EMBI Global Diversified Sovereign Yield, USA 10-year Bond Constant Maturity Yield.

Risks

EMD is a risk asset and, as always, high potential rewards come with high risks. The main risks of EMD investing include:

- *Downside risk.* Some of the most infamous sovereign defaults in the 20th century are of developing countries. Sovereign defaults in such magnitudes can rattle the entire global financial system. The 1997 Asian debt crisis hit EMD, with Thailand and South Korea affected particularly badly. EMD fell 29% in August 1998 during the Russian default crisis. Emerging markets have come a long way since then in terms of development, and developed countries have shown that their sovereign debt may be even riskier than that of emerging markets. Nevertheless, EMD still exhibits times of material drawdowns, such as October 2008 when EMD fell 14% in a single month during the 2008 crisis (negative sentiment can create supply and evaporate demand, causing prices to fall).

- *Currency risk.* EMD is exposed to currency risk when issues are denominated in local currency. The risk of local currency EMD can be dominated by currency risk. Issues in hard currency, such as the US dollar, still have currency risk for sterling-based investors, for example, but this risk is easily managed or hedged.

- *High volatility.* Due to wide swings in investors' risk-avoidance and risk-seeking related to stress in financial markets and in particular in emerging economies, EMD can exhibit high volatility (standard deviations of returns) that can average over twice that of developed debt and even higher than that of equities. High volatility is not a concerning risk per se for investors with a long investment horizon and a risk appetite, but it does mean extreme returns, both on the positive and negative side.

- *Liquidity risk.* At times of stress the EMD market can suffer from poor liquidity.

- *Thin volumes.* EMD of some issuers may be lightly traded and their price can be materially affected by trading activity of institutional investors, hedge funds and other large market participants. These price movements may be unconnected to economic fundamentals and difficult to predict. Securities traded in thin volume are exposed to the impact of trading by large investors or speculators.

- *Regulatory and political risk.* Emerging markets can change regulations (e.g. imposing tax on foreign investors). Changes in political policies and monetary policies by central banks can affect inflation, interest and currency exchange rates, with a material impact on EMD.

Investors tend to use collective investment schemes (or pooled funds) to invest in EMD, as many individual securities become more illiquid in secondary markets and bid-offer spreads are too wide to actively trade them. Collectives can offer the necessary diversification to reduce some of the risks of investing in EMD, as well as professional active management that is recommended for this asset class both because of alpha opportunities and the need to carefully manage risks.

Nevertheless, passive index trackers are also available (the TER for EMD ETF would be higher than an ETF tracking local bonds – for example, 45 basis points compared with 20 basis points). A do-it-yourself approach is not common for EMD since the asset requires thorough research, resources and knowledge of investing in sometimes complicated developing markets.

EMD investments can be customised and diversified across local and hard currencies, sovereign and corporate and inflation-linkers. Diversification within the asset class reduces some of the risks.

Expected return

Similar to other fixed income instruments, the long-term sustainable expected return of EMD is yield adjusted to expected loss due to defaults. The expected loss due to default is an important component and can be obtained from credit rating agencies such as Moody's and Standard & Poor's.

EMD return and risk characteristics

The dominant market indices for US dollar denominated EMD are the JPMorgan Emerging Market Bond Index Plus (EMBI+), JPMorgan EMBI Global index and JPMorgan EMBI Global Diversified index.

Figure 2.51 shows the cumulative performance of EMD since January 1994, as well as that of US equities. EMD has outperformed equities with a lower risk level. However, EMD does suffer from material drawdowns, as expected from a risk asset.

Figure 2.51: Cumulative performance of emerging market debt and US equities, January 1994 to December 2013

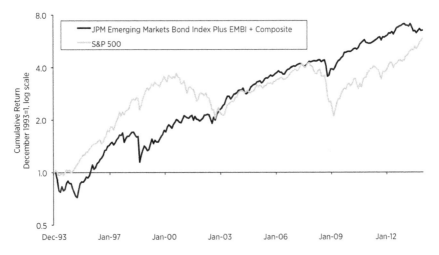

Source: Bloomberg, JPM Emerging Markets Bond Index Plus, S&P 500 Index.

Figure 2.52 shows the rolling 36-month correlation between EMD and US Treasuries and between EMD and US equities. EMD should provide diversification benefits when mixed with both asset classes, in particular with government bonds.

Figure 2.52: Rolling 36-month correlation between EMD and US Treasuries and equities, January 1997 to December 2013

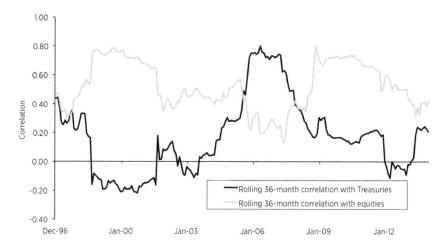

Source: Bloomberg, JPM Emerging Markets Bond Index Plus, Citigroup United States WGBI TR Index, S&P 500 Index.

Figure 2.53 shows the rolling 36-month volatility of the three asset classes. Clearly, EMD is a risk asset. Note the lower level of volatility of EMD since the beginning of the 2000s (except for the jump in volatility during the 2008 crisis).

The average 36-month rolling volatility of EMD until the end of 2002 was 18% and since 2003 the average is 9.6%. This illustrates a structural change in the characteristics of an asset. Looking solely at the numbers, however, is insufficient to spot a structural change. Investors need to understand the reasons behind it to confirm that indeed it is a structural change and not just a temporary alternation in a metric (e.g. level of return, volatility, correlation). In this case the development of emerging economies is the story behind the numbers.

Figure 2.54 plots the monthly returns of EMD against those of US equities, showing the high correlation between the two. Figure 2.55 shows the average return of EMD ranked by average decile returns of US equities. It can be seen that when equities fall EMD is expected to fall as well. EMD does add diversification benefits within portfolio context. However, as a risk asset, EMD should not be expected to provide a safety net in the form of positive returns when equities fall.

Figure 2.53: Rolling 36-month volatility of EMD and US Treasuries and equities, January 1997 to December 2013

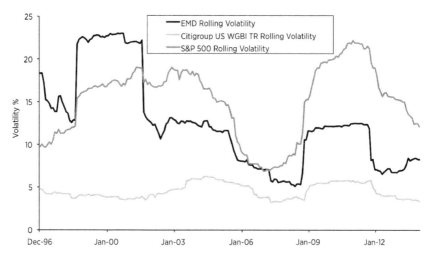

Source: Bloomberg, JPM Emerging Markets Bond Index Plus, Citigroup United States WGBI TR, S&P 500 Index.

Figure 2.54: Scatter plot of monthly returns of emerging market debt and US equities, January 1994 to December 2013

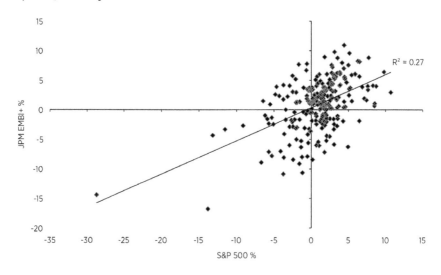

Source: Bloomberg, JPM Emerging Markets Bond Index Plus, S&P 500 Index.

Figure 2.55: Average performance of emerging market debt and US equities ranked by performance of US equities, January 1994 to December 2013

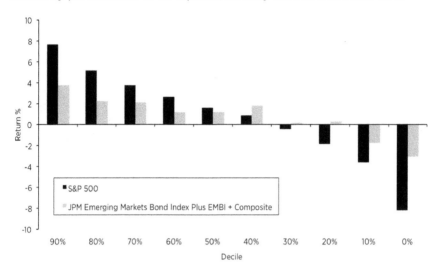

Source: Bloomberg, JPM Emerging Markets Bond Index Plus, S&P 500 Index.

Table 2.19 compares the risk and return analytics of the major asset classes since January 1999 (all asset classes are analysed over the same period). Table 2.20 shows the correlation matrix of the asset classes.

Over the measurement period, EMD delivered the highest returns, surpassing those of equities. While the long-term expected return of equities is normally higher than that of EMD, the realised returns depend on the specific time period. EMD has delivered its returns with lower risk relative to that of equities, making it the most efficient asset in Table 2.19, as indicated by its Sharpe ratio.

EMD does have a material downside risk, as indicated by its max drawdown and a combination of negative skewness and positive excess kurtosis.

As can be seen in the correlation matrix, EMD should provide diversification benefits, in particular when mixed with safe-haven assets, such as government bonds and global developed bonds. Interestingly, EMD has a lower correlation with most other fixed income assets than with equities, demonstrating that it is indeed a risk asset.

Table 2.19: Major fixed income asset classes and equity return and risk characteristics, January 1999 to December 2013. Sharpe ratio calculated using $ cash returns

	US Treasuries	US credit	High-yield	EMD	Global aggregate	US equities
Start month	Jan-1999	Jan-1999	Jan-1999	Jan-1999	Jan-1999	Jan-1999
Performance (% pa)	4.9	5.9	7.7	10.9	5.1	4.7
Volatility (%)	4.6	5.6	10.6	10.4	5.7	15.5
Skewness	-0.13	-1.10	-1.18	-0.75	0.01	-0.55
Kurtosis	1.44	5.62	7.73	2.99	0.38	0.83
Sharpe ratio	0.59	0.67	0.52	0.84	0.51	0.16
Max drawdown (%)	-5.0	-16.1	-34.2	-19.7	-9.8	-50.9

Source: Bloomberg, Global Financial Data, Citigroup United States WBGI TR Index, BofA Merrill Lynch US Corporate Bond Master TR Index, BofA Merrill Lynch Global High Yield TR Index, JPM Emerging Markets Bond Index Plus EMBI+ Composite, BofA Merrill Lynch Global Broad Market Index, S&P 500 Index.

Table 2.20: Correlation matrix, January 1999 to December 2013

Correlation matrix	US Treasuries	US credit	High-yield	EMD	Global aggregate	US equities
US Treasuries	1.00	0.58	-0.18	0.21	0.62	-0.31
US credit	0.58	1.00	0.57	0.61	0.69	0.21
High-yield	-0.18	0.57	1.00	0.62	0.34	0.66
EMD	0.21	0.61	0.62	1.00	0.45	0.50
Global aggregate	0.62	0.69	0.34	0.45	1.00	0.14
US equities	-0.31	0.21	0.66	0.50	0.14	1.00

Source: Bloomberg, Global Financial Data, Citigroup United States WBGI TR Index, BofA Merrill Lynch US Corporate Bond Master TR Index, BofA Merrill Lynch Global High Yield TR Index, JPM Emerging Markets Bond Index Plus EMBI+ Composite, BofA Merrill Lynch Global Broad Market Index, S&P 500 Index.

Conclusions

- Lending to the governments of developing countries is lending to the dominant political forces of the future.

- EMD is another way to access risk in portfolios.

- The fixed income side of portfolios may be diverse and include different risk assets, competing with equities for the role as the portfolio's growth engine.

- Fixed income is not boring, as some investors may think, and it can be spiced up using investments such as high-yield bonds and EMD.

Summary

- Emerging market debt (EMD) includes bonds issued by governments of emerging market countries and corporations operating in those countries. Sovereign EMD makes up the majority of the asset class.

- EMD issued in foreign currencies, such as the dollar and euro, is called hard currency. EMD issued in local currencies is called soft currency.

- EMD tends to have a lower credit rating than sovereign debt of developed countries because of the increased economic and political risks. However, developing countries have progressed considerably with economic and political reforms over the last few decades and their debt is not as risky as it used to be.

- EMD is a risk asset. The main reasons for investing in EMD include: growth; income; diversification; increased confidence in emerging economies; and opportunities for active management.

- EMD offers high potential reward with high risk. The main risks of EMD investing include: downside risk; currency risk; high volatility; liquidity risk; thin volumes; and regulatory and political risk.

Convertible bonds

Convertible bonds (convertibles or *converts*) are fixed income securities with an embedded option, giving investors the right to convert the bonds to common stock of the issuing company or cash at the option's strike price. Convertible bonds are sometimes classified as equities and sometimes as bonds. However, they are truly a hybrid security with features of both bonds and equities.

The interest rate on a convertible bond is typically lower than that of an equivalent standard bond because of the value of the embedded option that investors hold. The option allows investors to participate in the upside of the issuing company's stock, while benefiting from the limited downside of the bond.

Companies issue convertible bonds because they require lower interest payments relative to standard bonds, and when and if the bonds are converted to equity, the company's debt level (leverage or gearing) is reduced. However, if and when the convertible bonds are converted to equity, existing shareholders' holdings are diluted.

The largest convertible bond markets, in terms of outstanding debt levels, are those of the United States and Japan. In smaller convertible bond markets the securities may be illiquid and infrequently priced.

When the convert is issued, and its embedded option is out of the money, it behaves like a corporate bond with a lower yield than an equivalent corporate bond. If the stock of the issuing company performs poorly, the convert continues to behave like a corporate bond but with a lower interest rate. If the stock performs strongly, the value of the embedded option kicks in and the convert behaves more like equity. Generally, converts perform more like equities when equity markets rise and more like bonds when equity markets fall.

The *conversion ratio* or conversion premium determines how many stocks the convert can be converted into. It is expressed as a ratio or a conversion price. As the price of the underlying stock approaches the conversion price, the embedded option gets closer to the money and its value increases.

The convert's price behaves like that of a call option and the value of the embedded option benefits from factors that benefit a call option. Therefore, higher volatility in the underlying stock price increases the convert's value. Convertible bonds behave like corporate bonds when the underlying stock price is low (i.e. at maturity investors should get back the principal unless the issuing company defaults), and like a call option when the underlying stock price is high. They theoretically give investors unlimited upside with capped downside.

Normally, the issuing company has the right to call the convert or to force a conversion. Forced conversion usually occurs when the price is higher than the amount it would be if the convert were redeemed. This feature caps the convert's upside potential, and as such the sky is not the limit with converts as it is with equities.

The reasons for investing in convertible bonds

Convertible bonds play a role in portfolios as they provide the better of two worlds: upside participation in equities with the downside protection of corporate bonds. They can offer a higher potential return than bonds because of the participation in the equity market's upside, albeit with a lower interest rate than bonds. They can offer a higher running yield[66] compared to equities since their interest rate is typically higher than the dividend yield of equities.

---

[66] Running yield is the annual income from an investment divided by its current price. Running yield uses dividend payments from stocks and coupon payments from bonds to calculate the income and divides it by the market price of the security.

Converts can be used as a substitute for equities when uncertainty is high or when investors have constraints on investing directly in equities. High stock market volatility benefits converts since the value of their embedded option increases. The level of participation in the equity market (i.e. what portion of the equity market's return is captured by the convertible bonds) depends on the convert's *delta*.[67]

Convertibles have an imperfect correlation with other asset classes and therefore offer diversification benefits. Active managers can add alpha in the convertible bond market, either within long-only funds or hedge funds (convertible arbitrage). Alpha, which depends on manager skill and manager selection skill at the multi-asset portfolio level, is an uncorrelated source of return.

To model converts for SAA purposes their delta can be used to model them as a basket of equities and corporate bonds (e.g. if the delta is 0.60, the converts can be modelled as 60% equities and 40% corporate bonds).

Risks

As they provide the benefits of equities and bonds, converts also have the risks of both equities and bonds. Interest rate and inflation risks, for example, adversely affect the bond's value. Equity market risk, for example, adversely affects the embedded option's value. The forced conversion feature, the lower interest rate compared to equivalent standard bonds and the price move that the underlying stock must make before hitting the conversion price, are serious disadvantages of converts.

Rising interest rates and falling stock prices are the worst combination for convertible bonds since the price of the bond falls and the embedded option may get out of the money or further out of the money, meaning that the investor gets a lower interest rate than they would with the equivalent standard bond without any upside. By no means does a convertible bond offer a riskless potential reward (as always, there are no free lunches).

The equity-like upside potential means that converts offer a lower interest rate than that of normal equivalent bonds. Investors in convertible bonds forgo some of the interest that they could have otherwise received by investing in standard bonds. The longer the investor needs to wait until the convert is converted to common stock, the higher the interest forgone.

According to Jonathan Ingersoll,[68] a corporation should call its convertible securities as soon as their conversion value (i.e. the value of the common stock that would be received in the conversion exchange) rises to the effective call price. This strategy, if followed by corporations issuing convertible bonds, severely

---

[67] The delta is derived from the option pricing model of Black-Scholes and adjusted for continuous dividend payments in the way suggested by Merton. Delta values closer to 1 indicate a high sensitivity of the convertible for the underlying stock value, implying a high probability of conversion.

[68] Ingersoll, Jonathan, 'An Examination of Corporate Call Policies on Corporate Securities', *Journal of Finance* (1977).

limits the upside potential of converts. Under these circumstances, convertible bonds offer a higher return than non-convertibles only if the conversion value reaches the call price quickly.[69]

Convertible bond arbitrage

Convertible bond arbitrage is a market-neutral hedge fund strategy that aims to exploit mispricing between the bond and the underlying equity of convertible bonds. Convertible arbitrage started in the second half of the 19th century when the first convertible securities were issued.[70]

The arbitrage is based on taking a long position in the convertible bond and a short position in the underlying stock. The number of shares to short is a function of the conversion ratio (number of stocks into which the convertible bond converts), the sensitivity of the value of the embedded option to changes in the price of underlying equity (i.e. the option's delta), and the sensitivity of the delta to the changes in the price of underlying equity (i.e. the option's gamma).

If at the time of entering the arbitrage position the convertible bonds are underpriced, a potential for arbitrage profit exists. The strategy's premise is that sometimes the convertible is priced inefficiently relative to the underlying stock because of illiquidity, market psychology and the embedded option being a source of cheap volatility.

The *delta-neutral hedge ratio* (i.e. number of stocks to short) of the convertible arbitrage setup is time varying, since it depends on the stock price and delta. When the stock price approaches the conversion price, the delta of a convertible bond increases and the bond becomes more equity-like (i.e. the bond's price becomes more sensitive to the changes in the underlying equity's value). This means that more stocks need to be shorted in order to maintain the delta-neutral hedge ratio, which is defined as a product of the conversion ratio and delta. The opposite holds if the stock price goes down. The objective is for the combination of the long convert and short stocks to be insensitive to small price movements of the stock. The dynamic delta hedging process adds another source of potential return to the strategy.

Convertible arbitrage was one of the most successful hedge fund strategies of the late 1990s and the beginning of the 2000s. However, during the 2008 crisis convertible bond hedge funds delivered poor returns and were one of the worst performing hedge fund strategies. Generally, the large number of market participants pursuing the strategy has created intense competition and reduced its effectiveness.

---

[69] Bierman Jr., Harold, 'Convertible Bonds as Investments', *Financial Analysts Journal* 36 (1980).

[70] Calamos, Nick, *Convertible Arbitrage: Insights and Techniques for Successful Hedging* (John Wiley & Sons, 2003).

In theory, when a stock declines the associated convertible bond should decline less because of the downside protection of the bond. In the 2008 crisis, however, the confluence of factors – general risk aversion, causing a sell-off of convertibles; over-leveraged portfolios; illiquidity; large redemptions from investors, forcing hedge funds to sell illiquid positions; and deleveraging by banks and institutions, hitting the convertible bond prices – resulted in substantial losses on the convertible arbitrage strategy. The strategy recovered, however, following the crisis.

Convertible bond return and risk characteristics

Table 2.21 shows the performance and risk characteristics of convertible bonds, US credit, Treasuries and US equities. Table 2.22 is a correlation matrix of the different indices. While during the particular measuring period convertible bonds have outperformed other assets, such as equities, credit and government bonds, other metrics, such as volatility, max drawdown and the Sharpe ratio show that converts lie somewhere between credit and equities. This is as expected from this hybrid asset class.

The correlation of converts is positive with both equities and credit, but not perfect. Converts should behave differently to other assets within a multi-asset portfolio.

Table 2.21: Convertible bond return and risk characteristics, January 1999 to December 2013. Sharpe ratio calculated using $ cash returns

	Convertible bonds	US credit	US Treasuries	US equities
Start month	Jan-1999	Jan-1999	Jan-1999	Jan-1999
Performance (% pa)	7.6	5.9	4.9	4.7
Volatility (%)	12.8	5.6	4.6	15.5
Skewness	-0.77	-1.10	-0.13	-0.55
Kurtosis	4.22	5.62	1.44	0.83
Sharpe ratio	0.43	0.67	0.59	0.16
Max drawdown (%)	-35.4	-16.1	-5.0	-50.9

Source: Bloomberg, BofA Merrill Lynch US Convertible Bonds TR, BofA Merrill Lynch US Corporate Maser TR Index, Citigroup United States WBGI TR Index, S&P 500 Index.

Table 2.22: Correlation matrix, January 1999 to December 2013

Correlation matrix	Convertible bonds	US credit	US Treasuries	US equities
Convertible bonds	1.00	0.33	-0.24	0.76
US credit	0.33	1.00	0.58	0.21
US Treasuries	-0.24	0.58	1.00	-0.31
US equities	0.76	0.21	-0.31	1.00

Source: Bloomberg, BofA Merrill Lynch US Convertible Bonds TR, BofA Merrill Lynch US Corporate Maser TR Index, Citigroup United States WBGI TR Index, S&P 500 Index.

Figure 2.56 shows the cumulative performance of convertible bonds, US corporate bonds and US equities. The performance of converts seems to follow the long-term trend of credit with short-term influences from the equity market. In other words, converts behave like credit, but capture some of the upside and downside of equity markets.

Figure 2.56: Cumulative performance of convertible bonds, US corporate bonds and US equities, January 1999 to December 2013

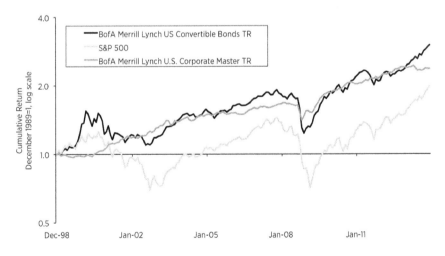

Source: Bloomberg, BofA Merrill Lynch US Convertible Bonds TR, S&P 500 Index, BofA Merrill Lynch US Corporate Maser TR Index.

Figure 2.57 shows the rolling 36-month correlation between convertibles and credit and between convertibles and equities. The correlation with equities is high, indicating the converts capture the movements in equity markets, but not necessarily the magnitude. Correlation is a measure of direction, not magnitude.

To capture both the correlation and magnitude a variability metric should be used, such as beta.

Figure 2.57: Rolling 36-month correlation between convertible bonds and US corporate bonds and US equities, December 2001 to December 2013

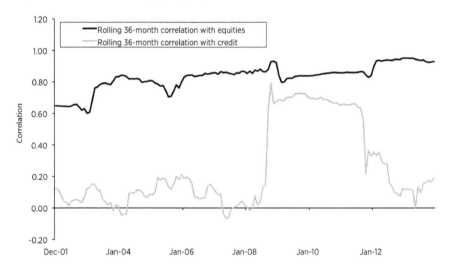

Source: Bloomberg, BofA Merrill Lynch US Convertible Bonds TR, S&P 500 Index, BofA Merrill Lynch US Corporate Maser TR Index.

Figure 2.58: Rolling 36-month volatility of convertible bonds, US corporate bonds and US equities, December 2001 to December 2013

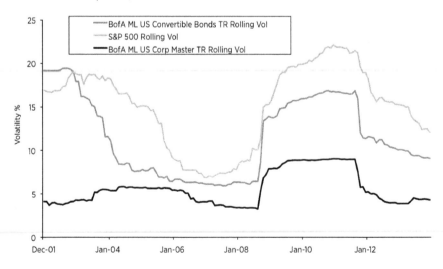

Source: Bloomberg, BofA Merrill Lynch US Convertible Bonds TR, S&P 500 Index, BofA Merrill Lynch US Corporate Maser TR Index.

Figure 2.58 shows the rolling 36-month volatility of the three asset classes. As expected, the risk of converts lies between that of credit and equities. When the volatility of equity markets spikes during market crashes, the volatility of converts jumps significantly (e.g. 2000 and 2008).

Figure 2.59 shows the average return of convertible bonds ranked by average decile returns of US equities. It can be seen that when equities fall convertibles are expected to fall as well, but they do exhibit lower drawdowns because of the bond protection. When equities rally, converts participate. When equities rally strongly, converts are likely to lag. For example, when equity markets fell in 2008, converts suffered a drawdown, but not as severe as that of equities. When equities, as well as credit, rebounded after the crisis, converts recovered strongly. More recently, in 2013, converts enjoyed a strong tailwind by participating in the rally of equities, surpassing the performance of credit.

Figure 2.59: Average performance of convertible bonds and US equities ranked by performance of US equities, January 1999 to December 2013

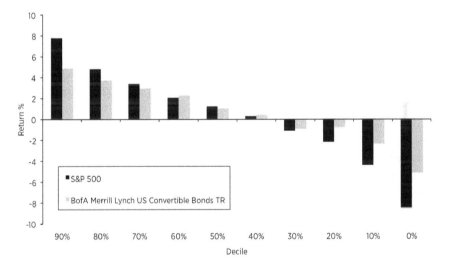

Source: Bloomberg, BofA Merrill Lynch US Convertible Bonds TR, S&P 500 Index.

Access

Accessing converts is possible through individual securities and collective investment schemes (funds). Trackers of convert indices are available, but with a much narrower choice compared to standard fixed income markets. The listed derivative market for converts is underdeveloped, so accessing the asset synthetically via listed derivatives is impossible.

CoCos

Contingent convertible bonds, also known as contingent convertibles or CoCos, are securities similar to traditional convertible bonds. They were issued by Lloyds Banking Group in November 2009. The difference between CoCos and traditional convertible bonds is that the convertibility of a CoCo to equity is *contingent* on a stipulated event, which can be specified depending on the issuer's particular need.

For example, a bank issuing a CoCo can make the convertibility contingent on the level of Tier 1 capital[71] falling below a given threshold. If Tier 1 capital falls below the threshold the CoCos will automatically convert to common stock and push Tier 1 capital up. When the stipulated event occurs, the conversion of the CoCos provides a boost to capital levels. Regulators hope that this form of capital could help support banks' finances in times of stress.

CoCos have an accounting advantage, as unlike other kinds of convertible bonds they do not have to be included in a company's diluted earnings per share until the bonds are eligible for conversion. CoCos usually allow the issuer to either hold on to the capital past the first repayment date or to skip paying coupons. This feature is a contractual flexibility for the issuer compared to regular bonds, for which skipping a coupon payment is considered a credit event. This is an example of the innovation and creativity that the fixed income market offers to issuers.

Regulators and bankers are keen to avoid a repeat of the 2008 financial crisis, during which risks of existing types of hybrid finance were revealed. A fundamental problem within banking finance is the risk of a *bank run*: when a bank needs to convert hybrid debt into equity, it sends a clear signal to investors that the bank is in trouble. These investors are then tempted to withdraw their investments, making the initial problem much worse. CoCos have been designed as an attempt to address this problem, but many issues are yet to be resolved, not least how to define the trigger that causes the bonds to convert automatically.

Conclusions

Sitting between equities and corporate bonds, convertible bonds may make sense in portfolios since they add diversification opportunities, they expand the investment opportunity set to an additional asset class, offer returns opportunities when they are underpriced and play a role when investors are uncertain whether equities or bonds are going to fare better. Investors can also add exposure to options and volatility via converts without the need to directly buy derivatives.

---

[71] Tier 1 capital is the core measure of a bank's financial strength from a regulator's point of view. It is composed of core capital, which consists primarily of common stock and disclosed reserves (retained earnings), but may also include non-redeemable, non-cumulative preferred stock.

Summary

- Convertible bonds are corporate bonds with an embedded option giving investors the right to convert the bonds into the issuing company's common stock or cash.

- Convertible bonds are a hybrid security, combining features of equity and corporate bonds.

- The interest rate on converts is lower than that on the equivalent corporate bond because of the value of the option that the investor holds.

- Convertible bonds behave like corporate bonds when the underlying stock price is low and like a call option when the underlying stock price is high. They theoretically give investors unlimited upside with capped downside. However, the issuing company typically can force conversion, capping the upside.

- The role of converts in portfolios is to provide upside equity potential with downside bond protection. At times of uncertainty, they can provide equity exposure with limited downside risk. Converts also provide diversification benefits and opportunities for active management to add alpha.

- As converts provide features of equities and bonds, they have the risks of equities (e.g. equity market risk) and bonds (e.g. interest rate risk and inflation risk).

- The worst combination for converts is rising interest rates and falling equity markets.

- Convertible bond arbitrage is a hedge fund strategy that aims to exploit mispricing between the convertible bond and the underlying stock.

- Converts can be accessed via individual securities and collective investment schemes (funds). Listed derivatives on indices of convertible bonds are not available.

- CoCos (contingent convertible bonds) are bonds that are converted to common stock when a stipulated event occurs, such as a bank's Tier 1 capital falling below a certain threshold.

CHAPTER 3: PREFERRED STOCKS

Preferred stocks or preferreds are technically an equity security and as such are a class of ownership in a corporation. Preferreds are generally considered a hybrid instrument as they have characteristics of both equity and debt.

Preferred stocks and bonds

Similarities

Preferreds share a few similarities with bonds. Preferreds are issued with a fixed par value and pay dividends based on a percentage of that par at a fixed rate. Just like bonds, which also make fixed payments, the market value of preferred shares is sensitive to changes in interest rates. If interest rates rise, the value of the preferred shares would need to fall to offer investors a better, competitive rate. If rates fall, the opposite would hold true. However, while the relative move of preferred yields is usually less dramatic than that of bonds, their prices do reflect the general market factors that affect their issuers to a greater degree than the same issuer's bonds, because the interest payments on preferreds require the issuer to be profitable.

Preferreds technically have a perpetual life because they have no fixed maturity date. However, they may be called by the issuer after a certain date (e.g. five years after issue). The motivation for the redemption is generally the same as for bonds: a company calls securities that pay higher rates than what the market is currently offering. Also, as is the case with bonds, the redemption price may be at a premium to par to enhance the preferred's initial marketability.

Like bonds, preferreds are senior to common stocks. However, bonds have more seniority than preferreds in terms of both the distribution of corporate earnings (as dividends) and the proceeds from liquidation of assets in the case of bankruptcy. In an issuing company's *capital structure*, preferreds give investors a claim to income and assets before investors in common stock but after debt holders. When a firm is liquidated, debt holders are paid first. If debt holders are made whole and value remains, preferred stock holders are paid up to their liquidation (par) value. Any residual value remaining after debt holders and preferred stock holders are paid is divided among the common stock holders.

Like bonds, preferred stocks are rated by the major credit rating agencies, such as Standard & Poor's and Moody's. The rating for preferreds is generally one or two tiers below that of the same company's bonds because preferred dividends do not carry the same guarantees as interest payments from bonds and they are junior to all creditors.

Differences

Preferreds are different from bonds due to several characteristics. Preferred stock is equity; bonds are debt. Preferreds pay fixed dividends, normally for the stock's life, but they must be declared by the company's board of directors and at the board's discretion. Similar to dividend-paying equity, preferred stocks' dividend payments are not a company's contractual obligation (as debt interest payments are).

Failure to pay preferred stock dividends does not constitute a default. As such, the same array of guarantees that are afforded to bondholders are not offered to investors in preferreds. This is because bonds are issued with the protection of an indenture. With preferreds, if a company has a cash problem the board of directors can decide to withhold preferred dividends; the indenture prevents companies from taking the same action on bonds.

Another difference between preferreds and bonds is that preferred dividends are paid from the company's after-tax profits, while bond interest is paid before taxes. This factor makes it more expensive for the issuing company to issue and pay dividends on preferred stocks.

A further difference to consider is that bond holders have a de-levered investment in the value of a firm, as they do not get rewarded when firm value increases, but are still guaranteed payment when the stock price declines. Declining firm value impinges on bond holders only after the firm value has substantially decreased to the extent that the stockholders' value has been driven to zero. Common and preferred stocks thus provide a buffer for bond holders in times of financial distress for the firm. Therefore preferred stocks do not have the same level of protection as bonds.

Information about a company's preferred shares is easier to access than information about the company's bonds, making preferreds, in a general sense, easier to trade (and they are perhaps more liquid). The low par values of the preferred shares also make investing easier, because bonds, with par values around $1,000, often have minimum purchase amounts.

Computing current yields on preferreds is similar to performing the same calculation on bonds; the annual dividend is divided by the price. For example, if a preferred stock is paying an annualised dividend of $1 and is currently trading in the market at $20, the current yield is $1.0/$20 = 5%. In the market, however, yields on preferreds are typically higher than those of bonds from the same issuer, reflecting the higher risk the preferreds present for investors.

Preferred stocks and common stocks

Except for the fact that preferred stocks and common stocks both fall under the equity of a company, these are two different securities. The most significant difference between preferred and common stocks is the potential for appreciation in value. This is where preferreds lose their attractiveness for many investors.

If, for example, a pharmaceutical research company discovers an effective cure for the flu, its common stock may soar, while the preferreds in the same company may only increase modestly. When the value of a firm is increasing, common stocks provide a substantial payoff to stock holders in the form of capital appreciation and at times dividend payments. Common stock holders thus have a leveraged investment in the value of the firm. Preferred stocks do not share in the upside potential of common stocks. The lower volatility of preferred stocks may look attractive, but preferreds will not share in a company's success to the same degree as common stock.

As with convertible bonds, preferreds can often be converted into the issuing company's common stock. This feature gives investors flexibility, allowing them to lock in the fixed return from the preferred dividends and, potentially, to participate in the capital appreciation of the common stock.

Many characteristics differentiate preferred and common stocks. Preferreds have fixed dividends and, although they are never guaranteed, the issuer has traditionally had a greater obligation to pay them. Common stock dividends, if they exist at all, are paid after the company's obligations to all preferred stockholders have been satisfied.

Historically, most preferred stocks were *cumulative*, meaning that all previously omitted dividend payments must be paid before common stock dividends can be paid. More recently, non-cumulative preferred stocks have become more prevalent. Dividends on non-cumulative preferred stocks can be omitted for years and only the current preferred stock dividend has to be paid before dividends can be paid to common stock holders. This development may have begun a trend of reducing the obligation to pay dividends on preferreds before those on common stocks.

Whereas common stock is often called voting equity, preferred stocks usually have no voting rights. Holders of preferreds therefore have no say in how the company is managed or on the direction that the management takes it in.

Preferred stock characteristics

Preferred stocks come in many types. The most common ones are:

- *Cumulative*. Most preferred stocks are cumulative, meaning that if the company withholds part, or all, of the expected dividends, these are considered dividends in arrears and must be paid before any other dividends.

Preferred stocks that do not carry the cumulative feature are called straight, or noncumulative, preferred.

- *Callable.* The majority of preferred shares are redeemable, giving the issuer the right to redeem the stock at a date and price specified in the prospectus.

- *Convertible.* The timing for conversion and the conversion price specific to the individual issue will be laid out in the preferred stock's prospectus.

- *Participating.* Preferred stocks have a fixed dividend rate. If the company issues participating preferreds, those stocks gain the potential to earn more than their stated rate. The exact formula for participation will be found in the prospectus. Most preferreds are non-participating.

- *Adjustable-Rate Preferred Stock (ARPS).* These relatively recent additions to the spectrum pay dividends based on several factors stipulated by the company. Dividends for ARPSs are keyed to yields on US government issues, providing the investor with limited protection against adverse interest rate markets.

A company may choose to issue preferreds for a couple of reasons. Preferred dividends may be suspended in case of corporate cash problems, offering the firm flexibility of payments. The majority of preferred stock is bought and held by institutions, which may make it easier to market at the initial public offering (IPO).

The reasons for investing in preferreds and their risks

The reasons for investing in preferreds include: potentially higher fixed-income payments than bonds or common stock; lower investment per share compared to bonds; priority over common stocks for dividend payments and liquidation proceeds; greater price stability than common stocks; and greater liquidity than corporate bonds of similar quality.

The disadvantages of preferreds include: callability; the lack of a specific maturity date, meaning that recovery of the invested principal is uncertain; limited appreciation potential; interest rate sensitivity; lack of voting rights; and risks such as industry concentration risk and credit risk. I will now look at these last two risks in more detail below.

Industry concentration risk

Prior to the 1980s, most preferred stocks were issued by regulated utility companies. In the mid-1980s, financial firms began to issue preferred stocks, but the explosive growth in preferred stock issued by financial firms did not occur until after the US Federal Reserve's 1996 ruling on Tier 1 capital. Financial institutions became the dominant issuers of preferred stocks by the late 1990s. While non-financial firms in aggregate have been issuing a steady 30 to 60 new preferred stocks a year over the past two decades, financial firms have dramatically increased the number of preferred stock offerings from nine in 1994 to over 500 in 2009.

Financial institutions issued $833 million or 44% of the $1.9 billion in preferred stock issued in 1994. By 2008, at the peak of preferred stock issuances, financial institutions issued $193 billion or 95% of the $201 billion in new preferred stock public offerings. The dramatic increase in preferred stock offerings by financial service firms was spurred by regulatory treatment of qualifying preferred stock as capital and the development of Trust Preferred Securities (TPS). TPS allowed firms to fund preferred dividend payments with interest payments, which the Inland Revenue Service (IRS) treats as a tax deductible interest expense.

The US Federal Reserve requires banks to maintain a certain level of permanent capital, or *Tier 1 capital*, to control their risk profiles and thus protect investors and the banks' depositors. This permanent capital is essentially equity capital since its holders do not have the right to demand periodic payments or repayment of any principal or face value. In 1996, the US Federal Reserve ruled that non-redeemable, non-cumulative preferred stock could be used to meet banks' capital requirements.

Today, Tier 1 capital includes common stock, retained earnings and non-cumulative, non-redeemable preferred stock. In addition to banks, other financial institutions issue significant amounts of preferred stocks. For example, in 2007 Freddie Mac and Fannie Mae raised $13 billion through two preferred stock offerings. Similar to banks, Fannie Mae and Freddie Mac have capital requirements that make preferred stocks an attractive source of capital. The Federal Housing Finance Agency (FHFA), which regulates Fannie Mae and Freddie Mac, requires them to maintain a level of 'core capital' comprised of common stock, retained earnings and perpetual, non-cumulative preferred stock.

Other non-bank financial institutions (e.g. brokerage firms) regulated by the US Securities and Exchange Commission (SEC) are required to maintain sufficient defined permanent capital. Similar to the US Federal Reserve and the FHFA, the SEC allows companies to treat some types of preferred stock as permanent capital.

Preferred stocks are an attractive source of capital for firms in part because they are generally less costly to issue than common stocks. In addition to lower issuance costs, preferred stocks allow financial institutions to reduce their capital servicing costs. By structuring preferred stock issues as TPS, a bank can pay preferred stock dividends before the money is taxed as income. This lowers the bank's taxable net income and effectively reduces the cost of using preferred stock as capital relative to using common stock as capital.

A primary risk of a portfolio of preferred stocks is therefore industry concentration risk. Since the vast majority of preferred stocks are issued by financial companies a portfolio of preferred stocks will almost always be concentrated in the financial services sector. For example, in the middle of 2009, the financial sector represented over 82% of the S&P U.S. Preferred Stock Index.

Credit risk

Industry concentration risk is not the only risk associated with preferred stocks – the credit risk of the issuing firm is also important. The payment of the dividend and the repayment of par value will depend on the issuing firm's viability. If it enters bankruptcy, the holders of preferred stocks (like the holders of debt) may not recover their investment fully. This effect is magnified for preferred stocks relative to debt holders since preferred stocks are junior to debt.

This magnification of credit risk for preferred stocks occurs essentially because of their payoff structure. If the firm is liquidated at a low value, all other debt holders are paid first and only then are the preferred holders paid. This credit risk is not rewarded with participation in the firm's upside as it is for common equity holders. Hence, when a firm's value becomes low, preferred stocks are more acutely exposed to credit risk than common stock holders. In such a situation of a low firm value, preferred stock prices can experience declines that are greater than that of common stock. During the 2008 financial crisis, financial firms encountered greater credit risk than non-financial firms; therefore the prospect of lower firm value became more likely and created larger risks for investors concentrated in preferred stocks.

Preferred stock return and risk characteristics

Figure 2.60 compares the cumulative performance of preferred stocks, US corporate bonds and US equities. Until July 2007, the S&P U.S. Preferred Stock Index was characterised by relative stability. Firm values of financial institutions were high and preferred stocks had returns that were similar to those of bonds.

Beginning in the summer of 2007, the volatility of returns of common stocks of financial firms increased significantly. After August 2007, the preferred stock index became more correlated with the S&P 500 Index and less correlated with the bond market. This increased correlation with common stocks and relatively low correlation with bonds is a direct consequence of the position preferred stocks hold in the capital structure of firms.

Figure 2.61 shows the rolling 36-month correlation of preferred stocks with US corporate bonds and US equities. The correlation with common stocks increased after the 2008 crisis and stayed above the correlation with corporate bonds. After the crisis the value of financial firms decreased, making investments in preferred stocks (that are dominated by financial firms) more dependent on the price of these stocks – due to the default risk – and less correlated with bonds.

Figure 2.60: Cumulative performance of preferred stocks, US corporate bonds and US equities, October 2003 to December 2013

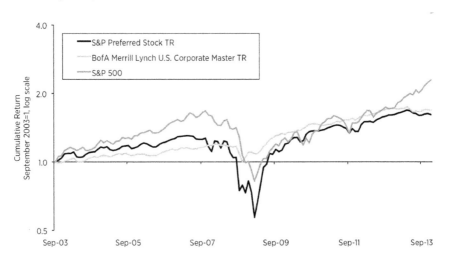

Source: Bloomberg, S&P Preferred Stocks Index, BofA Merrill Lynch U.S. Corporate Master TR Index, S&P 500 Index.

Figure 2.61: Rolling 36-month correlation between preferred stocks and US corporate bonds and US equities, October 2006 to December 2013

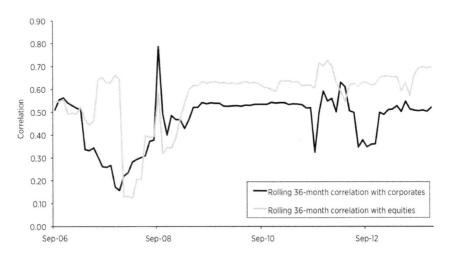

Source: Bloomberg, S&P Preferred Stocks Index, BofA Merrill Lynch U.S. Corporate Master TR Index, S&P 500 Index.

Since preferred stocks are junior to debt obligations in the capital structure hierarchy, preferred stocks are riskier than bonds. Figure 2.62 shows the rolling 36-month annualised volatility of the S&P Preferred Stock Index. Over a period of economic expansion, preferred stocks were more volatile than corporate bonds but less volatile than the broad equity market. During the period of economic contraction, the volatility of all asset classes increased. However, the volatility of preferred stocks increased far more than that of corporate bonds because preferred stocks are subordinated to bonds and have risk characteristics similar to common stocks in times of financial stress or uncertainty.

Before December 2007, when the market valued the financial firms highly enough, preferred stocks had volatility that was between that of the bond market and the broad stock market. However, when firm values declined, preferred stocks became more volatile; even more so than the broad common stock market.

This high volatility occurred primarily because preferred stocks take on the characteristics of common stocks in the presence of low firm values. The volatility was exacerbated because preferred stocks are concentrated in the financial sector.

Figure 2.62: Rolling 36-month volatility of preferred stocks, US Treasuries and US equities, October 2006 to December 2013

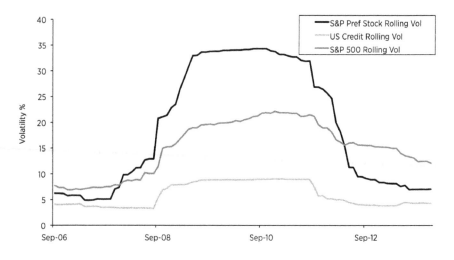

Source: Bloomberg, S&P Preferred Stocks Index, BofA Merrill Lynch U.S. Corporate Master TR Index, S&P 500 Index.

Table 2.23 shows the performance analytics of preferred stocks and Table 2.24 shows the correlations of preferred stocks, corporate bonds, government bonds and common stocks. While outperforming US Treasuries over the specific time period, the preferred index underperformed both US investment grade credit and equities. The volatility of preferreds was much higher than that of the other three asset classes, surpassing 19%. This means that the risk-adjusted return of preferreds was poor relative to that of govis, credit and equities (note the low Sharpe ratio). The negative skewness and high kurtosis of preferreds indicates that they were subject to fat-tail risk during the measurement period.

Table 2.23: Preferred stocks return and risk characteristics, October 2003 to December 2013. Sharpe ratio calculated using $ cash returns

	Preferred stocks	US corporates	US Treasuries	US equities
Start month	Oct-03	Oct-03	Oct-03	Oct-03
Performance (% pa)	4.8	5.2	4.1	8.4
Volatility (%)	19.1	5.9	4.3	14.6
Skewness	-0.91	-1.24	0.26	-0.88
Kurtosis	9.99	6.49	1.98	2.27
Sharpe ratio	0.17	0.62	0.57	0.47

Source: Bloomberg, S&P Preferred Stocks Index, BofA Merrill Lynch U.S. Corporate Master TR Index, Citigroup United States WGBI TR Index, S&P 500 Index.

Table 2.24: Correlation matrix, October 2003 to December 2013

Correlation matrix	Preferred stocks	US corporates	US Treasuries	US equities
Preferred stocks	1.00	0.50	-0.02	0.56
US corporates	0.50	1.00	0.46	0.35
US Treasuries	-0.02	0.46	1.00	-0.29
US equities	0.56	0.35	-0.29	1.00

Source: Bloomberg, S&P Preferred Stocks Index, BofA Merrill Lynch U.S. Corporate Master TR Index, Citigroup United States WGBI TR Index, S&P 500 Index.

Conclusions

Preferred stocks can behave like safe bonds for many years and then, just when the security of being a bond holder would be most valuable, become risky investments with behaviour like common stocks. The position of preferred stocks in corporate capital structures makes them riskier than bonds, but they do not share in the upside returns associated with common stocks.

In periods where firm values are low the credit risk of preferred stocks increases and these are the exact circumstances under which financial institutions are likely to issue preferred stocks in order to raise their core capital. In addition to the credit risk of the underlying issuers of preferred stocks, portfolios of preferred stocks almost invariably expose investors to industry concentration risk since the majority of preferred stock issuers are in the financial services industry.

Summary

- Preferred stock is technically an equity security with characteristics of both equity and debt and is generally considered a hybrid instrument.

- Similar to bonds, preferreds are issued with a fixed par value and pay dividends based on a percentage of that par at a fixed rate. They are commonly perpetual but callable.

- Like bonds, preferreds are senior to common stocks. However, bonds have more seniority than preferreds in terms of dividend distribution and rights to proceeds from liquidation of assets in case of bankruptcy.

- Preferreds pay dividends, which are not mandatory, although they have precedence over dividends on common stocks. Preferreds have no voting rights and no potential for price appreciation like that of common stocks.

- Preferreds are favoured by financial institutions so there is an industry concentration risk to financials in the asset class, as well as credit risk.

- The position of preferred stocks in corporate capital structures makes them riskier than bonds, but they do not share in the upside returns associated with common stocks.

CHAPTER 4: CASH

Cash is king, at least when most other asset classes lose value. Cash is considered a 'risk-free' asset as it is not supposed to lose money under any circumstances and in nominal terms cash should not have negative returns. This is not always true though. In the 2008 crisis many money market funds, which were benchmarked against LIBOR and classified as cash-equivalents, lost money since they invested in risky securities (such as asset-backed securities, ABS) to increase yield and outperform the LIBOR benchmark. The 2008 crisis drove these funds into negative territory, so they were clearly not risk-free.

In real terms, cash is not a risk-free asset since during many time periods cash returns have lagged inflation and experienced negative real returns. For example, if short-term interest rates are at a level of 0.5% and the inflation rate is at a level of 2%, then the real return on cash is -1.5%. Cash is also not a risk-free asset for investors with a liability profile with longer duration than that of cash since there is a duration mismatch between cash and the liabilities.

Cash invested in US Treasury bills (up to 3-month maturity) or UK Treasury bills is unlikely to lose money in nominal terms because countries like the United States and the United Kingdom should not default on their short-term debt obligations. Also, cash deposits held at large banks are virtually safe as these banks are too big to fail. This is as risk-free as it gets.

Cash is the ultimate source of liquidity in portfolios. It enables investors to meet expected and unexpected cash outflows and quickly invest in emerging opportunities. It provides coverage and margin to derivatives, and during times of 'normal' short-term interest rates (3% to 5%), it provides a steady source of returns.

Money market

The money market offers investors access to the marketplace in which large institutions and governments manage their short-term cash through a variety of different securities. The money market falls under the fixed income market. Money market investments (also called cash investments) include debt securities whose maturities are less than one year.

Money market securities are essentially IOUs issued by governments, financial institutions and corporations. The securities are liquid and normally have low risk (i.e. the issuing entities are unlikely to default on these short-term obligations). Most money market securities trade in high denominations, limiting access to individual investors. The money market is a dealer market, meaning that firms buy and sell securities in their own accounts at their own risk without a central trading floor or exchange. Deals are transacted over the phone or through electronic systems.

The easiest way to gain access to the money market is through collective investments schemes (CIS) or a money market bank account. The CIS and accounts pool together the investments of many investors to reach the scale to participate in the money market.

The main instruments in the money market include:

1. Treasury Bills

2. Certificates of Deposit (CDs)

3. commercial paper

4. Eurodollars

5. repurchase agreements (repos)

1. Treasury Bills

Treasury Bills (T-Bills) are the most common money market securities. T-Bills are used by governments (e.g. the US or UK governments) to borrow money from the public. T-Bills mature in less than one year. Investors purchase them for a price less than their par or face value and when they mature the government pays the holder the full par value. The interest is the difference between the purchase price and the par received at maturity (the same as a zero-coupon bond, which does not pay interest but is sold at a profit on maturity for its par value). For example, purchasing a 90-day T-Bill with a face value of $10,000 for $9,900 and holding it to maturity results in interest of $100 over 90 days.

The interest rate and price of T-Bills are affected by several factors:

- *Demand.* Demand for risk-free, short-term fixed income securities. For example, a flight to quality caused by concerns about default or liquidity risk in other financial markets may cause investors to shift to T-Bills to avoid risks.

- *Supply.* The government determines the supply of T-Bills based on its short-term funding needs. For example, the US federal budget surplus in the period 1998 to 2000 reduced the supply of some Treasury securities issues.

- *Economic conditions.* T-Bill interest rates typically rise during periods of business expansion and fall during recessions.[72]

---

[72] Rose, Peter, *Money and Capital Markets* (McGraw-Hill/Irwin, 1999).

- *Monetary policy.* While the interest rates on T-Bills and other money market instruments are determined by market forces, there is a close link between their rates and the rate set by central banks. In other words, actions by central banks affect the interest rates of T-Bills. Changes to the Federal funds rate, for example, are likely to affect the interest of other close substitutes, including short-term T-Bills.

- *Inflation and inflation expectations.* Periods of relatively high (low) rates of inflation are usually associated with relatively high (low) interest rates on T-bills.

Treasury Bills have a few advantages. They are issued in relatively low denominations (compared to other money market products), they are considered the investment with the lowest risk (the US and UK governments are not going to default on their short-term obligations) and they have tax advantages (they are exempt from state and local taxes in the US). The disadvantages of T-Bills are the relatively low return on offer (low risk, low return) and that if they are sold before maturity a capital loss may occur, depending on the prevailing price of the T-Bills.

2. Certificates of deposit (CDs)

A *certificate of deposit* (CD) is a time deposit with a bank (i.e. funds cannot be withdrawn on demand). CDs are generally issued by commercial banks and they have a specific maturity date (from three months to five years), a specified interest rate, and can be issued in any denomination, much like bonds.

CDs offer a modestly higher yield than T-Bills because of the slightly higher default risk for the issuing bank. The interest rate of the CD depends on a number of other factors such as the current interest rate environment, the amount invested, the CD's maturity and the particular issuing entity.

The advantages of CDs are their relative safety and known return. The disadvantages are their illiquidity (the funds are tied up until the maturity of the CD and redeeming before maturity involves a penalty) and lower returns than potential returns of higher risk investments (i.e. opportunity cost).

3. Commercial paper

Commercial paper is an unsecured, short-term loan issued by a corporation to finance its short-term financing needs (i.e. working capital, typically to finance accounts receivable and inventories). Commercial paper is usually issued at a discount reflecting the current market interest rates. Maturities of commercial paper are usually up to nine months. The reason corporations issue commercial paper is to avoid short-term borrowing from banks.

Normally commercial paper is a safe investment because the financial situation of the issuing corporation can easily be estimated over a few months.

Furthermore, typically only companies with high credit ratings and creditworthiness issue commercial paper. Cases of defaults on commercial paper are rare.

4. Eurodollars

Eurodollars are dollar-denominated deposits at banks outside of the United States. This market has evolved in Europe (specifically London) and hence the name. However, eurodollars can be held anywhere outside of the United States and not just in Europe. The eurodollar market is relatively light on regulations and therefore banks can operate on narrower margins than their counterparts in the United States. As a result, the eurodollar market has expanded largely as a way of circumventing regulatory costs.

The average eurodollar deposit is large (in the millions) and has a maturity of less than six months. A variation on the eurodollar time deposit is the eurodollar certificate of deposit (CD). A eurodollar CD is basically the same as a US CD, except that it is the liability of a non-US bank. As eurodollar CDs are typically less liquid they tend to offer higher yields.

5. Repurchase agreement

A *repurchase agreement* or a repo is a form of overnight borrowing. A dealer or other holder of government securities (usually T-bills) sells the securities to a lender and agrees to repurchase them at an agreed future date at an agreed price. They are usually short term, from overnight to 30 days or more. This short-term maturity and government backing means repos provide lenders with extremely low risk.

Repos are popular because they can virtually eliminate credit problems. Unfortunately, a number of significant losses over the years from fraudulent dealers suggest that lenders in this market have not always checked their collateralisation closely enough.

There are also variations on standard repos. A *reverse repo* is the complete opposite of a repo. In this case, a dealer buys government securities from an investor and then sells them back at a later date for a higher price. A *term repo* is exactly the same as a repo except the term of the loan is greater than 30 days.

The reasons for investing in cash

The main reasons for holding cash in portfolios are: a source of liquidity for expected and unexpected needs; a buffer to meet cash inflows and outflows; as collateral for derivatives; a way to reduce the portfolio's risk level (more cash less risk); and a reserve to quickly capitalise on investment opportunities, in particular after market falls. Warren Buffett has commented: "Cash combined with courage in a time of crisis is priceless."

Collective investment schemes usually have a limit on the maximum allowable cash level (e.g. 10%). This limit is meant to force portfolio managers to remain invested, while giving them some flexibility to reduce risk and manage liquidity. For example, a US long-only equity portfolio must stay invested in equities. If the manager has a negative view on the equity market the only ways to protect the downside are buying defensive stocks and holding a high level of cash.

Cash is the default holding in many cases. When an investment is sold, the proceeds normally come in cash and before buying new investments cash is held. Buying (spending cash) and selling (raising cash) investments involves transaction costs, while holding cash does not involve any material costs. Therefore, cash is a transition holding.

Risks

Even though cash is often said to be 'risk-less' there are risks associated with holding cash in portfolios:

- *Inflation risk.* Commonly the fundamental objective of long-term investing is maintaining the purchasing power of assets, but cash may fail in this objective. Cash does not always keep pace with inflation. When inflation is high, policymakers may lag in increasing short-term interest rates or maintain interest rates at low levels to stimulate the economy and in these circumstances cash can generate a negative real return.

- *Opportunity risk.* Holding cash is not investing. By not investing investors may lose out on potential returns from investing in other asset classes. If, for example, equities rally by 15% and the investor holds cash instead of investing in equities, the opportunity cost is 15% minus the interest on cash. Opportunity cost is commonly associated with regret risk.

- *Liability mismatch.* When assets are managed against liabilities whose duration is longer than that of cash, cash is not risk free. Risk-free investments should have the same duration as that of the liabilities. When there is a duration mismatch, interest changes introduce a potential deficit or surplus between assets and liabilities. For example, if the duration of cash is three months and the duration of liabilities is five years a 1% drop in interest rates means that the value of assets increases by 25 basis points, while the value of liabilities increases by 5%, meaning a 4.75% deficit (or a shortfall gap).

- *Cash drag.* When a portfolio receives a subscription in the form of a cash inflow the exposure to cash increases. If it takes time for the portfolio manager to invest the cash and markets rally, the excess allocation to cash drags performance downward, contributing to underperformance. If markets fall, on the other hand, the effect could be outperformance. Investing cash is a balancing act between transaction costs, minimum investments and exposure to cash.

Cash return and risk characteristics

Figure 2.63 shows the cumulative performance of nominal and real cash (US Treasury bills). During the 1970s, when inflation rates were high, the real return of cash was negative. Since the 2002 high-tech bubble burst, short-term interest rates have been at historical low levels and cash has struggled to keep up with inflation.

Figure 2.63: Nominal and real cumulative performance of T-Bills, January 1970 to December 2013

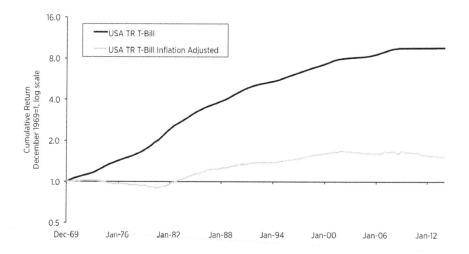

Source: Global Financial Data, USA TR T-Bill Index, US Inflation.

Table 2.25 show the performance analytics of US T-Bills, T-Bills returns adjusted for inflation (US T-Bills Real), Treasuries, US equities and inflation. Table 2.26 is the correlation matrix of these assets. When considering inflation, cash cannot be said to be risk free. While since the beginning of the 1970s the average annual return of cash was attractive (over 5%), this return should not be expected over the coming years as interest rates are so low. Imagine an asset returning 5% per annum with virtually zero volatility. These days are gone for now.

Cash is the closest that it gets to risk-free. Its volatility is below 1%, its skewness is positive and its max drawdown is nil. This changes, however, when inflation is considered, as can be seen by the drawdown of real cash return (-12.8%).

The Sharpe ratio of cash is blank since the numerator of the Sharpe ratio is the return of the asset minus the return of cash, which is nil in this case.

Table 2.25: Treasury Bills return and risk characteristics, January 1970 to December 2013. Sharpe ratio calculated using $ cash returns

	US T-Bills	US T-Bills real	US Treasuries	US equities	US inflation
Start month	Jan-1970	Jan-1970	Jan-1970	Jan-1970	Jan-1970
Performance (% pa)	5.3	1.0	7.2	10.4	4.2
Volatility (%)	0.9	1.2	4.8	15.5	1.3
Skewness	0.49	0.16	0.04	-0.45	-0.15
Kurtosis	0.44	1.94	0.73	1.87	3.50
Sharpe ratio	-	-3.60	0.70	0.33	-0.81
Max drawdown (%)	0.0	-12.8	-5.3	-50.9	-4.4

Source: Bloomberg, Global Financial Data, USA TR T-Bill Index, USA 10-year Government Bond Total Return Index, S&P 500 Index, US Inflation.

Table 2.26: Correlation matrix, January 1970 to December 2013

Correlation matrix	US T-Bills	US Treasuries	US equities	US inflation
US T-Bills	1.00	0.15	-0.01	0.46
US Treasuries	0.15	1.00	-0.01	-0.17
US equities	-0.01	-0.01	1.00	-0.09
US inflation	0.46	-0.17	-0.09	1.00

Source: Bloomberg, Global Financial Data, USA TR T-Bill Index, USA 10-year Government Bond Total Return Index, S&P 500 Index, US Inflation.

Conclusions

Most portfolios must hold some cash. Cash is the ultimate source of liquidity. It enables investors to meet expected and unexpected cash needs, cash inflows come in the form of cash and portfolios must have a positive cash balance, otherwise they are in overdraft (i.e. leveraged). Cash, however, is not investing. To make money from investing, investors need to invest cash in other assets.

Summary

- Cash is the ultimate source of liquidity and stable positive nominal returns.

- The main money market instruments include Treasury Bills, certificates of deposit, commercial paper, eurodollars and repos.

- While cash is often regarded as risk-free, it does have some risks. The main risks of cash are: inflation risk; opportunity risk; liability mismatch; and cash drag.

*   *   *

This concludes Part II. The traditional asset classes (equity, fixed income and cash) have been reviewed and their main characteristics and risks covered.

Traditional asset classes make up the bulk of most portfolios and they expose portfolios to the main systematic risks that are expected to be compensated by the market in the form of the main risk premiums: equity risk premium, maturity risk premium and credit risk premium. In addition to the risk premiums, most traditional asset classes can be a fertile ground for skilled active managers to add additional value in the form of alpha.

Part III moves away from traditional asset classes and ventures into the world of alternative investments. The main four categories of mainstream alternatives are real estate, commodities, private equity and hedge funds. These investments widen the universe of investment opportunities and add diversification benefits to the traditional asset classes.

PART III

ALTERNATIVE INVESTMENTS

INTRODUCTION

Alternative investments, alternatives or AI are best classified by negation as not traditional investments (equities, bonds and cash). There is no definitive definition of alternative investments and the assets included in this category change and evolve. For some assets it is unclear whether they are alternative investments or not, or whether they are an asset class at all.

Arguably, alternative investments include real estate (sometimes classified as a traditional investment), commodities, private equity and hedge funds (not considered an asset class). These might be referred to as *traditional* alternative investments. Art, timber, volatility, leveraged loans and insurance-linked securities are examples of novel, perhaps modern, types of alternative investments, and these will be covered in Part IV.

Alternatives have become increasingly popular since the 2000 equity market crash that followed the burst of the dot-com bubble. In the period 2000 to 2002 traditional risky assets, in particular equities, disappointed investors and their expected returns were subdued. While equity markets were falling, hedge funds delivered positive returns amid the equity carnage, attracting investors to include hedge funds in portfolios. The promise of absolute, equity-like returns with bond-like volatility sounded promising.

Famous university endowments in the United States, such as those of Harvard and Yale, have successfully used alternative investments to diversify their portfolios and boost returns. David Swensen showcased the use of alternatives in his book *Pioneering Portfolio Management*[73] about the Yale endowment. As the interest of institutional investors in alternative investments grew, assets under management (AUM) ballooned. Wealthy individuals followed the lead of institutional investors and alternatives have become more common investments.

Alternative investments were crushed, however, in the financial crisis of 2008. The toxic combination of aggressive risk taking, leverage, the credit crunch, a flight to quality and illiquidity saw the price of many alternative investments fall through the floor. For this reason we might refer to the period 2001 to 2007 as the golden age of alternatives.

Alternative investments have recovered in terms of asset under management over recent years. The current trends include exploring ways to gain a liquid, cheaper

---

[73] Swensen, David, *Pioneering Portfolio Management: An Unconventional Approach to Institutional Investment* (Free Press, 2000).

and regulated exposure to alternative investments. Hedge fund replication strategies, listed alternatives and alternative investments wrapped in regulated vehicles (e.g. UCITS[74] funds) are some examples of this trend.

Unlike traditional assets, alternative investments normally are not well represented by indices and accessing them usually requires actively managed portfolios. It is therefore harder to model alternatives for asset allocation, it is typically more expensive to invest in them, they are not as liquid as traditional asset classes and they are less frequently seen in portfolios compared to traditional assets. However, including alternative investments in portfolios improves diversification, expands the investment opportunity set and taps manager skill and a liquidity premium. Unless there are good reasons not to do so, portfolios should include alternative investments alongside traditional ones.

Characteristics of alternatives

Alternative investments share some common characteristics with each other. They normally have a low correlation with traditional asset classes, such as equities and bonds, because the return drivers or risk factors of alternatives are different. Alternatives may include both traditional equity and bond risk factors as well as *alternative betas*.

Most alternative investments are *strategies*, meaning that they are actively managed portfolios that offer a combination of alpha and betas. There is a continuum of returns along the spectrum from pure beta, on the one hand, to pure alpha, on the other. Along the spectrum there are multiple investments offering different degrees of alpha and beta exposures.

The *beta continuum* can represent the numerous ways that systematic risk premiums are packaged.[75] Different types of beta exist, ranging from the classic beta, which is known from CAPM, to other betas, which reflect systematic exposure to other defined facets of the market (e.g. commodity, real estate risk, as well as value, small cap and momentum risk factors). What may be perceived as alpha may simply be systematic exposure to some other style factor.

The main return drivers of hedge funds, for example, are market inefficiencies and arbitrage opportunities. Many alternatives, such as hedge funds and private equity, heavily depend on alpha from manager skill and manager expertise, not only on beta exposure to market risk. Hence, manager selection is critical for alternative investments.

---

[74] UCITS = undertakings for the collective investment in transferable securities.

[75] Anson, Mark, 'The Beta Continuum: From Classic Beta to Bulk Beta', *The Journal of Portfolio Management* 34 (2008).

Alternatives may behave differently to equity and bond markets, delivering *diversification* benefits and an expanded investment opportunity set to portfolios. However, since each alternative category behaves differently under different market conditions, including different alternatives enhances the diversification opportunities.

Some alternatives are relatively *illiquid*. Illiquidity is simultaneously a curse, since it is time consuming and costly to invest and disinvest, and a blessing, since it should deliver a liquidity premium over time. The illiquidity of alternatives means they are suitable only for investors with an appropriately long investment horizon.

The costs of purchasing and selling alternatives may be relatively high and a cost/benefit analysis is required before investing. Only when the investment horizon is long enough and/or the opportunity for returns surpasses the costs does the investment make sense. In addition, alternatives are less scalable than traditional assets and capacity constraints apply, in particular to newer alternatives.

It may be difficult to determine the current *valuation* of some alternatives. Most alternatives are not traded on regular exchanges and they lack ongoing, frequent market pricing. Their price is often based on appraisals and valuations. For example, the price of a house is usually based on the last price that was paid for it, prices paid for similar houses in the neighbourhood and appraisals by estate agents. This infrequent, valuation-based pricing causes the historic return series of real estate to have artificially low volatility (valuations do not drift by much from previous valuations), with the result that its true investment risk is underestimated.

Alternatives typically lack appropriate *indices* to reflect their historic returns and risk. This makes it more challenging to model them for asset allocation purposes and study their behaviour. Without reliable historic data, formulating CMAs for alternatives requires subjective assessment and assumptions. It is more difficult to establish CMAs for alternatives than it is for traditional asset classes.

Alternatives are normally more *opaque* than traditional asset classes. The publicly available information on real estate and private equity is not as easily available as the information on publicly traded equities. Also, hedge fund managers, for example, are normally reluctant to disclose their portfolio positions since they do not want to lose their competitive advantage and give away their trade secrets. Alternatives are commonly more complex than traditional investments and they have not been available for as many decades as traditional investments. These features may make investors hesitant to invest in alternatives, in particular when transparency is an important consideration.

The informational and market inefficiencies, and heterogeneous nature, of alternatives require that detailed investment analysis and research is undertaken. In some cases each alternative investment must be treated as unique and it is difficult to make any assumptions that are relevant for the entire asset class. Alternatives must be treated on a case by case basis, unlike traditional asset classes.

Directional and non-directional investments

Alternative investments are often classified as directional and non-directional. Directional investments exhibit a high correlation or beta with equity and/or bond markets. They have direct exposure to the market and they do not hedge all of it. Directionality is normally measured using the investment's beta with the relevant equity or bond market index. Long-only commodity investments, for example, are directional since they have no objective of removing the exposure to commodity market risk.

Non-directional investments exhibit a low beta with equity and/or bond markets. Non-directional investments are often called *market neutral* since their returns are independent of market returns. Absolute return funds are supposed to be non-directional since they aim to generate positive returns no matter what the market is doing. Because of the lack of exposure to beta or systematic risk, which is a source for long-term return, the performance of non-directional investments depends on their ability to add value (e.g. by security selection, market timing and/or exploiting arbitrage opportunities).

Figure 3.1 shows the betas of a range of indices with respect to the S&P 500 Index. Small caps are highly directional with a beta higher than 1.0 because of their higher volatility than large caps and high correlation with the S&P 500 Index. Direct real estate is not directional, with a beta close to zero. Managed futures have a slightly negative beta, still indicating a lack of directionality with respect to the equity market.

Non-directional alternatives should add the most diversification benefits to portfolios that are dominated by traditional equity and bond investments. They promise to deliver a return independent of market conditions. However, non-directional investments rely on manager skill and do not participate in the harvesting of beta returns (i.e. benefiting from the risk premiums on offer by taking systematic risks). Directional alternatives are more correlated with traditional assets, but they do benefit from beta returns. Each has advantages and disadvantages.

Figure 3.1: Betas of indices with respect to the S&P 500 Index, January 1994 to December 2013

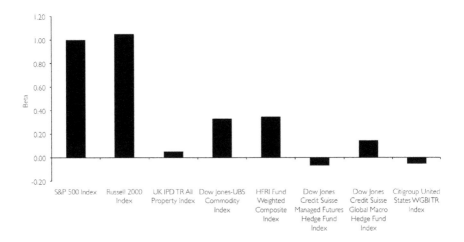

Source: Bloomberg, S&P 500 Index, Russell 2000 Index, UK IPD TR All Property Index, DJ-UBS Commodity Index, HFRI Fund Weighted Composite, Dow Jones Credit Suisse Managed Futures Hedge Fund Index, Dow Jones Credit Suisse Global Macro Hedge Fund Index, Citigroup United States WGBI TR Index.

Risk diversifiers and return enhancers

Alternative investments, as well as traditional asset classes, are often classified as either risk diversifiers or return enhancers. *Risk diversifiers* or risk reducers exhibit a low correlation with other asset classes and adding them to portfolios can reduce risk through diversification, usually at the cost of lower returns (lower risk normally comes with a lower return). However, some risk reducing strategies, such as fixed income arbitrage, may still be subject to material downside risk (e.g. the infamous fixed income arbitrage hedge fund Long-Term Capital Management) and they do not necessarily play a role of protection in portfolios.

Protection comes from assets that should perform strongly when equity and bond markets fall, such as certain government bonds and managed futures strategies. Risk reducers normally have a low or negative correlation with equity and bond markets; hence they are non-directional. Holding them on a standalone basis may have unattractive or modest returns and their benefit is within portfolio context. Risk diversifiers include certain hedge fund strategies, absolute return strategies and real estate in some cases.

Return enhancers aim to deliver attractive return opportunities. However, they may exhibit mediocre or poor returns during some time periods. These strategies are normally more directional and are highly correlated with the equity and bond markets or a source of high potential alpha. A fall in these markets may mean a negative return for return enhancer strategies. The role of such strategies in portfolios is to increase returns. Return-enhancing strategies include directional or aggressive hedge fund strategies, private equity, commodities and real estate in some cases.

Alternative betas

Traditional asset classes expose investors to traditional systematic risks or betas. The traditional betas are equity market risk, maturity (term or duration) risk and credit risk. Exposure to these risks is expected to be rewarded so investors are incentivised and compensated for assuming risk. Otherwise, no investor would take risk. The compensation comes in the form of a premium: equity risk premium, maturity risk premium and credit risk premium.

Alternative investments include varying degrees of exposures to the traditional betas. However, they also include a set of alternative betas. Alternative betas include all the systematic risks that are not the traditional three. Alternative betas include value, small cap, carry, momentum and volatility strategies, as well as mechanical merger arbitrage (i.e. going short the acquiring company and long the target company) and convertible arbitrage (i.e. going long the convertible bond and short the issuer's common stock). Other alternative betas include commodity risk and real estate risk, to which commodities and real-estate expose the portfolio.

The exposure to betas raises questions about *fees* and compensation paid to active portfolio managers. Alpha justifies high fees. Exposure to traditional betas does not justify high fees since they can be accessed passively and cheaply. The fees for alternative betas are probably somewhere in the middle.

Discretionary alpha generation warrants fees. Rule-based systematic beta risk taking warrants lower fees than those of discretionary alpha. When investing in investment products investors need to assess which kind of exposure they get and whether the fee level is appropriate.

One of the fundamental principles of multi-asset investing is to expose portfolios to different systematic risks to benefit from overall risk reduction due to diversification, utilise a wide investment opportunity set and harvest rewards from the different risk premiums on offer. Going beyond the traditional betas and including alternative betas improves the portfolio's reward-to-risk ratio. In other words, the efficient frontier moves upwards and more expected return can be generated for each level of risk.

Another fundamental principle of modern multi-asset investing is that the *exposures to betas should be dynamically managed* – and not left to a static buy-and-hold strategy – in order to manage risks and capitalise on opportunities. While buy and hold worked well during the 1990s when equity and bond markets trended upwards, the 2000s brought a new reality. Equities have traded sideways for a decade with two bear markets (2000 and 2008). Bonds have continued to rally until the yields on government bonds have reached close to all-time lows.

This new environment calls for dynamic allocations between beta sources and the inclusion of as many betas as possible to identify ways to generate returns and mitigate volatility. This is a brave new world that requires investors to be active.

Expected returns of alternative investments

Formulating the expected long-term returns of most asset classes is challenging. For traditional assets the most reliable method for formulating expected returns is using forward-looking observable indicators, such as yields and valuation ratios. These indicators contribute a large component of long-term returns and/or reflect the collective market view on future expected returns or current valuations. Alternative investments rarely have such indicators.

When forward-looking indicators are missing, the alternative method for formulating expected returns is breaking the return into building blocks and applying a premium to the building blocks for which expected returns can be formulated; for example, breaking expected return into inflation, real cash return and a risk premium.

The issue is that it is difficult to estimate the forward-looking risk premium. History may give some insight into estimating the premium, as is commonly done to estimate the long-term equity risk premium. However, many alternatives lack a reliable long history of returns. In addition, risk premiums are unstable as well as time-varying.

The conclusion is that in many cases the only way to estimate the expected returns of alternatives is using building blocks for which expected returns can be estimated and applying a subjective-based premium. The premium may reflect the potential or required return from alpha (e.g. for hedge funds and private equity). When costs are material a discount to reflect them may be appropriate as well (e.g. direct property). This is not an ideal, systematic methodology, but it may be as good as it gets in some cases.

Summary

- Alternative investments are best classified as *not* traditional investments (equities, bonds and cash).

- The classic alternative investments are real estate, commodities, private equity and hedge funds.

- It is more challenging to model alternatives for asset allocation purposes and to access them. However, including alternative investments in portfolios improves diversification, expands the investment opportunity set and taps the skill and liquidity premiums.

- Some common characteristics of alternatives include: a mix of alpha and beta returns; low correlation with traditional asset classes; illiquidity; lack of market pricing; lack of appropriate indices; limited transparency; and a need for comprehensive investment analysis.

- Alternatives are often divided into directional and non-directional. Directional investments have market exposure and a relatively high beta with the relevant market (e.g. equity and bond markets). Non-directional investments have a relatively low beta with the market.

- Alternative investments can be classified as risk diversifiers and return enhancers. The role of risk diversifiers is to reduce risk through low correlation with other assets. The role of return enhancers is to enhance the return of portfolios.

- Traditional betas include equity, term (maturity) and credit. Alternative betas include value, small cap, carry, momentum, technical merger arbitrage, technical convertible arbitrage, commodity risk and real-estate risk.

- Discretionary alpha warrants fees. Exposure to traditional betas can be accessed cheaply via passive vehicles. Exposure to alternative betas falls somewhere in the middle.

- One of the fundamental principles of multi-asset investing is exposing portfolios to different systematic risks to benefit from overall risk reduction due to diversification, utilising a wide investment opportunity set and harvesting rewards from the different risk premiums on offer.

- Exposures to betas should be dynamically managed and not left to a static buy-and-hold strategy to manage risks and capitalise on opportunities.

- Formulating long-term expected returns for alternatives is difficult since many lack forward-looking indicators such as yield and valuation ratios. The alternative is breaking the return into building blocks, estimating their expected returns and applying subjective premiums (e.g. alpha) and discounts (e.g. transaction costs).

CHAPTER 5: REAL ESTATE (PROPERTY)

Property is the fourth most popular asset class in portfolios, following equities, bonds and cash. Most investors are invested in real estate. For many individual investors their residential home is one of their largest investments, if not the largest.

However, owning real estate is more than an investment. An old English maxim says "an Englishman's home is his castle," and a Hebrew proverb puts it that "he is not a full man who does not own a piece of land." Often people say that the investment advice that they got from their parents was to buy real estate.

Real estate is brick and mortar, you can touch it. One of the worst economic situations is homelessness, so owning a property, a piece of land, a piece of the earth, a shelter, or a home has a metaphysical meaning; it is one of the fundamental conditions for living well in our world.

This brings up the question of whether a residential property is a home or an investment and the answer to this is not straightforward. A home involves both financial and emotional security considerations. Whatever the answer is, buying a home is a material financial commitment and the future of many investors depends on their home's value.

Many institutional investors own or rent office buildings and their property portfolio is one of their largest financial considerations. Indeed, many portfolios are heavily biased to real estate, whether it is a conscious investment decision or due to the need to own real estate. Donald Trump describes it like this: "Real estate is at the core of almost every business, and it's certainly at the core of most people's wealth. In order to build your wealth and improve your business smarts, you need to know about real estate." Trump also described his passion for real estate by saying: "It's tangible, it's solid, it's beautiful. It's artistic, from my standpoint, and I just love real estate."

For individual investors real estate usually means *residential property*, including their residential home and any properties owned for letting. Within investment portfolios real estate is usually focused on *commercial property* (e.g. office, industrial and retail buildings). Commercial property, which is also called investment or income property, refers to buildings and land intended to generate a profit from capital gains and/or income. Residential property with a large number of units may be classified as commercial property.

It is estimated[76] that in 2007 the value of US residential real estate amounted to $18 trillion and commercial real estate to $16 trillion. Other estimates[77] give US residential real estate in 2007 a value exceeding $30 trillion, a third of the global total. However, poor data due to the characteristics of the asset class (it is mostly traded in private markets, lacking publicly available data) and the lack of reliable indices make it challenging to research and model it. This means that real estate is relatively under-researched as an asset class.

Real estate may be more prone to bubbles than other assets due to the difficulty of determining fair value and the difficulty of short selling real estate assets, as well as the cost and infrequency of transactions. Due to the material absolute amount tied into real estate and the material relative amount tied into real estate as part of individuals' wealth, a real estate bubble may have devastating effects on the economy. A real estate bubble burst can hurt consumers and businesses across the economy.

An example of a property bubble was the one that burst in Japan in 1990. It had damaging effects on the Japanese economy and stock market, leading to Japan's *lost decade.*

The 2008 crisis was related to bursting of real estate bubbles around the world (e.g. United States, United Kingdom, Ireland and Spain). These bubbles began during the 2000s due to subprime lending and were fuelled by low interest rates and low mortgage borrowing rates. Securitisation of mortgages in different mortgage-backed securities (MBS) exacerbated the situation. When investors use their homes to amass leverage and use it in the stock market a property bubble can spill over into a stock market bubble.

The value of people's homes is part of the *wealth effect*, alongside the value of their stock portfolio and employment. The wealth effect is the degree to which people feel comfortable and secure about their wealth. This impacts the amounts people spend and consequently can drive the economy, and in turn the financial markets. The state of the housing markets, together with the labour market, are two important factors in the state of the general economy, affecting all asset classes.

Access

Historically, the two ways to access real estate were purchasing rights in direct real estate (i.e. owning buildings) and owning shares in listed real estate vehicles. Over the last two decades additional ways of access have become available; each with its own advantages and disadvantages, structures, liquidity, transparency and distinct risk/reward profile.

---

[76] Francis, Jack and Ibbotson, Roger, 'Contrasting Real Estate with Comparable Investments, 1978 to 2008', *The Journal of Portfolio Management* (2009).
[77] McKinsey Global Institute, 'Global Capital Markets: Entering a New Era', Annual Report 2009.

The main routes to access property are:

1. direct property

2. indirect property vehicles

3. real estate derivatives

4. Real Estate Investment Trusts (REITs)[78]

Each of these routes can be classified as a sub-asset class of real estate, with a different impact when included in a portfolio.

1. Direct property

Holding a portfolio of directly owned buildings provides a pure exposure to real estate. However, a number of factors – large lot sizes (making it difficult to diversify property specific or idiosyncratic risk); heterogeneity (location is a major driver of value and return, increasing specific risk); high transaction costs (leading to long holding periods and low trading volumes); high management costs; and illiquidity – make it challenging to construct a diversified portfolio of direct property (unless the portfolio's value is large).

Furthermore, a portfolio of direct properties does not track well a published property index. This means that it takes substantial capital to invest in direct property and the portfolio's risk/return characteristics may not match the modelling assumptions used for asset allocation purposes since they were probably based on a property index. In addition, directly owning real estate means that the investor is a landlord and needs to manage the property and collect rent from tenants, or hire an asset management company to do so.

The advantage of a pure exposure to direct real estate needs to be contrasted with the following disadvantages: illiquidity; the requirement of substantial investment to properly diversify; high costs; the need to materially invest in managing the portfolio or hire a professional asset manager; and the mismatch between asset class modelling assumptions and the actual portfolio.

Nevertheless, investors with large portfolios, sufficient resources, long investment horizons and appropriate liquidity needs should consider direct property since it provides the preferred features out of the available real estate investment routes in a portfolio context (e.g. diversification benefits with other asset classes and clean exposure to the real estate risk factor).

The average holding period of real estate in the United Kingdom at the end of the 1990s[79] was eight years and investors should plan to keep holding direct real estate investments for five to ten years.

---

[78] Commercial mortgage-backed securities (CMBS) and infrastructure also provide some exposure related to real estate.

[79] Collet, David, Lizieri, Colin and Ward, Charles, 'Timing and the Holding periods of Institutional Real Estate', *Real Estate Economics* 31 (2003).

Investors with a low appetite for illiquidity and a short investment horizon should stay away from direct property investment. Portfolios that require daily pricing of holdings should not invest in direct real estate either. UCITS-regulated portfolios cannot hold direct real estate, as per UCITS rules.

2. Indirect property vehicles

Indirect property investment means that investors invest in a vehicle that invests in real estate, not directly in the real estate itself. Indirect property vehicles are private, unlisted collective schemes (e.g. limited partnerships, unit trusts, private company structures and funds of funds),[80] mostly domiciled in tax havens.

The vehicles pool together many investors and provide some of the advantages of collectives, such as access to large properties that require large capital commitments, diversification, professional active management, lower search and monitoring costs (i.e. costs are shared among investors), and they permit investors who are excluded from borrowing to acquire leveraged real estate exposure.

Indirect property vehicles are classified by their target markets and risk/reward profile:

- *Core funds* typically have low leverage and target fully-let prime real estate (there is no single definition of prime real estate but it generally means high-quality property in terms of location, value, market and state of the building).

- *Core plus funds* may have higher levels of leverage and target markets with greater rental growth prospects.

- *Value added funds* look for more aggressive growth opportunities through releasing, repositioning and redevelopment.

- *Opportunity funds* utilise high levels of leverage and seek to generate returns by investing in distress assets, emerging markets and development projects.

As always, the higher the risk profile the higher the target returns.

Some issues with indirect property vehicles include calculation of management performance fees while performance is based on appraisals, the question of how to value fractional interests in properties, leverage and concerns about liquidity.

During the 2008 crisis the weaknesses of leverage and illiquidity of indirect property vehicles became vividly apparent. As property prices plunged, investors tried to rush out of the property market while lending conditions worsened. Indirect property vehicles, in particular the high risk ones, suffered poor returns and in some cases had to close the funds to redemptions since portfolio managers

---

[80] While funds of funds may provide diversification and professional manager selection, they have a layering of fees that dampens their benefits.

could not liquidate underlying properties to meet cash outflows. The toxic mix of illiquidity and risk aversion caused investors to sustain heavy losses.

3. Real estate derivative market

Property derivatives are normally written on property indices because of the illiquidity, information inefficiency and difficulty of pricing underlying direct properties. Commonly, property derivatives come in the form of property total return swaps (PTRSs). PTRSs can be funded, whereby one party pays the other party the notional amount in cash upfront in exchange for the future payments on the underlying property index. Funded PTRSs are a way to raise cash when portfolios have large property holdings that cannot be sold quickly.

Unfunded PTRSs (cash does not exchange hands between parties when entering the swap) is a way to increase or decrease the exposure to property in portfolios without raising or paying cash. Unfunded PTRSs do not solve cash or liquidity issues, but they can help to quickly alter the property exposure.

Property derivatives allow investors to gain exposure to diversified real estate returns with low entry costs, low transaction costs and low management costs. However, as always, there are disadvantages to using property derivatives. Using PTRSs in portfolios may introduce a basis risk, since the PTRS is written on a property index (such as IPD in the United Kingdom) and its returns are likely to be different than those of the actual properties held within portfolios. When portfolios hold a large, diverse portfolio of properties, with a relatively low tracking error to the property index, the basis risk of the PTRS is likely to be relatively low. When the property portfolio is less diversified, the tracking error between the PTRS and the portfolio is likely to be more substantial. Hence, PTRSs provide an imperfect hedge for the property exposure in the portfolio.

PTRSs also expose investors to other risks of using swaps, such as counterparty risk and liquidity risk (there is no organised secondary market for OTC swaps). However, the illiquidity of PTRSs is typically not as bad as that of direct property.

4. REITs

REITs (*Real Estate Investment Trusts*) are a corporate entity that invests in real estate. A REIT is a trust company that raises money through an IPO with the objective of managing a real estate portfolio and profiting from it. Investors in REITs own a portion of the real estate portfolio.

REITs offer a number of advantages to investors: diversification, income, relatively low transaction costs and liquidity. Since REITs pool together investments from many investors, they can manage a diversified portfolio of real estate. Directly investing in such portfolios would require substantial amounts of money.

The income from the real estate portfolio is distributed to the investors and the main use of REITs is as a source of income generation. Expected returns for securities with high income yields are relatively high, all else being equal.

In most countries REITs need to distribute large portions of their annual income (e.g. 90%) as legislation forces them to do so in order for the REITs to maintain their tax exempt status. This requirement is intended to create returns that are closer to those of the underlying real estate holdings and less dependent on management decisions.

REITs are subject to other qualifying rules specifying the nature of activities and asset base, ownership concentration and leverage structure (capital structure). The distributed income has a tax advantage compared to dividends on equities since it is deductible at the corporate level (no corporate tax) and generally taxed at a personal level.

The transaction costs on REITs are much lower than on direct property. In the United Kingdom the stamp tax on buying property is 4%, while it is 0.5% on REITs.

REITs are daily priced, listed vehicles (i.e. traded on exchanges), so they can provide liquidity in the property portfolio – as opposed to direct property, which is normally illiquid. However, REITs' liquidity comes at a price (indeed, whenever a liquid vehicle has underlying illiquid investments there is a catch, as liquidity cannot be created from nothing).

Compared to direct real estate REITs have a number of disadvantages, in particular higher volatility, which is augmented by short-term correlation with the equity market, and discounts and premiums relative to NAV and leverage. Investment in REITs exposes investors to a higher degree of volatility than direct property. The share price of REITs is affected not only by events in the property market, but also by those in the wider equity markets.

Since REITs are closed end funds their share price is affected by supply and demand. The price of shares is a function of the Net Asset Value (NAV) of the properties in which the REIT invests and the value that the market chooses to place on the share. The share price can trade either at a premium or discount to the NAV. The use of leverage augments the volatility of REITs. Investors in REITs must therefore accept their equity-like volatility.

REITs have a high correlation with equities over the short term and a higher correlation with direct property over the long term. Due to their equity-like volatility, REITs should not be considered as a short-term alternative to direct property investments. They are closer to a property sector within equities than to property in the short term.

However, REITs are a different asset class to equity. They pay high income, have low correlations with other asset classes and if investors look at the long term and accept high volatility, REITs do have a higher correlation with direct property. As they are frequently marked to market they look like equities, but over the long term accumulating and reinvesting interest should pay off.

Examining the *return determinants* of direct real estate and REITs, returns of REITs are found to be positively associated with stock and direct real estate returns, but negatively related to bond returns. Financial assets contribute greatly to the return variance of REITs, while the impact of direct real estate is limited.[81]

Examining the *integration* of direct real estate and REITs, the research is mixed. However, an article from 2005[82] finds that when controlling for property-type mix, leverage and appraisal smoothing, the mean and volatility of direct property and REITs are not different. This suggests that private and public real estate vehicles display long-term synchronicity. Other research[83] finds that *price discovery* occurs in the US and UK REIT markets and that this information does not transmit to the direct market for a year or more.

The conclusion is that REITs and direct real estate should be relatively good substitutes in a long-horizon investment portfolio.[84] This means, however, that when performance is frequently monitored (e.g. on a monthly basis) the performance of REITs relative to a direct property index can diverge materially. Investors must understand and accept this.

Drivers of property returns

The experience of investors in real estate is a function of rental income, return of the property market (i.e. capital gains or losses), the extent of leverage, the skill of the active property manager and the vehicle used to gain access to property (direct property, indirect property, derivatives or REITs).

The total return of property investing depends on the sector allocation (retail, office, industrial and residential), geography (location, location, location) and the specific properties. Due to the many choices and peculiar risk of each property, different property investments deliver a different experience, sometimes slightly and sometimes materially.

The opportunities for returns in the real estate market come from three main sources, excluding leverage:

---

[81] Hoesli, Martin and Serrano, Camilo, 'Securitized Real Estate and its Link with Financial Asset and Real Estate: An International Analysis', *Journal of Real Estate Literature* 15 (2007).

[82] Pagliari, Joseph, Scherer, Kevin and Monopoli, Richard, 'Public Versus Private Real Estate Equities: A More Refined, Long-Term Comparison', *Real Estate Economics* 33 (2005).

[83] Barkham, Richard and Geltner, David, 'Price discovery in American and British property markets', *Real Estate Economics* 23 (1995).

[84] Hoesli, Martin and Oikarinen, Elias, 'Are Reits Real Estate? Evidence from Sector Level Data', ERES Conference 2011.

1. *Income yield.* Rental income is the payments that the lease or property owner receives from the tenant. Rental yield is the rental income divided by the property purchase price. Yield from real estate should be stable and linked to inflation over the long term. Similar to bonds, income yield is a measure of property prices (i.e. yield is high when property prices are cheap and low when property prices are high). One of the advantages of investing in REITs is that they are a liquid source of income. However, income on REITs has been lower than that of bonds but with higher price volatility. REITs are neither a conservative asset class that should replace bonds nor a substitute for direct investment in real estate in portfolios when the investment horizon is not sufficiently long.

2. *Total return.* Total return from property includes the income yield plus the capital gain (or loss) realised when selling the property. When inflation rises quickly interest rates may rise as well and reduce the demand for property (higher mortgages rates), so adjustment to inflation may lag. Over the long term, however, property should provide a hedge against inflation. Ultimately, the price appreciation of property is determined by market forces. When demand for property is high there is a potential for capital gains. Normally, when the economy is doing well companies expand and rent more office space, manufacturers build factories and retailers open more shops. When the economy is doing poorly, the opposite occurs. Therefore, the total return of real estate is linked to GDP growth and the general state of the economy.

3. *Active management.* Real estate investments are informationally inefficient. Real estate prices do not price in all the public information on the market or on the intrinsic value of each specific property. Property is, therefore, an inefficient market, as well as illiquid and heterogeneous. These features provide opportunities for skilled active managers to outperform and for unskilled managers to underperform.

Relative performance is difficult to measure since there are no reliable property benchmarks. While in the United Kingdom the IPD[85] index (IPD UK Monthly Property Index) is published on a monthly basis, the NCREIF[86] index in the United States is published on a quarterly basis and the IPD Europe is published only on an annual basis. There is no reliable direct commercial property benchmark in Asia.

It is also impossible to track the benchmark because of the heterogeneous and illiquid nature of the asset class. Therefore, passive direct real estate investments are unavailable in the physical market; only synthetically through the derivative market (e.g. PTRS on the IPD index). Tracking REIT indices is much easier than tracking direct real estate investments. However, REITs are not a substitute for direct property investment, in particular over short investment horizons.

---

[85] IPD, Investment Property Databank, www.ipd.com.
[86] NCREIF, National Council of Real Estate Investment Fiduciaries, www.ncreif.org.

Identifying the factors that determine the returns of an asset class helps not only to understand its risks and returns, but also to understand how it should correlate with other asset classes in a multi-asset portfolio and how to model its expected returns for asset allocation purposes.

Unlike equities and fixed income, which are capital asset classes, real estate is a real asset class. Real estate is not used by companies to raise capital or for financing. Rather, real estate is used as a productive asset. Real estate is a different animal to equities and bonds.

According to research, the growth rate in per capita consumption, the real T-Bill rate, the term structure of interest rates and the unexpected inflation rate are financial and macro-economic fundamental drivers that systematically affect real estate returns.[87] Real estate prices are influenced by GDP growth rates.[88] Some of these factors are less dominant in equity and bond investing, making real estate a diversifying investment within multi-asset portfolios that are normally dominated by equities and fixed income.

Importantly, research[89] claims that a *real estate factor* is useful in explaining direct real estate returns in addition to stock and bond factors. Using a multi-factor analysis this real estate factor is a statistical factor that has a high load (beta) and is not common to factors of stocks and bonds. It is therefore not intuitive or easily explained by fundamental economics. This means that an allocation to real estate would expose the portfolio to this risk factor and provide diversification benefits as well as exposure to a unique systematic risk not available through other asset classes and which is expected to deliver a *real estate risk premium*.

Estimating real estate expected returns

Evaluating property's value quantitatively is based on the following four factors:

1. *Government bond yield.* Real estate investments should be bought only if they are expected to offer a yield above government bond yields with a similar maturity to the expected investment horizon of the real estate investments. Otherwise, property investments should be sold because they are riskier than government bonds and should offer a higher yield to compensate investors for the risk.

2. *Market supply and demand forecast and their influence on rental income.* The return on property is the discounted value of expected rental income, minus

---

[87] Naranjo, Andy and Ling, David, 'Economic Risk Factors and Commercial Real Estate Returns', *The Journal of Real Estate Finance and Economics* 14 (1997).

[88] Quan, Daniel and Titman, Sheridan, 'Do Real Estate Prices and Stock Prices Move Together? An International Analysis', *Real Estate Economics* 27 (1999).

[89] Mei, Jianping and Lee, Ahyee, 'Is There a Real Estate Factor Premium?', *Journal of Real Estate Finance and Economics* 9 (1994).

expenses, plus the discount value of the terminal value (the property selling price). The key variables are the rental income (normally expected to grow) and the discount factor, which should represent the risk of investing in property. Growth in rental income depends on assumptions about trends in the property market. The growth rate should be compared to the estimated growth in economy-wide inflation. Property should not be valued based on the cost of rebuilding it.[90] Property is expensive because rents are expensive, not because the land is expensive. The land is expensive because the rental income in the area is high.

3. *Tenant creditworthiness.* The required spread above government bond yield should consider the credit risk of the tenant and compensate investors for this risk.

4. *Property depreciation or obsoleteness.* This is a function of expected physical deterioration as well as the demand for the property and its location.

Determining the long-term expected return of property for asset allocation purposes is similar to determining the expected return of equities. The long-term expected return from property is the rental income yield, plus the expected growth in rental income yield (long-term GDP real growth plus inflation), plus the expected price change (appreciation or depreciation), minus transaction costs (expenses are material in property and cannot be ignored).

The most difficult factor to forecast is the expected price change. In a very simple way, it can be assumed to be the annualised convergence between current rental income yield and long-term average rental income yield (assuming mean-reversion in property valuations). The long-term expected return can then be calculated using the formula:

$$E(r) = I/P + GDP\ growth + inflation + I/P\ effect - expenses$$

where $E(r)$ is the expected return of property; I/P is rental income yield (I is income and P is the property price); GDP growth is the annual trend real GDP growth rate; inflation is the expected inflation; I/P effect is the contribution to return due to expected changes in rental income yield; and expenses are the annualised transaction costs of purchasing the property expressed as a percentage of the property price (all variables in the formula should be expressed as percentages). The formula can be adjusted to different property types and vehicles by including a subjective premium or discount.

The I/P effect[91] is calculated using the formula:

---

[90] *Tobin's Q* is the ratio of market value to replacement cost for a company's net assets or a house. Tobin, James, 'A General Equilibrium Approach to Monetary Theory', *Journal of Money Credit and Banking* 1 (1969).

[91] Rental yield is the inverse of the price-to-rent ratio. Rental yield is similar to earnings yield or dividend yield in equities. A current high (low) rental yield versus average means that the property is underpriced (overpriced) and if reverting to the mean its price will increase (decrease) over time.

$$\text{I/P effect} = (\text{I/P}_{Current}/\text{I/P}_{LT\ Avg})^{(1/n)}-1$$

where I/P effect is the annualised contribution to expected return due to changes in I/P; $\text{I/P}_{Current}$ and $\text{I/P}_{LT\ Avg}$ are the current and long-term average I/Ps, respectively; and n is the number of years in the investment horizon (e.g. n=10 for a 10-year horizon).

Inflation hedge

Real estate is one of the *real asset classes*, alongside commodities, inflation-linked bonds and infrastructure. These asset classes offer a hedge against inflation as they have a relatively high positive correlation with predicted and unpredicted inflation. However, this does not always hold.

Direct real estate should be positively correlated with long-term anticipated inflation through a link to real economic variables affecting supply and demand, because costs of construction materials normally increase with inflation, rents normally increase with inflation and inflation normally increases with economic growth, which normally leads to increased demand for real estate.

However, there is a weaker link between property prices and inflation over the short term, or unanticipated inflation, since property prices do not quickly adjust to inflation. The reasons are measurement issues (valuation-based prices are sticky, anchored around the last available prices and require time to adjust); the impact of lease contracts that prevent landlords from adjusting the rent on a regular basis; and policy actions by monetary authorities.

When inflation rises central banks normally react by increasing interest rates (real estate performance is strongly influenced by real interest rates), and the market expects interest rates to increase so the yields on long-term bonds increase. This increases the price of mortgages and makes property less affordable. Increasing inflation in this sense has an indirect negative effect on property prices.

The factor that has the largest impact on prices of commercial real estate is supply and demand. When vacancy rates are high they dominate the influence of inflation on real estate prices. Hence, real estate does not provide a hedge against inflation under all market conditions.

Illiquidity

Illiquidity is one of the major disadvantages of direct real estate investing. Much of the justification for the existence of REITs comes from their ability to enhance liquidity (as well as to diversify the portfolio and reduce transaction costs). However, the high value and indivisibility of real estate, the high transaction costs associated with real estate investing, and the lengthy and uncertain time taken to sell assets, all produce risk for investors.

Five main aspects of liquidity are used to characterise markets: the cost of liquidating a portfolio quickly; the ability to sell without affecting prices (market impact); the ability of prices to recover from shocks; the costs of selling now rather than waiting; and transaction costs (the direct and indirect costs of trading). These apply largely to publicly traded markets where depth and the presence of market makers ensure that adjustment to supply and demand occurs through the price mechanism. The price mechanism is not as efficient in the property market as it is for daily-traded markets such as equities and bonds. The importance and impact of these dimensions vary according to market conditions, across asset classes and within property by type of building, sector and location.

Given thin trading, a portfolio attempting to sell out of property may suffer losses due to forced sale prices. Large investors shifting their real estate weightings may influence prices. It often takes a long time to exit large real estate positions and the price may be lower than expected.

The ability to enter and exit the real estate market depends on how long it takes to buy or sell. The average time from initial purchase decision to completion in the United Kingdom is about ten months (there is considerable variation around this mean). In addition, marketing period times are often much longer in down markets and shorter in up markets.[92] The uncertainty over how long investors must stay in the market is an additional source of risk. During the time from the decision to sell until completion there is price volatility. Investors may be invested in real estate longer than desired and in the meantime prices can fluctuate.

Liquidity also has its advantages. Investors are concerned about liquidity both because of the additional *ex ante* uncertainty and because of potential difficulties in realising values quickly in order to meet unexpected liabilities (e.g. unexpected cash outflows that require cash to be raised by quickly selling assets). Since most investors face such risks, it is reasonable to expect a liquidity premium. Investors with long-term horizons and low liability risk may benefit from such a premium.

Risks

The main risk of direct property is its illiquidity. It is costly to buy a property and it may be costly, time consuming and uncertain, both in terms of price and time, to sell a property. Property illiquidity can have adverse effects on portfolio construction as the relative weight of property undesirably increases when the portfolio's assets diminish. Large lot sizes mean that real estate portfolios may be overly concentrated and not diversified enough.

---

[92] Fisher, Jeffrey, Gatzlaff, Dean, Geltner, David and Haurin, Donald, 'Controlling for the Impact of Variable Liquidity in Commercial Real Estate Price Indices', *Real Estate Economics* 31 (2003).

Managing a portfolio of buildings involves a number of risks. Tenants may be low quality, long vacancy periods may hurt income and costly repairs may be needed. Legal risks include the requirement for legal engagement for purchasing and selling property.

Worsening economic conditions, areas falling out of favour and disappointing returns from the real estate risk factor can all turn intended capital gains into actual capital losses. Real estate does not always appreciate as some investors think. During the 2008 crisis the prices of real estate around the world fell sharply.

When leverage is used another layer of risks is introduced. For their part, REITs add a full set of equity-like risks to the equation.

Real estate diversification

Similar to other asset classes, the possible diversification choices within real estate are geographic across countries or regions, and also across sectors. Two other impactful diversification options, more unique to real estate than other assets, are across different real estate vehicles and across specific buildings.

For indirect real estate, research[93] has found strong evidence that international real estate returns are correlated less strongly than international equity and bond returns. This means international indirect real estate portfolio diversification works better than for stocks and bonds. For direct real estate, research[94] has found that real estate returns are also less highly correlated with real estate returns in other countries than is the case of domestic stocks with international stocks, suggesting significant benefits from international real estate portfolio strategies too.

When investors have the resources and capabilities, real estate investment can be diversified across the United States, United Kingdom, Europe and Asia/Pacific (Japan, Australia and Asia). There are, however, practical issues in international direct real estate diversification. Asset allocation modelling relies usually on regional index returns. However, actual portfolio returns may substantially diverge from those of the indices. Due to information asymmetry and the need for local knowledge, higher research and monitoring costs are required. There is also currency risk.

In addition, most international real estate is likely to be concentrated in major cities in each country and this adds additional correlation to returns since global common demand factors affect returns in major cities (e.g. the demand for office

---

[93] Eichholtz, Piet, 'Does International Diversification Work Better for Real Estate than for Stocks and Bonds?', *Financial Analysts Journal* 52 (1996).

[94] Quan, Daniel and Titman, Sheridan, 'Commercial Real Estate Prices and Stock Market Returns: An International Analysis', *Financial Analysts Journal* 53 (1997); and Newell, Graeme and Webb, James, 'Assessing Risk for International Real Estate Investments', *Journal of Real Estate Research* 11 (1996).

space in financial centres around the globe may be affected by the state of the global economy).

While international diversification is beneficial, diversification by property type (sector) is more useful.[95] Property type should be the most important factor when constructing real estate portfolios as it is the most important dimension in determining different market behaviour.[96]

The role of real estate in portfolios

There are several reasons to include commercial real estate in portfolios, including diversification, a source of income and potentially attractive total returns that provide a hedge against inflation.

Not least, the rental income that comes from a portfolio of properties can be a solution for retirement, instead of relying on public or corporate pension schemes.

The challenge is how to determine the appropriate allocation to direct real estate in portfolios since it does not have a reliable benchmark to be used in SAA analysis. Real estate appears to deliver high returns relative to its reported risk. In other words, it has better risk-adjusted returns compared to equities and bonds and an asset allocation optimiser algorithm is likely to 'like' real estate because of that. However, real estate risk, as measured by volatility of returns, may be underestimated due to smoothing because values are based on appraisals and valuations and not on daily traded market prices, such as in the equity and bond markets. Correlations may also be inaccurate because of the smoothed returns.

Furthermore, real estate investing is exposed to risk factors that are not captured by traditional mean-variance optimisation, such as illiquidity, legal complications and potential agency problems of some of the ownership structures. Traditional risk adjusted performance measures, such as Sharpe ratio, do not take these risk factors into account and are inflated by the underestimated volatility of returns.

Three potential ways to tackle the issues are:

1. unsmooth the returns

2. use returns over long time periods to calculate the volatility (e.g. volatility of rolling 12 or 36-monthly returns)

3. adjust the risk to fat tails

---

[95] Eichholtz, Piet, Hoesli, Martin, MacGregor, Bryan and Nanthakumaran, Nanda, 'Real Estate Portfolio Diversification by Property Type and Region', *Journal of Property Finance* 6 (1995).

[96] Hoesli, Martin, Lizieri, Colin and MacGregor, Bryan, 'The Spatial Dimensions of the Investment Performance of UK Commercial Property', *Urban Studies* 34 (1997).

New technologies have increased the flow of information. It is now easier to collect information on properties. The modest increased efficiency of the market may have lowered the risk of investing in real estate and somewhat changed the expected returns from real estate.

Property can be relatively easily leveraged through a mortgage and so investors can borrow against their property. This enables them to increase the number of properties in the portfolio or use the money elsewhere. Leverage involves risks since properties can be foreclosed if investors cannot meet their mortgage obligations and capital losses can be intensified. Leverage should be treated with caution.

REITs have a reliable benchmark and they exhibit a low correlation with bonds and equities over the long term. The volatility of REITs is high due to leverage and their daily pricing. The volatility of underlying direct property is somewhere between that of REITs and bonds.

Portfolio construction and property

The illiquid nature of property has implications on portfolio construction. Multi-asset portfolios that hold property may be over-weighted to property, in particular when there are cash outflows from the portfolios. Most other asset classes, which are more liquid than property, can be sold to meet the cash outflows, but property cannot be sold quickly and portfolios may accumulate a larger relative allocation to property with time.

Take as an example a $100 million portfolio holding 50% equities, 40% bonds and 10% property. A $10 million cash outflow can be quickly met by selling $5 million equities and $5 million bonds. The portfolio's asset allocation has changed to 50% equities, 38.9% bonds and 11.1% property. The weight of property in the portfolio has increased.

The illiquidity of real estate can make rebalancing more difficult and costly, resulting in being undesirably overweight or underweight to property. An unwanted overweight to property can mean that cash in unavailable to invest in other assets. The result is a multi-asset portfolio with a different allocation to the desired one. This is another indirect cost of illiquidity.

The transaction costs of buying and selling property are relatively high. Therefore, before purchasing property investors need to think ahead about the implications of owning property and the impact on asset allocation in case changes are required. Two strategies to address the illiquidity of real estate are to use REITs, although they are not considered a real estate substitute over the short term, and the real estate derivative market.

Property indices

In the United States the common index for direct private commercial real estate is NCREIF and in the United Kingdom it is IPD. The returns of the indices are ungeared, represent a sub-set of investment quality real estate in the respective countries and are based on appraisals (valuations) of the real estate in each database, rather than on actual transaction prices. This last feature results in smoothed returns that underestimate volatility and distort correlations.

The US NCREIF provides only quarterly data. The index consists of properties acquired by tax-exempt institutions and held in a fiduciary environment. The index includes more than 5,000 buildings. The UK IPD provides monthly data and includes close to 4,000 buildings.

FTSE[97] provides a series of indices representing different REIT markets. The FTSE NAREIT US Real Estate Index Series, for example, is designed to represent a comprehensive family of REIT performance indexes that span the commercial real estate space across the US economy, offering exposure to all investment and property sectors.

The S&P/Case-Shiller Home Price Indices[98] measure the US residential housing market, tracking changes in the value of residential real estate both nationally as well as in 20 metropolitan regions.

Performance measurement performs three principal tasks:[99]

1. *Communications*. Informing stakeholders about the performance of the investment.

2. *Accountability*. Judging the performance of professional advisers and managers, usually in relation to pre-set targets.

3. *Research*. Investigating ways in which performance can be improved.

Real estate, and in particular direct real estate investing, presents issues in all of these areas. The development of indices such as NCREIF and IPD has improved the transparency of direct property returns. As the coverage expands and history of returns lengthens, more rigorous research of the asset class becomes possible, as well as comparing portfolio performance to those indices.

The reported returns of real estate indices suffer from two issues: valuation or appraisal smoothing; and non-normality of the return distribution. The statistical test of whether the returns of private UK real estate are normal is rejected (i.e.

---

[97] www.ftse.co.uk.
[98] www.standardandpoors.com.
[99] Brown, Gerald and Matysiak, George, 'Using Commercial Property Indices for Measuring Portfolio Performance', *Journal of Property Finance* 6 (1995).

the returns are not normally distributed).[100] This means that careful consideration is needed in the choice of risk measures. Standard deviation, for example, should be adjusted to fat-tail risk after the historic returns have been unsmoothed.

The returns reported in real estate indices represent unleveraged returns. However, most real estate private funds and REITs utilise debt. Leverage increases the potential volatility and adds interest rate risk. Comparison of listed real estate investments with the private real estate market should strictly adjust for the capital structure of the vehicle. Leverage should have no major impact on the correlation coefficients between real estate returns and the returns of financial assets.

Measuring real estate portfolios' performance relative to indices suffers from a number of issues. Firstly, real estate indices are normally reported in low frequency while performance is normally measured on a monthly basis. This means that between index publication times the relative performance is unknown.

Secondly, given the low frequency of indices and periodic portfolio valuations, demonstrating the statistical significance of the observed relative performance is problematic. Superior investment ability implies the ability to outperform the benchmark consistently.[101] Low frequency data creates large standard errors around the benchmark and portfolio return, making it near impossible to statistically prove outperformance or underperformance.

Tracking error measures are also problematic in direct real estate due to the appraisal-based nature of the indices and the challenges that face most investors in constructing a well-diversified portfolio of direct real estate investments.

The conclusion is that relative return and risk measures of direct real estate should be taken with a pinch of salt and investors should not rely on them too heavily to make investment decisions or to monitor portfolio managers.

Historical return and risk of property

Table 3.1 shows the performance and risk characteristics of direct UK property, US residential property,[102] REITs,[103] US equities and Treasuries. Table 3.2 is a correlation matrix of the different indices. The performance analytics are based on monthly returns.

---

[100] Young, Michael, Lee, Stephen and Devaney, Steven, 'Non-normal Real Estate Return Distributions by Property Type in the UK', *Journal of Property Research* 23 (2006).

[101] Deltner, David, Miller, Norman, Clayton, Jim and Eichholtz, Piet, *Commercial Real Estate Analysis and Investments*, 2nd ed. (South-Western Educational Publishing, 2007).

[102] Standard & Poor's Case-Shiller Home Price indices are measures for the US residential housing market. www.standardandpoors.com.

[103] FTSE NAREIT, www.ftse.com.

UK direct property has delivered an average return of close to 9% per annum over the measuring period, outpacing US Treasuries but lagging US equities by about 1%. Still, a return of 9% is equity-like and delivers growth in portfolios. The volatility of direct property seems very low (lower than that of Treasuries), however, it may not represent the true risk of the asset class due to smoothed appraisal-based returns. REITs have delivered the highest return out of the five asset classes, but with an equity-like volatility.

The correlation matrix demonstrates the low correlation of property (direct and REITs) with both equities and government bonds. Including property in multi-asset portfolios adds diversification benefits. The correlations among the three different property sub-asset classes (UK direct, US residential and REITs) show how each one should be considered as a separate asset, with its own return and risk characteristics.

Table 3.1: Property return and risk characteristics, February 1987 to December 2013. Sharpe ratio calculated using $ cash returns. All returns measured in $ except for UK IPD, which is measured in £

	UK IPD All Property	S&P Case-Shiller 10	FTSE NAREIT	US equities	US Treasuries
Start month	Feb-1987	Feb-1987	Feb-1987	Feb-1987	Feb-1987
Performance (% pa)	8.7	4.0	9.9	9.8	6.4
Volatility (%)	3.8	3.2	18.5	15.3	4.6
Skewness	-1.63	-0.56	-0.80	-0.92	-0.07
Kurtosis	6.75	0.76	8.97	2.62	0.70
Sharpe ratio	1.32	0.11	0.34	0.41	0.60
Max drawdown (%)	-36.7	-35.3	-68.3	-50.9	-5.3

Source: Bloomberg, Global Financial Data, UK IPD TR All Property Index, S&P Case-Shiller Home Price Composite 10 Index, FTSE NAREIT Equity TR Index, S&P 500 Index, Citigroup United States WGBI Index.

Table 3.2: Correlation matrix, February 1987 to December 2013

Correlation matrix	UK IPD All Property	S&P Case-Shiller 10	FTSE NAREIT	US equities	US Treasuries
UK IPD All Property	1.00	0.55	0.19	0.14	-0.17
S&P Case-Shiller 10	0.55	1.00	0.10	0.03	-0.04
FTSE NAREIT	0.19	0.10	1.00	0.57	-0.02
US equities	0.14	0.03	0.57	1.00	-0.07
US Treasuries	-0.17	-0.04	-0.02	-0.07	1.00

Source: Bloomberg, Global Financial Data, UK IPD TR All Property Index, S&P Case-Shiller Home Price Composite 10 Index, FTSE NAREIT Equity TR Index, S&P 500 Index, Citigroup United States WGBI Index.

Table 3.3 shows the performance analytics of NCREIF (US direct commercial property), REITs and US equities. Since NCREIF is available only on a quarterly basis, quarterly index returns are used for all three indices. The table includes the volatility adjusted for fat-tails (using the Cornish-Fisher approximation)[104] and analytics for unsmoothed returns (using an unsmoothing technique).[105] Table 3.4 shows the correlations among the asset classes.

Table 3.3: Property return and risk characteristics, March 1978 to December 2013. Based on quarterly returns

	NCREIF	REITs	US equities	Unsmooth NCREIF	Unsmooth REITs	Unsmooth US equities
Start month	Mar-78	Mar-78	Mar-78	Mar-78	Mar-78	Mar-78
Performance (% pa)	9.1	12.6	11.8	8.3	12.1	11.8
Volatility (%)	4.4	18.0	16.2	12.5	20.2	17.3
Skewness	-2.04	-0.75	-0.60	-2.04	-0.59	-0.55
Kurtosis	6.85	4.81	0.77	12.17	4.35	0.73
Adjusted volatility	6.2	23.5	18.5	20.1	25.7	19.6
Autocorrelation	0.78	0.12	0.07	-	-	-

Source: Bloomberg, NCREIF Index, FTSE NAREIT Equity TR Index, S&P 500 Index.

---

[104] Cornish and Fisher, 'Moments and Cumulants in the Specification of Distributions', *Review of the International Statistical Institute* (1937).

[105] Geltner, David, 'Smoothing in Appraisal-Based Returns', *Journal of Real Estate Finance and Economics* 4 (1991); and Geltner, David, 'Estimating Market Values from Appraised Values without Assuming an Efficient Market', *Journal of Real Estate Research* 8 (1993).

Table 3.4: Correlation matrix, March 1978 to December 2013. Based on quarterly returns

Correlation matrix	NCREIF	REITs	US equities	Unsmooth NCREIF	Unsmooth REITs	Unsmooth US equities
NCREIF	1.00	0.15	0.09	0.62	0.13	0.08
REITs	0.15	1.00	0.62	0.31	0.99	0.61
US equities	0.09	0.62	1.00	0.16	0.63	1.00
Unsmooth NCREIF	0.62	0.31	0.16	1.00	0.30	0.14
Unsmooth REITs	0.13	0.99	0.63	0.30	1.00	0.62
Unsmooth equities	0.08	0.61	1.00	0.14	0.62	1.00

Source: Bloomberg, NCREIF Index, FTSE NAREIT Equity TR Index, S&P 500 Index.

The volatility of direct real estate increases by 40% when adjusted for fat-tails (that of REITs increases by 30% and that of equities by 15%). When the returns are unsmoothed, the volatility of direct real estate jumps by more than 180% or almost triples (the volatility of REITs increases by 15% and that of equities by less than 10%). It can be seen that returns of direct real estate materially understate volatility and must be adjusted before relying on the numbers.

Figure 3.2 visually demonstrates the difference between reported and unsmoothed returns of direct US property. The performance line of the NCREIF Index is much smoother than the bumpier, unsmooth line. Both the volatility and drawdowns (e.g. 2008) are much more visible and their magnitude is amplified when performance is unsmoothed. Reported returns may be deceiving to the unsuspicious eye.

Figure 3.3 shows the cumulative performance of the UK IPD TR All Property Index since January 1987 (measuring performance of direct UK commercial property), the S&P Case-Shiller Index (measuring US residential home prices) and the FTSE NAREIT Equity Index (measuring performance of US REITs).

While the returns of direct property are smoothed due to appraisals and therefore their volatility is understated, the volatility of REITs looks much closer to that of equities than to that of direct property. However, the correlation between direct property and REITs over the long term is evident.

Figure 3.2: Cumulative performance of reported and unsmoothed US direct property, March 1978 to December 2013

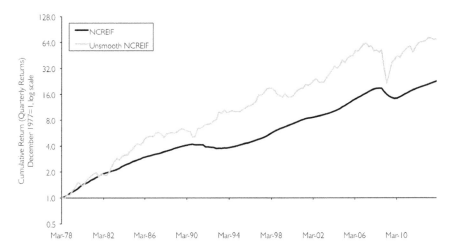

Source: Bloomberg, NCREIF Index.

Figure 3.3: Cumulative performance of property, January 1987 to December 2013

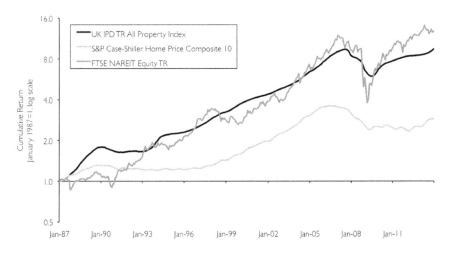

Source: Bloomberg, UK IPD TR All Property Index, S&P Case-Shiller Home Price Composite 10 Index, FTSE NAREIT Equity TR Index.

Figure 3.4 shows the rolling 36-month correlation between direct property and REITs, direct property and US equities, and REITs and US equities. Over most time periods the correlation between REITs and equities is higher than that between direct property and equities. However, this is because the correlation is measured over a relatively short time period of three years.

Figure 3.4: Rolling 36-month correlation of direct UK commercial property, REITs and US equities, January 1990 to December 2013

Source: Bloomberg, UK IPD TR All Property Index, FTSE NAREIT Equity TR Index, S&P 500 Index.

Figure 3.5 shows the rolling 36-month volatility of direct property, REITs and US equities. The volatility of REITs is much closer to that of equities than to that of direct real estate. This is both because REITs are traded daily, so their volatility captures short-term price changes, and the volatility of direct real estate is underestimated since it is appraisal-based. This chart demonstrates the difference between daily traded and infrequently traded assets.

Figure 3.6 plots the monthly returns of US equities and REITs. Figure 3.7 shows the average performance of REITs ranked by average decile performance of US equities. REITs are a risk asset, expected to have a high correlation with equities. However, we can see from the chart that when equities fall, REITs do not provide portfolio protection and tend to fall as well.

Figure 3.8 compares the cumulative performance of REITs and US equities based on monthly returns. Figure 3.9 adds direct US property based on quarterly returns. The charts show once again that REITs behave more like equities over the short term than like direct real estate. This means higher volatility. This can also mean higher returns. However, REITs do have material downside risk, as is evident from the 2008 crash, which was even more severe than that of US equities (although the following rebound was much stronger).

Figure 3.5: Rolling 36-month volatility of direct UK commercial property, REITs and US equities, January 1990 to December 2013

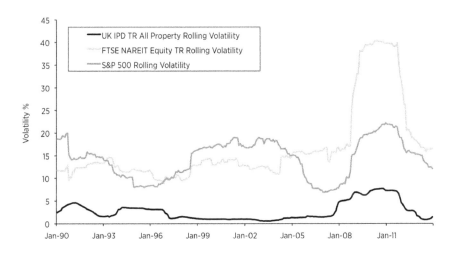

Source: Bloomberg, UK IPD TR All Property Index, FTSE NAREIT Equity TR Index, S&P 500 Index.

Figure 3.6: Scatter plot of monthly returns of REITs and US equities, January 1972 to December 2013

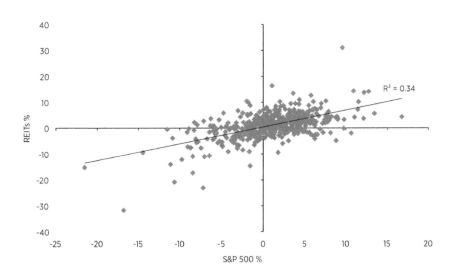

Source: Bloomberg, FTSE NAREIT Equity TR Index, S&P 500 Index.

Figure 3.7: Average performance of REITs and US equities ranked by performance of US equities, January 1972 to December 2013

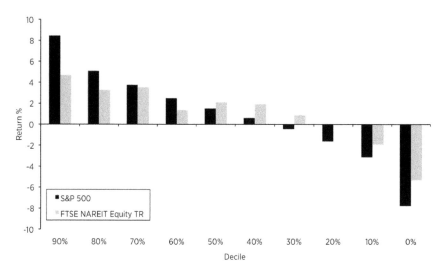

Source: Bloomberg, FTSE NAREIT Equity TR Index, S&P 500 Index.

Figure 3.8: Cumulative performance of REITs and US equities, January 1978 to December 2013

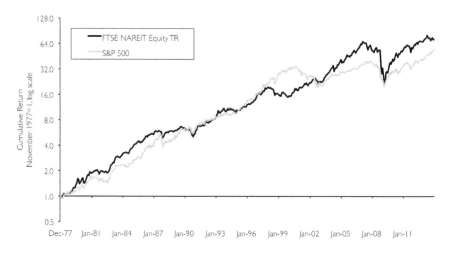

Source: Bloomberg, FTSE NAREIT Equity TR Index, S&P 500 Index.

Figure 3.9: Cumulative performance of direct property, REITs and US equities, March 1978 to December 2013. Based on quarterly returns

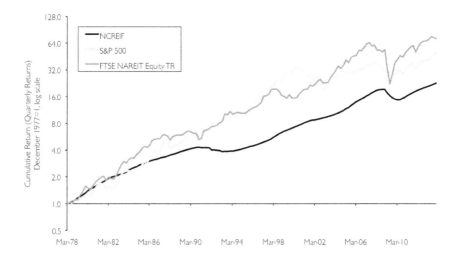

Source: Bloomberg, NCREIF, FTSE NAREIT Equity TR Index, S&P 500 Index.

Figure 3.10 shows the correlation between direct US property, REITs and equities. Figure 3.11 shows the rolling annualised volatility[106] of the three asset classes. All charts are based on quarterly returns. Direct real estate has a higher correlation with REITs than with equities most of the time, but not all of the time. During the 2008 crash, REITs fell dramatically, seeing their correlation with equities jumping, as well as their volatility. REITs are clearly a risk asset, in particular during a credit crunch, due to the leverage that REITs utilise.

---

[106] Annualising quarterly returns requires multiplying the standard deviation by the square root of 4.

Figure 3.10: Rolling 36-quarterly correlation of US direct property with REITs and US equities, January 1987 to December 2013. Based on quarterly returns

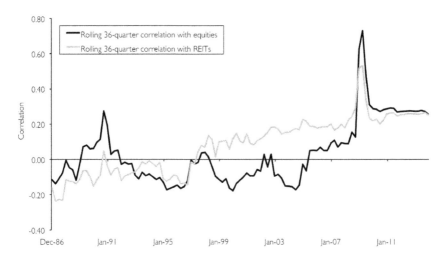

Source: Bloomberg, NCREIF Index, FTSE NAREIT Equity TR Index, S&P 500 Index.

Figure 3.11: Rolling 36-quarterly annualised volatility of US direct property, REITs and US equities, January 1987 to December 2013. Based on quarterly returns

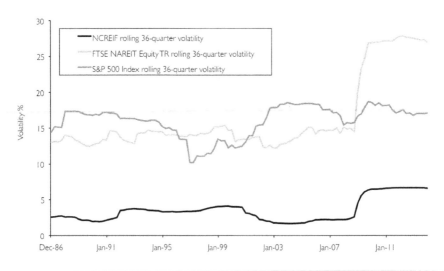

Source: Bloomberg, NCREIF Index, FTSE NAREIT Equity TR Index, S&P 500 Index.

Conclusions

People like to own property. You can live in it and you can touch it (it is bricks and mortar). Direct property is an expensive asset class, with high transaction costs and illiquidity costs. It does provide, however, unique features for long-term investors. The economy needs real estate; it is therefore a stable asset class (if crazy leverage is not used) and hence has a large potential profit.

REITs are not a substitute for direct property over the short term. They are, however, a separate asset class. REITs are a less known asset class and a neglected one, perhaps because they are relatively new and misunderstood.

Summary

- Most investors have exposure to real estate (in the form of a residential home, property portfolio of institutions or conscious investment in commercial real estate).

- Commercial property, investment property or income property refers to buildings and land intended to generate a profit from capital gains and/or income.

- The main routes to access property are direct property, indirect property vehicles, real estate derivatives and Real Estate Investment Trusts (REITs).

- Direct property gives the purest exposure to real estate. However, its disadvantages are: illiquidity; the requirement of a large investment to diversify; high costs; the need to invest in managing the portfolio or hire a professional asset manager; and the mismatch between asset class modelling assumptions and the actual portfolio.

- Indirect property pools together investments from many investors allowing for diversification, cost sharing and professional management. However, the disadvantages of indirect property are management fees, leverage and liquidity.

- Real estate derivatives, such as property total return swaps or PTRSs, are written on real estate indices. While they can offer liquidity and exposure to real estate, they suffer from large basis risk with actual real estate portfolios.

- REITs are listed pooled investment vehicles. They offer diversification, income and liquidity. However, REITs are more correlated with equities than real estate over the short term and they have equity-like volatility. They are a potential substitute for real estate only over long investment horizons.

- Rental income, total returns and active management are three sources of property returns (beyond leverage).

- While real estate returns are driven from risk factors common with other asset classes, a distinct real estate risk factor has been identified. This means that real estate exposes a portfolio to a systematic risk factor and a source of return not available from other asset classes.

- Real estate is one of the real asset classes, alongside commodities, inflation-linked bonds and infrastructure, providing a hedge against inflation. However, property does not provide a hedge against inflation in all market conditions. When high inflation results in higher interest rates and vacancy rates, property prices may drop and fail to hedge the inflation. Real estate prices do not quickly adjust to short-term inflation and unexpected inflation.

- Real estate is an illiquid investment with relatively very high transaction costs to get into and out of it. Therefore, before adding property to multi-asset portfolios investors must consider carefully the future allocation to real estate.

- The roles of property in portfolios are providing diversification, income yield and potentially attractive total returns, which provide a hedge against inflation.

- Direct property indices are based on appraisals and hence their returns are smoothed (i.e. reported return volatility is lower than true volatility).

CHAPTER 6: COMMODITIES

The quest to find asset classes with a low correlation with other investments, real returns (to act as a hedge against inflation) and positive performance when other markets are under stress and in turmoil has increased the interest in commodities in recent decades. Including commodities in portfolios expands the investable universe, broadens the investment opportunity set and enhances diversification, resulting in an improvement in the risk-adjusted return characteristics of these portfolios.

The Oxford Dictionary states that a commodity is "a raw material or primary agricultural product that can be bought and sold, such as copper and coffee." Commodities are essential resources and agricultural products. They are a class of basic, in-demand, commercially-used goods (some are input goods and some are intermediate goods) that are supplied without qualitative differentiation across the market.

Commodities have full or partial fungibility. This means that the market treats them as equivalent, or nearly so, no matter who produces them. A barrel of oil is a barrel of oil, no matter who produces it. Karl Marx[107] described this feature of commodities by saying, "From the taste of wheat it is not possible to tell who produced it, a Russian serf, a French peasant or an English capitalist." So we can say that one of the characteristics of a commodity is that its price is determined as a function of its market as a whole.

Well-established physical commodities have actively traded spot and derivative markets. The spot or cash market is a financial market where commodities are traded for immediate delivery. In contrast, the futures market is where commodities are traded for future delivery.

Commodities are divided into hard and soft commodities. *Hard commodities* are non-perishable real assets such as energy (oil, gas and coal), precious metals (gold, silver and platinum), industrial metals (aluminium and copper) and timber. *Soft commodities* are perishable and consumable real assets, such as agriculture (sugar, coffee beans, soybeans, rice and wheat) and livestock (lean hogs and live cattle).

---

[107] Marx, Karl and Engels, Frederick, 'A Contribution to the Critique of Political Economy', *The Collected Works of Karl Marx and Frederick Engels* 29 (1975).

Similar to real estate, commodities are part of a category of asset classes know as *real assets*. The link among these asset classes is the positive correlation with inflation. This should provide purchasing power protection or a hedge against inflation. Also, similar to real estate, and different to equities and bonds, commodities are not capital assets; they are not used by companies for raising capital.

Access

Unlike financial assets, for which the access is relatively clear (e.g. purchasing securities, funds or derivatives), it is less clear for commodities. The three main ways to gain access to commodities are:

1. direct physical investment

2. commodity-related equities

3. commodity futures

1. Direct physical investment

Direct physical investment means purchasing actual commodities. This route is normally impractical and expensive since physical commodities need to be transported, stored and insured, and some are perishable. Where are you going to store a herd of live cattle or 1000 lean hogs? The exception is precious metals (you can buy a piece of gold and store it in your safe, under your mattress, or wear it as a heavy necklace).

When selling physical commodities a willing buyer needs to be located, the commodities need to be inspected, their price may be discounted for quality and they need to be transferred. All these features make commodities cumbersome and inconvenient for investment as part of a portfolio of financial assets.

Some commodity exchange traded funds (ETFs) get around these issues with *physically-backed products*, which represent physical exposure to certain commodities without them ever being delivered to investors. This eliminates the cost of buying a commodity up front and worrying about who to sell it to when the time comes. Physically-backed exchange traded products do not have the potential complexity and need for expertise as do commodity futures, and investors never have to worry about delivery. Though storage costs are associated with physical ETFs, they are usually not material, allowing investors to keep the majority of their gains.

2. Commodity-related equities

Commodity-related equities are stocks issued by companies involved in commodity-related industries,[108] such as energy (e.g. oil and gas production and

---

[108] Examples of companies involved in commodity-related industries include PotashCorp (agriculture chemicals); Alcoa (aluminium); Freeport McMoran (copper); Barrick Gold Corporation (gold); Plum Creek Timber (lumber); BHP Billiton (metals); Petrobras (oil drilling and exploration); Silver Wheaton (silver); ArcelorMittal (steel); and Chevron and Exxon Mobil (oil).

oilfield services and equipment), non-ferrous metals, precious metals, agriculture and forest products. Often, collectives specialising in commodity-related equities are labelled *natural resources*. Such equities do not provide pure exposure to commodities as they include exposure to the companies that issue the stock. They may have a higher correlation with the general equity market than with commodity prices, which would defeat part of the objective of investing in commodities.

Companies may hedge their exposure to commodities, decreasing further the desired exposure to the asset class. For example, a gold mining company may hedge the effect of fluctuations in the gold price on its profitability by selling futures contracts on gold, thus stabilising the price of produced gold. Investors in the company's stocks are therefore less exposed to the gold price and more to the commercial fortunes of the company and the equity market. Nevertheless, a multi-factor analysis reveals that commodity-related equities do have exposure to a special risk factor not related to equities, so this does provide a diversification benefit.

Commodity-related equities should be considered as part of the allocation to equities. At times commodity-related equities may be slow to react to increases in commodity prices and may present an investment opportunity.

3. Commodity futures

Obtaining exposure to commodities is normally done via commodity futures because of the shortcomings of physical commodities and commodity-related equities. Each futures contract gives access to an individual commodity sector (e.g. oil, gold, gas, copper, corn). Commonly, commodity futures on different sectors are grouped into a commodity futures index, through which investors can access the asset class in a diversified way, rather than choosing specific commodity sectors.

A commodity futures contract is an agreement to buy (or sell) a specified quantity of a commodity at a future date at a price agreed upon when the parties entered into the contract (the futures price). The futures price is different from the value of a futures contract. When the buyer and seller enter into a futures contract, no cash exchanges hands between them; hence, the value of the contract is zero at its inception.

To obtain the commodity in the future, the alternative to buying a futures contract is to wait and purchase the commodity in the spot market at the point in the future when it is needed. The future spot price is obviously unknown today and so a futures contract locks in the terms of trade for future transactions.

In determining the fair futures price, market participants compare the current futures price with the spot price that can be expected to prevail at the futures contract's maturity. In other words, futures markets are forward looking and the futures price embeds expectations about the future spot price. If spot prices are expected to be much higher at maturity than they are today, the current futures price will be set at a high level relative to the current spot price. Lower expected spot prices in the future will be reflected in a low current futures price.[109]

Expected movements in the spot price are not a source of return to investors in futures because foreseeable trends in the spot markets are taken into account when futures prices are set. Long (short) investors in futures benefit when the spot price at maturity turns out to be higher (lower) than expected when they entered into the contract, and they lose out when the spot price is lower (higher) than anticipated.

A futures contract is thus a bet on the future spot price. By entering into a futures contract investors assume the risk of unexpected movements in the future spot price. Unexpected deviations from the expected future spot price are by definition unpredictable; for investors in futures, the deviations should average out to zero over time, unless an investor has the ability to correctly time the market.

Futures risk premium

Investors in futures expect to earn a payoff even if they do not benefit from unexpected spot price movements and are unable to outsmart the market. This payoff is the *risk premium*: the difference between the current futures price and the expected future spot price. If today's futures price is set below the widely expected future spot price, a purchaser of futures will, on average, earn money. If the futures price is set above the widely expected future spot price, a seller of futures will earn a risk premium. The total return of investing in futures is therefore the risk premium plus any unexpected deviation between the realised and expected future spot price.

Theoretical reasons have been developed to explain the risk premium. In the 1930s John Maynard Keynes[110] and John Hicks[111] postulated the theory of *normal backwardation*, which states that the risk premium will, on average, accrue to the buyers. According to the theory, market participants seek to hedge the future price of commodities (by going short commodity futures). On the other side of the hedges, speculators or insurance providers bear the commodity price risk (by taking the opposite long positions in the futures contracts) and demand a return for bearing this risk. It is therefore common for long-term futures contracts to trade at a discount beyond what all participants (hedgers and insurance providers) believe that the true price of commodities is going to be (the expected future spot price). By *backwardating* the futures price relative to the expected future spot price, speculators receive a risk premium from producers for assuming the risk of future price fluctuations.

[109] Black, Fischer, 'The Pricing of Commodity Contracts', *Journal of Financial Economics* 3 (1976).
[110] Keynes, John Maynard, *A Treatise on Money, Volume II* (New York: Macmillan & Co, 1930).
[111] Hicks, John, *Value and Capital* (Oxford University Press, 1939).

The theory of normal backwardation cannot be proven because the expectations of the market participants are unobservable. This means that the hedgers agree to pay a risk or insurance premium to the insurance providers. Commodity producers often hedge the commodity price volatility, more so than commodity consumers or processors, since producers commonly have higher inventories and fixed costs and hence a higher need for price stability. On average, the price of the futures contracts and the spot price converge as the futures near expiration and the insurance providers realise the risk premium.

Convenience yield

An alternative theory explaining the relationship between futures and spot price is the *theory of storage*. Nicholas Kaldor[112] reasoned that there are two types of yields for a holder of commodity inventory. One is the cost of financing and storing inventory and the other is the benefit of being able to use the inventory when it is commercially needed. The latter benefit became known as the *convenience yield* and is now a factor in commodity pricing theory. The equation connecting futures price and spot price is:

$$F - S = \text{storage costs} + \text{interest costs} - \text{convenience yield}$$

where F is the futures price; and S is the spot price.

This formula is used as the basis for futures pricing models. The difference between the futures price and the spot price is the cost of storing the commodity (the futures buyer saves the storage costs until maturity of the futures contract), plus the time value of money (futures are bought on margin and the full price is paid only at the maturity of the futures contract, hence the buyer saves the interest on the cash), minus the convenience yield (the futures buyer cannot use the commodity until the futures contract's maturity).

Drivers of commodity futures returns

The total return of a position in a fully collateralised commodity futures index (i.e. where the full notional amount is backed up by cash) is driven by three main factors or building blocks:

1. *Spot return.* This is the return from changes to the underlying commodity spot prices (also called price return).

2. *Roll return.* Roll return depends on the shape of the futures term structure. Commodity futures need to be rolled when the contract approaches its expiration. If the contract is not rolled, the investor may need to take physical

---

[112] Kaldor, Nicholas, 'Speculation and Economic Stability', *Review of Economic Studies* 7 (1939).

delivery of the underlying commodity or deliver them when holding a short position. You may end up with 1000 cows if you forget to roll your futures contract. Depending on the shape of the futures curve the roll-down process (i.e. swapping the immediately deliverable to the next deferred delivery contract) may result in a positive or negative carry to investors. This depends on whether the futures curve is in contango (the futures contract's price is trading above the expected spot price at contract maturity and generates negative roll return) or backwardation (the futures contract's price is trading below the expected spot price and generates a positive roll return).

3. *Collateral return.* When futures contracts are bought, collateral must be provided. The cash collateral (e.g. Treasury Bills) earns short-term interest rates.

Robert Greer's commodity futures pricing model

Robert Greer[113] developed a commodity futures pricing model that proposes the return drivers of commodity futures are:

1. expected inflation

2. insurance premium

3 convenience yield

4. diversification/rebalancing return

5. expectational variance

These return drivers are also helpful in understanding the return factors of other financial assets.

1. *Expected inflation.* Inflation affects both the collateral's return (e.g. when inflation is high, short-term interest rates are expected to increase and hence the return on collateral, such as Treasury Bills, is expected to increase as well) and the spot price of commodities. Increasing global industrial production and demand for commodities, for example, should inflate the prices of commodities over the long term.

2. *Insurance premium.* According to Keynes' theory of normal backwardation, investors in commodity futures earn a risk or insurance premium from commodity producers seeking to hedge future price fluctuations.

3. *Convenience yield.* The convenience yield[114] from Kaldor's theory of storage occurs as manufacturers bid up commodities' futures prices when they seek

---

[113] Greer, Robert, 'Commodity Indexes for Real Return and Efficient Diversification', *The Handbook of Inflation Hedging Investments* (McGraw-Hill, 2005).

[114] Kaldor, 'Speculation and Economic Stability'.

to guarantee supply of commodities that they require for their operations. The convenience yield drives up the futures price as contracts near their expiration.

The combination of the insurance premium and the convenience yield is the *roll return*. The interaction between hedgers and insurance providers or speculators depresses the price of long-maturity futures contracts. As the futures contracts near expiration their price may be bid up by manufacturers seeking to guarantee commodity supply. When the futures contracts near expiration, investors close out the futures positions since they normally roll them to the next set of contracts, avoiding delivery of the underlying commodities and staying invested. This means that investors buy low and then sell high when the futures contracts are rolled over. Over reasonably long time periods roll returns may be a major driver of commodity total returns.[115]

Roll return can, however, be negative. For commodities with seasonal price movement, for example, the current spot price can be higher than the expected futures price. For futures contracts with long maturities the insurance providers or speculators will demand a higher insurance premium because of the higher risk or expected volatility of the commodity price. As the insurance premium increases the price discount relative to the expected futures spot price is higher. Therefore, futures with longer maturities trade at a discount relative to futures with shorter maturities, resulting in a downward sloping term structure of futures contracts. When the futures term structure is downward sloping (contango), the roll return is negative.

4. *Diversification and rebalancing return.* Diversification return is the difference between a portfolio's geometric return and the weighted average of the geometric returns of the portfolio's components.[116] The reason for this difference is the benefits of diversification. Higher return volatility means a higher difference between the arithmetic and geometric return (geometric return equals approximately the arithmetic return minus half the variance). This is called variance drain.

    A well-diversified portfolio has lower standard deviation than the sum of its parts (when they are not perfectly correlated) and the variance drain is lower. Combining individual commodities in a portfolio has material diversification benefits because of the relatively low correlation among individual commodities (in particular when compared to the relatively high correlation among individual investments in other asset classes such as equities).

    Rebalancing a portfolio is a contrarian strategy of selling the winners and buying the losers. Rebalancing helps maintain the diversification of the

---

[115] Erb, Claude and Campbell, Harvey, 'The Tactical and Strategic Value of Commodity Futures', *Financial Analysts Journal* 62 (2006).
[116] Booth, David and Fama, Eugene, 'Diversification Returns and Asset Contributions', *Financial Analysts Journal* (1992).

portfolio over time and hence reduces its volatility. Without rebalancing, the drift from initial weights due to the disparity of returns among winners and losers increases, resulting in more concentrated, less diversified portfolios. The frequency of rebalancing has a material impact since too frequent rebalancing incurs transaction costs and too infrequent rebalancing can potentially lead to an increase in volatility. Empirically, annual rebalancing of a portfolio of commodity futures has increased returns while monthly rebalancing has decreased returns.[117]

5. *Expectational variance.* The final factor in Greer's commodity futures pricing model is expectational variance. The unobservable expected future spot price of a futures contract is unlikely to match the actual future spot price. It may be too high or too low. The expected future spot price includes an element of implicit commodity specific inflation forecast. Unexpected inflation, commodity related shocks and supply and demand forces affect the realised future spot price. Significant supply disruptions are more likely than supply abundance (e.g. droughts are more likely than surprisingly high harvests). Hence, the expectational variance tends to be positive.

Estimating commodity futures expected returns

Probably the most robust methodology for estimating the long-term expected returns of commodity futures is the building block approach. Other possible approaches are using CAPM and the Black-Litterman model. The shortcomings of these methods are the difficulty of measuring the beta of commodities with respect of the market portfolio (for CAPM) and the unknown market capitalisation of commodity futures (for Black-Litterman).

Futures contracts have zero market capitalisation as the long and short positions cancel each other out. Commodities do not have an equivalent of market capitalisation as do equities. Commodities are held in a variety of ways such as long futures positions, over-the-counter derivatives, purchasing contracts, physical inventory stored with the producer and so on. Complete accounting of capital dedicated to holding commodities is hence not feasible. These weaknesses leave the building block approach as the most viable method.

The expected long-term total return of a fully collateralised, well-diversified basket of commodity futures contracts, E(r), can be broken into three building blocks: spot return, roll return and collateral return, like so:

E(r) = Spot + Roll + Collateral

---

[117] Gorton, Gary and Rouwenhorst, Geert, 'Facts and Fantasies about Commodity Futures', *Financial Analysts Journal* 62 (2006).

The expected long-term *spot return* depends on the expected increasing demand for commodities from industrialising nations (e.g. China) and the inelasticity of supply. However, the expected price increases may not be evenly distributed across the entire commodity universe (e.g. crude oil, gold and wheat prices may behave differently) and high prices of commodities may slow down economic growth and further commodity price increases.

Another argument supporting continued increase in commodity prices is inflation. Many policy makers around the world are using monetary (both conventional and unconventional) and fiscal measures to support the global de-leveraging and their economies after the fallout of the 2008 crisis. When central banks reflate asset prices through accommodative monetary policy or quantitative easing (i.e. purchasing bonds and effectively printing money), inflationary pressures are created and commodity prices are inflated.

An optimistic or utopian view is that technological advances may change the supply side of commodities. For example, advances in agriculture technology may increase supply and agriculture commodity prices may drop, thus reversing the long-term trend of the increasing global population and the increasing demand for food. On the opposite side, a pessimistic or dystopian view is that the world is going to enter a long period of stagflation with diminishing demand for commodities. Under this scenario commodity prices are going to decrease. However, with increasing industrialisation, depleting commodity reserves and an increasing global population, the more likely scenario is continued long-term upward pressure on commodity prices.

While it is difficult to predict the expected long-term spot price return of commodities, it is reasonable to assume that the spot price will keep pace with inflation. If the long-term annual inflation rate is assumed to be 2.5%, for instance, then this can be used as the expected spot return.

Another way to forecast the spot return is to assume that commodity prices mean revert. The demand for commodities is cyclical and follows the economic cycle. The demand increases and decreases with economic activity as more or less commodities are required for manufacturers. The demand by speculators and investors is also cyclical as their risk appetite fluctuates.

Cyclicality is also on the supply side. When demand is strong, commodity prices rise and production increases. High commodity prices support expensive production since it is profitable. An increase in production means increased supply. Oversupply, coupled perhaps with a slowing economy, reduces commodity prices. Producers that were profitable before close down since lower commodity prices mean expensive production is unprofitable.

So, the cyclicality of commodity prices is driven by both demand (the general economic cycle) and supply (the cycle of increasing and decreasing production). Investors can assume that commodity prices mean revert to a five-year historic average. However, they should identify any structural changes that can cause prices to diverge from the historic mean (e.g. disruptive technologies or discoveries of abundant supplies).

Expected *roll return* depends on the shape of the commodity yield curve (backwardation or contango). Historically, the annual premium to a strategy taking long positions in futures in backwardation and short positions in futures in contango was 2.5%[118] per annum. This is a crude average long-term estimate and can be refined by considering the current shape of the yield curve rather than the long-term average.

The *collateral return* is relatively easy to estimate as it is the expected return of cash. Therefore, assuming a cash annual return of 0.5% in the current low interest rate environment, the expected total return of a fully collateralised, well-diversified basket of commodity futures is 2.5%+2.5%+0.5% = 5.5% per annum.

If cash return is 4% (arguably, a more 'normal' level), then the expected total return of commodities goes up to 9%. An expected return of 5.5% is close to that of bonds and 9% is close to that of equities. Clearly, the collateral return is an important factor in commodity futures' total return. In a high interest rate environment commodity expected returns are therefore higher and conversely in a low interest rate environment commodity expected returns are lower, all else being equal.

In addition, short-term interest rates are normally increasing when inflation is high and decreasing when it is low. Inflation, another factor in the return of commodities as part of the spot return, therefore may compound the effect of short-term interest rates on the returns of commodities. Strong economic growth normally goes with high inflation and positively affects the spot price of commodities. Weak economic growth has an opposite effect. All these factors cause commodity prices to behave cyclically as part of the economic cycle.

Alternatively, the three building blocks of commodities can be defined as cash return (collateral return), inflation (spot return) and a *commodity risk premium*. The commodity risk premium is unspecified and can be explained by the factors from Greer's commodity pricing model. Some attribute the premium mainly to diversification and rebalancing,[119] and others[120] attribute it mainly to the insurance premium from the backwardation theory of Keynes (roll return). The premium may be a combination of a few factors. If investors believe that history is a good guide to the future, an estimate for the premium can be extracted from historic experience (i.e. comparing commodity index total returns with T-Bills total returns) and added to the expected cash return and the inflation rate.

---

[118] Meketa Investment Group, 'Commodities: Strategic Allocation'.
[119] Erb, 'The Tactical and Strategic Value of Commodity Futures'.
[120] Gorton, 'Facts and Fantasies about Commodity Futures'.

An alternative methodology for estimating expected returns for commodities still focuses on the three building blocks (spot, roll and collateral), but uses a different way to calculate the expected returns. Under this methodology the broad commodity index is broken down into its separate commodity sectors. The Dow Jones-UBS Commodity Index, for example, currently consists of 22 commodity sectors as detailed in Table 3.5.[121] The weights within the index are published annually.

Figure 3.5: Dow Jones-UBS Commodity Index 2014 weights

Commodity	Weight
Natural Gas	9.4%
WTI Crude Oil	8.5%
Brent Crude Oil	6.5%
Unleaded Gasoline	3.6%
Heating Oil	3.7%
Live Cattle	3.3%
Lean Hogs	1.9%
Wheat	3.3%
HRW Wheat	1.2%
Corn	7.2%
Soybeans	5.7%
Soybean Oil	2.8%
Soybean Meal	2.7%
Aluminium	4.7%
Copper	7.5%
Zinc	2.3%
Nickel	2.1%
Gold	11.5%
Silver	4.1%
Sugar	4.0%
Cotton	1.6%
Coffee	2.3%

Source: DJ-UBS Commodity Index.[122]

---

[121] Out of a total of 23 eligible commodities.
[122] www.djindexes.com.

The expected total return of a long, fully collateralised futures position for each sector is estimated. Each expected total return is made of the three building blocks. Expected spot return is estimated using an econometric model to estimate the relationship between commodity prices and the economic factors with the strongest statistical link to commodity prices (e.g. inflation, term spread and GDP growth rate). The expected roll return is estimated based on historical relationships between realised roll yield and the roll yield implied by the current shape of the futures curve. The expected collateral return is the expected return of cash. The total commodity index expected return is calculated as the weighted average of the individual commodity sector expected returns.

Commodity management styles

Since commodity-investing is different to equity or bond investing, different methods are required to manage commodity portfolios. There are three main ways to manage commodity vehicles: passive indexing, systematic or enhanced indexing, and discretionary or active strategies:

1. *Passive indexing.* Passive investment in commodity futures indices is a well-established strategy although it has disadvantages. It does not maximise roll returns as it systematically buys the next available contracts, without considering the shape of the futures curve, instead of buying futures with shorter or longer maturities depending on the return from rolling them with a view to maximising the roll return. In some cases it can entail high exposure to some commodity sectors (e.g. the S&P Goldman Sachs Commodity Index has a high exposure to energy and it can result in higher volatility than a more balanced commodity index). The choice of index which the passive strategy tracks is important because commodity indices are often based on subjective factors to establish the index composition and its weights to different commodity sectors.

2. *Systematic or enhanced indexing.* These investments address some of the shortcomings of passive investments by applying rule-based strategies (i.e. revision to mean, roll maximisation and capturing seasonality) without applying subjective, discretionary views on different commodity sectors.

3. *Discretionary or active strategies.* Active strategies aim to outperform their benchmark by applying the portfolio manager's discretion and views on different commodity sectors based on economic models of supply and demand, and accessing less liquid commodity markets (such as coal futures). Active managers who have the flexibility to go long and short futures can enhance performance through profiting from negative views on commodity sectors and commodities in general, as well as from relative value positions and roll opportunities. Long/short managers, however, have a focus on alpha

and their performance is less correlated with inflation and the general commodity market. In other words, they have a lower beta with respect to the commodity risk factor or risk premium. These strategies, therefore, may play a role of alpha generation, rather than a role of accessing commodities as an asset class in portfolios. Their place within portfolios is under the absolute return bucket, rather than under the commodity bucket.[123]

There are three main active strategies to manage commodity futures, each aiming to exploit one of the three sources of commodity futures returns: price return strategies, roll return strategies and collateral return.

1. *Price return strategies.* There are several strategies under this category.

   - *Trend-following or momentum strategies* attempt to exploit the persistence of supply or storage shocks in particular commodities. There is evidence that trend-following strategies can add value given the unique nature of the commodity market.[124]

   - *Fundamental strategies* attempt to forecast commodity price movements, usually by aiming to construct supply and demand curves.

   - *Spread strategies* attempt to exploit mispricing between two substitute commodity curves (e.g. crude oil and natural gas).

   - *Mean reversion strategies* attempt to benefit from the mean reversion in commodity prices (i.e. overweight commodities whose price has dropped and overweight commodities whose price has appreciated). The risk with this strategy is that due to changes in supply or demand the price may not revert back to the mean (e.g. development and production of shale gas in the United States pushing the prices of natural gas downward).

All the strategies can be implemented using long and short futures positions. The strategies can include off-benchmark positions in less liquid commodity futures that are excluded from the benchmark (e.g. coal, lumber).

2. *Roll return strategies.* Roll returns are an important component of the total return of commodity futures strategies. One traditional way to outperform a commodity index is by rolling futures positions forward more cheaply outside the index period. A more sophisticated approach takes advantage of seasonality, which is present in several commodity markets, or systematically exploits the shape of the futures curves in order to maximise roll gains in backwardation or minimise carry charges in contango. Other strategies look at the shape of futures curves across commodities and go long those with largest roll gains and short those with the largest carry charges.

---

[123] Commodity Trading Advisors (CTAs) are covered under the section of managed futures later in the book.

[124] Schneeweis, Thomas, Kazemi, Hossein and Spurgin, Richard, 'Momentum in Asset Returns: Are Commodity Returns a Special Case?', *The Journal of Alternative Investments* 10 (2008).

The rolling approach of traditional commodity futures indices, such as the Dow Jones-UBS Commodity Index, is rolling futures to the nearby contract. This results in losses when the curve is in contango and drags down the total return even when price return is positive. Enhanced indexing strategies pursue superior roll strategies, such as simply more frequent rolling when the curve is in backwardation and more infrequent rolling when the curve is in contango.

3. *Collateral return.* A fully collateralised investment in a commodity index is not needed to gain access to underlying futures exposures because futures are purchased on margin. Opportunities to outperform commodity indices can be exploited by allocating cash not required to maintain underlying exposure to fixed income strategies designed to outperform cash returns. However, this would imply leverage as capital would be employed twice (i.e. the long futures positions are not fully covered by cash).

The unique return determinants of commodity futures and the features of commodity indices allow active and enhanced indexing strategies to add value and beat the commodity benchmarks. Therefore, this asset class offers opportunities for active management styles to add alpha.

However, the discretionary or active style heavily depends on the skill of the manager. As with other asset classes, predicting future specific commodity price changes requires talent, foresight and intuition, the result of which is that not many managers can consistently add value.

Commodity indices

The typical commodity indices are based on commodity futures contracts. There are three important differences between commodity indices and equity or bond indices:

1. *Collateral.* Commodity indices use futures in their construction and long futures positions require collateral. The major commodity indices assume that futures positions are fully collateralised using 3-month US Treasury bills (i.e. for every notional dollar invested in futures an actual dollar is invested in Treasury bills).

2. *Weighting.* Stock and bond indices are typically weighted by market capitalisation (some indices are price weighted). There is no accepted way to weight the exposure to commodities in the index. This is because all long futures positions are by definition offset by corresponding short positions. This implies that the market capitalisation of commodity futures is always zero. Different index providers use different ways to decide on the composition of the index, including equal weighting, worldwide production weighting or contract liquidity weighting.

3   *Futures roll methodology*. Commodity futures indices require a methodology to roll forward expiring futures contracts. Most indices roll forward expiring contracts to the next set of corresponding nearby contracts. For instance, at the beginning of November 2013 open positions in crude oil futures contracts for December 2013 delivery are rolled into contracts for January 2014 delivery (the next set of nearby contracts).

These differences between commodity indices and equity or bond indices mean that passive trackers of commodity indices do not track the performance of the commodities' spot price but rather the performance of commodity futures contracts.

The most commonly used commodity futures indices are the S&P Goldman Sachs Commodity Index (GSCI), the GSCI Energy Light and the Dow Jones-UBS Commodity Index (DJ-UBS).

GSCI has a high exposure to energy and therefore is more volatile than DJ-UBS (GSCI Energy Light addresses this by limiting the exposure to energy). In DJ-UBS the exposure to any sector (related group of commodities) is limited to 33%, including energy. DJ-UBS is less volatile and has a more balanced exposure to different commodity sectors relative to GSCI. Energy, however, tends to have high correlation with inflation and therefore GSCI may be a better hedge of inflation than DJ-UBS.

Commonly, three versions of commodity indices are published: excess return, total return and spot. The *excess return* index measures the returns accrued from investing in uncollateralised nearby commodity futures. Excess return does not include collateral return. The *total return* index measures the returns accrued from investing in fully collateralised nearby commodity futures. The spot index measures the level of nearby commodity prices.

The reasons for investing in commodities

There are a few arguments supporting the inclusion of commodities in portfolios.

- *Exposure to commodity systematic risk*. Investing in commodities exposes portfolios to commodity systematic risk or the commodity risk premium. Commodity systematic risk is a source of return. Unlike many other alternative investments (e.g. private equity and hedge funds), commodities do not require active management or manager skill to generate returns to justify inclusion in portfolios. While real estate also exposes a portfolio to a unique real estate risk factor, direct real estate does require active management and cannot be accessed passively as can commodities.

- *Diversification*. Commodities behave differently than other investments and commodity prices should benefit from situations that adversely affect other assets. Commodity prices are driven by supply and demand and in many cases *bad news* is good news for investors in commodities. Here are some examples:

- A drought that destroys wheat or cocoa bean production increases the prices of these commodities due to a squeeze on supply. A drought would normally have an opposite, negative effect on the economy and equity markets. Generally, disasters are good news for investors in commodities and bad news for the equity market.

- Higher inflation should increase the prices of commodities, while negatively affecting equities and bonds.

- A war in the Middle East may send the equity markets down but oil prices up due to disruptions of oil supply. A disastrous hurricane in the Gulf of Mexico can have similar effects. Spikes in oil prices may have negative effects on the profitability of corporations due to increasing energy costs and a reduction in the spending power of the consumer due to decreasing disposable income, further pushing stock prices downward.

- Emerging market governments may decide to nationalise their natural resources. This may reduce available supply and have a positive effect on commodity prices.

- *Hedge against inflation.* Commodity prices increase with inflation and therefore provide a hedge against inflation.

- *Expansion of the investment opportunity set.* Commodities bring into the investment universe a set of real assets that are not accessible through other investments.

- *Opportunities for active management.* Active and enhanced indexing strategies in commodities can add value and beat passive commodity indices.

- *Seasonality.* Many commodity prices exhibit seasonal price fluctuations. For example, heating oil prices are higher on average during the winter months in the Northern hemisphere when demand for heating increases. Fuel prices increase during the summer driving season when Americans drive on their holidays. The strongest performance of gold is usually in the autumn, driven by increased jewellery demand for the wedding season in India. Seasonality is an important factor in commodity trading and investing. Active commodity strategies can switch positions based on seasonal effects.

- *Fat-tail hedging.* Including some commodity sectors in portfolios may be used to hedge fat tail risks. Going long oil or gas, for example, can hedge geopolitical risks, such as a war in the Middle East or tensions with Russia. Going long gold can hedge stress in financial markets as a flight to quality pushes gold price upwards.

Risks

Commodities are a risk asset. They exhibit relatively high volatility of returns and can suffer from material drawdowns. The main risks of investing in commodities include:

- *Disappointing returns.* Over long time periods commodity returns have underperformed those of equities and bonds. When interest rates are low (low collateral return), the commodity futures curve is in contango (negative roll return) and inflation is subdued (low price return), and the total return of commodities may be disappointing.

- *Long cycles and high volatility.* Commodity returns may be more volatile than those of certain equity markets. Commodity returns follow long-term cycles (*commodity super cycle*) and can come in sudden, infrequent bursts after years of stagnant performance.

- *Bubbles and speculation.* Some commodities may experience bubble prices with their prices being driven by speculators. The price of oil reached an all-time peak in July 2008, surpassing $140 a barrel.[125] It subsequently fell by almost 40%. While the oil reserves in the world are depleting, the rise in oil during 2008 is explained by financial speculation, rather than true demand and supply. The price of gold reached $1,900 per ounce in May 2011. This was a rise of nearly 120% since the beginning of 2009. Even with increasing demand for gold from countries such as China and India, forces of demand do not explain this rise, but rather the explanation is a flight to gold by investors when conviction in other assets has diminished. More and more investors in commodities are speculators who seek a profit, rather than investors who need commodities for industrial use or productive consumption.

- *Roll risk.* Contango in the futures market can result in negative roll returns. Contango markets generate negative returns when investors buy futures at a premium to the expected spot price. Should long-only passive investors flood the market, futures prices may trade at a greater premium to the expected spot price and further diminish the opportunity to earn positive roll returns.

- *Technological innovation.* Technological innovations that increase the supply or decrease the demand for commodities may have an unexpected negative impact on commodity prices. If an alchemist finally discovers a way to transform industrial metal into gold, the price of gold will plunge. If cold fusion is invented and the need to continue consuming environmentally polluting fossil fuels finally ends, the price of oil will plunge, together with the equity markets of oil exporting countries. This is another example of the potential diversification and the contrarian nature of commodities.

---

[125] The oil price peaked at $147.30 per barrel in July 2008.

Technological innovation may be good news for equity markets, but bad news for commodities. Shale gas in the United States is a recent example of the technological impact on commodity prices. Led by the application of hydraulic fracturing technology and horizontal drilling, development of new sources of shale gas have offset declines in production from conventional gas reservoirs. The price of natural gas has consequently dropped, leading to losses for investors in gas. In this case good news for society means bad news for commodity investors. Another long-term trend with a potential impact for commodity prices is the melting of Arctic ice. The retreat of ice exposes new deposits of oil, gas, minerals and metals. This trend may push supply upward and prices downward for some commodities.

- *Disappointment in global demand.* Decreasing demand by consumers and countries due to sluggish economies, or finding alternatives to commodities, may have a negative impact on the prices of commodities. A material slowdown in China (hard landing), for example, can have a material negative impact on commodity prices due to a potential drop in demand.

- *Increased correlation with equities.* A slump in global demand due to an economic slowdown is bad news for both equities and commodities. In such instances the correlation between equities and commodities may increase and commodities will lose some of their diversification benefits. This is the time that diversification is needed the most and may fail.

- *Manager or strategy risk.* While there are ways to outperform a commodity index, systematic or active strategies may underperform. For example, strategies that were based on mean reversion suffered underperformance when the price of oil did not mean revert due to the development of shale gas. Like in any other asset, manager selection is critical. Since commodities require specific understanding of the asset class, manager due diligence requires specialisation.

Cornering the market

Cornering the market means that enough of a commodity is bought to enable the buyer to manipulate its price. Investors can buy a large number of futures contracts on a commodity and then sell them at a profit after inflating the price. Futures can be purchased on margin so the cornering effectively makes use of the leverage embedded in futures contracts.

In the 1970s and early 1980s the brothers Nelson and William Hunt attempted to corner the world's silver markets. They were holding at some stage the rights to more than half of the world's deliverable silver. During the cornering the price of silver rose from $11 an ounce in September 1979 to nearly $50 an ounce in January 1980. The silver price collapsed to below $11 an ounce two months later, mostly during a single day, known as *Silver Thursday*, due to changes in exchange rules regarding the purchase of commodities on margin. William Hunt lost a fortune, filed for bankruptcy and faced a series of lawsuits related to the cornering.

Socially responsible investing (SRI) and commodities

Socially responsible investing (SRI), also known as sustainable, socially conscious or ethical investing, is any investment strategy that considers both financial return and social good. In general, socially responsible investors encourage corporate practices that promote environmental stewardship, consumer protection, human rights and diversity. Some avoid businesses involved in defence, alcohol, tobacco, gambling and pornography; the latter four commonly referred to as 'vice'. The areas of concern recognised by the SRI industry can be summarised as environment, social justice and corporate governance (environmental social governance or ESG) issues. In addition to stock ownership either directly or through funds, other key aspects of SRI include shareholder advocacy and community investing.

The clash between commodity investments and SRI is due to the affects that commodity investing has on commodity prices. For example, agriculture commodities (e.g. wheat, rice) are used as a staple food source and as a source for employment for people in developing countries (e.g. coffee plantations in Africa). Pushing food prices up because of massive investments in commodities for financial gain may cause food prices to rise, increase stress on underprivileged populations and even starvation in some countries. Shorting commodities used as an employment source and pushing their prices downward may have an adverse impact on income for producers.

Another example is the impact of commodities on the environment. Artificially increasing the price of oil because of commodity investing may lead to increasing production of oil and other energy sources. This may lead to a negative impact on the environment and perhaps contribute to global warming. High prices of fossil energy sources lead to higher demand for nuclear energy. Nuclear energy may lead to another range of disasters, such as the Chernobyl disaster in Ukraine in 1986 and the Fukushima Daiichi disaster in Japan in 2011. A positive side of high energy prices is the push to develop sustainable, renewable or green energy sources, such as solar, wind and hydro energy.

Commodities are not financial assets, such as equities and bonds. They are necessary goods widely used across society and their price has a direct impact on everyone. Financial speculation on commodity prices may have a real impact on people's lives and therefore investing in commodities should be done responsibly.

Individual commodity assets

I will now discuss two of the principal commodity assets – gold and oil – looking at their background, investment benefits, risks and historical performance. While many commodities are important and deserve special attention, the focus here on gold and oil is because often investors choose to invest in them as separate asset classes, not necessarily as part of a broader investment in commodities.

Gold

Since the dawn of civilisation gold has been one of the most sought-after commodities. It has been commonly used as a medium of exchange, store of value, legal tender and unit of account. After World War II, gold was replaced as legal tender by a system of convertible currencies following the Bretton Woods system. Gold standards and the direct convertibility of currencies to gold were then abandoned by world governments when, on 15 August 1971, the United States unilaterally terminated convertibility of the US dollar to gold and it was replaced by *fiat currency* (which derives its value from government regulation or law, rather than from its intrinsic value, like gold). Switzerland was the last country to tie its currency to gold; gold backed 40% of the franc's value until the Swiss joined the International Monetary Fund (IMF) in 1999.

Besides its widespread monetary and symbolic functions, gold has many practical uses in dentistry, electronics and other fields. Its high malleability, ductility, resistance to corrosion and most other chemical reactions, and conductivity of electricity, lead to many uses for gold, including electric wiring, coloured-glass production and even edible gold leaf.

Gold does not pay dividends or income and therefore it is difficult to value. Commonly, valuation of financial assets is based on discounting expected future cash flows. However, without cash flows valuation lacks a basis.

One metric that can explain the majority of changes in gold prices is changes in real yields. Gold has no default risk and its price is linked with inflation over the long term. Investors compare the gold price with the level of 'risk-free' real yields, such as those of US Treasury Inflation-Protected Securities (TIPS). When the real yield is high (low), investors will demand a lower (higher) price of gold to increase (decrease) its potential long-term returns.

Figure 3.12 shows the price of gold and the real yield on 10-year TIPS (on an inverted scale). The chart clearly shows the inverse relationship between real gold price and real yield.

Figure 3.12: Gold price and real yield, January 2006 to December 2013

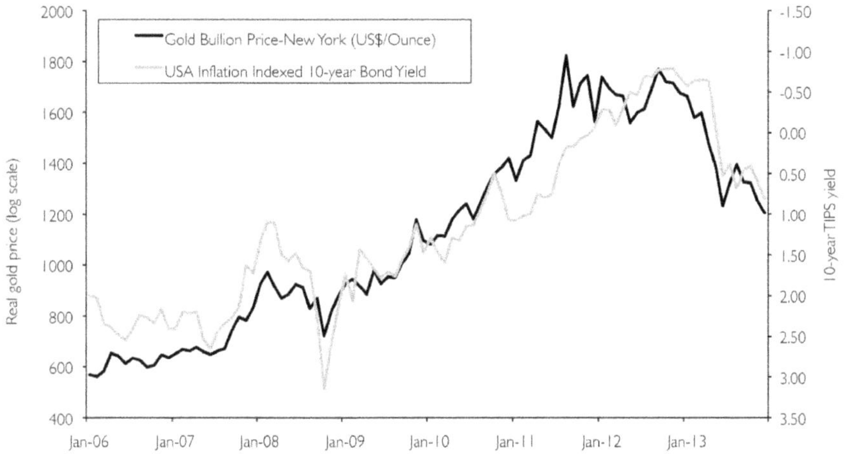

Source: Global Financial Data, Gold Bullion Price New York, US Bureau of Labor Statistics, US CPI-U.

The gold price should be driven by supply and demand. However, at times of financial stress gold is considered to be one of the safe-haven assets and its price may rally during flights to quality. The gold price tends to have a negative correlation with the US dollar and a positive correlation with inflation.

Access

Gold can be accessed in a variety of forms, including:

- physical gold coins, medals, jewellery, works of art, gold bars and bullion

- shares of gold mining companies

- exchange traded funds (ETFs)

- derivatives on gold (e.g. futures and options)

- gold trust receipts, structured notes and gold-backed bonds

Similar to other commodities, equities of companies in the gold industry include exposure to the commercial fortunes of the companies and the equity market. Physical gold gives exposure to the spot price of gold. Futures contracts on gold are a subset of the wider commodity futures universe.

The reasons for investing in gold

The main reasons for investing in gold are:

- *Purchasing power*. Historically, the price of gold has kept pace with inflation.

- *Intrinsic value*. While difficult to evaluate or determine its intrinsic value, gold has been a valuable commodity for centuries. Gold is a store of value.

- *Diversification*. Gold has exhibited a low correlation with other asset classes and therefore brings diversification benefits to portfolios.

- *Protection*. Gold tends to perform well during stressful times. As one of the safe-haven investments, during flights to quality investors rush to buy gold and this pushes its price upward when most needed (i.e. when most other investments fall).

- *Convenience benefits*. Gold is precious because of its industrial functions and emotional functions. Owning gold brings commercial benefits and satisfaction.

- *Physical form*. Gold is relatively easily stored and can be transferred in a physical form. It can be used as a means of physically storing wealth outside of the financial or banking system. In other words, in a similar way as with diamonds, gold can be used as a substitute for using cash.

Risks

Even investing in precious gold involves risks:

- *Volatility*. Gold can be a volatile investment. The gold bullion price has an annualised volatility of 20%, with significant drawdowns as large as 65% since 1970.

- *Storage*. Physical gold needs to be safely stored and insured.

- *Unknown fair-value*. Due to the lack of cash flows or income the fair-value of gold is unknown.

- *Lukewarm performance*. During long periods of economic stability gold prices may be range-bound and move sideways.

Gold return and risk characteristics

Figure 3.13 shows the price of gold ($/ounce) since January 1970 and the dramatic increase in its price since the early 2000s (as well as its fall since its peak).

Figure 3.13: Gold price $/ounce, January 1970 to December 2013

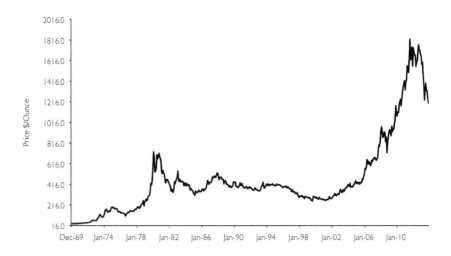

Source: Global Financial Data, Gold Bullion Price New York.

Figure 3.14 shows the rolling 36-month annualised volatility of the gold spot price. The chart shows that gold can be a volatile investment.

Figure 3.14: Rolling 36-month volatility of gold price $/ounce, January 1973 to December 2013

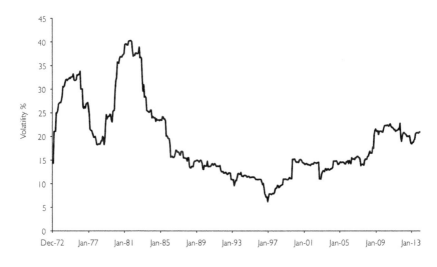

Source: Global Financial Data, Gold Bullion Price New York.

Figure 3.15 shows the rolling correlation of the gold spot price with US equities. As can be seen, gold has prolonged periods of negative correlation with equities. Within a portfolio context, investments that have a negative correlation with equities usually add the highest diversification benefits since most portfolios have a high exposure to equities in terms of weight (allocation) and risk exposure.

The correlation between gold and equities turns most negative at times of stress as gold is considered a safe-haven asset and investors rush to the safe hands of gold when equities and other assets crash.

Figure 3.15: Rolling 36-month correlation of the gold price $/ounce and US equities, January 1973 to December 2013

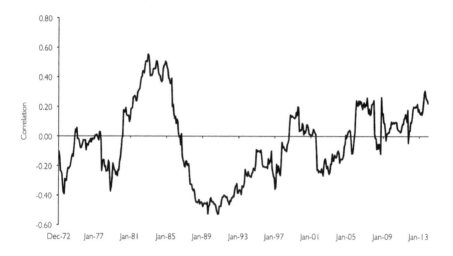

Source: Global Financial Data, Gold Bullion Price New York, S&P 500 Index.

Figure 3.16 shows the rolling correlation of gold with the US dollar. Normally, the correlation between gold and the dollar is negative. As the dollar weakens, the price of gold tends to increase since gold is denominated in dollars but widely used in global markets and by central banks of foreign countries. The negative correlation tends to break at times of crisis because both gold and the dollar are safe assets and at times of flight to safety the price of both is bid up by investors.

Figure 3.16: Rolling 36-month correlation of the gold price $/ounce and $, January 1976 to December 2013

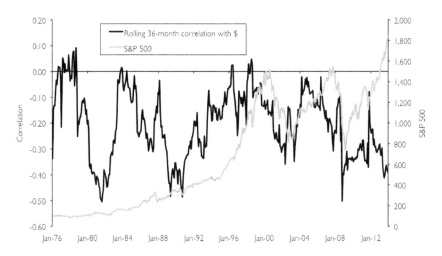

Source: Bloomberg, Global Financial Data, Gold Bullion Price New York, US Trade Weighted Broad Dollar January 1997=100, S&P 500.

Crude oil

Crude oil or petroleum (also known as black gold) is one of the most important commodities. It fuels the economy, as it satisfies 90% of vehicular fuel needs and makes up 40% of total energy consumption in the United States. Increases in oil prices can weigh on the entire global economy and sudden shocks in oil prices can cause an economic recession, as occurred in the 1970s.

The top three oil producing countries are Saudi Arabia, Russia and the United States. About 80% of the world's readily accessible reserves are located in the Middle East, with over 60% coming from the five Arab countries: Saudi Arabia, UAE, Iraq, Qatar and Kuwait. A large portion of the world's total oil exists as unconventional sources, such as bitumen in Canada and oil shale in Venezuela. While significant volumes of oil are extracted from oil sands, particularly in Canada, logistical and technical hurdles remain, as oil extraction requires large amounts of heat and water, making its net energy content quite low relative to conventional crude oil. Thus, Canada's oil sands are not expected to provide more than a few million barrels per day in the foreseeable future.

To put this in context, conventional crude oil production is around 89 million barrels per day (as of 2014). The World Energy Outlook 2013 of the International Energy Agency (IEA)[126] estimated that conventional crude oil production will increase by less than 1% per year until 2040.

---

[126] www.iea.org.

The World Energy Outlook 2012 of the IEA focuses on the emergence of a new global energy market landscape. The resurgence in oil and gas production in the United States, driven by upstream technologies that are unlocking light, tight oil and shale gas resources, have steadily changed the role of North America in global energy trade. The IEA expects that by around 2020 the United States is to become the largest global oil producer and North America is expected to become a net oil exporter by around 2030. This is a dramatic reversal of the current situation in which the United States imports around 20% of its total energy needs. Consequently, Asia is expected to become the main oil importer from the Middle East. Not only will these changes impact the global energy market, but they will also likely have geopolitical consequences as the United States may lose some of its interest in the Middle East and its politics.

The global energy market could be further reshaped by a retreat from nuclear power in some countries, continued rapid growth in the use of wind and solar technologies, and by the global spread of unconventional gas production. Taking all new developments and policies into account, however, the world is still failing to put the global energy system on to a more sustainable path.

The IEA forecast under its central scenario that global energy demand will grow by more than one-third over the period to 2035, with China, India and the Middle East accounting for 60% of the increase. Energy demand barely rises in OECD countries, although there is a pronounced shift away from oil, coal (and, in some countries, nuclear) towards natural gas and renewables.

Despite the growth in low carbon sources of energy, fossil fuels remain dominant in the global energy mix. Oil is expected to continue to fuel the global economy for years to come.

Access

Investing in crude oil can be done through:

- futures (e.g. futures on Light Sweet Crude Oil or Brent Crude)

- stocks of exploration, pipeline and refining companies[127]

- exchange traded funds (ETFs). ETFs are available on crude oil futures or stocks of companies in the oil industry. ETFs that track futures may have different strategies for addressing futures rolls and should be carefully researched before investing. As always with commodities, investing in oil-related equities is equity investing, not pure exposure to oil.

---

[127] For example: Exxon Mobil, British Petroleum, Chevron, ConocoPhilips, Royal Dutch Shell, Transocean, Anadarko Petroleum, Petrochina, Petroleo Brasilerio, Halliburton, Apache.

Oil return and risk characteristics

Figure 3.17 shows the price of oil ($/barrel) since January 1970 and the dramatic fluctuations in its price since the early 2000s. The oil price is sensitive to geopolitical events, in particular wars in the Middle East. The 1973 Yom Kippur War, the 1979 Iranian revolution and the 1990 Iraqi invasion of Kuwait are all examples of oil price shocks linked to events in the Middle East.

The energy crisis of the 2000s, however, was mostly caused by other factors. Commentators attributed the oil price increases during the 2000s to many factors, including those related to supply and demand of oil, such as reports from the United States Department of Energy and others showing a decline in petroleum reserves, worries over *peak oil*,[128] Middle East tensions, and factors related to financial markets, such as the depreciation of the US dollar and oil price speculation. The global energy market has changed over the last decade and is expected to further change over the next couple of decades.

Figure 3.17: Oil price $/barrel, January 1970 to December 2013

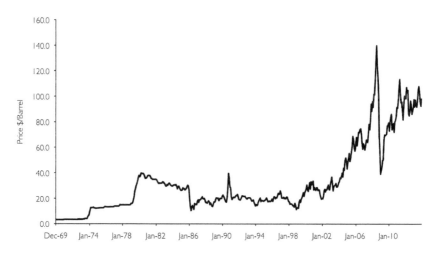

Source: Global Financial Data, West Texas Intermediate Oil Price.

Commodity prices and the US dollar

Commodities typically have a negative correlation with the US dollar. When the dollar strengthens (weakens) against other major currencies, the prices of commodities typically depreciate (appreciate).

---

[128] Peak oil is the point in time when the maximum rate of petroleum extraction is reached, after which the rate of production is expected to enter terminal decline.

One reason for this relationship is that commodities are priced in dollars. When the value of the dollar drops, it takes more dollars to buy commodities. This is not a casual reason for the relationship, but rather explains why the number of dollars per commodity increases when the dollar depreciates. Another reason is that commodities are traded around the world. Buyers outside of the United States purchase US commodities (corn, soybeans, wheat, oil) with dollars. When the value of the dollar drops, they have more buying power and demand typically increases as prices drop when measured in the foreign currency. For example, for a UK-based investor the price of US-produced commodities drops when the pound appreciates versus the dollar, since they are priced in dollars.

Figure 3.18 shows the rolling correlation between commodities and the dollar. Since the correlation tends to be negative most of the time, multi-asset portfolios with high exposure to the US dollar and currencies correlated with the dollar can benefit from diversification into commodities.

Figure 3.18: Rolling 36-month correlation of commodities and $, January 1994 to December 2013

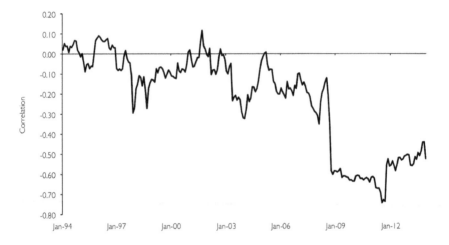

Source: Bloomberg, DJ-UBS Commodity Index, US Trade Weighted Broad Dollar January 1997=100, S&P 500.

Historic return and risk characteristics of commodities

Table 3.6 shows the performance and risk characteristics of commodities, gold, oil, US equities and Treasuries. Table 3.7 is a correlation matrix of the different indices.

The average annual return of commodities has been disappointing over the measuring period. With equity-like volatility, the risk-adjusted performance of commodities has been poor (the Sharpe ratio is actually negative for the DJ-UBS index). The return of gold and oil was better, but with equity-like volatility for gold and twice the volatility of equities for oil.

While the average return of commodities over this time period is low, there are times when commodities perform much better and, as indicated by the correlation matrix, commodities offer diversification benefits in a multi-asset portfolio.

Table 3.6: Commodities return and risk characteristics, February 1991 to December 2013. Sharpe ratio calculated using $ cash returns

	DJ-UBS Commodities	S&P GSCI	Gold	Oil	US equities	US Treasuries
Start month	Feb-1991	Feb-1991	Feb-1991	Feb-1991	Feb-1991	Feb-1991
Performance (% pa)	1.3	3.5	5.0	6.8	9.9	6.1
Volatility (%)	14.8	20.6	15.6	30.2	14.7	4.5
Skewness	-0.55	-0.39	0.23	-0.07	-0.65	-0.14
Kurtosis	2.65	1.98	1.22	1.72	1.31	1.08
Sharpe ratio	-0.12	0.02	0.13	0.12	0.47	0.70
Max drawdown (%)	-54.5	-67.6	-65.0	-72.0	-50.9	-5.3

Source: Bloomberg, Global Financial Data, DJ-UBS Commodity Index, S&P Goldman Sachs Commodity Index, Gold Bullion Price New York, West Texas Intermediate Oil Price, Citigroup United States WGBI TR Index, S&P 500 Index.

Table 3.7: Correlation matrix, February 1991 to December 2013

Correlation matrix	DJ-UBS Commodities	S&P GSCI	Gold	Oil	US equities	US Treasuries
DJ-UBS Commodities	1.00	0.89	0.43	0.71	0.30	-0.07
S&P GSCI	0.89	1.00	0.25	0.87	0.24	-0.07
Gold	0.43	0.25	1.00	0.18	-0.01	0.11
Oil	0.71	0.87	0.18	1.00	0.15	-0.14
US equities	0.30	0.24	-0.01	0.15	1.00	-0.13
US Treasuries	-0.07	-0.07	0.11	-0.14	-0.13	1.00

Source: Bloomberg, Global Financial Data, DJ-UBS Commodity Index, S&P Goldman Sachs Commodity Index, Gold Bullion Price New York, West Texas Intermediate Oil Price, Citigroup United States WGBI TR Index, S&P 500 Index.

Figure 3.19 shows the cumulative performance of the DJ-UBS Commodity Index and US equities since February 1991. Commodities can have long periods of attractive performance (e.g. 2002 to the middle of 2008), competitive to that of equities. However, commodities can also have long periods of disappointing returns (e.g. 1991 to 2001), as well as severe drawdowns (e.g. 2008).

Figure 3.19: Cumulative performance of commodities and US equities, February 1991 to December 2013

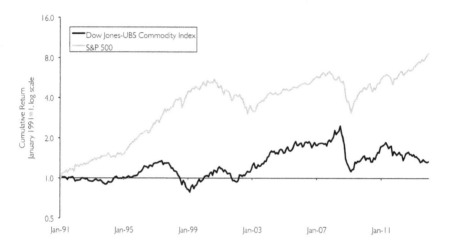

Source: Bloomberg, DJ-UBS Commodity Index, S&P 500 Index.

Figure 3.20 compares the performance of GSCI and DJ-UBS. While their performance is highly correlated, GSCI is more volatile than DJ-UBS due to the higher exposure to energy.

Figure 3.21 shows the rolling 36-month correlation of DJ-UBS with US equities and Treasuries. Until the 2008 global financial crisis, commodities were a diversifier to both equities and government bonds with a correlation hovering around 0.0 with both asset classes. After the crisis, the correlation between commodities and equities jumped, while it turned more negative with govis. Commodities did not provide diversification with equities when it was needed the most. The two main conclusions are that first commodities are a risk asset and second the characteristics of assets are dynamic.

Figure 3.20: Cumulative performance of two commodity indices, January 1970 to June 2012

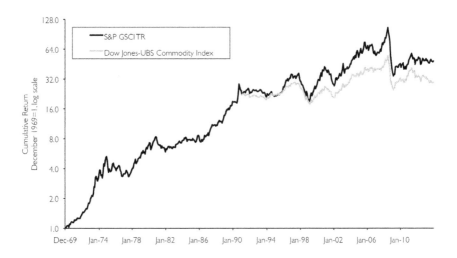

Source: Bloomberg, DJ-UBS Commodity Index, S&P Goldman Sachs Commodity Index.

Figure 3.21: Rolling 36-month correlation of commodities, US equities and Treasuries, January 1994 to December 2013

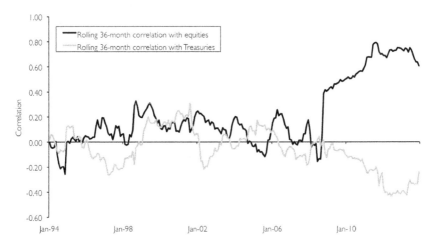

Source: Bloomberg, DJ-UBS Commodity Index, Citibank United States WGBI TR Index, S&P 500 Index.

Figure 3.22 shows the rolling 36-month volatility of DJ-UBS, GSCI and US equities. GSCI is the most volatile asset out of the three, due to the high exposure to energy. The volatility of DJ-UBS is broadly in line with that of equities, but has been higher since 2006.

Figure 3.22: Rolling 36-month volatility of commodities and US equities, January 1994 to December 2013

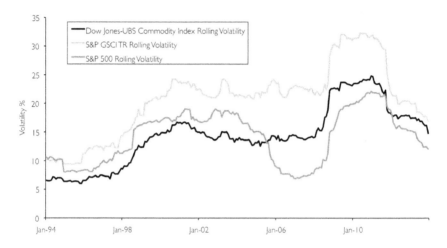

Source: Bloomberg, DJ-UBS Commodity Index, S&P Goldman Sachs Commodity Index, S&P 500 Index.

Figure 3.23 shows the average performance of DJ-UBS and GSCI ranked by average inflation deciles. The chart bears out the fact that commodities are positively correlated with inflation. When inflation is negative, commodities generate negative returns, on average.

Figure 3.24 shows the drawdown of DJ-UBS using nominal returns and real returns. While the returns of commodities are positively correlated with inflation, inflation reduces the value of the returns. Therefore, the inflation-adjusted returns are worse than the reported returns.

Figure 3.23: Average performance of commodities ranked by average inflation deciles, February 1991 to December 2013

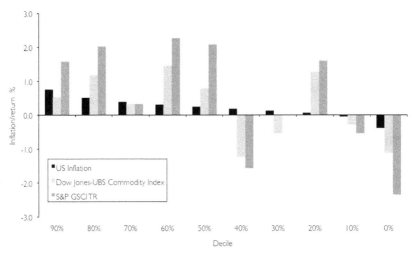

Source: Bloomberg, DJ-UBS Commodity Index, S&P Goldman Sachs Commodities Index, US Inflation.

Figure 3.24: Drawdowns of commodity nominal and real returns, January 1991 to December 2013

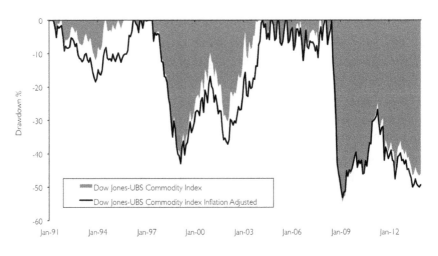

Source: Bloomberg, DJ-UBS Commodity Index, US Inflation.

Conclusions

The main advantage of commodities in a portfolio context is that they typically behave differently to other common investments in portfolios, such as equities and bonds. Commodities are liquid and they can be accessed easily and relatively cheaply, offering exposure to a commodity risk factor. While commodities are a risk asset, even a small allocation to commodities can improve the risk-adjusted performance of portfolios because of diversification benefits, as well as providing a long-term hedge against inflation.

Summary

- Commodities are basic resources and agricultural products lacking differentiation qualities – they are the same no matter who produces them.

- Commodities are part of the real asset classes (together with real estate, inflation-linked bonds and infrastructure).

- In many instances bad news for equities is good news for commodities (e.g. inflation, disasters and wars). This means commodities offer diversification benefits when held with other asset classes, since factors negatively affecting other investments may positively affect commodities.

- Commodity prices exhibit seasonality that drives demand patterns.

- The three ways to invest in commodities are direct physical investment, commodity-related equities, or commodity futures.

- The most common and practical way to gain access to commodities is through commodity futures (investing in physical commodities is impractical and equity-related commodities have significant equity exposure).

- Foreseeable trends in the spot markets are taken into account when futures prices are set so expected movements in the spot price are not a source of return to investors in futures.

- The total return of investing in futures is a risk premium plus unexpected deviation between realised future spot price and expected future spot price.

- Commodity futures have three sources of return: spot return, roll return and collateral return (i.e. interest on cash or bonds held as collateral).

- Spot return is the change in prices of underlying commodities.

- When the futures curve is in *contango* (the futures contract price is trading above the expected spot price at contract maturity) the roll return is negative and when the curve is in *backwardation* (the futures contract price is trading below the expected spot price) the roll return is positive.

- Collateral return is the return on the collateral posted to back the futures positions (e.g. Treasury Bills), which are assumed to be fully collateralised.

- The Greer commodity futures pricing model proposes that the return drivers of commodity futures are expected inflation, an insurance premium, a convenience yield, diversification/rebalancing return and expectational variance. Insurance premium plus convenience yield make up the roll return.

- The expected long-term total return of a fully collateralised, well-diversified basket of commodity futures contracts, E(r), can be broken into spot return, roll return and collateral return. E(r) = Spot + Roll + Collateral.

- The three strategies for commodity vehicles are passive index tracking, systematic enhanced indexing and discretionary active management.

- Active long/short commodity portfolios may aim to generate alpha and may lack exposure to commodity systematic risk or have a negative correlation with inflation. Their place in portfolios is under the absolute return bucket, rather than under commodities.

- The differences between commodity indices and equity or bond indices mean that a passive tracker of a commodity index will not track the performance of the spot price of commodities.

- The reasons for investing in commodities include: exposure to commodity systematic risk (i.e. commodity risk premium); diversification; hedge against inflation; expansion of the investment opportunity set; opportunities for active management; seasonality; and fat-tail hedging.

- The main risks of investing in commodities are: disappointing returns; long cycles and high volatility; bubble prices; contango; technological innovation; slump in global demand; increased correlation with equity markets; and manager or strategy risk.

- Cornering the market means that enough of a commodity is bought to enable its price to be manipulated.

- Socially responsible investing (SRI), also known as sustainable, socially conscious or ethical investing, is any investment strategy that considers both financial return and social good.

- Investing in commodities may have an adverse impact on society. Commodity investing requires responsibility.

- Gold is a safe-haven asset whose price often benefits from times of crisis. Due to generating no cash flows, gold is difficult to evaluate. However, changes in the 10-year real yield can explain the majority of changes in gold price.

- Oil is one of the most important commodities and shocks in oil prices can drag the global economy into a recession.

- Commodities tend to be negatively correlated with the US dollar.

CHAPTER 7: PRIVATE EQUITY

The term private equity indicates that it includes equities (as well as debt and convertible securities) that are not publicly traded on a stock exchange, or are issued by companies whose securities are not publicly traded; hence it is private. Private equity investments are primarily made by private equity firms, venture capital firms or angel investors,[129] providing finance capital to target companies.

Private equity boomed in the 1990s and early 2000s. Assets under management grew from under $100 billion in 1990 to over $600 billion in 2000 (riding the high-tech bubble), peaking above $2 trillion in 2007, just before the 2008 crisis. Venture capital was especially popular in the 1990s with the success stories of renowned investors, such as the endowment of Yale University, and the internet revolution of the late 1990s.

The burst of the high-tech bubble in 2000 was a setback for the venture capital industry as valuations of technology start-ups collapsed. While the private equity industry then struggled for two years, from 2003 it started to recover (as did public equities) and up to 2007 it enjoyed one of its best periods. The period from 2003 to 2007 is considered the Golden Age of private equity, ending with 2008's hard landing.

Private equity can be divided into two separate investment strategies: *venture capital* and *leveraged buyouts*. The asset class can be further classified across expansion or growth capital, distressed investments and mezzanine capital.

Venture capital

Venture capital (VC) is an equity investment, normally in young private companies, for the start-up, early development or expansion of their business. The VC industry fulfils an important role in the economy by financing companies at the beginning of their road and supporting entrepreneurship. Often, such young companies cannot get financing from banks since they lack tangible assets (commonly their only assets are intellectual property) and revenues to pledge as collateral for bank loans. These companies are usually not ready to tap the public equity market through a public offering for equity financing because they are not yet profitable or close to being so. Hence, VCs are their prominent financing route.

---

[129] An angel investor is a wealthy individual providing capital for a business start-up, usually in exchange for equity or convertible debt.

Venture capital is often associated with new technologies, services or products that are in development stages and have not yet been tested on the wider market. There is, therefore, a high risk in venture capital investing as the investee companies are immature and unproven. However, there is also a potential for high reward when investing in new technologies, services or products that are successful once introduced to the market. VC investing in a start-up is high risk with high potential reward. It resembles purchasing a call option on the company. If it fails the entire investment is lost. If it succeeds the rewards are high.

VC can be categorised by the development stage of the investee. *Early stage capital* is used to support start-up companies and *expansion capital* is used to finance the expansion of existing companies.

By financing companies at an early or expansion stage the VC can purchase a large equity stake in the company. Since the companies are typically not profitable yet, their valuation and share price are relatively modest. As the companies are not publicly traded, their share price is not quoted on a stock exchange and needs to be estimated through a valuation model. A VC needs the expertise of evaluating companies and identifying companies with the potential to succeed. The success of VCs is highly dependent on skill.

VCs need to overcome the *asymmetry of information* between them and the management of companies seeking financing. Typically, the management prepares a business plan with *pro forma* financial accounts based on their expectations for the business. Management aims to draw a rosy picture to attract investors and increase the company's valuation. Management may be too optimistic. The VCs need to objectively assess the company's potential in order to pick potential winners and avoid overpaying.

When investing in private equity the venture capitalist should have an *exit strategy* for each investment. The exit strategy can be a private placement of the holdings (acquisition by another investor) or Initial Public Offering (IPO) of the company's stocks, including the venture capitalist's holdings. Private equity investments are illiquid and cannot be sold on public markets. The only way for investors to cash in on the investments is to find a willing buyer on the private market or to sell the shares to the general public through an IPO.

VC firms normally hold a portfolio of companies in which they invest. Diversification is critical since most companies are unlikely to succeed and the venture capitalist will lose on these investments. Well-constructed portfolios mean that the success of a small number of investments is enough to make a profit on the overall portfolio.

VC is invested and exposed to the latest hot things. High exposure to technology in 2000, for example, resulted in high losses for many VC firms. Venture capital may therefore be exposed to bubbles and private equity investors must be cautious not to join the bandwagon just before a crash.

Expansion or growth capital

Growth capital is a private equity investment in relatively mature companies (as opposed to young companies for VC) seeking capital to expand or restructure their business, penetrate a new market or expand through an acquisition. Such companies are looking for the capital from minority private investors (as opposed to large stakeholders for VC) since they are not in a position to tap capital markets and they prefer an equity investor to taking debt, either due to instability of earnings or existing debt levels. Most expansion capital investments are in the form of equity (common stock or preferred stocks), but some investors use hybrid securities, such as convertible bonds, to combine ownership with interest payments.

Leveraged buyouts

The goal of leveraged buyout (*LBO*) funds is turning public firms into private companies, restructuring them, creating value and selling the investments at a profit. Typical LBO transactions involve a private equity firm purchasing a majority equity control of an existing company using leverage to finance the purchase.

The private equity firm partners with a sponsor, who acquires the majority equity holdings in a company, while using leverage to finance some of the capital needed for the acquisition. The company whose equity is acquired normally generates cash flows, which the acquirer can use to pay the interest and principal payments on the debt.

LBOs are often structured with no recourse to the sponsor's other assets and therefore fit the needs of private equity limited partners. LBO investors need only to provide some of the required capital and can benefit from enhanced returns due to leverage. The high levels of leverage also mean that the transaction has material leverage risk. The sponsor, once having a majority stake in the company, can initiate restructuring (such as replacing management, reducing costs, selling assets) with the objective of increasing the value of the company and selling it for a profit.

The most famous LBO is the $25 billion takeover of RJR Nabisco by private equity firm Kohlberg Kravis Roberts (KKR) in 1989. The deal was the subject of a subsequent book and an HBO television movie *Barbarians at the Gate*.[130] RJR Nabisco was an American conglomerate. In those days, many companies used LBOs to purchase undervalued companies only to turn them around and sell off the assets (these acquirers were known as corporate raiders). Today, however, LBOs are increasingly used as a way to turn mediocre companies into successful ones.

---

[130] Burrough, Bryan and Helyar, John, *Barbarians at the Gate: The Fall of RJR Nabisco* (Harper & Row, 1989).

Distressed investments

Distressed refers to investment in equity and/or debt securities of financially distressed companies. One common strategy is purchasing debt of a company with the objective of assuming control of its equity following a restructuring.

Another common strategy is investing in equity and debt (often at a large discount), therefore providing financing for the distressed company, with the objective of turning it around and benefiting from its success and consequent increase in its equity and debt prices.

Mezzanine capital

Mezzanine capital is subordinated debt or preferred equity that is senior only to common stock in the company's capital structure. In other words, mezzanine capital is junior to all other debt holders.

Mezzanine capital enables companies without access to the high-yield bond market to finance their activities beyond borrowing from banks and other finance providers. Investors in mezzanine capital expect high returns to compensate them for the high risk taken through the subordinated investments. If the company fails and goes through bankruptcy, the holders of mezzanine capital are likely to lose most or all of their investment.

Access

Most investors do not invest directly in companies that require private equity investments since they do not have the expertise and resources to complete due diligence on the opportunities, structure the deals and monitor the investments. Unlike public equity, where investors can directly invest in individual stocks, in private equity the normal route for investors is via private equity funds.

For investors with sufficient assets, private equity investments can be diversified across a range of private equity funds. Large investors can directly co-invest in private equity investments alongside the private equity funds. Investors with smaller portfolios can invest in a fund of funds to diversify their holdings. The downside is that funds of funds have a dual layer of fees, which are already high.

Listed private equity funds are also available. However, while offering perceived liquidity these are closed-end funds that may trade at large premiums or discounts to their net asset value (NAV), introducing more volatility and potential drawdowns due to expanding discounts.

Another way to access private equity is through investing in shares of public companies operating in the private equity industry (i.e. listed private equity firms).[131] These, however, are public equities and therefore have high exposure to the public equity market (even more so than private equity, which is highly correlated with public equity). These investments should be part of the allocation to public equities and should be viewed as a sector within equities (i.e. private equity sector). This is similar to investing in gold, for instance, through companies operating in the gold industry. Investing in private equity firms has its advantages: it is relatively cheap, liquid and transparent.

Investment vehicle and structure

The typical structure of a private equity fund is a *limited partnership* in which the private equity firm serves as the *general partner* and acts as the investment manager. The private equity firm raises the equity capital through private equity funds, which are typically closed-end funds. Each investor provides funding as a *limited partner*. Large investors may instead co-invest with the private equity firm.

Private equity investments are made in two stages. During the first stage the limited partner makes a commitment of capital to the general partner. During the second stage capital is deployed by the general partner. The general partner can make a call on the committed capital when investment opportunities arise and capital needs to be invested. After committing their capital, the limited partners have little say on how the general partner deploys the investment funds, as long as the basic covenants of the fund agreement are followed. Common covenants include restrictions on how much fund capital can be invested in any one company (limit concentration), the types of securities in which a fund can invest and the debt at the fund level (as opposed to unrestricted debt at the portfolio company level).

The fund typically has a fixed life (e.g. ten years), but it can be extended for additional years (e.g. three years). The private equity firm normally has up to five years to invest the fund's committed capital into companies and then has an additional five to eight years to return the capital plus potential profits to investors. If the private equity fund loses money, the limited partners may get back less than the committed capital.

Returns of private equity are normally only realised after a relatively long time, depending on the investment strategy. During the first few years when commitments are drawn down from the portfolio to finance investments, investors experience negative returns. Potentially, after a few years, investments start to pay off and the return profile turns positive. This behaviour is commonly referred to as the *J-curve* because of the shape of the chart describing the profit and loss of investing in private equity (as illustrated in Figure 3.25).

---

[131] Some of the largest listed private equity firms include Blackstone Group (United States), Onex Corporation (Canada), Partners Group (Switzerland), Melrose plc (United Kingdom), KKR & Co. (United States), Ratos AB (Sweden), Wendel (France), HAL Trust (the Netherlands or Curacao), 3i (United Kingdom) and Leucadia National Corporation (United States).

Investors should understand the private equity return profile. Education, patience and expectation management are important because no investor should be surprised with the losses over the first few years and with the long investment horizon that is required.

Figure 3.25: J-curve

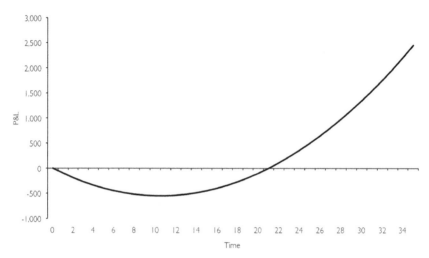

Source: The author.

Illiquidity

Private equity is an illiquid investment that is not traded or priced on a daily basis or at regular intervals. These attributes prevent many portfolios, which require liquidity or frequent pricing, from investing in private equity. This illiquidity means private equity is appropriate only for investors with a long-term investment horizon.

The 2008 crisis demonstrated the danger of illiquidity. The commitments of portfolios to invest in private equity reduce portfolio liquidity and flexibility. Capital calls during times of dry liquidity and bear markets may force investors to sell other assets at depressed prices to raise cash to satisfy the calls. As the percentage of assets invested in alternatives rises, the amount of liquid equities and bonds available to meet spending requirements, capital calls and margin calls plummets.[132] Investors missing capital calls may lose their prior investments and legal action may be taken against them.

---

[132] Siegel, Laurence, 'Alternatives and Liquidity: Will Spending and Capital Calls Eat Your "Modern" Portfolio?', *The Journal of Portfolio Management* 35 (2008).

Private equity's low liquidity and long holding periods have disadvantages and advantages. The disadvantage is the lack of flexibility. Private equity is a long-term commitment. The advantages are enabling the private equity firm sufficient time to accomplish its goals with its investees and rewarding investors with a liquidity premium.

When an LBO firm takes a public company private the share price should be discounted for the illiquidity. This discount creates a hurdle to be overcome before investors in the LBO generate positive returns.

Private versus public equity

Private equity, as the name implies, is equity that is private instead of public. A comparison between the two is called for.

The main advantage of private over public equity is better corporate governance, such as closer supervision of management. Private equity firms normally hold a relatively large portion of the investee company's equity. Consequently, as a large shareholder and normally the main source of capital they can take an active role in creating value in their investments (e.g. by improving operating efficiency). They can also exploit the tax shelter on interest payments on leverage.

Public equity portfolios, on the other hand, typically aim to generate returns through buying and selling equities; their activism is limited. Most active portfolio managers investing in public equities are subject to a zero-sum-game (i.e. for every winning position there is a losing position on the other side). Investing in public equities does not create value (e.g. investors do not improve operating efficiencies of investees).

Private equity firms utilise different kinds of activism, such as board and management reorganisation, balance sheet restructuring or the utilisation of private equity firm industry-specific skills. Activism can add economic value or be purely earnings management-driven (without value creation). Both buyout and venture capital firms invest with varying degrees and types of activism.[133] Some private equity firms actually create value, so private equity is not a zero-sum-game.

Performance comparison

It is difficult to compare the performance of private and public equity. First, returns of private equity are based on valuations (similar to those of direct real estate) and are therefore smoothed. The volatility of returns and their correlations are distorted.

---

[133] Rauch, Christian, Umber, Marc and Furth, Sven, 'Private Equity Shareholder Activism', SSRN working paper (2012).

Second, performance of private equity is typically quoted as an *internal rate of return (IRR)*, which is based on the *dollar-weighted* rate of return. IRR is not directly comparable with the *time-weighted* rate of return (total return), which is used for performance calculations of public equity. The time-weighted rate of return measures the compound rate of growth in a portfolio and it eliminates the impact of cash flows on performance. The dollar-weighted rate of return does not eliminate the impact of cash flows on performance. Therefore, comparing time-weighted and dollar-weighted returns is comparing apples and oranges – they are not based on the same methodology. IRR is used since mark-to-market prices are not available, and the *dollar-weighted* rate of return used in IRR is appropriate since the timing of deploying capital (cash flows) is an important decision of the private equity portfolio manager.

Internal rate of return (IRR) is the rate that discounts all future cash flow to the current price. Therefore:

$$P_0 = \sum CF_t/(1+IRR)^t$$

where P_0 is the current price; CF_t is cash flow at time t; and IRR is the internal rate of return. IRR is similar in concept to yield-to-maturity in fixed income.

While it is challenging to compare the performance of private and public equity, there have been attempts to do so. Academic research on private equity does not find performance advantage for the *average* private equity firm over the public equity market. One piece of research[134] reports after-fee average returns for limited partners no better than those from investing in the S&P 500 Index over the period 1980 to 2001.

Other research[135] adjusts private equity returns for *selection bias* because unsuccessful funds tend to choose not to report their performance to fund databases, which are based on voluntary reporting. Adjusting for the estimated impact of a lack of reporting, the researchers claim that private equity lags the S&P 500 Index by 3% per annum. High fees explain the underperformance and by adding back fees, gross private equity returns are claimed to outperform those of the S&P 500 by 3% per annum (fees are assumed at a level of 6%).

While private equity managers may be skilful, the high fees are a material hurdle. Charging fees on committed but uncalled capital attracts most criticism. Another earlier piece of research[136] found that once the selection bias is overcome there is little that is special about venture capital per se and that the smallest NASDAQ stocks have similar return and risk to those of venture capital.

---

[134] Kaplan, Steven and Schoar, Antoinette, 'Private Equity Performance: Returns, Persistence, and Capital Flows', *The Journal of Finance* 60 (2005).

[135] Phalippou, Ludovic and Gottschalg, Oliver, 'The Performance of Private Equity Funds', *Review of Financial Studies* 22 (2009).

[136] Cochrane, John, 'The Risk and Return of Venture Capital', *Journal of Financial Economics* 75 (2005).

Given the higher risks of private equity due to leverage, high volatility, high equity market beta, lack of transparency and illiquidity, a premium is warranted compared to public equity. Academic research fails to find the existence of a required and justified premium.

The success of private equity investing

Despite the apparent lack of premium, private equity does attract investors. There are several possible explanations. Brand-named, experienced and successful private equity firms do generate attractive, top-quartile returns, beating those of public equities. These successes attract investors to the asset class, and investors with manager selection skill and the capacity to access the success stories benefit.

The media focuses on the successful stories and this creates a perception of high returns. Some investors believe that the historical track record of private equity is much better that it really is. Other investors have a lottery tendency; believing that they will invest in the next Google.

The key to generating superior returns in private equity is gaining access to information. In this sense private equity is similar to hedge funds; manager skill is essential for generating superior returns and compensating investors for risks. There are no passive vehicles for accessing the private equity market and active funds are the only choice.

When investing in private equity, manager selection is critical since it is an information and skill-based asset class. If skilled managers cannot be accessed there is no justification for investing in private equity instead of the cheaper, more liquid, less volatile public equity market.

Top-quartile managers do generate returns in excess of public equity markets. There is also evidence of return persistence across different funds raised by the same private equity firm.[137] Investing in past winners has a higher likelihood of future success. The key is not investing in the average fund but investing in a good fund.

The type of investors in the private equity firm can also affect results. Research[138] has found that private equity firms with endowments as limited partners outperform the average fund by nearly 14%. In contrast, firms with banks as limited partners underperform the average fund by 10%.

---

[137] Kaplan, 'Private Equity Performance'.

[138] Lerner, Josh, Schoar, Antoinette and Wong, Wan, 'Smart Institutions, Foolish Choices? The Limited Partner Performance Puzzle', *The Journal of Finance* 62 (2007).

Expected return

Returns of private equity are likely to be better in the early stages of bull markets when investment opportunities and financing conditions are attractive but competition for deals is not yet excessive. There is not too much money chasing too few opportunities at these times.

After strong years, investors tend to chase performance and commit capital to private equity firms. This pattern hampers subsequent performance. The excessive inflows into private equity during the 2000 and 2007 peaks were a warning signal just before the collapses. In contrast, the years during which recessions ended (1991, 2001 and potentially 2009) were vintage years for PE.

The long-term performance of private equity can be explained by public equity market performance, financing costs when leverage is deployed, fees, a discount due to competitive pressures (when the private equity industry is in excess, subsequent returns are lower) and a premium on public equity returns. A premium over public equity is assumed since this is the only way to justify investing in private equity. While the average private equity fund may not generate a premium, top-quartile funds do generate one. The premium represents the alpha or skill-based return that the private equity firm is expected to generate, as well as the liquidity premium when illiquid private equity firms are used.

$$E(r) = \text{Equity Return - Interest Cost - Fees} + (\text{Premium - Discount})$$

To estimate the volatility of private equity returns the reported valuation-based returns should be unsmoothed. The unsmoothed return series can be used to estimate correlations with other investments.

The reasons for investing in private equity

There are a few good reasons for including private equity in portfolios.

- *Exposure to private equity risk.* The small capitalisation risk factor can be a source of outperformance in public equities as it attracts a risk premium. Private equity exposes a portfolio to a risk factor of companies with a smaller market capitalisation than even listed micro caps.

- *Opportunity to invest in emerging successes.* Private equity investing allows investors to participate in tomorrow's success stories.

- *Alpha.* Investors with manager selection skills and the capacity to access top-performing private equity funds can benefit from material excess returns. Private equity is a skill-based investment and without accessing skilled managers there is no justification for investing in private equity instead of the much cheaper and liquid public equity market.

- *Liquidity premium.* Private equity's illiquidity should be compensated by the market. Investors who can bear illiquidity (e.g. endowments with perpetual investment horizon) can benefit from the liquidity premium.

Risks

The main risks of private equity relative to public equity are illiquidity and bias to micro, small and mid capitalisation stocks. Volatility of private equity should be comparable to that of public equity. However, venture capital is not as diversified as the broad public equity market and it is subject to specific concentrated risks of the companies in the portfolio. LBOs utilise leverage that increases volatility. Private equity therefore has a higher volatility than that of quoted equities. For a well-diversified portfolio of private equity an assumption of twice the volatility of quoted equities is reasonable. For a concentrated portfolio, the volatility can be three times that of quoted equities.

Investors should expect higher returns from private equity to compensate them for the higher systematic risk relative to public equity. Private equity should also include alpha from manager skill and this alpha should be the justification for the relatively high fees that private equity firms charge.

Venture capital has high equity market beta exposure if the smoothed returns due to valuations are adjusted. VCs therefore offer lower diversification benefits to a multi-asset portfolio with material exposure to equities compared to other alternatives.

Other risks include leverage risk of LBOs and the risk of investing in immature businesses for VC funds. Private equity portfolios tend to be concentrated and activist, meaning material opportunities with material risks.

Role in portfolios

Private equity is clearly a risk or growth asset aiming to generate high returns. It is a return enhancer rather than a risk diversifier because of its high correlation with public equities, which usually dominate the risk of multi-asset portfolios. Its main role is generating high returns over the long term.

Private equity is predominantly an equity or equity-like investment and therefore should be considered as part of the allocation to public equities, potentially alongside some hedge fund strategies such as equity long/short. However, many investors choose to include private equity as part of the allocation to alternative investments, alongside hedge funds, commodities and sometimes real estate.

Diversification across companies, regions, sectors and investment strategies within private equity is recommended, as it is for public equities. However, when private equity is included as part of the allocation to public equities the diversification can be partly achieved through diversifying the public equities. This is a cheaper and more liquid way to achieve proper diversification. Public equity can complement private equity. The diversification through public equity should not come, however, at the expense of diversifying the private equity companies to reduce unique risk.

Once a commitment to private equity is made there are restrictions on the sale of the investments and the secondary market is not well developed. Since private equity funds have discretion on timing of calling commitments and distributing profits to investors, the cash flows of private equity funds are unpredictable, uncertain and are not controlled by the investor. This can lead to misallocation to private equity in portfolios and a challenge of keeping the allocation at the desired level. Portfolios may be underinvested while part of the committed capital has not been called yet, leading to a performance drag. On the other hand, portfolios may become overinvested by making commitments that are too large, which can lead to a liquidity shortfall in the portfolio.

Addressing the underinvestment before commitments are drawn is easily done through investing in passive public equity funds, ETFs or futures to gain liquid public equity exposure (i.e. equitising the committed but uncalled capital). This exposure is a substitute to the private equity exposure and can be reduced quickly and cheaply when capital is called for private equity investing. Managing the allocation to private equity within portfolios needs careful planning and investors need to prepare recommitment strategies.[139]

Secondary market

Private equity secondary markets (often called private equity secondaries) refer to trading existing commitments to private equity. The seller sells not only the investment in the fund but also the remaining unfunded commitments. As the private equity market is illiquid and investments are not normally traded on exchanges, secondaries provide some liquidity. Secondaries can be considered a distinct asset class or sub-asset class with its own cash flow profile, which is different to that of private equity.

Private equity indices

Cambridge Associates[140] produces the most commonly used index of private equity investments. Cambridge Associates has a proprietary database of institutional

---

[139] de Zwart, Garden, Frieser, Brian and van Dijk, Dick, 'Private Equity Recommitment Strategies for Institutional Investors', *Financial Analysts Journal* 68 (2012).
[140] www.cambridgeassociates.com.

quality private investment funds tracking the performance of more than 4700 institutional quality private partnerships and more than 64,000 portfolio company investments. This data is used to derive the private investment benchmarks. The Cambridge Associates U.S. Venture Capital Index and the Cambridge Associates Private Equity Index are published on a quarterly basis. These indices represent the majority of institutional quality capital raised since 1981.

The S&P Listed Private Equity Index[141] is comprised of 30 leading globally listed private equity companies. These are publicly traded private equity firms. Investing in these companies exposes portfolios to the general public equity market and the firms' commercial fortunes. While the fortunes of the firms are driven by their private equity investments, investing in them is like investing in the private equity sector within the public equity asset class and therefore does not provide a pure exposure to private equity.

Private equity return and risk characteristics

Figure 3.26 shows the cumulative performance of the S&P Listed Private Equity Index since December 2003, as well as that of the S&P 500 Index. The listed private equity index represents the returns of listed private equity firms, not the performance of the underlying private equity investments. Publicly traded private equity companies provide a way to measure the performance and risk of the asset class. However, the performance of publicly traded private equity companies is greatly affected by that of the public equity market.

As can be seen, the correlation between the general public equity market and the listed private equity sector is high. Since listed private equity is more concentrated and private equity firms are affected greatly by the general direction of the public equity market, the listed private equity index is more volatile, exhibiting more severe drawdowns, as well as stronger upturns, than the general public equity market.

---

[141] The top ten companies in the index as of the end of December 2013 were The Blackstone Group LP, KKR & Co., Bookfield Asset Management Inc., Ares Capital Group, 3i Group, American Capital Ltd, Wendel, Partner Group Holdings, Prospect Capital Corp and Intermediate Capital Group. www.standardandpoors.com.

Figure 3.26: Cumulative performance of listed private equity and US equities, December 2003 to December 2013

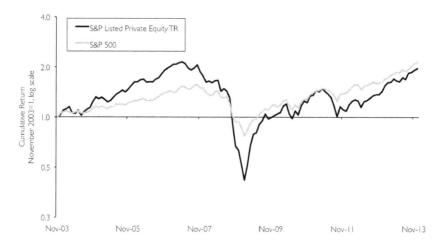

Source: Bloomberg, S&P Listed Private Equity Index, S&P 500 Index.

Table 3.8 shows the performance analytics of Cambridge Associates Private Equity and U.S. Venture Capital indices, as well as US equities. The Cambridge Associates indices are available only on a quarterly basis, so quarterly index returns are used for the S&P 500 Index as well. The table includes the volatility adjusted for fat-tails (using the Cornish-Fisher approximation) and analytics for unsmoothed returns (using an unsmoothing technique).

Over the specific time period both private equity and VC outperformed public equity. The volatility of reported returns of private equity seems much lower than that of public equities. However, this is due to the smoothed valuation-based private equity returns. The unsmoothed volatility of venture capital is more than twice that of public equity.

VC has a unique distribution of returns as it is positively skewed with very high excess kurtosis. This means that VC has had some exceptionally high quarterly returns – this is the positive side of fat-tail risk. VC's volatility adjusted for fat-tails is blank since the skewness and kurtosis numbers result in a negative volatility using the Cornish-Fisher approximation.

Table 3.9 shows the correlations among the asset classes. The correlations show that private equity, VC and public equities are unique asset classes, whose combination has diversification benefits.

Table 3.8: Private equity return and risk characteristics, June 1986 to December 2013. Based on quarterly returns

	Private equity	Venture capital	US equities	Unsmooth PE	Unsmooth VC	Unsmooth US equities
Start month	Jun-86	Jun-86	Jun-86	Jun-86	Jun-86	Jun-86
Performance (% pa)	13.5	13.8	9.4	12.8	6.7	9.1
Volatility (%)	9.9	22.5	16.8	14.9	45.7	17.6
Skewness	-0.38	3.74	-0.63	-0.16	3.38	-0.57
Kurtosis	2.16	24.76	0.83	1.75	26.71	0.76
Adjusted volatility	11.4	-	19.3	16.4	12.4	20.0
Autocorrelation	0.39	0.61	0.04	-	-	-

Source: Bloomberg, Cambridge Associated Private Equity Index, Cambridge Associates U.S. Venture Capital Index, S&P 500 Index.

Table 3.9: Correlation matrix, June 1986 to December 2013. Based on quarterly returns

Correlation matrix	Private equity	Venture capital	US equities	Unsmooth PE	Unsmooth VC	Unsmooth US equities
Private equity	1.00	0.67	0.69	0.92	0.52	0.68
Venture capital	0.67	1.00	0.40	0.59	0.80	0.39
US equities	0.69	0.40	1.00	0.72	0.45	1.00
Unsmooth PE	0.92	0.59	0.72	1.00	0.61	0.72
Unsmooth VC	0.52	0.80	0.45	0.61	1.00	0.46
Unsmooth US equities	0.68	0.39	1.00	0.72	0.46	1.00

Source: Bloomberg, Cambridge Associated Private Equity Index, Cambridge Associates U.S. Venture Capital Index, S&P 500 Index.

Figure 3.27 shows the cumulative performance of the Cambridge Associates Private Equity Index and U.S. Venture Capital Index and compares them with that of the S&P 500 Index. Cambridge Associates indices are published only on a quarterly basis, so the cumulative performance of the S&P 500 Index is also based on corresponding quarterly returns. As private equity is based on valuations, the returns of the Cambridge Associates indices are smoothed and appear less volatile than those of the S&P 500 Index.

Figure 3.27: Cumulative performance of US private equity and US equities (quarterly returns), March 1986 to December 2013

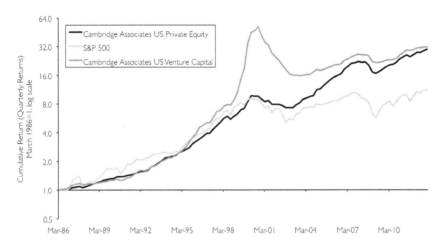

Source: Bloomberg, Cambridge Associates Private Equity Index, Cambridge Associated U.S. Venture Capital Index, S&P 500 Index.

Figure 3.28 compares the cumulative returns of three indices: Cambridge Associates Private Equity Index, S&P Listed Private Equity Index and S&P 500 Index. As can be vividly seen, listed private equity – as represented by S&P Listed Private Equity Index – behaves much more like public equity than directly invested private equity – as represented by the Cambridge Associates Private Equity Index.

Conclusions

Private equity is similar to public equity in many ways. However, when a skilful private equity fund is identified and can be used, the potential rewards can be attractive. Private equity requires a long time and patience and as such it is suitable only for investors with a long investment horizon and an appetite for illiquidity.

Figure 3.28: Cumulative performance of listed private equity, US private equity and US equities (quarterly returns), September 2003 to December 2013

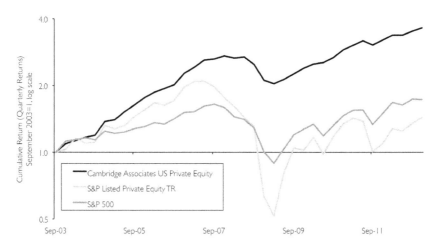

Source: Bloomberg, Cambridge Associates Private Equity Index, S&P Listed Private Equity Index, S&P 500 Index.

Summary

- Private equity mainly involves investing in equities, as well as debt and convertible securities, which are not publicly traded on stock exchanges.

- Venture capital (VC) and leveraged buyouts (LBOs) are the two most common private equity strategies. Distressed and mezzanine capital are two other private equity strategies.

- VC invests in private companies with the aim of either taking them public through an IPO or selling their equity to another investor at a profit.

- The goal of leveraged buyout (LBO) funds is turning public firms into private companies, restructuring them, creating value and selling the investments at a profit.

- Most investors access private equity through private equity funds. Other access routes are funds of funds, listed private equity funds and shares of listed companies operating in the private equity industry. Listed private equity funds are closed-end funds and suffer from more volatility due to premiums and discounts to NAV. Listed companies in the private equity industry expose the portfolio to public equity market risk.

- Private equity funds are structured as a partnership with the private equity firm as the general partner, managing the fund, and the investors as the limited partner, providing the capital.

- Normally, returns of private equity investments are negative in the first few years, as commitments are drawn, and then potentially turn positive in later years as investments mature. This is known as the J-curve.

- Private equity is an illiquid, infrequently priced asset class. It is suitable only for portfolios with a long-term investment horizon.

- The main advantage of private over public equity is better corporate governance, such as closer supervision of management. Private equity funds can create value by improving operating efficiency and exploiting the tax shelter on interest payments on leverage.

- Direct comparison of private and public equity returns is difficult since private equity returns are based on valuations and therefore smoothed. They are also based on IRR, which is difficult to compare to public equity's time-weighted returns.

- Internal rate of return (IRR) is based on current price, cash flows and the timing of cash flows. IRR is the discount rate that equates the present value of future cash flows with current price.

- Academic research finds that the *average* private equity firm does not beat the general public equity market. The key is investing with top-quartile firms.

- Manager skill is critical in private equity for generating superior returns. Passive private equity vehicles are unavailable. Return persistence means that investing in private equity firms with top-quartile funds has a higher likelihood of generating excess returns.

- Private equity is a skill-based investment and without accessing skilled managers there is no justification for investing in private equity instead of the much cheaper and liquid public equity market.

- The long-term expected return of private equity is the public equity market expected return minus financing costs when leverage is deployed, minus fees, minus discount due to competitive pressures (when the private equity industry is in excess subsequent returns are lower), plus a premium to public equity returns. A premium over public equity must be assumed since this is the only way to justify investing in private equity.

- Similar to direct real estate, to estimate the standard deviation and correlation of private equity the reported returns must be unsmoothed.

- The main reasons for investing in private equity include: exposure to private equity risk; opportunity to invest in emerging successes; alpha; and liquidity premium.

- The main risks of private equity are illiquidity, high volatility, concentration, investing in immature companies and leverage risk of LBOs.

- Private equity is more volatile than publicly traded equities because of the concentration risk of VCs and leverage of LBOs. The higher volatility should be compensated by higher returns, as well as alpha from manager skill.

- Private equity can be part of the alternative assets in a portfolio but it should be part of the general allocation to equities in portfolios.

- Diversification is critical to reducing idiosyncratic risk. Public equities can complement the private equity exposure and diversify it.

CHAPTER 8: HEDGE FUNDS

Hedge funds are not considered an asset class but rather a type of private, pooled investment vehicle that is actively managed by a professional fund manager who can flexibly utilise a wide array of investment strategies and techniques. In practice, however, investors normally allocate part of their portfolio to hedge funds, effectively treating them as a kind of asset class.

Hedge funds are not widely distributed to the general public like retail collective investment schemes (more than 60% of hedge fund investments come from institutional investors), so they are less regulated. Consequently, they are less constrained than retail funds and can utilise investment strategies and techniques such as *leverage*, *short selling* and *derivatives* more freely. There are, however, some regulated hedge funds that are UCITS[142] compliant vehicles.

Hedge funds do not normally have a benchmark to measure and constrain or anchor them. They commonly aim to deliver absolute returns, equity-like returns with bond-like volatility, or other target returns. While some hedge funds succeed in meeting their objectives, not all hedge funds do.

It is unclear when the first hedge fund was launched. During the Roaring 1920s a number of investment vehicles with similar principles to those of hedge funds were on offer in the United States. The vehicle from that time that is best known today is the Graham-Newman Partnership, mainly because one of its partners was Benjamin Graham. The first investment vehicle that was actually called a 'hedge fund' was launched in 1949 by Alfred Jones and this was designed solely to neutralise the effects of a bear market on an investment portfolio.

Some hedge funds aim to hedge losses and downside risks. Hedging, however, is not always included in the investment objectives of hedge funds and their name may be misleading since they may not aim to hedge any risk. Hedge funds may hedge unwanted risks to maintain a purer exposure to wanted risks or to isolate arbitrage opportunities.

Some hedge funds market themselves as aiming to generate equity-like returns with bond-like volatility. However, this may be misleading as well. The volatility may be understated and exclude other risks, such as liquidity, derivative, operational and manager risk.

---

[142] UCITS is Undertakings for the Collective Investment of Transferable Securities.

The hedge fund industry has grown rapidly in the past few decades and is estimated to have close to $2 trillion in assets under management (AUM). Hedge funds gained popularity during 2000 after the high-tech bubble burst when disappointing returns from equities put hedge funds under the spotlight as an alternative to equities. Hedge funds' popularity was dented, however, in the 2008 crisis as many disappointed investors with poor performance and illiquidity that caused some funds to restrict investors' withdrawals. The year 2011 was another disappointing one for hedge funds, with the second worst annual performance of broad hedge fund indices over the last decade.

Hedge fund performance

The historic performance of hedge fund indices shows that hedge funds as a group have produced higher net returns and risk-adjusted returns (i.e. Sharpe ratio) than traditional equity and fixed income investments and have outperformed cash. Cash is arguably the appropriate benchmark for hedge funds with an absolute return objective.

Based on hedge fund index returns,[143] hedge funds have produced positive net alpha after fees. Fees on hedge funds are relatively high so it appears that hedge funds have generated high gross returns. These results differ from the results of long-only active funds that as a group tend to lag their benchmarks net of fees and costs.

There are a few *a priori* arguments that support the expected positive results of hedge funds and their superior results when compared to long-only portfolios:

- *Flexibility*. With fewer constraints than long-only managers and the ability to freely short sell, use leverage and use derivatives, hedge funds have more opportunities to generate alpha. Short selling allows hedge funds to benefit from negative views on securities and markets and to hedge unwanted risks to isolate alpha opportunities. Some of the classic arbitrage strategies, such as convertible arbitrage, require short selling. Leverage allows higher returns to be extracted from profitable decisions. For example, small expected profits from arbitrage trades can be amplified using leverage. Derivatives allow a wide range of strategies to be utilised, including those with asymmetric payoffs using options. Derivatives also allow the manager to synthetically short sell and leverage positions. Some hedge funds can invest across different asset classes and markets (they are multi-asset portfolios) and therefore have a wide investment opportunity set. Hedge fund managers have many more options and strategies at their disposal than long-only managers.

---

[143] For a discussion on hedge fund indices see Lustig, *Multi-Asset Investing*.

- *Investment horizon.* Some hedge funds have lock-ups and restrictions on redemptions, giving them a longer investment horizon to generate value. They do not need to meet redemption requests shortly after making an investment as long-only managers often have to do. More time means potentially more money.

- *Access to a wide range of risk premiums.* Hedge funds can access both traditional systematic risks (equity, maturity and credit) and alternative systematic risks, such as value, small cap, momentum and volatility. This gives hedge funds a wide array of risk premiums. By holding illiquid assets hedge funds can also benefit from the liquidity risk premium.

- *Motivation.* Hedge fund managers can earn high performance fees and many invest their own wealth in the funds that they manage, better aligning their interests with those of investors. The high fees attract the most talented portfolio managers and investment professionals to hedge funds, at the expense of long-only portfolios.

- *Rewards for economic functions.* Hedge funds earn rewards for certain economic functions that they offer, such as capital provision, risk sharing and management, liquidity provision, insurance provision and market completion. Hedge funds, in aggregate, tend to invest in underpriced investments and sell or short overpriced investments. This process moves market prices towards fair-values and facilitates an efficient allocation of capital in financial markets.

- *Lumpy cash flows.* Hedge funds normally have large minimum investments. Hedge fund managers do not need to deal with frequent small cash inflows and outflows that may hurt performance, as long-only managers need to do.

The alternative explanation for the apparently good results of hedge funds as a group and their superior results over long-only portfolios is that the results are just wrongly reported and deceiving. The explanation can be divided into two reasons: biases in hedge funds indices and hedge fund risks.

Hedge fund indices are based on voluntary reporting of hedge fund results. The results of the indices are affected by reporting biases (e.g. survivorship and backfill biases) that probably overstate the reported returns and understate risk as measured by standard deviation. The returns of fund of fund (FoF) indices are less affected by biases,[144] but include a double layer of fees. Failing hedge funds may choose not to report their performance and their poor results are not included in the indices.

On the risk side, many hedge funds are exposed to different risks that are not captured by standard deviation. Alternative beta risks, illiquidity, leverage, fat-tail risk, operational risks, derivative-related risks and a lack of transparency are

---

[144] Fund, William and Hsieh, David, 'Hedge-Fund Benchmarks: Information Content and Biases', *Financial Analysts Journal* (2002).

a few risks that are not reflected in risk-adjusted measures, such as the Sharpe ratio. Some hedge funds are short volatility and this is like selling financial downside risk protection or insurance, resulting in a portfolio exposed to extreme negative returns.

The reported returns of some hedge fund indices are smoothed because many hedge funds invest in illiquid investments whose prices are based on valuations, not ongoing market pricing. Smoothed returns underestimate true volatility.

Hedge funds' strong results may reflect aggressive risk taking rather than skill. The results of hedge funds may not be pure alpha and may also be driven by exposure to alternative betas. For example, maintaining an exposure to small caps over time may generate superior returns. However, this is a permanent style tilt and risk taking, rather than skill. Investors are probably willing to pay hedge fund managers high fees for alpha and not for exposure to alternative betas and in particular to traditional betas.

Performance analysis

Table 3.10 shows the annual performance since 2000 of the four main hedge fund strategies (global macro, equity hedge, event-driven and relative value), the overall hedge fund industry (hedge fund composite), US equities and Treasuries. Hedge fund returns are represented by hedge fund indices, which do not represent the performance of any individual hedge fund.

As can be seen, during 2000 to 2002 the returns of equities were negative and those of most hedge fund strategies positive. Hedge funds made their name at this time. During the equity bull run of 2003 to 2007 some hedge fund strategies delivered returns that were competitive with those of equities. This is impressive since it is challenging to compete with equities when they are on a positive run.

2008 was a dreadful year for most hedge fund strategies, in particular those that used leverage and illiquid investments (e.g. event-driven and relative value) or had directionality with the equity market (e.g. equity hedge). Following the 2008 crisis, it seems that hedge funds have not returned to their previous glory, with some hedge fund strategies delivering disappointing returns (e.g. global macro).

The performance of hedge funds depends heavily on the skill of their managers. Whether it is a fundamentally research driven or mathematical systematic model using sophisticated algorithms (black boxes), the performance depends on the skill of the people (the person behind the machine). The relatively high hedge fund fees are supposed to be a compensation for that skill. You do not pay to get market exposure; you can buy this cheaply through passive investments. You pay for alpha, or skill.

Table 3.10: Hedge funds, US equities and Treasuries annual returns %, January 2000 to December 2013

Year	Global Macro	Equity Hedge	Event-Driven	Relative Value	HF Composite	US equities	US Treasuries
2000	2.0	9.1	6.7	13.4	5.0	-9.1	13.5
2001	6.9	0.4	12.2	8.9	4.6	-11.9	6.8
2002	7.4	-4.7	-4.3	5.4	-1.4	-22.1	11.7
2003	21.4	20.5	25.3	9.7	19.5	28.7	2.3
2004	4.6	7.7	15.0	5.6	9.0	10.9	3.5
2005	6.8	10.6	7.3	6.0	9.3	4.9	2.8
2006	8.2	11.7	15.3	12.4	12.9	15.8	3.1
2007	11.1	10.5	6.6	8.9	10.0	5.5	9.0
2008	4.8	-26.6	-21.8	-18.0	-19.0	-37.0	13.9
2009	4.3	24.6	25.1	25.8	20.0	26.5	-3.7
2010	8.1	10.5	11.9	11.4	10.2	15.1	5.8
2011	-4.1	-8.4	-3.3	0.2	-5.2	2.1	9.6
2012	-0.1	7.4	8.9	10.6	6.4	16.0	2.0
2013	-0.5	14.3	12.6	7.0	9.2	32.4	-2.7

Source: Bloomberg, HFRI Macro Index, HFRI Equity Hedge Index, HFRI Event-Driven Index, HFRI Relative Value Index, HFRI Fund Weighted Composite Index, Citigroup United States WGBI TR Index, S&P 500 Index.

The number of hedge funds in the world is large (about 8000). Here, manager selection is probably more important than in the long-only world (since returns are supposed to be driven mostly by alpha and not by beta exposure) and more difficult to undertake properly. Many hedge funds use complex trading techniques and do not follow an orderly investment management process. This makes it more difficult to assess the skill for an outsider, such as a manager research analyst.

It is challenging, but possible, to evaluate hedge funds and add value through manager and fund selection. Indeed, as in less researched and less efficient stock markets, which may provide more opportunities for active managers, the hedge fund industry is a less researched and less efficient market for manager selection. In addition, research has found evidence of performance persistence in hedge funds. Past performance is no guarantee of future results, but it gives some indication of future performance, with the persistence stronger in small, young funds.[145]

---

[145] Boyson, Nicole, 'Hedge Fund Performance Persistence: A New Approach', *Financial Analysts Journal* 64 (2008).

Hedge fund fees

Hedge funds normally pay handsomely for skilled managers. Hedge funds provide more freedom to managers to utilise skill, if the manager indeed has skill. Freedom is a double-edged sword though. The relative freedom of a hedge fund in the hands of an unskilful manager, who relies more on luck than skill to get the job done, is a risky adventure. The fees that hedge funds charge are relatively high to compensate managers for skill, and hopefully investors do not pay high fees for just luck.

The remuneration of hedge fund managers typically consists of an asset management fee and a performance fee. *Asset management fees* are calculated as a percentage of the fund's Net Asset Value (NAV) and typically range from 1% to 4% per annum (1% to 2% is the standard). The *performance fee* is typically 20% of the fund's excess return over a benchmark or cash, but it can range from 10% to 50%. The ratio of 2-and-20 is the norm for hedge funds, meaning 2% management fee and 20% performance fee. Performance fees are meant to provide an incentive for the hedge fund manager to generate attractive returns for investors.

There are a few potential pitfalls with the fee structure of hedge funds. As the fund's assets under management (AUM) rise, it is more difficult for managers to generate excess returns as the fund reaches its capacity and more money is chasing the same number of investment opportunities. Many hedge funds invest in illiquid opportunities from which only limited capital can be efficiently deployed to benefit (e.g. arbitrage opportunities in derivatives with limited liquidity). Managers may therefore be more incentivised to focus on growing AUM for higher management fees instead of focusing on generating excess returns for investors to earn performance fees.

When the fund is young and AUM is low, performance fees can lead fund managers to take excessive risks because hedge funds share only the profits and not the losses. This asymmetry means that performance fees can create an incentive for high risk taking (principle/agent issues).

A compensation structure linking each fund manager's compensation to the hedge fund's profitability instead of to the performance of any one fund can address some of these issues. Such a structure reduces the incentive to accumulate assets in a single fund since inflows should be deployed in the best funds to enhance the firm's profitability. The manager is less prone to excess risk taking since it has less of an impact on their direct compensation and it puts at risk the profitability of the entire firm.

Performance fees may include a *high watermark*, meaning that performance fees apply to returns above the highest level of the NAV previously achieved. A fund whose NAV reached 110 in a year, then fell to 100 in the subsequent year, will not get a performance fee until the NAV surpasses 110 again. A return of 10% or less will not reward the hedge fund manager with a performance fee because of the 10% loss in the previous year. This prevents managers from receiving fees for volatile performance or for performance below the peak (i.e. not recouping previous losses).

Hedge fund managers sometimes close a fund that has suffered serious losses (known as being deep underwater) and launch a new fund, resetting the watermark. Otherwise, they need to recover the losses, occasionally over a long time period, before receiving performance fees again.

Performance fees may include a *hurdle rate* or a benchmark. In this case the performance fee is paid only on the fund's excess return over the benchmark. The benchmark ensures that managers are rewarded only for returns that investors could not have gained by investing simply in the benchmark. Most hedge funds, however, do not have an explicit performance objective to beat a benchmark.

Hedge funds sometimes charge a redemption fee to apply *lock-in periods* (typically one to three years). Many hedge funds invest in illiquid investments, and redemptions may force liquidation of positions to the detriment of remaining investors due to transaction costs and lost opportunities. Redemption fees compensate remaining investors for the costs of liquidating those positions.

When hedge fund managers invest personal money in the fund it is a sign that they should be more motivated to generate higher returns and/or not take excessive risks. That is, putting money where their mouth is. Close alignment of interests between the principal and agent is a way to alleviate some of the compensation issues.

Hedge fund strategies

Hedge funds are unconstrained and can utilise a wide array of investment strategies and techniques. Retail funds or long-only funds typically cannot short (hence long-only), cannot use leverage and have limitations on utilising derivatives (normally, derivatives are permitted for *efficient portfolio management*, EPM, purposes only). Hedge funds do not have these constraints.

On top of that, they do not need to diversify their investments, as some retail funds have to do, and may hold concentrated portfolios. These features enable hedge funds to pursue a wide spectrum of different investment strategies.

The four main categories of hedge fund investment strategies are:

1. global macro
2. equity long/short (equity hedge)
3. event-driven
4. relative value (arbitrage).

The hedge fund industry is evolving and new strategies and innovations are constantly developed. The industry must innovate because arbitrage opportunities tend to disappear once identified and exploited. When too much smart money chases the same investment ideas, deviations from fair-value quickly disappear as do alpha opportunities.

For example, a stock is priced at $80, while its fair-value is $100. If many investors identify the opportunity and buy the stock, its price will increase because of demand. As the number of investors buying the stock increases and the amount they use to buy the stock increases, its price will move up faster. This means that the buying opportunity disappears quickly, making it harder to benefit from it.

Multi-strategy hedge funds can use more than one investment strategy or a combination of a few hedge funds, each following a different strategy. An *absolute return* strategy seeks positive returns without reference to any benchmark and independent of market movements. A *market neutral* strategy seeks returns that have a low correlation or beta with market movements. *Directional* strategies have a higher correlation or beta with respect of markets (beta is often used to measure directionality).

Hedge funds can use an investment process that aims to add value either through fundamental analysis of securities and markets or through a systematic process, which relies on quantitative models (often referred to as black boxes). The variety of hedge funds and their strategies is almost endless.

I will now look at the four main strategies mentioned above in more detail.

1. Global macro

Global macro hedge funds invest in the global equity, fixed income, commodity and currency markets to benefit from macroeconomic events and developments. Global macro funds tend to use leverage and they tend to be directional. Some global macro funds identify investment opportunities through fundamental analysis of economies. This is a similar process to that of global tactical asset allocation (GTAA) funds that look for mispricing opportunities across markets. Other global macro funds employ quantitative models that generate signals to inform the fund manager of potential investment opportunities.

Global macro funds can be divided into funds that benefit from trends and momentum in markets and funds that benefit from reversal of trends. Global macro funds typically invest in highly liquid derivative markets and therefore do not have material illiquidity risk.

Global macro among the most flexible and least restrictive of the major hedge fund styles. The strategy aims to identify and capitalise on the best global reward/risk opportunities across all asset classes (it is a subset of multi-asset investing). This investment flexibility, coupled with the use of liquid and cost efficient derivatives, enables global macro to adapt quickly to new economic conditions.

The top-down approach of global macro is different from the typical bottom-up approach of most other hedge fund styles and long-only funds. Global macro therefore can offer strong diversification opportunities in portfolios. However, the success of a global macro strategy heavily depends on manager skill and hence manager selection is crucial.

Figure 3.29 shows the average returns of the S&P 500 Index over different deciles and the corresponding average performance of the HFRI Macro Index. Global macro has had a flat average return during equity crashes, indicating the potential ability of the average manager to protect the downside when equity markets fall.

Figure 3.29: Average performance of global macro and US equities ranked by performance of US equities, January 1990 to December 2013

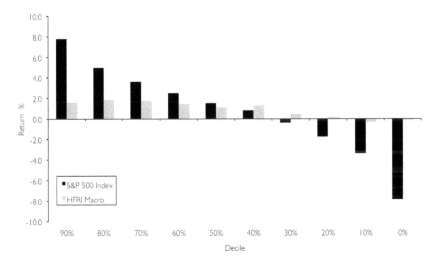

Source: Bloomberg, HFRI Macro Index, S&P 500 Index.

Figure 3.30 shows the cumulative performance of the S&P 500 Index and the HFRI Macro Index. The average performance of global macro hedge funds has not only been superior to that of US equities over the measuring period, but also it has been uncorrelated and much less volatile. The returns of the global macro index during the two major equity bear markets of 2000 and 2008 are particularly impressive. However, global macro in general has struggled to add value over the last few years.

Figure 3.30: Cumulative performance of global macro and US equities, January 1990 to December 2013

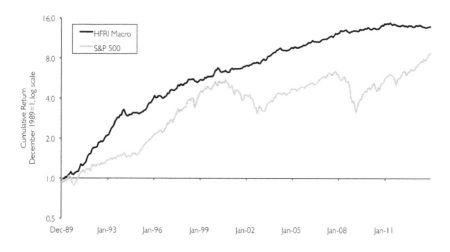

Source: Bloomberg, HFRI Macro Index, S&P 500 Index.

Figure 3.31 shows the rolling 36-month correlation between the HFRI Macro Index and the S&P 500 Index. When equity markets crashed in 2000 and 2008 the correlation between global macro hedge funds and equities materially fell. This indicates that macro hedge funds reduced their directionality with equity markets when equity markets fell.

Figure 3.31: Rolling 36-month correlation between global macro hedge funds and US equities, January 1990 to December 2013

Source: Bloomberg, HFRI Macro Index, S&P 500 Index.

Based on past performance of an index representing macro hedge funds, global macro hedge funds have been successful. However, since 2011 the global macro index has delivered negative returns. Perhaps at a time during which the actions of policymakers in Europe, aiming to tackle the European sovereign debt crisis, and in the United States, aiming to support the economic recovery following the 2008 crisis and address the mountain of public debt, the ability of global macro funds to generate alpha has been hurt. It is much more challenging to predict policy actions than financial market movements.

2. Equity long/short

Equity long/short funds can take both long and short positions in equity securities across different markets. The ability to short securities enables fund managers to add value not only through buying equities of companies in which managers have conviction, but also through shorting equities of companies that managers believe are going to fall. Managers can benefit from both sides of stock research, the positive and negative views on stocks. Long-only funds, on the other hand, can only benefit from the positive side and invest in equities that the managers believe are going to outperform the market.

Equity long/short funds can hold large amounts of cash and increase the short bias when market prospects are negative. Long-only funds can typically only hold up to 10% of NAV in cash and must remain invested, even when managers believe equity markets are going to fall. They can outperform on the downside by security selection and holding maximum cash, but not more. Equity long/short funds therefore have more flexibility than long-only equity portfolios.

Equity long/short funds invest in equities and therefore hold liquid positions. These strategies are less exposed to illiquidity risks than other, less liquid hedge fund strategies.

The funds can either broadly invest across equity markets or specialise in a specific segment of the equity market, such as emerging market equity long/short. *Short bias funds* maintain a short position on equity markets (hence the name short bias). These funds tend to underperform other strategies when equity markets rise. However, they have a negative correlation with equities and therefore can add diversification benefits in portfolio context. Since equity markets tend to generate positive returns over the long term, short bias funds tend to generate negative returns over the long term.

130/30 funds have 130% long positions and 30% short positions and therefore a net 100% long position. Often they have a UCITS or regulated fund structure. These funds are appropriate for investors who cannot or do not wish to invest in unregulated hedge funds.

Equity long/short hedge funds often short futures, which are mostly written on large capitalisation stocks or indices, and short large capitalisation stocks, which are liquid and easy to short. The funds tend to have a long bias to small capitalisation stocks, which are less liquid and more difficult to short. This creates a small cap bias, which should generate excess returns over time (*Fama and French model*).[146]

Figure 3.32 shows the cumulative performance of equity long/short and US equities. Equity long/short funds demonstrated a much lower downside risk than long-only equities (S&P 500 Index) during the 2000 and 2008 equity crashes. Protecting on the downside and keeping up on the upside is a recipe for long-term value creation.

Figure 3.32: Cumulative performance of equity long/short hedge funds and US equities, January 1990 to December 2013

Source: Bloomberg, HFRI Equity Hedge Index, S&P 500 Index.

Figure 3.33 shows the rolling 36-month correlation between the HFRI Equity Hedge Index and the S&P 500 Index. The correlation has been increasing over the years, indicating that the funds in general have become more directional.

---

[146] Fama, 'Common Risk Factors in the returns on stocks and bonds'.

Figure 3.33: Rolling 36-month correlation between equity long/short hedge funds and US equities, January 1990 to December 2013

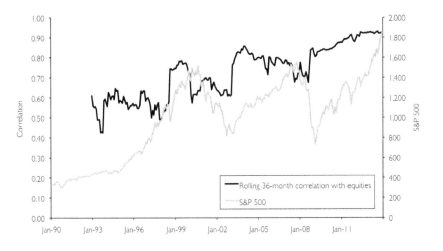

Source: Bloomberg, HFRI Equity Hedge Index, S&P 500 Index.

3. Event-driven

Event-driven funds aim to benefit from financial events, such as corporate activity (e.g. mergers, acquisitions and bankruptcies). Fund managers take long and short positions related to the event before it occurs based on predicted price movements of securities post the event. Event-driven strategies can be divided into three sub-categories: distressed, risk arbitrage and special situation.

1. *Distressed* strategies invest in loans or bonds of companies facing financial distress. The loans and bonds are sold at a discount to reflect the issuer's default risk. If the hedge fund can prevent the issuer's bankruptcy or liquidation, the loans or bonds can appreciate in value and generate a return. Distressed debt hedge funds have a number of advantages over long-only high-yield bond funds, such as more flexibility in utilising hedge techniques to reduce beta exposure and the ability to lend to corporations and have more sense of ownership and influence. They can also impose lock-up periods on their investors and therefore have more control over cash flows and prevent short-term investors from forcing them to hold investments for a short time. This provides the funds more stability in managing illiquid assets and extracting value from them.

2. *Risk arbitrage or merger arbitrage* strategies aim to benefit from corporate restructurings such as mergers, acquisitions and liquidations. When a company acquires a target company, for example, typically the equity price of the acquiring company falls and that of the target company rises. One reason

for this phenomenon is the general view that the acquirer usually overpays for the target company. Often, investment banks that evaluate the stock price of the acquired company overestimate it. Fund managers can benefit from the event by going long the target's equity and short the acquirer's equity. If the two companies are in the same industry, the long and short positions can have minimum beta if correctly structured. The risk of this strategy is that the event does not happen. Managers need to conduct research to assess the risk of the event's incompletion.

3. *Special situations* are events that impact on the price of a company's equity, such as corporate actions or restructuring (e.g. spin-offs, share buybacks and security issuance). Fund managers need to predict the event and position the fund accordingly to benefit from it.

Figure 3.34 compares the cumulative performance of event-driven hedge funds, US equities and Treasuries. As can be seen, the index representing event-driven strategies has delivered better returns than those of equities and government bonds. While correlated with equity, the even-driven index suffered from a much lower drawdown in the 2008 equity market crash and avoided almost entirely the 2000 equity market crash.

Figure 3.34: Cumulative performance of event-driven hedge funds, US equities and Treasuries, January 1990 to December 2013

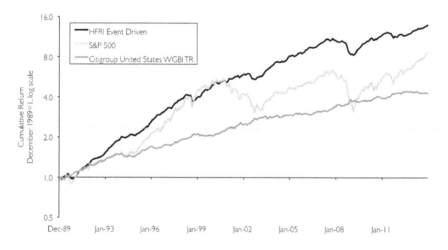

Source: Bloomberg, HFRI Event Driven Index, S&P 500 Index, Citigroup United States WGBI TR Index.

Figure 3.35 shows the rolling correlation between event-driven hedge funds and US equities and Treasuries. While in theory event-driven funds are supposed to be non-directional, their correlation with US equities as a group has been higher than expected and has increased over the last few years. Investing in equity-related events and completely hedging the equity market beta may be more challenging than expected.

Figure 3.35: Rolling 36-month correlation between event-driven hedge funds and US equities and Treasuries, January 1990 to December 2013

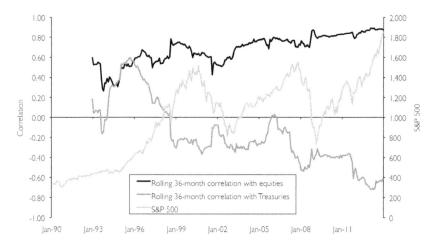

Source: Bloomberg, HFRI Event Driven Index, S&P 500 Index, Citigroup United States WGBI TR Index.

4. Relative value

Relative value (RV) arbitrage takes advantage of relative mispricing of investments. The mispricing can occur between related securities, a derivative and its underlying security, or a security and the market. Hedge fund managers use different valuation models to determine the true valuations of investments and if the valuations are different to the current price then managers can take advantage of the discrepancy.

Success depends on the convergence between the market price and value, as evaluated by the hedge fund. If the discrepancy in prices expands, instead of converging, then the strategy may lose on the trade. If the mispricing is small, managers often use leverage to enhance the potential return. Some relative value strategies have small directionality while others are market neutral, aiming to have no directionality.

Relative value hedge funds follow many different strategies exploiting pricing discrepancies in many different markets. Common relative value strategies include: fixed income arbitrage; equity market neutral (maintaining a long/short hedged position with small directionality); convertible arbitrage (exploiting pricing discrepancies between convertible bonds and related equities); statistical arbitrage (identifying pricing discrepancies using mathematical and statistical models); and volatility arbitrage (exploiting discrepancies in implied volatility and related derivatives).

Fixed income arbitrage, for example, can take advantage of anomalies in fixed income markets while minimising interest rate risk by taking long and short positions in related securities while utilising leverage. Convertible bonds are a natural area for arbitrage opportunities. Convertible arbitrage hedge funds held approximately 75% of all the convertible bonds available in 2005. Many of the convertible bond funds faced difficulties in 2008 because liquidity almost completely dried up.

Index arbitrage is a strategy that buys stocks that are going to be added to equity indices and shorts stocks that are going to be deleted from indices. Passive index trackers and ETFs, which need to replicate the indices, buy the additions and sell the deletions, and the fund can benefit from these trades. The trick is hedging away the directional equity market risk. Otherwise, general equity market movements can overwhelm performance.

Arbitrage in financial theory means a risk-free opportunity to make a profit. This is the classic free lunch. However, the concept is used more loosely in the hedge fund world since arbitrage here is certainly not risk free. Arbitrage in its loose definition is offsetting positions that should hedge each other. In reality, the positions do not always hedge each other and may be risky, in particular when their impact is amplified through leverage.

Figure 3.36 compares the cumulative performance of relative value hedge funds, US equities and Treasuries. Over the specific period, the relative value index delivered equity-like returns with bond-like volatility. The index is expected to underperform equities when they rally. However, mitigating downside risk has paid off during the measurement period.

Figure 3.37 shows the rolling correlation between relative value hedge funds and US equities and Treasuries. In the middle of the 1990s there was a low correlation with equity markets but this has materially increased. It appears that relative value hedge funds as a group are highly correlated with equities; this is not the characteristic that investors seek.

Figure 3.36: Cumulative performance of relative value hedge funds, US equities and Treasuries, January 1990 to December 2013

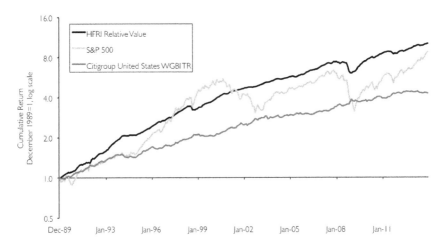

Source: Bloomberg, HFRI Relative Value Index, S&P 500 Index, Citigroup United States WGBI TR Index.

Figure 3.37: Rolling 36-month correlation between relative value hedge funds and US equities and Treasuries, January 1990 to December 2013

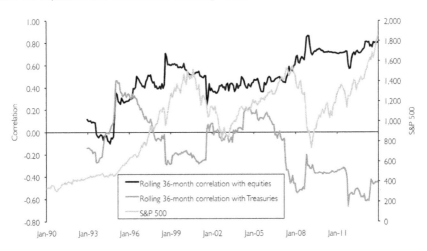

Source: Bloomberg, HFRI Relative Value Index, S&P 500 Index, Citigroup United States WGBI TR Index.

Funds of hedge funds

Funds of hedge funds or funds of funds (FoFs) are hedge funds that invest in hedge funds. The advantage of funds of funds is that their managers select the single manager funds following a due diligence process, monitor the underlying funds and manage the portfolio risk. The portfolio of funds is usually constructed to provide diversification across different strategies (multi-strategy and/or multi-manager).

The Achilles heel of FoFs is the double layer of fees; one at the FoF level and the second at the underlying single fund level. FoFs may be an expensive proposition that requires a high hurdle rate to deliver performance net of fees.

During 2008 the Madoff fraud was revealed. FoFs had been investing in the fund of Madoff (see page 302), failing miserably to detect the fraud. This led to intensified criticism of FoFs. Not only that they charge a fee in addition to the fees of the underlying funds, but that they may also fail in delivering robust due diligence. Since this event, the point of investing in FoFs has become less convincing.

FoFs may still play a role for small investors who do not have sufficient assets to properly diversify across single manager/single strategy funds.

Role of hedge funds in portfolios

Hedge funds follow a diverse range of investment strategies and deliver different profiles of returns, risks and correlations with other assets. Hedge funds can be divided into *risk diversifiers* and *return enhancers*. Some hedge fund strategies offer returns that have a relatively low correlation with other assets and can add diversification benefits to portfolios, hence risk diversifiers. Non-directional strategies should be uncorrelated with markets, offering diversification. Some hedge funds should benefit from adverse market movements and add material diversification or protection to portfolios that are predominately exposed to long equity and fixed income market movements. Other hedge fund strategies, on the other hand, are speculative, directional and/or aggressive and can potentially enhance portfolio returns.

Hedge funds enhance the investment opportunity set of portfolios as they provide access to *alternative systematic risks* (betas), investment strategies and techniques that are not available through traditional asset classes. For example, volatility cannot be accessed via traditional long-only funds and one of the only ways to access this risk through a professionally-managed fund is via hedge funds (alternatively, investors can use derivatives to access volatility as an asset class; however, the 'do it yourself' method is not professionally managed and requires expertise).

Importantly, hedge funds provide access to manager skill or *alpha*. Alpha is a non-correlated source of return and can both enhance diversification and generate returns. Indeed, some of the skilled and most successful long-only managers have moved to work for hedge funds, attracted by the lucrative compensation and flexibility that hedge funds offer. However, alpha may be negative as well. Even the most successful hedge funds and hedge fund managers cannot guarantee to deliver on their investment objectives.

Some hedge fund strategies should form part of the asset class to which they have systematic exposure. For example, equity long/short offers equity market risk plus manager skill or credit arbitrage that may form part of the credit allocation. Other strategies, which are not associated with any other asset class, should be part of a separate allocation (alternative investments, absolute return or simply hedge funds).

One of the principles of multi-asset investing is that investors should look for as many different sources of market risks and returns as possible and then decide how best to combine these sources based on risks, opportunities and interdependencies. Many hedge fund strategies are similar to selling insurance. Selling insurance provides a steady stream of returns (collecting premiums) until an insurable event happens. For example, hedge funds can provide liquidity to the market (selling insurance) and when liquidity dries up in a shock (insurable event), the hedge funds suffer. This is one of the reasons that hedge fund returns are asymmetric and exhibit fat tails (insurable events). Nevertheless, selling insurance is an uncorrelated source of risk that should add to risk diversification in portfolios.

Risks of investing in hedge funds

In many countries hedge funds are not distributed to the mass retail market, but rather sold selectively to sophisticated qualified investors. These investors are deemed to understand investment risks, in particular the risks of investing in hedge funds, and have the recourse to hire professional investment advisers.

Normally, regulations require retail funds to disclose risks through prospectuses and factsheets. The regulations also impose strict investment constraints on retail funds, such as limitations on short selling, leverage, use of derivatives, concentration and cash holdings. Funds that are managed relative to a published index normally have relative risk constraints and therefore their risks are aligned with those of the index.

Hedge funds expose investors to a wide range of risks, some of which are different to those of retail, long-only funds.

Operational risk

When selecting hedge funds, it is not only recommended to do an investment due diligence, but also an operational due diligence. Operational failings are a reason for a large proportion of hedge fund failings or a contributing factor to these failings. Hedge funds are relatively small, unregulated or lightly regulated businesses so they are exposed to many operational risks. Since the investment techniques that hedge funds utilise are sophisticated, their operational infrastructure needs to be assessed.

Some of the areas operational risk should cover include: mark-to-market valuation techniques; back-office; prime broker; risk measurement; risk management; behaviour and incentives of individuals; liquidity mechanisms; legal aspects; security of assets; performance reporting; and systems, controls and processes. Since hedge funds are lightly regulated relative to long-only funds, the risk of fraud should be evaluated carefully.

One of the most infamous hedge fund fraud scandals broke in December 2008 when Bernard Madoff admitted that the wealth management arm of his business was a Ponzi scheme. The size of the fraud was estimated to be more than $64 billion. Investors in Madoff's fund included funds of hedge funds, which are supposed to conduct thorough, professional due diligence on their investments. Even professional investors operating FoFs fell into the Madoff trap. Following the 2008 crisis, new regulations were introduced in 2010 in the United States and the European Union requiring hedge fund managers to report more information, leading to enhanced transparency.

Liquidity risk

Some hedge funds include *lock-up periods* that prevent investors from redeeming their investment during an agreed period. Lock-up periods or early redemption fees protect investors from the high transaction costs of trading illiquid positions. This is similar to the dilution levy or swing price of some long-only collectives.

When hedge funds face large redemptions while holding illiquid assets or need to sell assets that cannot be evaluated reliably, *side pockets* may be created. Funds segregate the illiquid assets and do not allow redemptions until the assets can be sold. New share classes that have rights only to the assets within the side pocket are issued. Once the assets are sold investors get their investment or what is left of it. The mechanism allows hedge funds to sell the illiquid assets in an orderly manner. This protects the shareholders in the funds from being disadvantaged when other shareholders redeem their holdings before the illiquid assets can be sold. It prevents the redeeming shareholders from receiving a higher price for their shares at the expense of the remaining shareholders, who wait until the illiquid assets can be sold.

Side pockets were common following the collapse of Lehman Brothers in September 2008. Many markets stopped functioning and hedge funds remained holding investments that could not be sold or evaluated. Side pockets were created during this emergency to enable the funds to sell the assets over time.

Prime broker risk

Prime brokerage is a term used to describe the services offered by investment banks and security firms to hedge funds. The features of the prime brokerage relationship and the important prime brokerage services are:

1. clearing and settlement

2. financing

3. custody

Clearing and settlement services enable transactions to be executed with multiple executing brokers, while centralising clearing and settlement through a single prime broker so the hedge fund's collateral requirements are netted across all deals handled by the prime broker. Financing is typically provided through margin loans, security loans (e.g. for short selling), repurchase agreements and OTC derivatives (via intermediation and embedded leverage). For convenience and to support access to financing as collateral, hedge funds often place assets in the custody of a prime broker.

The fall of Bear Stearns and Lehman Brothers demonstrated the reality of prime broker insolvency risk. Utilising prime brokerage services exposes a hedge fund to prime broker insolvency risk; generally, in the amount of that hedge fund's assets held by the prime broker and available for its rehypothecation (the practice by banks or brokers to use for their own benefit assets that have been posted as collateral by their customers). Prime brokerage insolvency may mean that not only the hedge fund needs to urgently find another prime broker to continue functioning, but also the hedge fund's assets held by the insolvent prime broker may be frozen or lost.

Valuation risk

When hedge funds hold illiquid holdings, valuation risk may be an issue. Similar to real estate and private equity, the NAV of hedge funds is based on valuations because some of the holdings are not regularly priced by the market.

Valuation risk includes the risk of inaccurate NAVs. This means that investors who purchase units in hedge funds may pay too much (or too little and dilute the incumbent investors) and investors who sell units may get paid less than the true NAV. Another aspect of valuation risk is the understatement of risk as measured by historic returns because the valuation-based returns are smoothed.

Manager risk

The main reason to invest in hedge funds is to access manager skill but of course managers can make unsuccessful investment decisions. There are plenty of examples of spectacular losses of hedge funds due to risky investment decisions that turned against them. In 2006 Amaranth Advisors lost in excess of $6.5 billion on natural gas trading. In 1998 Long-Term Capital Management (LTCM) famously lost $4.6 billion following the Russian debt crisis. Anyone can make a mistake or a wrong investment decision; when a manager has the flexibility to speculate virtually without limitation using derivatives and leverage, losses can be spectacular.

Leverage risk

Hedge funds that use leverage are exposed to leverage risk. Leverage is borrowing money or trading on margin to increase the exposure to investments beyond the money that was invested by investors. Leverage can amplify potential returns and potential losses, as well as require interest payments.

For example, a fund with $100 million in assets borrows $50 million and invests $150 million in an S&P 500 Index tracker. If the index rises by 10% the fund made a profit of $15 million or 15% on the $100 million of assets. If, however, the index falls 10%, the fund has lost $15 million: a loss of 15%. A leverage of 50% has enhanced returns and losses by 1.5 times since 1.5 times assets are invested.

In addition to the gain or loss, the fund needs to pay interest on the loan. Annual interest on the loan is an additional payment of $0.5 million per annum.

Capacity risk

Hedge funds have capacity risk because they often pursue investment opportunities that may disappear when enough money is chasing them (too much money chasing too few investments), or invest in investments that are so illiquid that the movement of sufficient amounts of money may significantly move their price. There is a limit on the amount of assets that hedge funds can manage efficiently. Many hedge funds choose to close to new investors when reaching capacity to ensure that they can continue to manage their assets efficiently. However, some hedge fund managers accept too much in new assets, stretching beyond capacity, perhaps motivated by management fees. This may hurt performance.

Concentration risk

Hedge funds are normally not managed relative to a benchmark and have no tracking error limit, so they may hold concentrated portfolios. Concentration risk is the exposure to a number of investments without proper diversification. This allows funds to take a high risk with a potential high reward, but also to suffer from large drawdowns.

There is nothing wrong with concentration in the hands of talented investors per se. However, concentrated portfolios tend to be riskier than diversified ones, all else being equal, because of the risk-reducing feature of diversification.

Construction of hedge fund portfolios

When constructing hedge fund portfolios, the challenge is that most quantitative measures for portfolio construction are unreliable. Volatility is understated; returns are not normally distributed; analytics based on betas, such as SAA, are inaccurate; historic returns lack predictive power; the track record is short; and alpha estimates are a guesstimate. There are many sophisticated, quant-driven methodologies for hedge fund portfolio construction. However, in many cases these methodologies are black boxes for most investors and their added value is questionable.

A practical approach should be more qualitative, allocating money to a few categories that logically have a low correlation with each other. One solution is allocating across the four main hedge fund strategies: global macro, equity long/short, event-driven and relative value.

The allocations to the different strategies can change if there is a reliable source for views on the expected relative performance of the four strategies, as well as decisions based on the conviction in the funds under each strategy. This ability can add a strategy rotation process across the four strategies.

The hedge fund portfolio can also be changed based on its role within the wider multi-asset portfolio (e.g. risk diversifier or return enhancer) and its interaction with other assets. The portfolio can be supplemented by managed futures, which can improve its risk profile (i.e. adding an element of protection and contrarianism, as well as changing the distribution of returns by reducing negative skewness and decreasing excess kurtosis).

Hedge fund replication

Both academics and practitioners have tried to explain and replicate hedge funds' returns using different techniques, such as multi-factor models. The motivation is clear: achieving hedge fund-like returns at fee levels of passive strategies and at high levels of liquidity.

Hedge fund returns are driven by three components:

1. traditional beta (attributed to long-only exposure to traditional market factors, such as equities and bonds)

2. alternative beta (attributed to alternative factors such as currency carry and equity momentum)

3. alpha (attributed to individual manager skill).

The first two components can potentially be replicated, while the third one cannot be easily captured.

In 2004 William Fung and David Hsieh published[147] a seven factor model with the aim of replicating hedge fund returns. These factors explain up to 80% of the monthly return variation in a diversified portfolio of hedge funds.

The seven factors are:

1. market (S&P 500 Index)

2. small cap minus large cap spread (Wilshire 750 Index minus Wilshire 1,750 Index)

3. change in 10-year constant maturity Treasury bond yield

4. change in spread between 10-year Treasury bond yield and Moody's Baa bond yield

5. portfolio of lookback options on bonds

6. portfolio of lookback options on currencies

7. portfolio of lookback options on commodities.

A *lookback straddle* is a derivative security that pays its holder the difference between the maximum and minimum price of the underlying asset over a given time period. The lookback straddle is a combination of a lookback put (an option to sell the underlying at its maximum price) and a lookback call (an option to buy the underlying at its minimum price). The idea is that the lookback straddle benefits from the dominant trend in the underlying's price over the given time period. A large spread between the maximum and minimum, or high volatility in the underlying's price, are profitable.

Lookback straddles are one example of an alternative beta. Other alternative betas include *currency carry* (long high-yielding currencies and short low-yielding currencies); *equity momentum* (long well-performing stocks and short poorly performing stocks); and *merger arbitrage* (long acquired companies and short acquiring companies).

The multi-factor model used for the hedge fund replication should use a combination of *time-varying* beta loading factors. Hedge fund indices are used as the benchmarks for replication of the different strategies. The best hedge fund indices should be asset-weighted (as opposed to equally-weighted) because they better reflect the opportunities that exist and where investments are directed by underlying hedge funds. Strategy specific indices should be used (e.g. global macro, equity long/short

---

[147] Fung, William and Hsieh, David, 'Hedge Fund Benchmarks: A Risk Based Approach', *Financial Analysts Journal* 60 (2004).

as opposed to broad indices) since each strategy has different investment techniques, instruments and markets, and different factors are used to replicate them (the composition of the broad index also changes, so it is more difficult to model).

The multi-factor model should be a *parsimonious* model (i.e. with the least number of parameters). This ensures that the model avoids the negative effects of *data mining*. The best approach is to identify factors that make intuitive and economic sense, rather than factors that just have high statistical explanatory power.

Supporters of hedge fund replication techniques claim that they should work since when individual managers' views are aggregated in an index, they tend to cluster into common themes that drive the index performance. The large number of decision makers reduces the frequency of changes of views, enabling the index performance to be replicated.

While the performance of replicating strategies is systematically inferior to that of actual hedge funds[148] (depending on fund selection) and hedge funds seem to add alpha,[149] then hedge fund replication strategies, also known as *liquid alternative beta*, have advantages in portfolios. Investors can build the allocation to hedge funds more cheaply and efficiently; the positions offer transparency, daily liquidity and valuations; investors can change the exposures tactically (due to liquidity and relative low transaction costs); the passive hedge fund exposure can be used in the passive core of a core/satellite approach; capacity constraints are minimal; the replication strategies can be used during transitions; they can be used to replicate the short of the index and enable long hedge fund positions to be hedged; they reduce *headline risk* (risk associated with an individual manager or the possibility that negative news involving a manager may have a harmful impact on investors); and they can enable investors who have constraints on purchasing hedge funds to gain exposure to hedge funds.

The hedge fund replication industry is rapidly developing, in particular because it is a lucrative business for investment banks. Investment banks are well positioned to offer investment products that are rule-based (as opposed to discretionary) and they benefit from hedge fund replication on three levels: fees on the products, commissions on trading instruments for the hedge fund replication strategies and prime brokerage. The increasing popularity of hedge funds regulated by UCITS has also boosted the investment bank business in the hedge fund space.

---

[148] Hasanhodzic, Jasmina and Lo, Andrew, 'Can Hedge-Fund Returns be Replicated?: The Linear Case', *Journal of Investment Management* 5 (2007); and Amenc, Noel, Martellini, Lionel, Meyfredi, Jean-Christophe and Ziemann, Volker, 'Performance of Passive Hedge Fund Replication Strategies', EDHEC Risk and Asset Management Research Centre (2009).

[149] Ibbotson, Roger, Chen, Peng and Zhu, Kevix, 'The ABCs of Hedge Funds: Alpha, Betas and Costs', *Financial Analysts Journal* 67 (2011).

Expected returns

Estimating a single expected return for a heterogeneous and diverse group of investments such as hedge funds is too simplistic. One expected return for a hedge fund strategy (e.g. equity long/short, global macro, relative value and event-driven) is also too simplistic.

A quick and crude estimate is assuming that the expected long-term return of hedge funds is the average between the expected return of equities and bonds. For example, if the expected return of equities is 8% and that of bonds is 4%, then the expected return of hedge funds would be 6%. This is based on the assumption that hedge funds are unlikely to do as well as equities are expected to do but they should outperform bonds. This is, however, one size fits all and unlikely to reflect reality.

The recommended way to estimate hedge fund long-term expected returns is a granular approach. Each hedge fund should be treated separately on a case by case basis. The expected returns of funds should be based on their return objectives.

The expected return of funds with an absolute return objective is the absolute return objective. For example, a fund targeting LIBOR + 4% has an expected return of the expected cash return, say 1%, plus the outperformance target, giving 5%.

The expected returns should be net of fees, which may be substantial (e.g. 1% or 2% management fees plus a 20% performance fee). Using the stated return objective means a high degree of confidence in the ability of the fund to meet its objectives. However, only high conviction hedge funds should be used, implying a high degree of confidence in their ability to meet their objectives.

Hedge fund indices

Hedge fund indices are based on hedge fund databases that capture only a subset of the hedge fund universe while the indices capture only a subset of the database. However, the indices should contain less systematic biases than do broader databases and contain higher quality data.

The Dow Jones Credit Suisse (DJCS)[150] hedge fund index data (based on the Lipper TASS database) starts in 1994. Since 2000, the DJCS index has been run on a real-time basis, so there should be little survivorship or backfill bias after that point. The HFR[151] index goes further back (published data start in 1990), but in the early years at least it was not adjusted for survivorship bias.

The DJCS is a value-weighted index and should exhibit milder biases than equally-weighted fund indices such as the HFR. Both index families offer indices representing different hedge fund styles.

---

[150] www.hedgeindex.com.
[151] www.hedgefundresearch.com.

Hedge fund historical return and risk characteristics

Figure 3.38 shows the cumulative performance of the four main hedge fund strategies (global macro, equity long/short, event-driven and relative value) since January 1991 using the HFRI indices. The returns are correlated since they are influenced to different degrees by similar risk factors, such as the equity risk factor. However, the different hedge fund strategies deliver a different return and risk profile. Relative value is the least risky (it has the smoother line) and it has delivered the lowest return. Global macro seems to have fallen out of favour over recent years.

Figure 3.38: Cumulative performance of global macro, equity long/short, event-driven and relative value hedge funds, January 1990 to December 2013

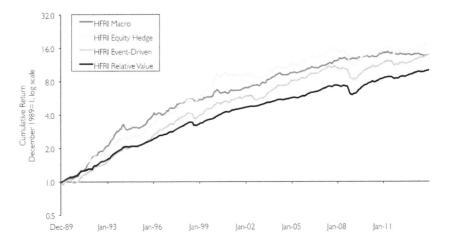

Source: Bloomberg, HFRI Macro Index, HFRI Equity Hedge Index, HFRI Event-Driven Index, HFRI Relative Value Index.

Figure 3.39 shows the rolling 36-month volatility of global macro and equity long/short compared with the rolling volatility of US equities and Treasuries. The volatility of most hedge funds falls most of the time between that of government bonds and equities. However, the volatility of each hedge fund should be analysed separately since different hedge funds can have different characteristics. The volatility of equity long/short is greatly affected by that of equities. The volatility of global macro has fallen over recent years and is now in line with that of Treasuries.

Figure 3.39: Rolling 36-month volatility of global macro and equity long/short hedge funds, and US equities and Treasuries, January 1992 to December 2013

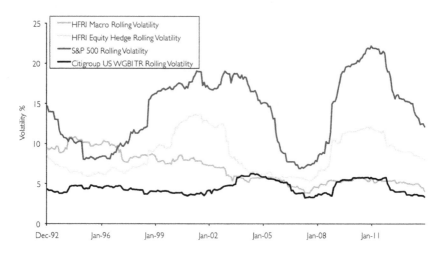

Source: Bloomberg, HFRI Macro Index, HFRI Equity Hedge Index, HFRI Event-Driven Index, HFRI Relative Value Index.

Table 3.11 shows the return and risk characteristics of hedge fund strategies, managed futures, US equities and US bonds and Table 3.12 shows the correlation matrix among the indices. All the analytics are based on published index returns. Over the entire measurement period hedge fund strategies have delivered impressive results with returns matching those of equities and volatility close to that of government bonds. The Sharpe ratios of hedge funds are all high.

However, there are four main caveats to the data shown here. First, the performance of each individual hedge fund may differ to that of the index. Second, the performance of the index may be boosted by biases. Third, risk is understated. Fourth, the return depends heavily on the measurement period. Investors should not just look at reported numbers but should try to understand the story behind them.

The correlations of hedge fund strategies with equities and Treasuries are attractively low, so including hedge funds in portfolios should deliver diversification benefits. However, once again, correlations change and they depend on each individual hedge fund.

Table 3.11: Hedge fund and managed futures return and risk characteristics, January 1994 to December 2013. Sharpe ratio calculated using $ cash returns

	Global Macro	Equity Long/Short	Event-Driven	Relative Value	Managed Futures	US equities	US Treasuries
Start month	Jan-1994	Jan-1994	Jan-1994	Jan-1994	Jan-1994	Jan-1994	Jan-1994
Performance (% pa)	7.6	10.3	10.4	8.4	5.1	9.2	5.4
Volatility (%)	6.5	9.2	6.7	4.2	11.6	15.2	4.6
Skewness	0.25	-0.24	-1.30	-2.89	0.02	-0.71	-0.11
Kurtosis	1.14	2.17	4.42	16.60	-0.02	1.10	1.19
Sharpe ratio	1.73	0.81	1.12	1.31	0.16	0.42	0.57
Max drawdown (%)	-10.7	-30.6	-24.8	-18.0	-17.7	-50.9	-5.3

Source: Bloomberg, HFRI Macro Index, HFRI Equity Hedge Index, HFRI Event-Driven Index, HFRI Relative Value Index, Dow Jones Credit Suisse Managed Futures Hedge Fund Index, Citigroup United States WGBI TR Index, S&P 500 Index.

Table 3.12: Correlation matrix, January 1994 to December 2013. Correlations with Managed Futures, January 1994 to June 2012

Correlation matrix	Global Macro	Equity Long/Short	Event-Driven	Relative Value	Managed Futures	US equities	US Treasuries
Global Macro	1.00	0.55	0.51	0.32	0.48	0.32	0.18
Equity Long/Short	0.55	1.00	0.87	0.73	0.01	0.76	-0.21
Event-Driven	0.51	0.87	1.00	0.82	-0.03	0.73	-0.24
Relative Value	0.32	0.73	0.82	1.00	-0.07	0.58	-0.18
Managed Futures	0.48	0.01	-0.03	-0.07	1.00	-0.09	0.26
US equities	0.32	0.76	0.73	0.58	-0.09	1.00	-0.18
US Treasuries	0.18	-0.21	-0.24	-0.18	0.26	-0.18	1.00

Source: Bloomberg, HFRI Macro Index, HFRI Equity Hedge Index, HFRI Event-Driven Index, HFRI Relative Value Index, Dow Jones Credit Suisse Managed Futures Hedge Fund Index, Citigroup United States WGBI TR Index, S&P 500 Index.

Figure 3.40 shows the rolling 36-month correlation between the HFRI Fund Weighted Composite Index and the S&P 500 Index with the linear trend line. Over recent years hedge funds have become more directional and correlated with equities. In other words, hedge funds now generally have higher equity risk beta than in the past.

The correlation of event-driven and relative value hedge funds with equities has materially increased over the years. These hedge fund strategies, as a group, fail to deliver their diversification benefits and non-directionality. This trend in correlation between indices reinforces the need to evaluate each hedge fund separately to determine whether it has a role in portfolios and what this role is.

Figure 3.40: Rolling 36-month correlation between hedge funds and US equities, January 1993 to December 2013

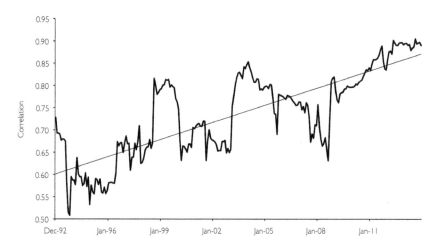

Source: Bloomberg, HFRI Fund Weighted Composite Index, S&P 500 Index.

Managed futures

Managed futures are a type of alternative investment that can take both long and short positions in futures contracts and options in global commodity, interest rate, equity and currency markets. Managed futures have different return profiles than the underlying investments as a result of manager skill and systematic factors.[152]

Managed futures are classified as a sub-strategy within hedge funds by some (because of the similar limitation on marketing to investors, fee level and

---

[152] Schneeweis, Thomas, 'Dealing with Myths of Managed Futures', *The Journal of Alternative Investments* (1998).

potential risk level, although the risk depends on the specific investment), or as a separate type of investment by others (because of the more regulated nature of managed futures and their legal structure that may be a separate managed account, rather than a fund). While there are arguments to support each view, what matters the most is the characteristics of each investment, less so whether it is defined as a hedge fund or managed futures. Hence, managed futures are discussed here, under the chapter on hedge funds.

Managed futures are commonly managed by licensed commodity trading advisors (CTAs), which are regulated in the United States by the Commodity Futures Trading Commission and the National Futures Association. During the late 1970s a number of CTAs were established, inaugurating the managed futures industry. In the latter two decades of the 20th century and on into the 21st century the managed futures industry has exhibited rapid growth; as of the middle of 2012, it was estimated that the total assets under management in the managed futures (CTA) industry were over $330 billion.

Managed futures can use a number of investment strategies, the most common of which is *trend following*. Trend following involves buying markets that are making new highs and shorting markets that are making new lows. Variations in trend-following managers include duration of trend captured (short term, medium term, long term); definition of trend (i.e. what is considered a new high or new low); and money management and risk management techniques. Other strategies that managed futures use include discretionary strategies, fundamental strategies, option writing (e.g. writing out-of-the-money call options and collecting premium payments), pattern recognition, arbitrage strategies and so on.

Figure 3.41 shows the average performance of a managed futures index ranked by average decile performance of US equities. As can be seen, managed futures tend to perform strongly when equity markets fall.

Figure 3.41: Average performance of managed futures and US equities ranked by performance of US equities, January 1994 to December 2013

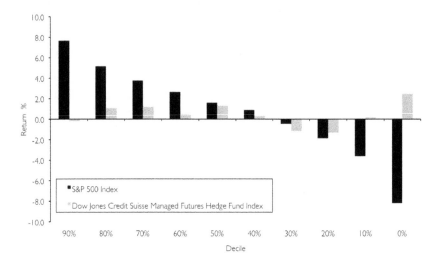

Source: Bloomberg, Dow Jones Credit Suisse Managed Futures Hedge Fund Index, S&P 500 Index.

Reasons for investing in managed futures

The main reasons for investing in managed futures include:

- *Diversification.* Managed futures tend to have a low correlation with other assets, both traditional and alternatives, including hedge funds. They therefore offer diversification opportunities.

- *Protection.* Managed futures tend to perform well during times of financial stress and turmoil.

- *Wide investment opportunity set.* Managed futures may utilise futures contracts traded on many global exchanges involving a wide range of underlying assets or indices, including equity indices, financial instruments, commodities and currencies. They offer potential trading and investing opportunities across a broad spectrum of assets and markets.

- *Active management.* Managed futures offer wide flexibility for active managers to add value.

- *Liquidity.* The underlying futures contracts are liquid.

- *Return distribution.* Managed futures tend to have positive skewness and can help favourably shape the return distribution of portfolios. Managed futures may have positive skewness and negative excess kurtosis.

Risks

The risks of investing in managed futures include:

- *Disappointing performance.* During sideways moving, choppy or directionless market conditions, managed futures can suffer and deliver negative and volatile returns.

- *Complicated.* Managed futures normally use sophisticated trading techniques and instruments. Some investors may find it difficult to understand them. Some managed futures strategies are opaque black-boxes.

Managed futures historical return and risk characteristics

Figure 3.42 shows the cumulative performance of managed futures and US equities since January 1994. As can be seen the index representing managed futures has delivered a return profile different than that of equities. Managed futures seem to perform the best when equities perform the worst, making managed futures an interesting addition to multi-asset portfolios.

Figure 3.42: Cumulative performance of managed futures and US equities, January 1994 to December 2013

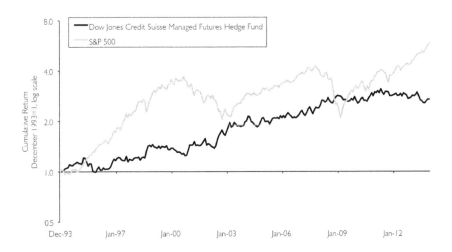

Source: Bloomberg, Dow Jones Credit Suisse Managed Futures Hedge Fund Index, S&P 500 Index.

Figure 3.43 shows the rolling 36-month correlation between managed futures and US equities. The correlation seems to drop when equity markets drop (2000 and 2008). This pattern of correlation is what investors should be seeking in defensive assets.

Figure 3.43: Rolling 36-month correlation of managed futures and US equities, January 1997 to December 2013

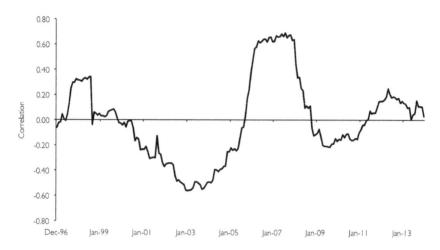

Source: Bloomberg, Dow Jones Credit Suisse Managed Futures Index, S&P 500 Index.

Conclusions

Hedge funds and managed futures offer a wide array of flexible investments. They are heavily dependent on manager skill and are therefore typically expensive because talent costs money. They offer portfolios exposure to alternative betas as well as alpha. Investors who have the capability of choosing and monitoring hedge funds should consider including them in their portfolios because of the diversification benefits and potential for enhanced returns.

Summary

- Hedge funds are not a separate asset class. They are unregulated, pooled, professionally managed and unconstrained vehicles, and they can use a variety of investment techniques such as leverage, short selling and derivatives.

- In practice, investors normally allocate part of their portfolio to hedge funds, effectively treating them as a kind of asset class.

- Hedge funds are normally not tied to a benchmark and can aim to deliver return objectives such as absolute return or equity-like returns with bond-like volatility.

- The name hedge fund may be misleading since some hedge funds do not aim to hedge any risk.

- Hedge fund returns depend on manager skill. Manager selection is challenging but has more opportunities to add value with hedge funds than with long-only strategies.

- Historically, hedge fund indices have delivered better results than long-only managers. However, biases in hedge fund indices (e.g. survivorship and selection) overstate returns. Hedge funds expose investors to risks that are not captured by standard risk measures (e.g. standard deviation), including illiquidity and fat-tail risks.

- Hedge funds charge high fees, normally combining an asset-based fee (1% to 2% per annum) and a performance fee (20%). The fee structure may skew the manager incentives. A high watermark is common to prevent compensating managers for performance below previous peaks. Lock-in periods protect incumbent investors from redemptions by other investors.

- The four main categories of hedge fund investment strategies are global macro, equity long/short, event-driven and relative value (arbitrage).

- Funds of hedge funds offer manager selection, monitoring, risk management, diversification and portfolio construction at the expense of a double layer of fees.

- The roles of hedge funds in multi-asset portfolios can be broadly divided into risk diversifiers and return enhancers, depending on the hedge fund strategy.

- Hedge funds expand the investment opportunity set of portfolios through accessing manager alpha, alternative betas, different investment techniques, unique asset classes (such as volatility) and unique risks (such as insurance selling).

- The light regulations, flexibility and unconstrained portfolios of hedge funds expose investors to a wide array of risks. The main risks include operational risk; liquidity risk; prime broker risk; valuation risk; manager risk; leverage risk; capacity risk; and concentration risk.

- Hedge fund portfolio construction can be based on a qualitative approach of diversifying the exposure across the four main hedge fund strategies: global macro, equity long/short, event-driven and relative value. The portfolio can be supplemented by an exposure to managed futures.

- The expected returns of hedge funds should be assessed on a case by case basis and should be matched against the return objectives of each hedge fund.

- The correlation of event-driven and relative value hedge funds with equities has materially increased over recent years. These hedge fund strategies, as a group, fail to deliver their diversification benefits and non-directionality.

- The trend in increasing correlation between hedge funds and equities reinforces the need to evaluate each hedge fund separately to determine whether it has a role in a multi-asset portfolio and what this role is.

- Managed futures are a type of alternative investment that can take both long and short positions in futures contracts and options on global commodity, interest rate, equity and currency markets.

- Managed futures offer many potential benefits for multi-asset portfolios, including diversification, protection, a wider investment opportunity set, alpha from active management, liquidity and favourably changing the distribution of returns.

*　*　*

This concludes Part III. The four mainstream types of alternative investments (real estate, commodities, private equity and hedge funds) have been reviewed. These alternative investments are not novel any more. Most multi-asset portfolios should include these investments for diversification, widening the investment opportunity set and enhancing performance, as long as these investments are appropriate. This depends on the constraints of the portfolio, such as a sufficiently long investment horizon, liquidity needs, cost budget and so on.

Part IV ventures into the area of new alternative investments. These are investment types and techniques that are not covered by traditional and mainstream alternative investments. Many of these investments are relatively new and less familiar than the investment types that have been covered up to this point; the investment management universe is always expanding.

PART IV

NEW ALTERNATIVE INVESTMENTS

INTRODUCTION

Alternative alternatives

The list of alternative investments gets longer and longer as more types of investments are added. The reasons for the ever-extending list are the continued search for diversifying assets and financial innovation, making more investments investable and accessible.

Another reason is the disappointment with equities, which broadly moved sideways for more than a decade up to 2012, and the subdued expected returns from bonds, given their low yields. Investors are on the lookout for new sources of investment returns. Yet another reason for the addition of new investment types is the ongoing search of the investment management industry to come up with new products to sell to customers.

Currency has always been part of global portfolios but only over the last couple of decades has it started to be treated as a separate asset class. Infrastructure has become another alternative asset class with increasing popularity in the last few years. Volatility may also be classified as an alternative investment, in particular with the advent of innovative ways for accessing it.

Art, wine, antiques, coins, stamps, forestry, catastrophe bonds, life settlements and loans are some other examples of alternative alternatives that have become more popular over the last decade. Some of these investments have been in existence for centuries. Art, for instance, is certainly not new and the older it is usually the more valuable it gets. However, only recently have these investments started to be treated as part of investment portfolios; hence my use of the term *new* alternatives. Modelling these investments as part of the overall asset allocation is still in its infancy.

Most of these investments are not traded on regulated exchanges, they have no appropriate indices and there is no publicly published, reliable track record of their performance. Therefore, most of these investments are highly illiquid (it is challenging to build large positions and trade them); their markets are relatively inefficient (creating opportunities for expert investors); they are likely to have a low correlation with other assets (adding diversification opportunities in portfolio context); and it is difficult to model them for SAA purposes since their capital market assumptions (CMAs) are mostly based on qualitative, subjective judgment. Most of them are therefore suitable for a relative small allocation within portfolios and investing in them requires a high level of expertise. These investments are not for everyone.

Some of the new alternative investments are not separate asset classes but rather the result of financial engineering and innovation. Structured products, for example, combine asset classes with derivatives to create a new type of investment. Structured products are not an asset class on their own but rather a way to invest in asset classes to deliver a different return and risk profile. Structured finance securities, such as asset-backed securities (ABS), mortgage-backed securities (MBS) and collateralised debt obligations (CDOs), are basically methods for packaging securities or financial instruments to create new securities.

The key advantages of most of the new alternative investments is that they offer exposure to risk factors and return drivers that are not accessible through traditional asset classes or standard alternative investments. Infrastructure, loans, volatility, art, insurance-linked securities and timber each have unique return drivers not found elsewhere. One of the fundamental premises of multi-asset investing is exposing portfolios to imperfectly correlated systematic risks to harvest risk premiums. New alternative investments add to the list of these systematic risks and improve the risk-adjusted performance of portfolios.

Summary

- Infrastructure, volatility, currency, art and forestry are examples of new alternative investments.

- New alternative investments include investment types that are not part of traditional asset classes and mainstream alternative investments.

- The search for uncorrelated investments and financial innovation has expanded the list of alternatives to more esoteric asset classes.

- Investments such as art are highly illiquid and difficult to model for SAA purposes, but offer opportunities for active, expert management as well as diversification benefits.

- Some of the new alternative investments are not separate asset classes but rather the result of financial engineering and innovation, packaging asset classes and financial instruments in particular ways to create new securities.

- The key advantages of most of the new alternative investments is that they offer exposure to risk factors and return drivers that are not accessible through traditional asset classes or standard alternative investments.

CHAPTER 9: CURRENCY

Currency or foreign exchange (forex or FX) is an integral part of international investing. It is the world's largest, most actively traded and most liquid financial market. Participants include large banks, central banks, institutional investors, asset managers (e.g. hedge funds) and retail investors.

Each day nearly $4 trillion of foreign exchange changes hands on average. Of the $4 trillion about $1.5 trillion is in spot transactions (agreement to exchange currencies for an agreed price for settlement on the spot date, which is normally T+2 days) and about $2.5 trillion is traded via derivatives.[153] The global currency market is active 24 hours a day. Trading in the United Kingdom accounts for over 35% of the total volume, while trading in the United States accounts for about 18% and in Japan for about 6%.

Table 4.1 shows the most traded currencies by value. The four major currencies are the US dollar, euro, Japanese yen and British pound. Together they account for nearly 80% of daily trading volume.

Table 4.1: Most traded currencies, April 2013

Currency	ISO 4217 Code (Symbol)	Daily share (%)
United States dollar	USD ($)	87.0
euro	EUR (€)	33.4
Japanese yen	JPY (¥)	23.0
British pound sterling	GBP (£)	11.8
Australian (Aussie) dollar	AUD ($)	8.6
Swiss franc	CHF (Fr)	5.2
Canadian dollar	CAD ($)	4.6
Mexican peso	MXN ($)	2.5
Chinese yuan (renminbi)	CNY (¥)	2.2
New Zealand (kiwi) dollar	NZD ($)	2.0
Swedish krona	SEK (kr)	1.8
Russian rouble	RUB (k)	1.6
Hong Kong dollar	HKD ($)	1.4
Norwegian krone	NOK (kr)	1.4
Singapore dollar	SGD ($)	1.4
Other		12.2

Source: Bank of International Settlements. The total sum is 200% since each currency trade always involves a currency pair.

---

[153] Bank of International Settlements, www.bis.org.

When investors hold international investments or assets denominated in foreign currencies they effectively make two investments: one in the underlying investment and a second in the currency in which the investment is denominated. The foreign currency exposure can and should be treated as a separate asset class.

When foreign currency exposure is part of a foreign investment it may be an unintended by-product of investing internationally. Investors usually have the choice of whether to assume the currency risk or to hedge it to their base currency and mitigate it almost completely (currency risk is a manageable risk).

Investors can, on the other hand, intentionally gain exposure to foreign currencies with the objective of making a profit. This is easily achieved through deposits in foreign currency, purchasing foreign bonds or through the derivative market, most commonly via FX forward contracts.

The currency market is becoming increasingly transparent. Globalisation is integrating the global economy and the number of pegged exchange rates is decreasing. The number of non-tradable currencies is also declining. This means that, in addition to traditional currencies, new investment opportunities are emerging in growth markets such as Asia and Latin America. The currency investment opportunity set is expanding.

Foreign exchange investing is effectively investing in the economic development of a country or group of countries. Factors such as GDP growth, trade balances, interest rates, industrial output and the political stability of a country or region all have a decisive effect on exchange rates.

The exchange rate is the price of a currency pair or the value of one currency for the purpose of conversion to another. For example, if the exchange rate between the US dollar and the British pound is 1.60 £/$ it means that it cost 1.6 dollars to buy one pound. Exchange rates can be confusing and investors should pay attention to which amount of one currency is converted to a single unit of the other currency.

History

One feature that all assets have in common is that their price is determined by free market forces. Their price is not set or controlled by any single entity; otherwise their expected returns and risks are artificially set and not driven by economic forces. The prices of assets should be driven by market forces.

This was not the case with foreign exchange in the past. In July 1944 the Bretton Woods agreement was signed. According to the agreement, each country that was part of the agreement was obliged to adopt a monetary policy that maintained the exchange rate by tying its currency to the US dollar. The International Monetary Fund (IMF), which was established by the agreement, was given the ability to bridge temporary imbalances of payments. The agreement meant that exchange rates were fixed or *pegged* to the dollar, which was based on the gold standard. In other words, the prices of currencies or their exchange rates were set by governments, not by market forces.

In August 1971 US President Richard Nixon unilaterally suspended the convertibility of dollars into gold, effectively ending the gold standard. In December 1971 the *Smithsonian agreement* was signed and the era of fixed exchange rates ended. In June 1973 the *free floating* of currencies commenced. This marked the birth of currency as an asset class since the value of currencies started to fluctuate driven by the foreign exchange market forces of supply and demand and not because of the way the price was controlled by governments (as is the case under a fixed exchange rate regime). Even though people have exchanged currencies since ancient biblical times, the global foreign exchange market as we know it today is a modern phenomenon; about 40 years old.

Determinants of exchange rate

A prominent theme in academic studies is that currency returns are not forecastable and hence long-term currency expected returns are zero. However, some academic studies have reported empirical evidence of a currency risk premium[154] and others have documented that various currency trading strategies (e.g. the carry trade and technical analysis-based strategies) have been profitable. This means that assuming currency risk may be profitable over time as it is rewarded by a risk premium and therefore active currency trading can add alpha.

In addition, academic papers have documented that the returns from currency trading strategies are weakly correlated with other asset classes (e.g. equities, bonds and real estate), making currency desirable as a *zero beta* asset.

Attempts have been made to explain the fluctuations in exchange rates using different factors. The factors can be divided into:

1. financial and economic theories
2. economic factors (economic policy and economic conditions)
3. political conditions
4. market psychology

Forecasting currency movements is difficult, in particular over the short term, since some theories are disconnected from empirical reality and the effects, weighting and timing of the different factors are difficult to predict. Also, political developments and sentiment (market psychology) are virtually unpredictable.

---

[154] Dumas, Bernard and Solnik, Bruno, 'The World Price of Foreign Exchange Risk', *Journal of Finance* 50 (1995); de Santis, Giorgio and Gerard, Bruno, 'How Big is the Premium for Currency Risk?', *Journal of Financial Economics* 49 (1998); and Lustig, Hanno and Verdelhan, Adrien, 'The Cross-section of Foreign Currency Risk Premia and Consumption Growth Risk', *American Economic Review* 97 (2007).

1. Financial and economic theories

A number of *financial and economic theories* attempt to explain the fluctuations in exchange rates under a floating exchange rate regime. The theories are divided into international parity conditions, a balance of payments model and asset pricing models.

International parity conditions

A number of economic parities provide a logical explanation for exchange rates between currencies. However, similar to many economic theories, they fail in practice as they are based on unrealistic assumptions (e.g. free flow of goods, services and capital).

Purchasing Power Parity (PPP) states that the same amount of money is required to purchase the same goods and services across national borders and can be used to calculate the implicit exchange rate. PPP is based on the *law of one price*, stating that in an efficient market all identical goods must have only one price (otherwise arbitrageurs push the prices to equilibrium). The *Big Mac Index* is an example of PPP since a Big Mac in McDonald's restaurants around the world should cost the same since effectively it is the same product.

A Starbucks latte is another example of a product that should have the same price irrespective of the currency and location. If, for instance, a latte costs £2 in London and $3 in New York City then the £/$ exchange rate should be 1.50 so the two cups of latte have the same price across the Atlantic.

The reality, however, is that international markets for goods and services are not efficient and PPP does not necessarily hold. One issue is that goods are not always transferable. You cannot buy a cheaper latte in London, fly it to New York City and sell it for a riskless profit. In other words, arbitrage forces do not move the prices in London and New York City into equilibrium. Nevertheless, PPP can be helpful in forecasting fair-value or equilibrium exchange rates over the long term.

Uncovered interest rate parity is a no-arbitrage condition representing an equilibrium state under which investors will be indifferent to available interest rates on bank deposits in two countries. This would imply that if the interest rate on a dollar deposit is higher than the interest rate on a euro deposit, the euro should appreciate versus the dollar to make investors indifferent between the two deposits, and vice versa. That is, according to the parity, currencies with lower (higher) interest rates should appreciate (depreciate).

According to an approximation of the uncovered interest rate parity:

$$i_L = i_F * \Delta FX_{L,F}$$

where i_L is the interest rate on the local currency; i_F is the interest rate on the foreign currency; and $\Delta FX_{L,F}$ is the change in the exchange rate between the local and foreign currencies. According to the parity the change in exchange rate is equal to the ratio between the interest rates.

The empirical reality, however, is that the currencies with a higher interest rate tend to appreciate (not depreciate as implied by the uncovered interest rate parity) since a high interest rate attracts investors and the demand for the currency pushes its relative value higher. The empirical reality is opposite to theory in this case.

The *International Fisher effect* is similar to uncovered interest rate parity and suggests that differences in nominal interest rates reflect expected changes in the spot exchange rate between countries. According to the international Fisher effect:

$$E(_{FX}) = (1+i_L)/(1+i_F)-1$$

where $E(_{FX})$ is the expected change in exchange rate; i_L is the interest rate on the local currency; and i_F is the interest rate on the foreign currency.

For example, if the current exchange rate between the dollar and pound is 1.60, the interest rate on the dollar is 2% and that on the pound is 4%, then the expected exchange rate is $1.4*(1+2\%)/(1+4\%) = 1.57$. The currency with the lower interest rate – in this example the dollar – is expected to appreciate versus the pound (it takes fewer dollars to buy each pound). In reality, however, similar to the uncovered interest rate parity, currencies with higher interest rates tend to appreciate, not depreciate.

Balance of payments model

This model focuses largely on tradable goods and services, ignoring the increasing role of global capital flows. According to the model, a current account deficit should cause the currency to depreciate. The value of imports exceeds the value of exports. Hence, the demand for foreign currency to purchase the imports is higher than the demand for the local currency to purchase the exports, causing the local currency to fall in value. A current account surplus causes the reverse and the local currency should appreciate.

Asset pricing models

The international capital asset pricing model (ICAPM)[155] is an example of an asset pricing model that attempts to determine the required return on risky assets, measured in local currency. Theoretically, ICAPM should offer investors sufficient returns for taking on systematic or market risk on the world market of

---

[155] Merton, Robert, 'An International Capital Asset Pricing Model', *Econometrica* 4 (1973).

investable securities, measured in the same currency as the one in which the asset's return is attempted to be measured.

The models view currencies as an asset class for constructing investment portfolios. Assets' prices are influenced mostly by the willingness of market participants to hold the existing quantities of assets and this depends on their expectations of the future worth of these assets. The equilibrium-based asset pricing model of exchange rate determination states that the exchange rate between two currencies represents the price that balances the relative supply and demand with respect of the assets denominated in those currencies.

In practice none of these theories can be reliably used to correctly predict the movements of exchange rates. Currency prices are driven by market forces of supply and demand. These forces are influenced by economic factors, political conditions and market psychology.

2. Economic factors

Economic factors that explain fluctuations of exchange rates include economic policy and economic conditions. *Economic policy* includes government fiscal policy and monetary policy. In an open economy, *fiscal policy* affects the exchange rate and the trade balance. In the case of a fiscal expansion, the rise in interest rates due to government borrowing and potential public spending and investments in infrastructure, for example, attracts foreign capital. As they buy more local currency to invest, foreigners bid up the price of the local currency, causing an exchange rate appreciation in the short run. This appreciation makes imported goods cheaper and exports more expensive abroad, leading to a decline in the merchandise trade balance. Foreigners sell more to the country than they buy from it and, in return, acquire ownership of the country's assets (including government debt).

In the long run, however, the accumulation of external debt that results from persistent government deficits can lead foreigners to distrust the country's assets and can cause a depreciation of the exchange rate.

Monetary policy sets the cost of money through the interest rate. The mechanism for transmitting monetary policy to the demand for goods and services became increasingly important after 1973, when foreign exchange rates were allowed to float, and obstacles to international movements of capital began to disappear. An increase in local interest rates relative to those in foreign countries draws capital into local currency assets (investors seek higher yield) and raises the value of the currency through demand. The country's goods become more expensive relative to foreign goods, for buyers both at home and abroad. Declines in exports and increases in imports reduce aggregate demand for domestic production.

Unconventional tools of monetary policy include *quantitative easing* (QE). QE is used by central banks to stimulate the economy when conventional monetary policy has become ineffective. A central bank can implement QE by purchasing financial assets from commercial banks and other private institutions with newly created money in order to inject a pre-determined *quantity* of money into the economy. This is distinguished from the more usual policy of buying or selling government bonds to keep market interest rates at a specified target value.

QE increases the excess reserves of banks, raises the prices of financial assets bought, and lowers the yield of these assets. Since the central bank prints money, thereby increasing the money supply, the currency tends to depreciate. This feature of QE benefits exporters and debtors whose debts are denominated in that currency, for as the currency devalues so does the debt. However, it harms creditors and holders of the currency as the real value of their holdings decreases. Devaluation of a currency also harms importers as the cost of imported goods is inflated by the devaluation of the currency.

Economic conditions that can affect exchange rates are diverse and include:

- *Government budget.* The market usually reacts negatively to a widening government budget deficit (where the government's expenditures exceed revenue, mainly from taxes) and positively to a narrowing budget deficit. The impact is reflected in the value of a country's currency.

- *Balance of trade levels and trends.* The trade flow between countries illustrates the demand for goods and services. In turn, it indicates demand for a country's currency to conduct trade. Surpluses and deficits in the trade of goods and services reflect the competitiveness of a nation's economy. For example, trade deficits (where the value of imports exceeds the value of exports) may have a negative impact on a nation's currency.

- *Inflation levels and trends.* Typically a currency will lose value if there is a high level of inflation in the country or if inflation levels are perceived to be rising. This is because inflation erodes purchasing power and thus the demand for that particular currency diminishes. However, a currency may sometimes strengthen when inflation rises because of expectations that the central bank will raise short-term interest rates to combat rising inflation.

- *Economic growth and health.* Reports such as GDP growth, employment levels, retail sales, capacity utilisation and others detail the levels of a country's economic growth and health. Generally, the more healthy and robust a country's economy, the better its currency will perform.

- *Productivity of an economy.* Increasing productivity in an economy should positively influence the value of its currency. Its effects are more prominent if the increase is in the tradable sector. The tradable sector in a country's economy consists of sectors whose output of goods and services can be traded internationally. It covers mainly the manufacturing industry. The non-tradable sectors' output cannot be traded internationally, and consists mainly of services, such as health, education, retail and construction. Increased productivity in the tradable sector means increased export and demand for the local currency.

3. Political conditions

Political conditions that influence the exchange rates among currencies include internal, regional and international political conditions and events. All exchange rates are susceptible to political instability because political upheaval and instability can have a negative impact on a nation's economy. Similarly, in a country experiencing financial difficulties, the rise of a political faction that is perceived to be fiscally responsible can have the opposite, positive effect. Also, events in one country in a region may spur positive or negative interest in a neighbouring country and, in the process, affect its currency.

Political decisions may have a substantial impact on currencies. Examples include the decisions of the United States in 1971, the British government in 1992 and the European Union future decisions about the euro. The 1998 Russian financial crisis was partially due to a political crisis and saw the ruble plummet versus the dollar. Politics can change the way currencies are traded (fixed or floating), central banks can intervene in the currency markets to control the exchange rate even under a free floating regime and political decisions can determine the future existence of currencies (e.g. the creation of the euro and its potential future breakup). Political analysis is an important part of forecasting currency movements and this makes currency movements even more difficult to predict since political decisions are often unpredictable.

4. Market psychology

Market psychology and perceptions influence the foreign exchange market in a variety of ways as they can drive supply and demand. Market psychology, sentiment and the way market participants interpret the other factors can ultimately determine the direction and level of exchange rates. Some examples of market psychological factors include:

- *Flights to quality.* Unsettling international events can lead to a flight to quality and capital flows into safe-haven investments. This may lead to demand and a higher price for currencies perceived as stronger than their counterparts. The US dollar, Swiss franc and Japanese yen have been traditional safe-haven currencies during times of political or economic uncertainty. Factors contributing to safe-haven status include stability of purchasing power, political and fiscal condition and outlook, and the policy of the country's central bank.

- *Long-term trends.* Currency markets often move in long-term trends (momentum). Although currencies do not have an annual growing season like physical commodities, business cycles do make themselves felt. Cycle analysis looks at longer-term price trends that may arise from economic or political trends.

- *Market reaction.* Markets often tend to overreact to news and be oversold or overbought. Market efficiency and standard finance are replaced by temporary inefficiency and behavioural finance.

- *Technical trading considerations.* As in other markets, the accumulated price movements in a currency pair such as EUR/USD can form apparent patterns that traders may attempt to use. Many traders study price charts (i.e. technical analysis) in order to identify such patterns.

* * *

As we can see, exchange rates are affected by a wide range of factors, making it difficult to forecast currency movements.

Reasons for investing in currencies

Foreign currency exposure is part of international investing and often investors consider it a necessity rather than a choice. There are a few good reasons to embrace exposure to foreign currencies in portfolios:

- *Diversification.* Movements in foreign exchange rates have a relatively low correlation with movements in equities and bonds, which normally make up the bulk of multi-asset portfolios. While most assets move independently of each other, currencies move in pairs. This means that when one currency appreciates another currency must depreciate, meaning that if one currency is correlated with assets, the other one is negatively correlated.

- *Level playing field.* Unlike stocks, the news that drives currency prices is available to everyone on a real-time basis. In theory, there are no insiders in the foreign exchange market, which operates 24 hours a day around the world. Since currency valuations are driven by actual monetary flows and events that influence the country's economic health, investors can do their own analysis on how these events might impact currencies. One example of insider dealing in currencies is tipping off on future movements and decisions of central banks or politicians that can affect exchange rates.

- *Global economic hedge.* The currency market allows investors to select currencies based on how they perceive their relative values will change over time. Investors can bet both ways, either long or short, depending on which direction they think a particular currency is headed. They can allocate their risk across the currencies of several countries, allowing them to profit from changing global macroeconomic conditions.

- *Capital appreciation.* Currencies are akin to commodities and stocks because they offer the potential for capital appreciation. If the value of currencies rises against the base currency of the portfolio, it will profit. If the value of currencies falls relative to the base currency, the portfolio will be negatively impacted.

- *Hedge against political and event risk.* Currencies can be played against each other based on investors' tactical assessment of important events going on around the world. Examples are changes in top leadership, interest rate fluctuations, currency revaluations, wars and conflicts, political upheavals, trading sanctions, new tariffs, monetary policy changes, trade deficits, recessions, tax changes, import restrictions and health-related epidemics.

- *Currency risk premium.* If foreign currency risk is rewarded by a risk premium by the market, then currency is a way to expose portfolios to a systematic risk, which is imperfectly correlated with other systematic risks. This risk premium should generate returns over time, can be accessed passively without the need to pay high fees for active management, reduces portfolio risk through diversification and expands the investment opportunity set.

- *Carry.* Gaining exposure to high-yielding foreign currency via deposits or bonds can generate a carry or a yield. The risk is a depreciation of the foreign currency.

Risks

With potential rewards come risks. The main risk of foreign currencies is that the exchange rate can change, sometimes materially and quickly. Negative currency movements can generate losses and wipe out returns on foreign assets. Most models used to forecast exchange rate movements are unreliable since currencies can move because of actions of market participants, including actions by central banks to control the price of currencies. Active currency funds or mandates can disappoint investors, so manager risk is important.

Pegged currencies

A pegged currency maintains a fixed exchange rate with respect of another currency, a basket of currencies or gold. Two examples of pegged currencies are the Singapore dollar and Chinese renminbi (whose primary unit is the yuan).

Singapore issued the first Singapore dollar in 1967. Initially, the Singapore dollar was pegged to the British pound. This peg lasted until the demise of the Sterling Area in the early 1970s, after which the Singapore dollar was linked to the US dollar for a short time. As Singapore's economy grew and its trade links diversified to many other countries and regions, it moved towards pegging its currency against a fixed and undisclosed trade-weighted basket of currencies from 1973 to 1985.

From 1985 onwards, Singapore adopted a more market-oriented exchange regime, classified as a Monitoring Band, in which the Singapore dollar is allowed to float (within an undisclosed bandwidth of a central parity), but closely monitored by the Monetary Authority of Singapore (MAS) against a concealed basket of currencies of Singapore's major trading partners and competitors. This in theory allows the Singaporean government to have more control over imported inflation (inflation due to an increase in the price of imports) and to ensure that Singapore's exports remain competitive (by keeping a competitively priced local currency).

For most of its early history, the Chinese renminbi (RMB) was pegged to the US dollar at 2.46 yuan per dollar. When China's economy gradually opened up in the 1980s, the RMB was devalued in order to improve the competitiveness of Chinese exports. The RMB has moved to a managed floating exchange rate based on market supply and demand with reference to a basket of foreign currencies.

The daily trading price of the US dollar against the RMB in the inter-bank foreign exchange market is allowed to float within a narrow band of 0.5% around the central parity published by the People's Bank of China (PBC). China has stated that the basket is dominated by the US dollar, euro, Japanese yen and South Korean won, with a smaller proportion made up of the British pound, Thai baht, Russian ruble, Australian dollar, Canadian dollar and Singapore dollar.

Figure 4.1 shows the exchange rates between the US dollar and the Singapore dollar (SGD) and Chinese renminbi (CNY) from 1981 to 2013. The SGD is pegged to a basket of currencies, including the dollar. Therefore, its exchange rate with the dollar varies within a bandwidth. The exchange rate of the CNY is controlled. Therefore, it goes through periods of complete stability versus the dollar and moves only when the Chinese policymakers allow it to move.

Figure 4.1: Exchange rates of Singapore dollar (left-hand axis) and Chinese yuan (right-hand axis) against the US dollar, January 1981 to December 2013

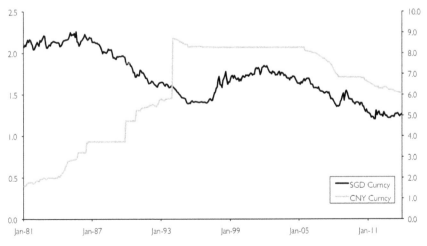

Source: Bloomberg, SGDUSD, CNYUSD.

Currency mandates

Two types of mandates

There are two basic types of currency mandates. An *absolute return mandate* seeks to earn a positive return, usually in excess of some benchmark, and subject to a specified risk level (e.g. tracking error, standard deviation or VaR). A *currency overlay mandate*, on the other hand, is added to a portfolio with exposures to currencies with the objective to either entirely eliminate currency risk from the portfolio or partially reduce currency risk while opportunistically seeking to generate returns.

Currency mandates are either *passive* or *active*. A passive mandate is constrained to track a predefined benchmark and does not seek to generate excess returns. Most benchmarks are constructed from a clearly articulated investment process which means that a passive manager often follows a systematic or rule-based approach.

For an absolute return mandate, trading designed to mimic benchmarks based on carry trading, trend following, value trading strategies or volatility are all examples of passive strategies. For a currency overlay mandate, always fully hedging the currency position in a fixed income portfolio or always hedging 50% of the foreign currency value of the position are typical examples of passive strategies.

On the other hand, an active mandate has discretion to implement a variety of trades based on the manager's views. For an absolute return mandate, the active manager seeks to add value in excess of the benchmark and can do so by entering into trades that deviate from the benchmark. For example, an active currency overlay manager who thinks that a foreign currency has a strong chance of appreciating can hedge only 25% of the foreign currency exposure in a fixed income portfolio instead of 100% in an attempt to add extra return. Whether under an absolute return or currency overlay mandate, an active manager may adopt a systematic or rule-based investment process, a discretionary investment process or a combination of both.

Allowed currencies

A currency mandate agreement typically constrains the manager to operate within a set menu of *allowed currencies*, perhaps restricted to the G3 currencies (US dollar, euro and Japanese yen) or currencies of the G10[156] countries where financial markets offer greater depth, or G20 countries, or emerging market countries where markets are less liquid, but where a wider investment opportunity set may lead to greater profit opportunities.

---

[156] G10 or the group of ten includes 11 countries, namely Belgium, Canada, France, Germany, Italy, Japan, Netherlands, Sweden, Switzerland, the United Kingdom and the United States.

A wider range of allowed currencies may be more valuable in the case of an absolute return mandate (wider breadth), although some managers may prefer to limit themselves to only those currency pairs where they have greater expertise. In a currency overlay, the allowed currencies are often limited to those in the underlying portfolio, although not always, as cross-hedging[157] can be a useful tool.

Permitted instruments

Another dimension for the currency mandate is *permitted instruments*. A currency mandate agreement may specify which instruments the manager is permitted to use. The manager may be allowed to trade spot and forward contracts only, or may be permitted discretion to use plain vanilla currency options or other derivative instruments such as exotic currency options (e.g. barrier or basket options).

In the case of a currency overlay agreement, derivatives may offer a more efficient way of hedging particular risks in the underlying portfolio, or of taking asymmetric trades that leave the underlying portfolio unharmed if the currency moves in one direction, but allows the manager to benefit if the currency moves in a way that was forecast. In the case of an absolute return mandate, derivative instruments are often a more efficient way to obtain leverage and so whether or not they are permitted may be linked to how much leverage is allowed by the mandate.

Leverage

The degree of *leverage* allowed is an important consideration for absolute return mandates as well as for currency overlays that have an element of a return-seeking objective. A manager can be constrained to use limited leverage, or allowed discretion to vary leverage up to some limit, depending on market conditions. For an absolute return mandate, leverage up to a factor of 10 is typical, but greater leverage is feasible and sometimes observed in certain hedge funds. Rather than specify leverage, a currency mandate can instead specify target volatility, expected return or worst permitted drawdown.

Performance measurement

A currency mandate needs to specify *performance measurement* or how outperformance is measured and compensated. For an absolute return mandate, when a manager is given trading authority over a pool of funds, the benchmark for performance on those funds could be LIBOR, LIBOR plus, or some other index denominated in the portfolio's base currency. Investing the assigned assets at LIBOR is essentially risk free, while benchmarks above LIBOR entail risk.

---

[157] Cross-hedging is taking an opposite position in another asset that is correlated but not similar to the hedged asset.

When the manager receives only a line of credit against funds that are invested elsewhere, then the benchmark for performance can be zero, a percentage target or another measure of performance. A manager who never draws on the credit line, and never takes a currency position, will earn zero return and incur zero risk. Active use of the credit line in the pursuit of positive returns entails risk.

Performance benchmarks for a currency overlay manager are usually designed to reflect the returns from a continuum of hedging choices from no hedging through to continuous hedging of the entire underlying position. The returns from a strategy of a continuous 50% hedge are often taken as a naïve benchmark for a currency overlay manager.

Manager compensation

Manager *compensation* often has several parameters, almost always including an annual management fee and a performance incentive fee based on annual returns. For retail investors and funds of funds that invest in currency hedge funds, the most common fee structure is a 2% per annum management fee (based on assets under management) and a 20% share of profits earned over the year. Institutional investors and high net worth individuals are likely to negotiate management fees that are far lower while still being subject to the 20% performance fee.

In addition, compensation is usually governed by a high-watermark rule such that annual performance fees are paid only to the extent that returns push the manager's cumulative returns above the previous high-watermark.

Funded vs unfunded mandate

Another choice for currency mandates is between a *funded* and *unfunded* mandate. In a funded mandate, the investor designates specific funds that are placed in custody accounts where the manager is permitted to trade. For example, a pension fund sponsor may allocate $10 million to a currency fund manager. If the mandate allows for ten times leverage, the currency manager can have up to $100 million exposure to invest using derivatives, while the cash is used to cover their margin requirements. These funds would be placed on deposit earning LIBOR unless otherwise committed to a foreign currency trading strategy. If the pension fund sponsor had begun with $100 million in global equity holdings, carving off $10 million for currency would change the sponsor's exposure to $90 million in global equity, and $10 million to $100 million in currency, depending on the degree of leverage devoted to currency.

In an unfunded mandate, the plan sponsor retains custody of the underlying assets, but earmarks some of those assets to collateralise a trading account for use by the currency manager. In this case, initially the currency manager has no assets and so faces a zero return unless trading positions are established.

In principle, an absolute return mandate could be executed through either a funded or unfunded structure. A currency overlay mandate is more commonly implemented using an unfunded structure as the plan sponsor may wish to retain the ability to trade the underlying foreign currency assets that require the overlay.

Active currency investment strategies

Four investment strategies are commonly utilised by active currency managers:

1. The *carry trade* involves borrowing the low interest rate currency in a pair (e.g. Japanese yen) and investing in the high interest rate currency in a pair (e.g. New Zealand dollar). The risk is that the high interest rate currency may depreciate and possibly by more than the interest rate differential. This would result in a loss.

2. *Trend following* involves buying currencies that are appreciating and/or shorting currencies that are depreciating. The risks to this strategy include sudden reversals of trends or patterns, trading based on false signals and excessive trading costs.

3. A *value* strategy involves taking a longer-term horizon and relying on a value benchmark to gauge when currencies are over or under valued. Purchasing Power Parity (PPP) is one way to represent long-term equilibrium value. Empirically, currencies often overshoot their PPP values in the short term and show a tendency to revert back toward PPP in the longer run. A simple trading strategy is to identify currencies that are substantially misaligned with the expectation that they will move closer to PPP over time. The risks in this strategy include the possibility that currency values may become still more misaligned, that exchange rates will be slow to revert toward PPP or that the currency's long-run real exchange rate has changed consistently with a new PPP.

4. *Volatility-based* strategies involve gaining exposure to volatility risk by not only taking open currency positions, but also by using options and other derivatives whose prices are sensitive to volatility. The risk is being long (short) volatility when it declines (increases).

Currency historical return and risk characteristics

The return and risk analytics below consider the currency effect on a US-based investor whose base currency is the US dollar.

Table 4.2 shows the return and risk characteristics of currencies, US equities, US bonds and US cash and Table 4.3 shows the correlation matrix among the indices. The average annual return from currencies over the measurement period is low – it is lower than the return of cash (T-Bills). This is in line with the academic view that the long-term expected return on currency should be zero. The volatility of currencies is around 10% – much higher than the risk level of cash.

These return and risk characteristics suggest that investing in currency over this long-term period (at least from the perspective of investors with a US dollar base currency) would not have been worthwhile. The Sharpe ratio for all three currencies is negative. Investing in currencies is time dependent and requires dynamic management to add value.

The correlation matrix shows that the returns of currencies were weakly correlated with those of other assets. This confirms the academic view that currency is a zero beta investment. Including currency exposure in a global portfolio comes with diversification benefits. So hedging currency typically reduces risk but this reduction is offset by the increased risk due to losing some diversification benefits.

Table 4.2: Currency return and risk characteristics, January 1985 to December 2013. Sharpe ratio calculated using $ cash returns

	GBP	EUR	JPY	US equities	US Treasuries	US T-Bills
Start month	Jan-1985	Jan-1985	Jan-1985	Jan-1985	Jan-1985	Jan-1985
Performance (% pa)	1.2	2.3	3.0	11.3	8.0	3.9
Volatility (%)	10.3	10.8	11.5	15.4	7.8	0.7
Skewness	-0.11	-0.19	0.58	-0.82	0.15	-0.12
Kurtosis	2.85	0.62	2.14	2.43	0.85	-1.08
Sharpe ratio	-0.25	-0.14	-0.07	0.48	0.53	-

Source: Bloomberg, Global Financial Data, GBPUSD, EURUSD, JPYUSD, S&P 500 Index, USD 10-year Government Bond TR Index, USA TR T-Bill Index.

Table 4.3: Correlation matrix, January 1985 to December 2013

Correlation matrix	GBP	EUR	JPY	US equities	US Treasuries	US T-Bills
GBP	1.00	0.71	0.35	0.06	0.05	0.05
EUR	0.71	1.00	0.43	0.09	0.17	0.03
JPY	0.35	0.43	1.00	-0.06	0.21	0.01
US equities	0.06	0.09	-0.06	1.00	-0.01	0.07
US Treasuries	0.05	0.17	0.21	-0.01	1.00	0.11
US T-Bills	0.05	0.03	0.01	0.07	0.11	1.00

Source: Bloomberg, Global Financial Data, GBPUSD, EURUSD, JPYUSD, S&P 500 Index, USD 10-year Government Bond TR Index, USA TR T-Bill Index.

Figure 4.2 shows the exchange rate of the US dollar with the British pound, euro and Japanese yen. Exchange rates can oscillate around a certain value for long time periods. For instance, the pound and the dollar have been hovering around 1.64 since the middle of the 1980s. However, there are periods of sharp currency movements that do not revert back to prior levels. For example, the dollar sharply appreciated versus the pound and yen from the mid-1970s to the mid-1980s. This highlights the need to spot structural changes in the currency market that can shift the relative value of currencies. The modern currency market was born only in 1973 when the free float commenced, so in 1975 the market was still adapting to its new evolutionary conditions.

Figure 4.2: Exchange rates of the British pound, euro (LHS) and Japanese yen (RHS), January 1975 to December 2013

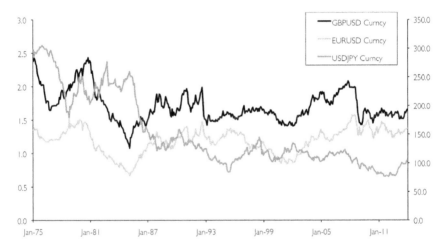

Source: Bloomberg, GBPUSD, EURUSD, JPYUSD.

Figure 4.3 shows the rolling correlation between the GBP/USD exchange rate and US equities and Treasuries. While the correlation of changes in exchange rates with the returns of asset classes is not stable, currency returns are imperfectly correlated with those of other assets. A correlation within the range of -0.40 and 0.40 means diversification benefits. Finding assets with a negative correlation with others is uncommon and can be valuable.

Figure 4.3: Rolling correlation of the British pound/US dollar spot exchange rate with US equities and Treasuries, January 1974 to December 2013

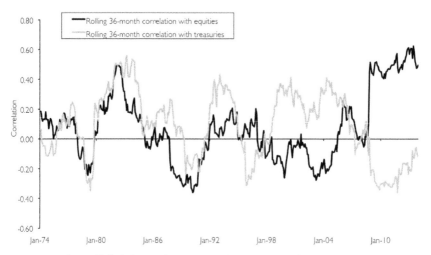

Source: Bloomberg, Global Financial Data, GBPUSD, S&P 500 Index, USD 10-year Government Bond TR Index.

Figure 4.4 shows the rolling volatility of the GBP/USD, EUR/USD and USD/JPY exchange rates. Based on their level of volatility, currency investing is a risk asset. Volatility should not be regarded as a risk per se for investors with a long investment horizon. Rather it is drawdowns and unrecoverable losses that are the true risk for investors.

Figure 4.4: Rolling volatility of exchange rates of British pound, euro and Japanese yen, January 1974 to December 2013

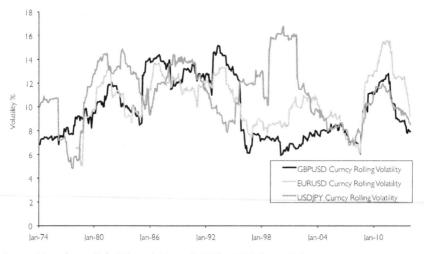

Source: Bloomberg, Global Financial Data, GBPUSD, EURUSD, JPYUSD.

Conclusions

Every investor who invests globally must understand currencies. One question that investors need to answer is whether to hedge or unhedge currency exposure to international investments. Another question that investors need to answer is whether to include currency exposure in their portfolios.

Currencies are a source of potential return and diversification, they are accessible through a wide variety of financial instruments, they are easily hedgeable, they are liquid and they are part of every global portfolio. Investors should use currencies for the benefit of their portfolios.

Summary

- Foreign currency exposure comes with investing abroad. When investing in foreign assets, investors make one investment in the asset itself and a second in the foreign currency.

- Investors usually have a choice of hedging unintended currency risk. Investors can choose to gain exposure to foreign currencies.

- Attempts have been made to explain the fluctuations in exchange rates using many different factors. The factors can be divided into financial and economic theories, economic factors (economic policy and economic conditions), political conditions and market psychology.

- Forecasting currency movements is difficult since some theories are disconnected from empirical reality and the effects, weighting and timing of the different factors are difficult to predict.

- The reasons for investing in currencies include diversification, a level playing field, a global economic hedge, capital appreciation, a hedge against political and event risks, the currency risk premium and carry.

- The risk of currency investing is that foreign exchange rates can move, sometimes materially and quickly. This can result in material losses.

- Two types of currency mandates are the absolute return mandate and a currency overlay mandate. They can be offered with a variety of features, including active/passive, allowed currencies, permitted instruments, leverage, performance measurement, compensation structure and the choice between a funded and an unfunded mandate.

- Active currency strategies include carry, trend, value and volatility.

CHAPTER 10: INFRASTRUCTURE

Infrastructure is the basic physical and organisational structures and facilities (e.g. buildings, roads and power supplies) needed for the operation of a society or enterprise. In other words, infrastructure is the underlying networks and services that are necessary for the proper functioning of global economies. Infrastructure includes the physical assets, facilities and systems that provide essential services to society.

It is one of the most commonly used asset classes out of the new alternative investments and is increasingly found in portfolios of institutional investors, in particular those with long investment horizons and an appetite for illiquid assets.

Infrastructure can be divided into two major groups:

1. *Economic infrastructure* refers to transportation (roads, toll-roads, railroads, airports, seaports, bridges and tunnels); energy and utility (power generation facilities, electricity grids, gas, water systems, sewage and renewable energy); and communications (cable networks, satellite networks and communication towers).

2. *Social infrastructure* refers to healthcare facilities, correctional facilities (prisons), housing and subsidised housing, waste facilities and stadiums.

Infrastructure includes real assets that often require considerable investment to construct and maintain and typically generate a relatively steady stream of cash flows that should increase with inflation.

Within the infrastructure universe there are assets with different characteristics. At one end, toll-road operators face virtually no competition and extremely high barriers to entry. At the other extreme, communication networks and power generation operate in a much more competitive environment and investments in these areas are more similar to private equity.

While the nature of the underlying assets can vary considerably, most infrastructure assets share some common features:

- *Stability*. Infrastructure assets are often monopolies, enjoy high barriers to entry or provide essential services so they have a captive customer base. This insulates them from the impact of the economic cycle relative to other assets. Consumer demand for services provided through infrastructure assets is typically price inelastic[158] and most infrastructure assets have a low risk of

---

[158] Price inelasticity means that the supply and demand are unaffected by changes to price. When the price for an infrastructure service increases, its demand does not change by much since it is an essential service.

technological obsolescence. However, the degree of stability depends on the asset type and whether it earns established revenues. Investment in the construction phase of infrastructure assets has a much lower degree of stability.

- *Yield and predictable cash flows.* The running yield[159] provides the bulk of the return on a portfolio of infrastructure assets. The running yield is often a function of predictable cash flows from concession arrangements and other forms of long-term contracts whereby a large proportion of prices and revenues are set by regulations. Investment in the construction phase of infrastructure assets has a much lower degree of predictable cash flows.

- *Inflation and GDP linkage.* Regulation and concessions typically underpin pricing and often result in inflation-linked cash flows. While tariffs are linked to inflation, usage of infrastructure assets tends to be linked to GDP growth. However, while inflation linkages are typically embedded in concessions, GDP growth linkages are not guaranteed and depend on the long-run correlation between usage and GDP growth and the correlation between usage and GDP during the economic cycle.

- *Long duration.* A typical lifespan of infrastructure assets is more than 30 years. The long-term lifespan of infrastructure assets means that any related investment has a long duration.

Infrastructure developments are carried out across the world in both developed and developing countries. The core developed countries include the European Union (EU), North America and Australia. The developing countries include China, India, Russia and countries in Latin America, Eastern Europe and the Middle East.

Different markets have different risks. Political risk is material in Latin America. Government reputation is a risk particularly in China and Russia. The regulatory framework is a risk especially in China. Corruption is a risk particularly in India and Africa. Moving away from the core developed markets (the EU, North America and Australia) entails significant political and governance risks. In some potentially high risk markets the demand for infrastructure is so high that it justifies the risks. In other high-risk markets there are market niches that have lower risk.

Infrastructure investments may be used by governments to stimulate economic growth. During the Great Depression of the 1930s, many governments undertook public infrastructure development projects to create jobs and stimulate the economy. The construction of the Hoover Dam in the United States is one example. John Maynard Keynes provided a theoretical justification for this policy in *The General Theory of Employment, Interest and Money.*[160] Following the 2008 global financial crisis, some governments proposed investing in infrastructure as a means of stimulating the economy.

---

[159] Running yield is the income generated from a portfolio as a percentage of the portfolio's market value (income/market value).

[160] Keynes, *The General Theory of Employment, Interest and Money.*

The Canada Pension Plan Investment Board (CPPIB), one of the most established infrastructure investors, summarises the key attributes it seeks in infrastructure investments as follows:[161]

> "We generally are interested in infrastructure assets that provide relatively stable long-term returns, operate in strong regulatory environments, have relatively low technology replacement risk, and possess minimal substitution risks. We look for long-term assets that can be held for periods of 20-30 years. The types of global infrastructure assets that have these characteristics include: electricity transmission and distribution, gas transmission and distribution, water and sewage companies, and certain transportation assets, such as toll roads, bridges and tunnels, airports, and ports. Regardless of the type of asset, however, we generally seek out investments that operate under long-term contractual agreements, or within transparent and dependable regulatory frameworks that balance the needs of both ratepayers and investors."

Due to its link with inflation, infrastructure belongs to the category of *real assets*. Real estate and commodities are two other real asset classes that are also tangible assets. These three asset classes are not capital or financial assets, such as equities and bonds, and all three are essential for the functioning of the economy and society (inflation-linked bonds are also a real asset but unlike infrastructure they are an intangible financial asset).

Infrastructure as a separate asset class in portfolios should exclude assets that are already included elsewhere. For example, infrastructure buildings may already be included under commercial real estate and utilities may already be included under public and private equities.

Access

Similar to private equity and real estate, infrastructure assets are not traded on exchanges as securities, as are equities for example. The four main ways to gain access to infrastructure are:

1. *Direct investment.* Direct investment means that the investor directly buys rights in the infrastructure assets. For example, equity investment in a private company constructing and operating a toll-road. This type of investment typically requires material investment of capital and therefore diversification is available only for large investors and normally involves concentration risk. Infrastructure assets are typically highly regulated and hence direct investment entails regulatory risk. The advantage of direct investment is control over the investment. However, direct control means that investors need expertise to manage the investment. The disadvantages include concentration risk, large capital requirements, regulatory risk and illiquidity

---

[161] CPP Investment Board, Backgrounder on Infrastructure Investing, February 2008.

risk. This is not a viable investment route for most investors seeking to include infrastructure as part of their portfolios.

2. *Private equity funds and partnerships.* These funds or partnerships invest directly in infrastructure assets on behalf of their shareholders, limited partners or investors. The pooling of money from multiple investors enables diversification and lower capital commitments from each individual investor. The investment is still illiquid but offers more liquidity compared to direct investment. Many of the funds or partnerships use leverage, which can amplify returns as well as risks. This investment is similar to private equity as investors (limited partners) commit capital to an investment pool and the capital is drawn down by the general partner as required for investment opportunities along with periodic management and operating fees. Private equity funds may be offered as a fund of funds (FoF). FoFs specialise in due diligence and diversification, but they may be more expensive due to the double layer of fees (one at the FoF level and a second at the underlying fund level). This is a viable route to get exposure to infrastructure for investors who have an appropriate long investment horizon and appetite for illiquidity. The conditions for making this type of investment are similar to those for private equity investing.

3. *Listed infrastructure vehicles.* These vehicles are listed on exchanges and invest in infrastructure assets. The advantages of these vehicles are that they pool together money of multiple investors and hence require a lower investment compared to direct infrastructure; they are diversified; they are publicly traded on exchanges; they are more liquid than direct infrastructure; they have relatively low transaction costs; they are professionally managed; and they are regulated by the exchange. The disadvantages are that these vehicles are typically closed-end funds, which can trade at a premium or discount to NAV (this may be an advantage if the investment is made at a discount); and investing in these vehicles or disinvesting from them may have a material price impact, hence their liquidity may be misleading. Similar to REITs versus direct property, listed infrastructure vehicles have equity-like volatility and a high correlation with equities over the short term. Over the long term, however, their correlation with the underlying infrastructure assets increases. Listed vehicles may be appropriate for relatively small investments. However, when the multi-asset portfolio and the investment in infrastructure are both large, the price impact and illiquidity of these vehicles may be a serious disadvantage. This means that when the investment is large relative to the assets in the vehicle the demand for shares can push their price downward, creating a discount to NAV.

4. *Infrastructure-related equities.* Equities of publicly traded corporations[162] whose business is directly related to infrastructure assets can be accessed directly

---

[162] The largest corporations in the infrastructure sector include Enterprise Products Partners (United States), National Grid (United Kingdom), TransCanada Corporation (Canada), Enbridge (Canada), American Tower Corporation (United States), Hong Kong and China Gas (China), The Williams Companies (United States), Kinder Morgan Energy Partners (United States), Crown Castle International (United States) and Spectra Energy Corporation (United States).

through investing in individual stocks, collective investment schemes or ETFs on infrastructure equity indices. Since the stock prices are priced on a daily basis they can trade at a premium or discount to the value of the underlying infrastructure assets. These premiums and discounts are different to those of closed-end funds since they reflect the difference between the equity value of the companies and the value of the underlying infrastructure assets. These are equities and are exposed to equity market risk. The equities may be of companies that have a wider business unrelated to infrastructure (i.e. the infrastructure-related business can be just one piece of a larger conglomerate operation). This is not a pure exposure to infrastructure but rather an exposure to the infrastructure sector within equities and should be part of the equity allocation of a portfolio (this is similar, for instance, to investing in commodity-related equities instead of in commodity futures). The advantages of infrastructure-related equities are liquidity, a relatively low price, transparency and a high correlation with infrastructure assets over the long term.

Government involvement

Historically, infrastructure assets were under the complete purview of governments. However, due to the widening investment gap (i.e. lack of public funds to finance infrastructure projects), governments are increasingly allowing private capital to flow into infrastructure.

Infrastructure assets could be split into two types by the degree of government involvement:

1. *Limited government involvement.* Private investors buy the assets through privatisation or from another private company, assuming full control of the assets as well as the full risk exposure. Government involvement is usually limited to a regulatory role. This type of investment is similar to private equity investing as it involves managing a business, albeit within a regulated sector with more predictable cash flows. However, there are still areas where management can make a difference to cash flows to investors (e.g. operational efficiency, pricing of services outside the scope of concessions and so on).

2. *Active government involvement.* The government is actively involved in the management of the infrastructure assets. In the case of Public-Private Partnerships (PPPs), the government retains ownership and control of the infrastructure assets but one or more private players are hired to finance and operate assets with an agreed payment framework. In the case of Public Finance Initiative (PFIs), infrastructure assets are owned by a private company and the government makes annual payments to the private company that provides the associated services. This type of investment is closer to fixed income as cash flows are more predictable and management has more limited flexibility (particularly in PPPs).

Infrastructure and other asset classes

Infrastructure shares some features in common with other assets but also displays some unique characteristics:

- *Fixed income and infrastructure.* Reliance on cash yield expectation and cash flow predictability are common features. The inflation uplift is similar to inflation-linked bonds. However, infrastructure investments do not provide the security associated with debt instruments and are associated with equity-like upside potential. Moreover, unlike conventional fixed income, infrastructure is highly capital intensive and involves leverage, as the purchase of infrastructure assets requires large capital commitments.

- *Private equity and infrastructure.* Both are investments in the equity capital of unlisted companies and both require active operational management. However, unlike infrastructure, private equity returns are largely driven by capital appreciation, rather than income, as private equity funds typically invest in start-up companies with material upside potential or companies in need of a radical turnaround, and such companies do not pay income in the form of dividends.

- *Real estate and infrastructure.* Both involve the purchase of tangible underlying assets providing a running yield from users or tenants and both often employ leverage. However, infrastructure cash flows are more predictable because the length of concessions is longer than real estate leases and concessions are backed by government guarantees rather than contracts with private sector tenants. Moreover, the value of infrastructure assets is more predictable because these are typically monopolistic businesses with high barriers to entry, whereas property values are affected by supply and demand in a given region or sector.

- *Unique to infrastructure.* The purchase of monopolistic underlying assets with high barriers to entry is a unique feature of infrastructure investing. Alongside this comes the requirement to assess regulatory and sovereign risk (i.e. the risk of losing concessions or governments defaulting on their obligations). This is a different type of risk from the sovereign risk embedded in government bonds as governments are more likely to force renegotiation of infrastructure concessions than they are to default on sovereign debt.

The similarities with other assets help investors to understand and model infrastructure investing. The dissimilarities mean that infrastructure as an asset class offers investors exposure to unique risks and sources of return and therefore provides diversification opportunities and an expansion of the investment opportunity set.

Phases of infrastructure investing

Investing in established infrastructure comes with earning established revenues. By contrast, investments in the construction stage of infrastructure assets have a different risk-return profile.

Infrastructure investing has three principal project stages:

1. Construction of assets (no revenue received until completion).

2. Assets maturing (assets are operational and earning revenue; however, long-term utilisation and cost structure are unclear).

3. Assets earning established revenues (long-term predictable revenues and cost structure).

The first two stages are termed *growth infrastructure* and the third stage is termed *income infrastructure* or *mature infrastructure*. The risk-return profile of growth infrastructure is different to that of income infrastructure – this will be explained further in the Risks section below.

Infrastructure is a potentially attractive asset class from a risk-return perspective. However, it should not be deemed a low-risk investment similar to certain fixed-income investments because, in spite of the relative stability of cash flows, most infrastructure funds apply a high degree of leverage, not only enhancing potential returns but also increasing risk (potentially above that of equities).

One example of leverage and financing risk is one of the biggest infrastructure projects in Europe's history – the Eurotunnel. In 1986 Groupe Eurotunnel was formed to finance, construct and operate a tunnel connecting Britain and France. The 50km railway was financed entirely by private funds and its construction cost was about £9.5 billion, around twice the estimated cost. In its first year of operation in 1994 the group lost nearly £1 billion because of disappointing revenues and heavy interest charges on its debt. The degree of leverage of the group was unsustainable so in 2006 the group started a series of restructurings to avoid bankruptcy. This is a classic case study of large infrastructure projects, as well as of corporate finance and the risks of debt.

There is also a wide variation in expected returns across funds, largely driven by differences in cash yields (though other factors such as dilution, projected leverage gains and fees also play an important role). Two stocks of the same company are identical, two stocks of two companies in the same industry are similar, but like real estate, each infrastructure asset is unique and requires a case-by-case due diligence.

Reasons for investing in infrastructure

The main reasons for investing in infrastructure include:

- *Income.* Infrastructure is an income source. Due to its monopolistic nature and government backing, infrastructure is a source of stable income.

- *Inflation hedge.* As a real asset class, the value of infrastructure investments appreciates with inflation and provides a long-term hedge against inflation.

- *Diversification.* Infrastructure is not highly correlated with other assets, such as equities and bonds. Therefore, including it in multi-asset portfolios reduces risk through diversification.

- *Asset/liability matching.* Its long duration means infrastructure can be used to match long-term liabilities. At the very long horizons (above 20 years) it is challenging to find bonds to hedge liabilities. Investors with long-term liabilities need to look for alternatives to bonds, such as derivatives and infrastructure investing.

- *Opportunities for active management.* As a relatively new, under-researched and inefficient asset class (similar to real estate and private equity), infrastructure needs active management and opens the door for active managers to add value.

Role of infrastructure in portfolios

Infrastructure can play a number of roles within portfolios. Infrastructure is one of the real or inflation-linked assets, alongside linkers, commodities and real estate. As such, it can provide a hedge against inflation. Its long duration and inflation hedge means that infrastructure can be used in asset-liability management (or Liability Driven Investing, LDI). Infrastructure can be used as a source of stable cash flows (income) or as a growth asset.

The chosen investment characteristics must be in line with the desired role of the investment within the portfolio. For investors with a long investment horizon, as well as an appetite for illiquidity, infrastructure can provide diversification benefits for portfolios.

Risks

Infrastructure investing has different characteristics to those of other assets. With this comes a long list of different risks. The main risks of infrastructure investing include:

- *Emerging asset class and managers.* Despite some history of infrastructure investing – accumulated mostly by Australian managers and Canadian pension funds – infrastructure remains an emerging asset class, lacking robust data that can be modelled for asset allocation purposes. As a consequence, the majority of managers do not have a long enough track record to be able to assess them properly, making manager selection challenging.

- *Competition.* Despite the infancy of the market, there has been a surge of interest in infrastructure from institutional investors and sovereign wealth funds. This has led to the launch of numerous new infrastructure funds. One potential risk is that funds under pressure to put money at work outbid each other and end up overpaying for infrastructure assets with associated lower initial yields (too much money chasing too few opportunities). Alternatively, funds may remain holding cash for longer than expected while waiting for the right deal, with their returns suffering from a cash drag.

- *Regulatory risk.* Cash flows for many projects are regulated or even contractually guaranteed by a particular government. Potential changes in government policies, particularly in countries with a less established legal and regulatory framework, are a risk. These types of risks are amplified when the investment is highly leveraged as changes in regulatory pricing may make infrastructure assets unable to service their debt payments. Regulatory risk at the extreme can mean nationalisation of infrastructure assets. Some examples include the nationalisation of railways in the United Kingdom in 1948, rail corporations in the United States in the 1970s and different industries in Venezuela in 2007 to 2010 under the leadership of Hugo Chávez.

- *Reputational risk.* Infrastructure assets are important to society and in the public domain. In the event that the asset does not deliver its services there is a risk that the investors can be viewed in a negative light. This risk is substantially reduced if investments are not held directly but through a fund.

- *Event risk.* As infrastructure projects are usually single business assets and building a diversified portfolio is difficult, infrastructure is particularly exposed to single events. For instance, the September 11 terrorist attacks detrimentally affected airports as customers were reticent to fly for an extended period of time.

- *Concentration risk.* Due to the capital intensive nature of infrastructure projects, individual projects may account for 20% to 30% of a single fund's assets. This creates significant exposure to project specific risk. This risk can be mitigated by investing with a number of managers focusing on different segments and geographies.

- *Leverage risk.* Infrastructure projects usually involve high levels of financial leverage and, as the asset matures, the level of leverage increases. Cash flows from infrastructure assets are likely to absorb potential increases in the interest rates but this may happen with a time lag. In addition, there is financial distress risk associated with any highly leveraged asset. Leverage is generally not employed at the fund level but debt is widely employed to finance the purchase of individual infrastructure assets.

- *Interest rate risk.* As the valuations on infrastructure investments are usually based on long-term discounted cash flows, the value of infrastructure assets is susceptible to rising real yields as valuations decrease when the real interest rate increases. Due to their typical long horizons, infrastructure assets have a long duration, which is sensitive to changes in interest rates. This should not be a major risk for investors with a long investment horizon but affects the implied marked-to-market volatility of infrastructure assets.

- *Construction risk.* Given the scale and complexity of infrastructure projects, investments in *green field* projects bear significant risks of construction delays and development errors. This risk is usually passed through from investors to subcontractors and becomes a subcontractor default risk.

- *Operational risk.* Feasibility studies often tend to be modest on costs so cost overruns are a significant risk for growth infrastructure. This risk is usually passed through from investors to asset operators and becomes an operator default risk.

- *Patronage risk.* Much like construction risk, given the start-up nature of growth infrastructure projects the demand for many projects (such as toll-roads and ports) cannot be accurately gauged in advance. This may lead to a revenue shortfall, which is a risk that is difficult to pass through.

- *Growth infrastructure investing is a speculative proposition.* There is a large potential premium to offset this because of the expected price appreciation embedded in the development stage (much like in real estate), but this remains a risky proposition for the inexperienced investor.

- *Illiquidity.* There is no organised secondary market for direct and private infrastructure investments. The price of listed infrastructure closed-end funds may move to a discount to NAV when trying to sell them. As is the case with direct real estate, illiquidity is one of the major risks of infrastructure investing.

- *Long horizon to generate returns.* Similar to the J-curve of private equity, it may take years until the returns on infrastructure materialise. In the first few years committed capital is drawn for investing and the infrastructure investment shows negative returns. Only after a few years, when the infrastructure assets are operational and generating revenues, may investors begin to see positive returns. Patience and expectation management are needed.

Investing in infrastructure requires a long investment horizon, ability to invest in illiquid investments and expertise. Investors with a short investment horizon, no appetite for illiquidity and no access to a good professional infrastructure manager should probably avoid the asset class altogether.

Infrastructure indices

Direct, pure infrastructure lacks indices. The only indices are for global infrastructure-related equities (i.e. indices of public equity of corporations in the infrastructure sector). The degree to which these indices accurately reflect the risk and return characteristics of direct infrastructure is unclear. Conceptually, using indices of stocks of listed infrastructure corporations to proxy direct infrastructure is analogous to the use of indices of REITs to proxy direct commercial real estate. The behaviour of the infrastructure indices is probably close to public equities over the short term and more like direct infrastructure over the long term.

The Macquarie Global Infrastructure Index[163] is a free float-adjusted, market capitalisation-weighted index designed to track the performance of globally listed infrastructure-related stocks. The index "is designed to reflect the performance of the worldwide market in the shares of companies whose principal activity is the management, ownership and/or operation of infrastructure and utility assets."

Other indices of globally listed infrastructure-related equities are offered by MSCI,[164] Standard & Poor's[165] and Dow Jones Brookfield.[166] The different indices have different exposures to infrastructure sectors (pipelines, utilities, communications, transportation and social) and geographies (North America, United Kingdom, Continental Europe, Japan, Asia ex Japan, Latin America, Middle East and Africa). The largest differentiator across indices is the exposure to utilities.

Capital market assumptions for infrastructure

Setting up risk and return capital market assumptions for infrastructure as an asset class is a challenge because of three factors: the unavailability of long-term historical data to assess volatilities and correlation; the only available data refers to listed infrastructure-related equities; and each infrastructure fund has a different strategy, it targets a different degree of concentration and leverage and has a different fee structure. This implies that assumptions need to be tailored to the chosen investment vehicle.

One approach to set the expected long-term returns of infrastructure is using the CAPM. Investors can try to estimate the market capitalisation weight of infrastructure in the market portfolio, together with the weights of other asset classes, and use reverse optimisation to calculate the implied expected return.[167]

---

[163] www.ftse.com/products/indices/Macquarie.

[164] www.msci.com/products/indices/thematic/infrastructure.

[165] www.standardandpoors.com.

[166] www.djindexes.com/infrastructure.

[167] Sharpe, William, 'Imputing Expected Security Returns from Portfolio Composition', *Journal of Financial and Quantitative Analysis* (1974).

The challenges are estimating the weights of infrastructure and other asset classes, such as real estate and commodities, in addition to the shortcomings of using the CAPM.

An alternative approach, like for most other asset classes, is estimating the long-term expected returns for infrastructure based on a building block methodology. The building block approach for most assets is based on income yield (e.g. dividends for equities or interest rates for bonds), growth of yield (e.g. earnings growth for equities) and necessary adjustments (e.g. style or cap size adjustments for equities or maturity or default adjustments for bonds). The adjustments apply premiums or discounts to the expected return. When material costs are involved (e.g. transaction costs for real estate or fees for hedge funds) they need to be subtracted from the expected return.

The expected return for infrastructure is made of the initial yield plus expected growth in income minus depreciation, dilution for not being invested initially and fees. Consistent with the way other assets are modelled, this expected return does not incorporate an allowance for alpha from manager skill. It also disregards projected gains from leverage as the use of gearing at the asset level to boost income is best thought of as a source of alpha. I will now look at these various elements in more detail.

- *Initial yield.* Unlike fixed income, the yield is harder to establish at the outset because infrastructure assets are not being acquired when a new fund is launched. Different funds may also have different approaches to dividend payments. Moreover, as part of an in-depth due diligence it is important to assess whether the initial yield is sustainable because, unlike other assets, there is a potential risk of it being manipulated (i.e. the use of proceeds from borrowings to pay out distributions to investors). An initial yield of 8% is used as an example.

- *Expected growth in income.* This is hard to assess as it depends on factors such as the geographical and sector composition of the infrastructure fund and the extent of inflation or GDP linkages to future revenues. The expected growth is calculated as a function of the proportion of infrastructure with inflation and/or GDP growth linkages and the fund's geographical breakdown. For instance, it is reasonable to assume that 80% of revenues from transport assets grow in line with GDP as a result of the connection between GDP and usage whilst 100% of revenues of utilities are linked to inflation as GDP growth participation is more limited. An expected growth of 3% is used as an example. It lies between the 2.5% long-term inflation rate and the 3.5% long-term GDP growth rate.

- *Depreciation.* The life of infrastructure assets can vary widely (e.g. for a toll-road it can be as low as 30 years but can go up to over 50 years for assets like water utilities). Assuming a 40-year horizon, the depreciation rate would be

2.5% per annum. Depreciation may be classified as the required level of annual capital expenditure to maintain or upgrade the infrastructure asset. In practice, this can vary depending on the type of assets and the rules embedded in the concession, which typically prescribe a residual life at the end of the concession period. Depreciation is also difficult to evaluate because some managers argue that initial yield numbers are already net of capital expenditure to maintain and upgrade infrastructure assets. An annual depreciation rate of 2.5% is assumed as an example.

- *Dilution for not being invested initially.* Most funds do not have seed assets and they need time after the initial close to be fully invested (i.e. the time between committing the capital and calling and investing the capital). Assuming that full investment is achieved after one year, an expected dilution factor of 0.5% is reasonable, assuming that money committed but not drawn is invested in cash.

- *Fees.* A management fee of 1.5% per annum is assumed as an example.

The result is an expected return of 6.5% (8.0%+3.0%-2.5%-0.5%-1.5%). This expected returns lies between that of fixed income and equities. It makes sense since infrastructure shares some characteristics with fixed income and some with equities.

The expected volatility of infrastructure investments is difficult to evaluate as it is an illiquid asset class with no readily available market prices. Based on historical returns of indices representing listed infrastructure-related equities, the historical annualised volatility is 14% per annum. Historical returns have been based on the Macquarie Global Infrastructure Index since July 2000. However, when volatility is adjusted using the Cornish-Fisher approximation to reflect downside risk (i.e. historical fat tails) the expected volatility goes up to 17% per annum. This volatility is that of equities related to infrastructure, not of the underlying infrastructure assets, and therefore it reflects equity's volatility.

The correlation of infrastructure calculated using the Macquarie index since July 2000 is 0.66 with US equities, -0.07 with Treasuries and 0.13 with cash. The Macquarie index is based on listed infrastructure-related equities, which have a much higher correlation with the general equity market than unlisted infrastructure.

The expected return, risk and correlation of equity-related infrastructure are easier to formulate. Investors can use the published indices and their fundamental data (e.g. dividend yield, price/earnings ratio) to formulate CMAs in a similar way to any other equity market.

Manager selection

Manager selection has a potentially large impact on results in infrastructure investing because of the many investment choices (the asset class is heterogeneous), its inefficiencies and because of its relative infancy. There are many different investment philosophies among managers – they can focus on different areas of expertise and the asset class can exhibit investment characteristics of private equity, fixed income and real estate. Each specific product or portfolio can offer a different return and risk profile. Manager selection is hence critical.

Infrastructure return and risk characteristics

Figure 4.5 shows the cumulative performance of listed infrastructure-related equities since July 2000. Listed infrastructure is materially different to direct infrastructure, which is accessed through private funds or directly. Listed infrastructure is much more correlated with equity markets and has a similar volatility level to that of the general equity markets.

Figure 4.5: Cumulative performance of listed infrastructure and US equities, July 2000 to December 2013

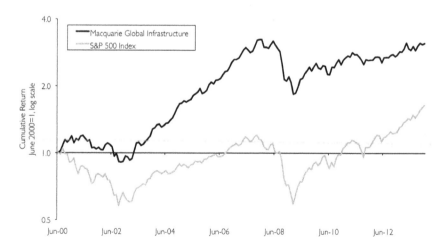

Source: Bloomberg, Macquarie Global Infrastructure Index, S&P 500 Index.

Figure 4.6 shows the rolling correlation of listed infrastructure with equities and bonds. Figure 4.7 shows the rolling annualised volatility of listed infrastructure and equities. As the two charts demonstrate, listed infrastructure has a high correlation with equities and volatility similar to that of equities. This is simply because listed infrastructure is infrastructure-related equity and not a pure infrastructure asset.

Figure 4.6: Rolling 36-month correlation of listed infrastructure with US equities and US Treasuries, June 2003 to December 2013

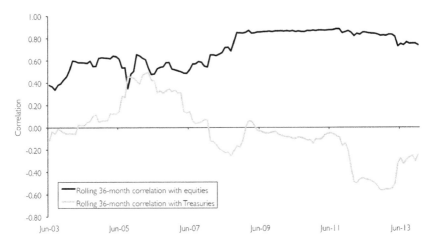

Source: Bloomberg, Macquarie Global Infrastructure Index, S&P 500 Index, Citigroup United States WGBI TR Index.

Figure 4.7: Rolling 36-month volatility of listed infrastructure and US equities, June 2003 to December 2013

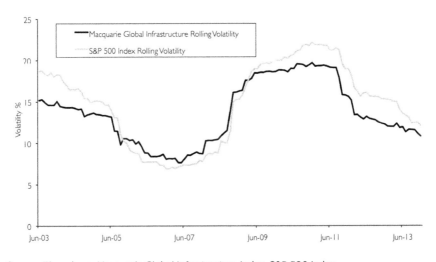

Source: Bloomberg, Macquarie Global Infrastructure Index, S&P 500 Index.

Conclusions

Similarly to other new alternatives, infrastructure investing is different; in fact it is unique among asset classes. This means exposure to a different set of risk factors, diversification, expansion of the investment opportunity set and a potential liquidity premium. Investors who can accept the illiquidity and long investment horizon should consider including this asset class in their portfolios.

Summary

- Infrastructure includes physical assets, facilities and systems that provide essential services to society.

- Four common features of infrastructure investing are relative stability through the economic cycle; yield and predictable cash flows; inflation and GDP linkage; and long duration.

- Infrastructure is a real asset, alongside real estate, commodities and inflation-linked bonds.

- Infrastructure includes assets that often require considerable investment to construct and maintain and typically generate a relatively steady stream of cash flows that should increase with inflation.

- Infrastructure as a separate asset class in portfolios should exclude assets that are already included elsewhere (e.g. infrastructure buildings under commercial real estate and utilities under public and private equities).

- The four ways to access infrastructure investments are: direct investments (this requires a large capital commitment and they are very illiquid, so impractical for most investors); private equity funds and partnerships (normally the recommended way to gain pure, diversified exposure to the asset class); listed vehicles (typically closed-end funds that may trade at material premiums and discounts to NAV); and infrastructure-related equities (exposure to the equity market).

- Different infrastructure investments can be distinguished by the level of government involvement and the stage of project across construction, maturing assets and assets earning established revenue.

- Infrastructure shares some similar features with fixed income, private equity and real estate. However, it also has unique features.

- Different infrastructure investments and different vehicles can have different risk/return profiles depending on the underlying assets and leverage – the asset class is heterogeneous and each investment has unique characteristics. The risk of infrastructure could be higher than that of equities. Therefore, each infrastructure investment should be carefully evaluated.

- The reasons for adding infrastructure to multi-asset portfolios include: income; as an inflation hedge; diversification; asset/liability matching; and opportunities for active management.

- The risks in infrastructure investing include infant asset class risk (lack of return history and manager track records); competition; regulatory risk; reputation risk; event risk; concentration risk; leverage risk; interest rate risk; construction risk; operational risk; patronage risk; unique risks for growth infrastructure; illiquidity; and a long horizon to generate returns.

- Direct, pure infrastructure lacks indices. The only available indices are for global listed infrastructure-related equities (i.e. indices of public equity of corporations in the infrastructure sector).

- Infrastructure's expected return is initial yield, plus income's expected growth, minus depreciation, minus dilution for not being invested initially, minus fees.

- The many choices in infrastructure investing (the asset class is very heterogeneous), the inefficiencies of the asset class and its relative infancy mean that manager selection has a potentially large impact on results.

CHAPTER 11: STRUCTURED FINANCE

Structured finance relates to securitisation of cash flows from underlying pools of usually illiquid financial instruments (e.g. mortgages, loans and credit card receivables) into liquid, transferable financial securities.

These securities are essentially fixed income, since they promise to pay interest to their investors. However, unlike government and corporate debt, which is used to finance its issuers through borrowing, structured finance securities repackage existing financial instruments and sell them. They are not used to raise debt by their issuer and they exhibit different return and risk behaviour compared to other, more traditional fixed income securities.

For example, a bank lends money to buyers of residential real estate (i.e. houses) and holds a book of mortgages on its balance sheet. The mortgages are an asset (cash receivable) on the bank's balance sheet. The bank receives a steady stream of cash flows in the form of interest and principal payments from the mortgage holders. The downside for the bank is that it is going to receive the cash payments from the mortgages over time (not at present) and it cannot easily sell the illiquid mortgages. Securitisation comes to the rescue.

The bank can package the cash flows from the mortgages into new securities (i.e. securitisation) and then sell them to investors. Investors get paid interest on the securities directly from the underlying mortgage payments (known as *pass through*). The bank is able to receive a cash flow now from investors who buy the newly created securities instead of the future stream of cash flows from the mortgages.

The bank has transferred the mortgages' risk to the investors and replaced the future mortgage receivables with current cash on its balance sheet. The bank's credit is transformed into tradable securities. The pass through structure exposes investors directly to the underlying cash-flow stream of the underlying asset pool.

Tranching refers to creating different investment classes for the new securities with different risks and rights on the cash flows from the underlying assets. Different investors can buy different classes based on their risk appetite. Each tranche has a different credit rating, with the senior tranches having the highest, then mezzanine, junior and finally the *equity tranche* with the lowest credit rating. The equity tranche receives payments only after all the more senior tranches have received their cash flows in full.

The Committee on the Global Financial System[168] has explained tranching as follows:

> "A key goal of the tranching process is to create at least one class of securities whose rating is higher than the average rating of the underlying collateral pool or to create rated securities from a pool of unrated assets. This is accomplished through the use of credit support (enhancement), such as prioritization of payments to the different tranches."

Credit enhancement is a way to create a security that has a higher credit rating than the issuing company. Credit enhancement techniques include issuing subordinated bonds, which are allocated any losses from the collateral before losses are allocated to the senior bonds, thus giving senior bonds a credit enhancement. Another technique is *overcollateralisation*, where the balance of the assets is greater than the balance of the issued securities. For example, the principal amount of an issue may be $100 million while the principal value of the underlying assets may be $120 million (overcollateralisation of $20 million).

Asset-backed securities (ABS)

Asset-backed securities (ABS) are structured securities whose cash flows and value are backed by a collateralised pool of underlying assets. The assets in the pool are illiquid and cannot be easily sold without the ABS structure, but using this structure they can be sold to investors. Through the securitisation of the asset pool the institution, such as a bank, can transfer the risk of the asset pool to willing investors. The underlying asset pool can include a wide range of assets that pay cash flows, such as mortgages, student loans, credit cards and so on.

Often, a separate legal entity called a *Special Purpose Vehicle* (*SPV*), is incorporated and the underlying assets are sold to it. The SPV holds the underlying asset pool, repackages the assets and then issues them as interest-bearing fixed income securities (ABS). Alternatively, a *bankruptcy-remote* trust is used instead of or in addition to the SPV. The institution that originated the underlying assets (the sponsor) sells them to the SPV or the trust to achieve *bankruptcy remoteness*, insulating the SPV or trust from the sponsor. The SPV sells the ABS and pays the proceeds from the sale to the sponsor. In other words, the investors in the ABS have no recourse to the sponsor since the SPV or trust stands between the investors and the sponsor.

When the credit risk of the underlying assets is transferred to the SPV the originating institution can remove them from its balance sheet (taking them *off balance sheet*). The institution receives cash from the SPV when the ABS are sold.

---

[168] Bank of International Settlements, 'The Role of Rating in Structured Finance: Issues and Implications', report submitted by a Working Group established by the Committee on the Global Financial System, www.bis.org (January 2005).

This transfer of the asset pool away from the balance sheet of the institution can reduce the risk of its balance sheet, improve its credit rating (hence reducing the interest it needs to pay on its debt) and reduce its capital requirements.

The ABS credit rating is based on the SPV credit rating and can be higher than that of the originating institution since the SPV is a separate legal entity. Credit enhancements are often used to increase the SPV credit rating. A higher credit rating means that the SPV needs to pay lower interest rates on the ABS to investors.

A *mortgage-backed security* (*MBS*) is an ABS whose asset pool is mortgages. *Collateralised debt obligations* (*CDOs*) or *collateralised loan obligations* (*CLOs*) are ABS whose asset pool is bonds or loans. *Synthetic CDOs* gain exposure to the underlying asset pool via derivatives and not through holding the physical underlying assets. Often synthetic CDOs are more liquid than physical ones.

MBS and the financial crisis

Low quality MBS backed by subprime mortgages played a major role in the 2008 global financial crisis. In some markets, such as those for securities backed by risky subprime mortgages in the United States, the unexpected deterioration in the quality of some of the underlying assets undermined investors' confidence. Both the scale and persistence of the attendant credit crisis seem to suggest that securitisation, together with poor credit origination, inadequate valuation methods and insufficient regulatory oversight, could severely hurt financial stability. By 2012 the market for high quality MBS had recovered and was once again a profitable business for banks.

Risks

As with all fixed income securities, the prices of ABS fluctuate in response to changing interest rates. When interest rates fall prices rise and vice versa. Prices of ABS with floating rates are much less sensitive to interest rate risk because the index against which the ABS rate adjusts (e.g. LIBOR) reflects external interest-rate changes.

Prepayment risk is a risk related to interest rate risk and particularly affects MBS. This is the risk of an early repayment of the mortgages in the underlying asset pool when mortgage holders refinance their mortgages to a lower interest rate. The refinance is possible because either the credit rating of the mortgage holders has improved or interest rates have decreased. In either case, the interest payments to investors in the MBS are lower than before and they face reinvestment risk.

Refinancing typically happens when interest rates decline since at these times borrowers have opportunities to refinance to mortgages with lower interest rates. The MBS' value, therefore, declines when interest rates decline, unlike most other fixed income instruments, whose values increase when interest rates decline.

When interest rates increase, there are no refinancing of mortgages and hence no prepayments. Investors in MBS are exposed to downside prepayment risk, but rarely benefit from it. MBS have a *negative convexity* (or concavity, unlike most fixed income investments, which have a convexity)[169] and hence when interest rates fall the duration of MBS increases, enhancing the fall in price. This means that MBS must pay a higher interest rate than comparable standard bonds to compensate investors for this risk.

Typically, nonmortgage consumer assets, such as credit card receivables, auto loans, student loans and so on, are not highly sensitive to fluctuations in interest rates. Thus, ABS backed by such assets are not usually subject to prepayment risk due to declines in interest rates.

Since the cash flows from the underlying asset pool are passed through to the investors in the ABS, the default risk is minimised through diversification. The asset pool includes hundreds or thousands of individual cash flow generating assets and the specific risk of each asset is low. However, one risk that cannot be diversified away is *systemic risk*.

Systemic risk is the risk of collapse of an entire financial system or entire market, as opposed to risk associated with any one individual entity, group or component of a system. When an event hits the entire market and causes all the assets in the pool to default or drop in value, the ABS will stop passing through the full expected cash flows, adversely affecting the interest payments to investors. This means that the risk of default in the ABS market is a failure of the collateral or the underlying asset pool.

ABS, MBS and CDOs attracted considerable criticism during the 2008 crisis after credit rating agencies assigned the highest credit ratings to these structures and failed to warn investors of their true credit risk. The prices of many structured securities collapsed during the crisis. It emerged in many instances that the credit ratings were inflated, ABS could not pay their obligations and their liquidity disappeared. In some cases money market funds invested in AAA-rated ABS structures to enhance returns. When the value of these securities collapsed, the money market funds' returns turned negative.

ABS have revolutionised the way banks manage risk and capitalise their balance sheets, and have added a substantial stream of revenues for investment banks. With the shattered confidence in this market, or some segments thereof, the implications for the profitability and risk management tools of banks are material.

---

[169] Convexity means that when interest rates rise the bond price falls at a slower rate than that at which the bond price rises when interest rates decline. Graphically, the relationship between bond price and interest rates is convex instead of a straight line (linear).

Role of ABS in a portfolio

ABS are a source of yield. Often, ABS pay higher yields compared to equivalent government bonds and corporate bonds with the same credit rating. The issue is whether the credit rating of the ABS truly reflects their risk. The higher yields from ABS often come with higher risks.

ABS normally have relatively short duration risk so they can be used as a source of yield and return during a rising interest rate environment.

MBS can be tactically included in portfolios as part of the fixed income allocation. When long-term interest rates fall MBS underperform equivalent government bonds. Conversely, when interest rates increase, MBS outperform equivalent government bonds.

There is no natural clear strategic or permanent role for ABS in portfolios. While ABS can offer diversification benefits, investors should invest in ABS only if they understand the risks and potential rewards. Investors who rely on advice from advisors who work for investment banks, which sell ABS, should seek a second, independent opinion since the banks are profiting from selling the ABS and the advisors may be in a conflict of interests.

Some investors use ABS to get around restrictions on investing in below investment grade bonds, as the senior tranches of the ABS may have an investment grade rating. This can be another role for ABS in some portfolios.

Some ABS should be considered *toxic waste*. Their risks cannot be easily modelled and their contribution to the returns and risks of portfolios are unclear. Their high credit rating may be misleading.

Investors who are not experts or cannot hire experts in structured securities should avoid them. If investors do want exposure to these securities, a professional portfolio manager should be used to manage a diversified portfolio of ABS.

ABS return and risk characteristics

Figure 4.8 compares the cumulative performance of ABS (Barclays Asset-Backed Securities Total Return Index),[170] US Treasuries and US corporate bonds. Figure 4.9 shows the rolling annualised standard deviation of the three asset classes. Figure 4.10 shows the rolling correlation of ABS with Treasuries and corporate bonds.

Over time, ABS have performed in line with Treasuries and corporate bonds. However, the systemic credit crunch of 2008 saw ABS decouple from Treasuries. Treasuries gained in the crisis due to a flight to quality while ABS and corporate bonds fell.

---

[170] The Barclays Asset-Backed Securities Index is the ABS component of the Barclays Capital US Aggregate Index. The ABS index has three subsectors: credit and charge cards, autos, and utility. The index includes pass-through, bullet and controlled amortisation structures. The ABS index includes only the senior class of each ABS issue and the ERISA-eligible B and C tranche. The manufactured housing sector was removed as of 1 January 2008 and the home equity loan sector was removed as of 1 October 2009.

Figure 4.8: Cumulative performance of ABS, Treasuries and corporate bonds, January 1992 to June 2012

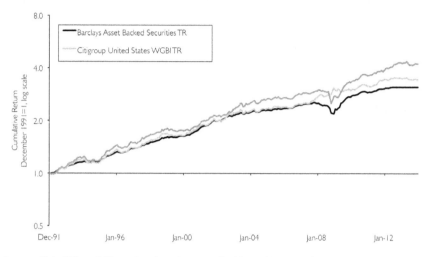

Source: Global Financial Data, Barclays Asset-Backed Securities TR Index, Citigroup United States WGBI TR Index, BofA Merrill Lynch U.S Corporate Master TR Index.

Figure 4.9: Rolling 36-month volatility of ABS, Treasuries and corporate bonds, January 1995 to June 2012

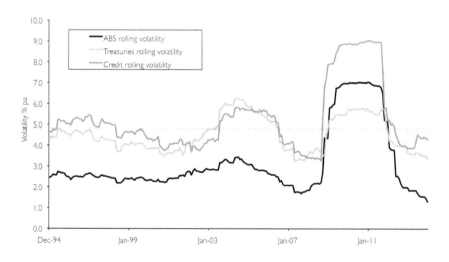

Source: Global Financial Data, Barclays Asset-Backed Securities TR Index, Citigroup United States WGBI TR Index, BofA Merrill Lynch U.S Corporate Master TR Index.

Figure 4.10: Rolling 36-month correlation between ABS and Treasuries and ABS and corporate bonds, January 1995 to June 2012

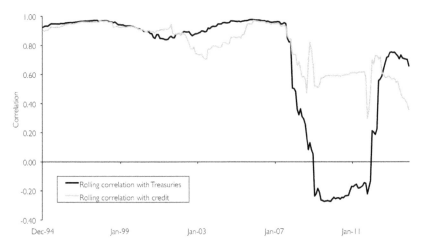

Source: Global Financial Data, Barclays Asset-Backed Securities TR Index, Citigroup United States WGBI TR Index, BofA Merrill Lynch U.S Corporate Master TR Index.

Figure 4.11 plots the monthly returns of an MBS index (Bank of America Merrill Lynch Mortgage Master)[171] and US 10-year Treasuries. The chart demonstrates the close relationship between MBS and Treasuries.

Figure 4.11: Scatter plot of MBS and 10-year Treasury monthly returns, January 1982 to December 2013

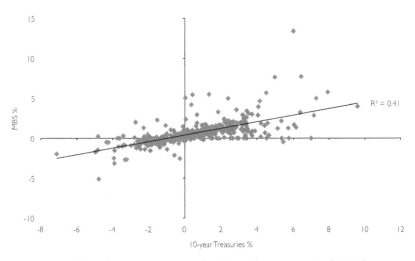

Source: BofA Merrill Lynch Mortgage Master, USA 10-year Government Bond TR Index.

[171] This index tracks the performance of US dollar-denominated fixed rate and hybrid residential mortgage pass-through securities issued by US agencies in the US domestic market having at least $5 billion per generic coupon and $250 million outstanding per generic producing year.

As Figure 4.12 demonstrates, the long-term cumulative performance of MBS and 10-year US Treasuries is similar.

Figure 4.12: Cumulative performance of MBS and 10-year Treasuries, January 1982 to December 2013

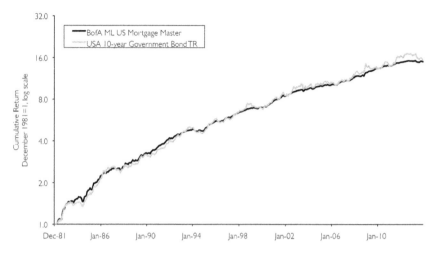

Source: BofA Merrill Lynch Mortgage Master, USA 10-year Government Bond TR Index.

Figure 4.13: Rolling 36-month correlation between MBS and 10-year Treasuries, January 1985 to December 2013

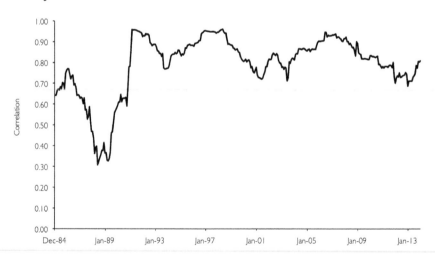

Source: BofA Merrill Lynch Mortgage Master, USA 10-year Government Bond TR Index.

Figures 4.13 and 4.14 show MBS, as represented by the Bank of America Merrill Lynch Mortgage Master, have maintained a high correlation with Treasuries and their volatility has remained relatively steady over the last 15 years. The 2008 crisis did not adversely affect MBS as it affected ABS.

Figure 4.14: Rolling 36-month volatility of MBS and 10-year Treasuries, January 1985 to December 2013

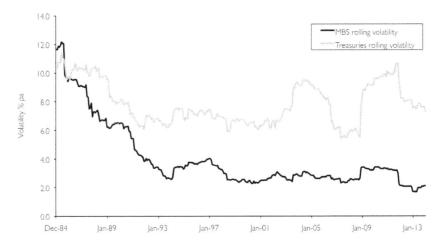

Source: BofA Merrill Lynch Mortgage Master, USA 10-year Government Bond TR Index.

Covered bonds

Covered bonds are securities that are backed by cash flows from public sector loans or mortgages. They are similar to ABS since the cash flows from a pool of assets are backing them. However, unlike ABS, covered bonds remain on the issuer's balance sheet.

Covered bonds typically have relatively high credit ratings since in the case of default they have recourse to both the issuer and the pool of assets backing them if the issuer becomes insolvent. Their credit rating is a function of the issuer's credit rating and the quality of the pool of loans (cover pool) backing them.

Covered bonds are often attractive to investors looking for high-quality debt that offers high yields. Since the bonds remain on the balance sheet of the issuer, it must ensure that the cover pool constantly backs them.

The interest of the covered bonds is paid from an identifiable source of projected cash flows and not out of the general cash flows generated from the operations of the issuer. Non-performing loans or prematurely paid debt must be replaced in the pool, so the success of the product for the issuer depends on its ability to evaluate the assets in the pool and to rate and price the bond.

Access

Typically, only professional or sophisticated investors purchase individual ABS since they require research on the underlying asset pools and structures of the ABS. Investors can access ABS through actively managed dedicated collective investment schemes. Passive trackers (ETFs) of MBS and covered bond indices are available. Many fixed income funds can have a small allocation to ABS, so many investors in these funds have some exposure to the ABS market, sometimes without realising it.

Conclusions

ABS and MBS have characteristics that differentiate them from other asset classes. Including them in portfolios may expand the investment opportunity set and improve diversification. However, investors must be wary. The credit rating of ABS and MBS may be misleadingly high because of the creativity of securitisation and the investment bankers behind it.

Summary

- Structured finance relates to securitisation of cash flows from underlying pools of usually illiquid financial instruments (e.g. mortgages, loans and credit card receivables) into liquid, transferable, interest-bearing financial securities.

- Securitised securities are fixed income instruments but they have different risk and return characteristics compared to more traditional fixed income securities, such as government and corporate bonds.

- Securitisation means packaging cash flows from underlying cash flow generating assets (e.g. mortgages), creating different investment classes through tranching, enhancing credit quality through credit enhancement techniques and selling the newly created securities to investors, who are exposed to the cash flows from the underlying pool of assets through the pass through structure. Investors can choose the risk level by buying different investment classes.

- ABS are based on any underlying asset pool. MBS and CDOs are sub-categories of ABS based on the underlying assets (mortgages for MBS and bonds and loans for CDOs and CLOs, respectively).

- Interest rate risk affects ABS as a fixed income instrument. Prepayment risk is one of the risks of MBS. Default risk means that the value of the underlying asset pool (collateral) has fallen or the assets in the pool default on their cash flow payments. The risk of an individual asset failing is diminished through diversification. However, systemic risk is not diversified away.

- The 2008 credit crunch demonstrated that the high credit rating of ABS, MBS and CDOs can be completely misleading.

- ABS can be a source of yield. The high yield comes with high risk.

- ABS do not have a natural role in multi-asset portfolios. They can be included as part of the fixed income allocation, in particular during an increasing interest rate environment due to their relatively low duration risk. Some ABS are just risky and opaque and should be considered toxic waste. ABS should be accessed through a professional portfolio manager who knows the risks of these instruments and can manage a properly diversified portfolio.

- Covered bonds are similar to ABS since they are backed from a cash flow of loans or mortgages. However, they remain on the balance sheet of the issuer, meaning the investors have recourse to both the underlying asset pool and the issuer.

- ABS can be accessed through individual securities (mostly relevant for professional and sophisticated investors), funds, trackers of MBS and covered bond indices, and as part of fixed income funds.

CHAPTER 12: LEVERAGED LOANS

Introduction

Leveraged loans (or simply loans) fall under the broad category of fixed income, alongside structured finance, government bonds, investment grade corporate bonds and high-yield bonds. The US leveraged loan market is almost as large as the high-yield bond market, with over $800 billion of outstanding loans as of May 2010.[172] In Europe companies borrow predominantly via bank loans rather than by issuing bonds.

Unlike bonds, loans are not tradable securities. They settle through execution of bilateral legal contracts between parties (the lending bank and borrowing company). They have historically been less accessible to small investors compared to other fixed income securities such as corporate and high-yield bonds. However, investors can increasingly access loans via actively managed portfolios specialising in loans.

When companies borrow from banks they typically do so through loans. Banks lend to investment grade companies at rates normally lower than those available to such companies at the bond market. The incentive for the banks is to offer these companies other services (e.g. foreign exchange, derivatives and advisory) and charge fees to compensate for the lower interest rates applied to the loans.

The sub-investment grade market is different. Many sub-investment grade borrowers have been subject to leveraged buyouts (LBOs) and the interest on the loans is higher to reflect the higher risk due to leverage and credit risk. Loans to sub-investment grade companies are known as *leveraged loans*.

In a typical LBO transaction a private equity sponsor pays between 30% and 70% of the company's purchase price and arranges an underwriting for a syndicated bank loan to finance the balance. Once the transaction goes through, the underwriting bank seeks to syndicate the loan to other banks and institutional investors. Most loans do not have a public credit rating and investors need to determine the borrower's creditworthiness through extensive due diligence.

---

[172] Credit Suisse Leveraged Finance Update, May 2010.

Leveraged loans and high-yield bonds are issued by similar companies. High-yield bond borrowers need a diverse pool of investors and this requires the borrower to be known, have a business that can be easily understood, to disclose key financial information and typically to have a public credit rating. Loans, in contrast, are syndicated to a small group of investors who can conduct the required due diligence themselves.

Comparing loans and bonds

Loans usually have a number of different characteristics to bonds. Loans are secured on the operating assets of the borrower (*secured loans*). Bonds are generally unsecured. Loans have priority over bonds on the issuer's assets in the case of a default.

Loans typically have higher *recovery rates*[173] relative to bonds at default. Recovery rates on loans typically range from 50% to 100% while those for bonds typically range from 0% to 50%. The higher recovery rates of loans mean they have lower volatility compared to bonds in the secondary market (a sign of stress causes bond prices to react more severely than those of loans).

Loans typically pay *floating interest rates*, while the interest rate of most bonds is fixed. Similar to floating rate notes (FRNs), loans do not have duration or interest rate risk. In a rising interest environment fixed rate bonds may lose value while loans may not.

Both loan and bond legal documents include restrictive *covenants*. For example, covenants can limit the issuer's gearing (ratio of debt to equity or debt to earnings) and require a minimum level of interest rate coverage ratio.[174] The covenants on loans are usually tested more frequently than those of bonds, and loan agreements usually give investors more flexibility to change the legal documents than bonds do.

Leveraged loans provided a steady stream of returns to investors until the financial crisis that started in 2007. When the subprime market collapsed, collateral backing margin lines was called and because loans were more liquid than other assets, it caused a sell-off of loans. Deleveraging of excessive leverage of borrowers exacerbated the situation, causing an unprecedented drop in prices of leveraged loans. In 2009 loan prices recovered strongly, indicating that prices overshot the level that fairly represented the level of stress of borrowers and the likely recovery rates at default.

---

[173] The recovery rate is the amount recovered by a creditor through foreclosure of collateral or bankruptcy procedures in the event of default, expressed as a percentage of the face value of the loan or bond.

[174] The interest rate coverage ratio indicates the ability of a company to pay interest on its outstanding debt. The ratio is calculated by dividing the company's earnings before interest and taxes (EBIT) by the company's interest expenses.

Benchmark

The S&P/LSTA Leveraged Loan Index[175] is a common benchmark for leveraged loans covering the loan market in the United States. S&P/LSTA offers a series of loan indices, including coverage of the European market. The index series is published by a partnership of S&P and the Loan Syndications & Trading Association (LSTA). Each index reflects the market-weighted performance of institutional leveraged loans in its respective market based upon real-time market weightings, spreads and interest payments.

Role of loans in a portfolio and their risks

Loans can be a source of yield, they can perform better than other fixed income investments during a rising interest rate environment and they can enhance diversification due to their relatively low correlation with other assets, including fixed income investments such as government bonds.

The risks of loans are that normally they have a below investment grade rating (i.e. credit risk), they are illiquid and they can undergo periods of severe drawdowns, such as in 2008. An additional risk is that loans are likely to underperform longer-duration fixed income investments in a declining interest rate environment.

Access

The three primary types of investors buying loans are banks, finance companies and institutional investors. Institutional investors mainly cover Collective Loan Obligations (CLOs) and Collective Investment Schemes (CIS) investing in loans. Hedge funds, high-yield bond funds, pension funds, insurance companies and other proprietary investors participate in the loan market.

The wider retail market can access the asset class through CIS specialising in the loan market. CIS can be open-end funds with daily trading, closed-end funds with monthly or quarterly trading and exchange-traded closed-end funds. Most recently, ETFs on the S&P/LSTA Leveraged Loan 100 Index have been launched. Loans can also be accessed through CLOs although these fall under structured finance and can have a different return and risk profile to that of loans.

---

[175] www.lsta.org.

Leveraged loan return and risk characteristics

Figure 4.15 shows the cumulative performance of the US leveraged loan market, alongside global high-yield bonds and US equities. The 2008 crash and the subsequent recovery of the loan market are vividly evident.

Figure 4.15: Cumulative performance of US leveraged loans, global high-yield bonds and US equities, January 1998 to December 2013

Source: Bloomberg, S&P/LSTA Leveraged Loans Index, Barclays Capital Global High Yield TR Index, S&P 500 Index.

Tables 4.4 and 4.5 show the return and risk characteristics of US leveraged loans, global high-yield bonds, US Treasuries and US equities and their correlation matrix. Over the measurement period loans have delivered an average annual return comparable to that of equities and Treasuries, with volatility closer to that of Treasuries than to that of equities. Global high-yield was the best performing asset out of the four, benefiting from a tailwind of declining rates. Going forward, if rates are to increase, the short duration of loans can boost their performance relative to that of high-yield bonds.

Table 4.4: Leveraged loans return and risk characteristics, January 1998 to December 2013. Sharpe ratio calculated using $ cash returns

	Loans	Global High-Yield	US Treasuries	US equities
Start month	Jan-1998	Jan-1998	Jan-1998	Jan-1998
Performance (% pa)	5.2	7.4	5.2	6.0
Volatility (%)	6.5	10.4	4.6	15.9
Skewness	-2.03	-1.14	-0.12	-0.65
Kurtosis	20.09	7.66	1.45	0.97
Sharpe ratio	0.44	0.48	0.62	0.23

Source: Bloomberg, S&P/LSTA Leveraged Loans Index, Barclays Capital Global High Yield TR Index, Citigroup United States WGBI TR Index, S&P 500 Index.

Table 4.5: Correlation matrix, January 1998 to December 2013

Correlation matrix	Loans	Global High-Yield	US Treasuries	US equities
Loans	1.00	0.76	-0.37	0.43
Global High-Yield	0.76	1.00	-0.19	0.64
US Treasuries	-0.37	-0.19	1.00	-0.32
US equities	0.43	0.64	-0.32	1.00

Source: Bloomberg, S&P/LSTA Leveraged Loans Index, Barclays Capital Global High Yield TR Index, Citigroup United States WGBI TR Index, S&P 500 Index.

Figure 4.16 shows the rolling annualised volatility of loans, high-yield bonds and Treasuries. Figure 4.17 shows the rolling correlation of loans with high-yield bonds and of loans with Treasuries. The risk level of loans lies between that of Treasuries and that of high-yield bonds. At times of stress, the volatility of loans can jump, as happened in 2008. Normally, however, they have volatility in line with that of Treasuries.

Figure 4.16: Rolling 36-month volatility of US leveraged loans, global high-yield bonds and US equities, January 2001 to December 2013

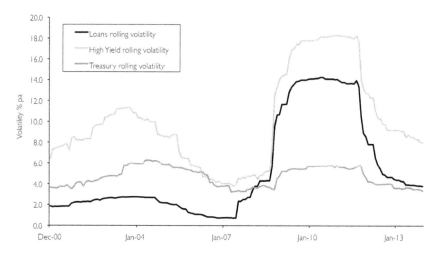

Source: Bloomberg, S&P/LSTA Leveraged Loans Index, Barclays Capital Global High Yield TR Index, Citigroup United States WGBI TR Index.

Figure 4.17: Rolling 36-month correlation between US leveraged loans and global high-yield bonds and between loans and Treasuries, January 2001 to December 2013

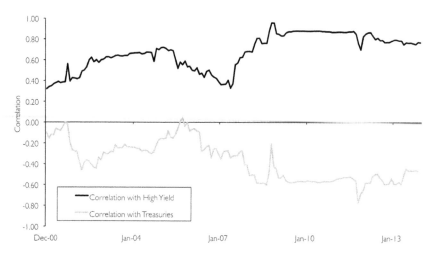

Source: Bloomberg, S&P/LSTA Leveraged Loans Index, Barclays Capital Global High Yield TR Index, Citigroup United States WGBI TR Index.

Conclusions

While less common than high-yield bonds, loans normally offer a stream of income to investors with relatively low volatility and interest rate risk. Loans can play a role in portfolios, in particular in a rising interest rate environment when fixed interest rate bonds may suffer.

Summary

- Leveraged loans are bilateral agreements between lending banks and borrowing companies. They can be accessed by retail and small institutional investors via professionally managed funds or by large institutional investors via loan syndication.

- Loans are secured on the operating assets of the borrower; have higher recovery rates compared to high-yield bonds; have lower volatility than that of high-yield bonds; pay floating interest rates; and have more flexibility to review covenants.

- The roles of loans in a portfolio are a source of income, a source of return in particular during rising interest rates conditions and diversification. The main risks are below investment grade credit risk, illiquidity and downside risk.

CHAPTER 13: STRUCTURED PRODUCTS

Introduction

Structured products are designed to customise the cash flow profile and risk/reward characteristics of investments or portfolios, typically using a combination of standard investments, such as bonds and equities, and derivatives, such as options, futures and swaps. Structured products can be customised to specific investor needs, usually if investors have sufficient money to justify customisation (i.e. to make it economically worthwhile for the originating institution). Many financial institutions, in particular investment banks, create standard structured products and then sell them to their clients.

The underlying standard investments can be a single security, a basket of securities, indices or a basket of indices, covering a wide array of asset classes such as equities, bonds, commodities and currencies. Each structured product has its own risk/reward profile. It is therefore impossible to classify structured products as an asset class and each product or family of similar products should be treated individually.

Similar to hedge funds, structured products are a way to access different asset classes and create a new investment by changing the risk and return profile or cash flows of the underlying investments. Different to hedge funds, structured products are based on combining different investments and derivatives to create a predefined cash flow profile that is not dependent on the discretion or talent of an active portfolio manager but rather usually on a set of rules (i.e. it is rule-based).

The United States Securities and Exchange Commission (SEC) Rule 434[176] defines structured securities as "securities whose cash flow characteristics depend upon one or more indices or that have embedded forwards or options or securities where an investor's investment return and the issuer's payment obligations are contingent on, or highly sensitive to, changes in the value of underlying assets, indices, interest rates or cash flows".

---

[176] US Securities and Exchange Commission, www.sec.gov.

Principal protected note (PPN)

The structure and cash flow profiles of some structured products are straightforward. A common structured product is a *principal protected note (PPN)*. For example, a PPN can give investors 80% of the appreciation of the S&P 500 Index (*participation rate*) and 100% capital return guaranteed if the product is held to maturity. This means that if the S&P 500 Index rises by 10%, the investor's return on the structured note is 8%. If the S&P 500 Index falls by 10% the investor's return is 0% and the principal investment is paid back to the investor. The investor has lost only the opportunity cost of not investing the principal in a deposit and earning an interest rate, as well as the fee on the structured product.

Figure 4.18 illustrates the performance of such a theoretical PPN with a maturity of three years. The chart compares the 3-year rolling total return of the S&P 500 Index and the total return of the PPN (assuming a total fee of 2%). In this case the average 3-year return of the S&P 500 Index was 16% and that of the PPN was 16.6%. The PPN outperforms when equity markets fall and underperforms when equity markets generate positive returns.

Figure 4.18: Illustrative rolling 36-month return of the S&P 500 and a principal protected note with 80% participation, 100% principal protection and 2% total fee, January 2003 to December 2013

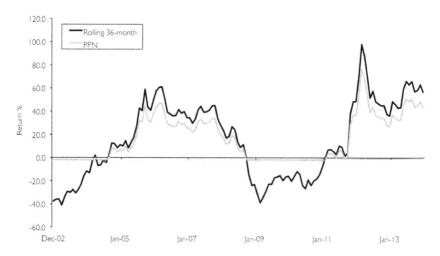

Source: Bloomberg, S&P 500 Index.

This principal protected product is fairly simple to structure. The originating institution sells each note for $1,000, buys a zero coupon bond (ZCB) for $900 and call options on the S&P 500 Index for $98 (the institution collects $2 as fees). The zero coupon bond pays back the $1,000 at maturity so the principal is guaranteed. The call option returns 80% of the return of the S&P 500 Index if the index appreciates, or expires worthless if the index declines.

The terms of such a structured product depend on market volatility (the higher the volatility, the more expensive the options and the lower the participation rate) and the level of interest rates (the lower the interest rate, the lower the interest on the ZCB and the lower the available cash to buy the options). A combination of a volatile market environment and low interest rates is the worst for principal protected products. Also, the level of credit risk of the ZCB determines the level of its yield, and hence the amount available to purchase the call options.

More complicated structured products

The structure and cash flow profiles of some structured products are complex. A *rainbow note* offers exposure to more than one underlying asset. This can be the average of a few equity indices, for example. In a *lookback note* the value of the underlying asset is based not on its final value at maturity, but rather on an average of values from specific times during the term of the note (similar to an Asian option).

Some structured products offer an attractive payment as long as a certain underlying index does not breach a certain floor or cap at the maturity of the note or at any time during its term. Other notes may pay high levels of interest or dividends as long as an underlying index is trading within a certain range.

The variety of structures is endless. Some are straightforward but others may offer returns that are dependent on many conditions. This makes predicting and understanding their cash flow profile challenging.

Exchange traded notes (ETNs)

Exchange traded notes (*ETNs*) are debt securities that can be used to offer standardised structured products that are traded on the market (similarly to ETFs) and have much better liquidity. An ETN is a senior, unsecured, unsubordinated debt security issued by an underwriting bank. Similar to other debt securities, ETNs have a maturity date and are backed only by the credit of the issuer. ETNs are designed to provide investors access to the returns of various indices or strategies, less fees.

When an investor buys an ETN, the underwriting bank promises to pay the amount reflected in the underlying index or strategy, minus fees upon maturity. Unlike an ETF, if the underwriting bank goes bankrupt, the investment may lose value, the same way a senior debt would. Though linked to the performance of indices or strategies, ETNs are not equities or index funds, but they do share several characteristics with them. Similar to equities, they are traded on an exchange and can be sold short. Similar to index funds, they can be linked to the return of an index. However, as debt securities, ETNs do not actually own anything that they are tracking.

Risks

One risk of structured products is *liquidity risk*. In principal protected products the guarantee is contingent upon holding the product to its maturity. The products are not traded on an exchange. To sell them, investors need to find a willing buyer, or the originating institution may offer a secondary market.

The *credit risk* of the issuer of structured products is another risk. If the originating institution fails, the investor payments are at risk. In principal guaranteed products that are based on a ZCB, the counterparty of the ZCB introduces *counterparty risk*. The word "guaranteed" is not foolproof since it depends on the ZCB not defaulting. Since structured products use derivatives, all the risks of derivatives are imbedded in the product as well.

When volatility is high and interest rates are low, the maturity of structured products is extended since the interest on the ZCB is low and call options are expensive. The way to improve yield is to buy long-maturity ZCBs. When maturity is extended, duration risk (*interest rate risk*) on the ZCB is higher and illiquidity risk is higher, since the product needs to be held for a longer time.

Structured products are normally expensive. The fee structure is normally opaque, in particular when the products are not plain vanilla. Investment banks are notorious for the steep fees that they ask for the products and services that they sell and structured products are not an exception. Plain vanilla structured products can be replicated by sophisticated investors without the need to purchase them from banks.

Role in portfolio

Structured products can be used to achieve specific cash flow profiles that cannot be achieved using standard investments. Principal protection, for example, may be a desired feature for risk averse investors who still want exposure to the equity market, but do not want to risk their capital. This feature costs money in the form of fees and limited participation in equity market upside. Structured products may also be used to gain access to some markets that are inaccessible otherwise.

If the product is opaque, complex, overly expensive and/or its expected performance and risk are difficult to understand or model, it normally means it does not have a clear role in the portfolio. In some instances banks create structured products that fit the positions that they wish to hedge on their balance sheets.

A bank offering a product must hedge the market risks of the product so the bank does not expose itself to the movements of the underlying securities or indices, while it can benefit from the fees. Some banks offer products that do not necessarily fit investors' needs but rather enable the bank to hedge positions due to other products or transactions. Investors should be wary of such products.

Conclusions

Structured products are a diverse and heterogeneous universe of financial products that package securities and financial instruments to create a new risk/return and cash flow profile. Based on a case by case analysis they can add value to portfolios. However, investors need to consider their risks, some of which are not obvious, and their usually steep fees.

Summary

- Structured products use underlying investments and derivatives to change the risk/return profile and cash flows of investments or portfolios.

- Each structured product or a family of structured products should be modelled separately since they may not have any commonalities.

- A principal guaranteed product is affected by market volatility and interest rates. High volatility and low interest rates is the worst combination for principal guaranteed products.

- The main risks of structured products are liquidity risk, credit risk of the issuer, counterparty risk, derivative risk and interest rate risk.

- Structured products are commonly expensive and the fees should be carefully considered.

- Structured products can play a role in a portfolio since they can customise the cash flows from investments.

CHAPTER 14: ALTERNATIVE BETAS

Alternative or smart betas are based on methodologies of reweighting and reconstruction of existing asset indices to produce more efficient investments (not to be confused with alternative betas that are the systematic risks accessed through alternative investments).

Since the first market capitalisation weighted (cap-weighted) index was introduced by Standard & Poor's in 1923, they have become the dominant indexing methodology. The vast majority of index trackers, such as exchange traded funds (ETFs) and passive funds, and derivatives on indices, such as index futures, are based on cap-weighted indices. Cap-weighted indices are the most representative gauge of the market (i.e. they represent the value that the market assigns to each security) and they have the lowest implementation costs due to their capacity (large caps have a high weight in the index and high liquidity). Nevertheless, the development of alternative betas has mainly resulted from the criticism of cap-weighted indices.

One criticism is that cap-weighted indices have an inbuilt size bias that often produces portfolios that are heavily concentrated in specific sectors or companies. For example, material exposure to technology, oil or financials has developed during different time periods. For instance, the FTSE 100 had an exposure of over 9% to BP just before the Macondo well explosion in the Gulf of Mexico. BP's share price dropped by 50% following the incident, shedding 5% from the value of the entire FTSE 100 Index. This is an example of a constituent concentration risk.

Also, because assets with higher valuations have a higher weighting in the market cap weighted indices, they are more vulnerable to market sentiment and asset price bubbles (as the weight of inflated stocks increases) and subsequent corrections. For example, the weight of financials in the S&P 500 Index ballooned between 2000 and 2007. When the global financial crisis hit in 2008, the index was tilted towards the most vulnerable sector and companies.

Market cap indices are exposed to risk factors that do not attract risk premiums. Large and mega capitalisation securities make up a large portion of market cap indices. However, it is the small and mid cap risks that attract risk premiums, not large cap risk. Growth stocks make up a large portion of the index, although it is the value risk factor that is rewarded by a risk premium, not the growth risk factor (at least not low quality growth; high quality growth stocks can be rewarded).

In the case of fixed income indices, companies with large amounts of outstanding debt receive a large relative weight in the index. However, these companies are more susceptible to idiosyncratic default risk, which may not attract a risk premium since it is a diversifiable risk (unlike credit risk).

The mechanics of cap-weighting lead to trend following strategies, which provide an inefficient risk/return trade-off. As the price of a security increases, its market-cap increases and so does its weight in the index. The index rebalances from losers to winners (sell low, buy high), chasing performance. One classic example is the tilt to technology stocks during the build-up of the high-tech bubble during the 1990s and its eventual burst in 2000.

All these shortcomings in cap-weighted indices resulted in the development of different smart beta strategies that aim to overcome them, using a range of methodologies. The different alternative beta index methodologies can be divided into diversification strategies (e.g. equal weighting), low volatility strategies (i.e. risk focused) and fundamental weighting schemes.

Diversification strategies

The simplest way to avoid a size bias is to equally weight every asset in the portfolio. In an *equally-weighted* index (known as naïve diversification) the return is simply the arithmetic mean of the returns of its constituents (i.e. each stock has the same weight). If equally-weighted indices are properly rebalanced then they avoid the worst effects of asset pricing bubbles. However, rebalancing such an index can be costly due to the exposure to illiquid small and mid cap stocks.

Figure 4.19 compares the cumulative performance of the S&P 500 Index and an equally-weighted index comprised of the 500 constituents of the S&P 500 Index. The equally-weighted index outperformed the cap-weighted index over the measurement period. The equally-weighted index was less susceptible to bubbles, such as the high-tech bubble at the end of the 1990s, as the weight of appreciating sectors and stocks does not grow. However, the equally-weighted index is exposed to crashes, such as that of 2008, due to its large weight in small and mid caps. Small and mid caps should outperform large caps over the long term; however, they are more sensitive to market downturns.

Equal risk contribution and diversity-weighting strategies also aim to reduce stock specific risks by constructing portfolios with lower concentration than cap-weighted portfolios. These strategies do not apply to stock selection, but rather reweight and include all the securities in the index's universe.

Figure 4.19: Cumulative performance of the S&P 500 Index and an S&P 500 equally-weighted index, January 1990 to December 2013

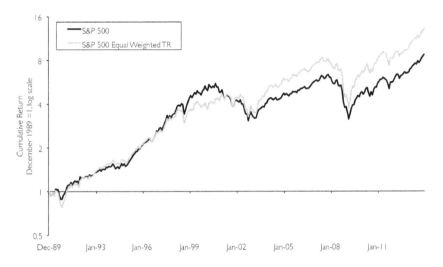

Source: Bloomberg, S&P 500 Index, S&P 500 Equal Weighted Index.

The *equal risk contribution* approach[177] considers both the weights of stocks and their marginal risk contributions so each stock contributes equally to the portfolio's total risk. The *diversity-weighted* portfolio takes the market-cap weights of individual securities and raises individual weights to a power between zero and one. This method essentially represents a middle ground between cap-weighted and equal-weighted portfolios. The diversity-weighted strategy has lower turnover and active risk than the equal-weighted strategy (*diversity* is a measure of the level of market concentration).[178]

The diversification strategies systematically overweight small cap stocks relative to cap-weighted portfolios and they have negative exposure to momentum because of their disciplined rebalancing away from stocks with higher past returns. They therefore have an inherent contrarian bias.

Low volatility strategies

One of the fundamental principles of investing is that high risk is expected to be rewarded with high return. However, the low-volatility effect or anomaly challenges the traditional equilibrium asset pricing theory (CAPM) that an asset's return is directly proportional to its beta or systematic risk. Contrary to that

---

[177] Maillard, Sébastien, Roncalli, Thierry and Teïltche, Jérôme, 'The Properties of Equally Weighted Risk Contribution Portfolios', *Journal of Portfolio Management* 36 (2010).

[178] Fernholz, Robert, Garvy, Robert and Hannon, John, 'Diversity-Weighted Indexing', *Journal of Portfolio Management* 24 (1998).

theory, the empirical evidence of a few academic studies[179] has illustrated that low-volatility investing tends to outperform the broad market as well as high-risk strategies over a long-term investment horizon, with much lower realised volatility.

A simple way to construct a low volatility index is the *ranking-based* approach. The approach weighs each asset in proportion to the inverse of its historical volatility (i.e. the least volatile securities receive the highest weights), or selects the assets with the lowest historical volatility from the entire universe. The S&P Low Volatility Index is an example of such an index.[180] This is a non-optimised approach and is based on the premise that stock volatility tends to cluster (i.e. stocks with lower past volatility may continue to exhibit lower volatility in the following period). The shortcoming is that this method assumes that all assets are equally correlated or ignores the correlation among stocks.

A more sophisticated approach is to run an optimisation algorithm (mean-variance optimisation) to find the weights that minimise the portfolio's risk. The result is the *minimum variance portfolio* that considers both risk and correlation. Mean-variance optimisation requires an estimate to be made of stocks' excess returns and the covariance matrix. A simplified method assumes that all stocks have the same expected returns.

Fundamental weighting strategies

Fundamental weighted indices (FWI) use balance sheet and financial account information (e.g. sales, cash flows, dividends and book value) to select stocks within the index. Proponents of FWI argue that fundamental weighting removes biases in traditional indices caused by reliance on market valuations.[181]

Another fundamental weighting approach is GDP-weighting. In a GDP-weighting, a country's weight depends on the relative size of its economy as measured by its gross domestic product (GDP). With a backdrop such as that of the European sovereign debt crisis, for instance, GDP-weighting appealed to bond investors because instead of weighting a country according to the size of its debt pile, GDP-weighting effectively weights each country according to its ability to service its debt.

FWI schemes can either select the index constituents from the whole stock universe based on fundamental measures or reweight all the constituents of the cap-weighted index based on fundamental measures, without making any stock selection. Indices that include a stock selection element may have a stronger value tilt and greater exposure to small cap stocks relative to indices that do not include stock selection and cover the entire stock universe.

---

[179] Baker, Malcolm, Bradley, Brendan and Wurgler, Jeffrey, 'Benchmarks as Limits to Arbitrage: Understanding the Low Volatility Anomaly', *Financial Analysts Journal* 67 (2011).

[180] www.standardandpoors.com.

[181] Arnott, Robert, Hsu, Jason and Moor, Philip, 'Fundamental Indexation', *Financial Analysts Journal* 61 (2005).

Understanding alternative equity betas

The key to understanding and evaluating alternative equity beta strategies is that equity returns can be explained by their beta or factor exposures. The first factor is the *market factor*; this is the beta from the capital asset pricing model (CAPM). Fama and French[182] expanded on the CAPM and developed a three-factor model using market, *small cap* and *value* factors. *Momentum* has been identified as another factor[183] because of the persistence in the relative performance of past winners and losers. The fifth factor is *volatility*. Contrary to theory, empirical evidence suggests that holding high volatility stocks has not been compensated by higher long-term returns more than holding low volatility stocks.[184]

Small cap, value and momentum have historically been associated with material positive returns, while the volatility factor has historically offered negative returns. However, similar to the market factor, these factors are volatile and the potential reward derived from systematically tilting the portfolio to these factors can vary significantly from one time period to another. In other words, they can result in material outperformance and underperformance relative to traditional market indices. These five common equity factors have partly motivated the development of different alternative equity beta strategies.

A 2011 survey[185] found that the alternative equity beta strategies outperform their market cap-weighted counterparts largely owing to exposure to value and size factors. Almost entirely spanned by market, value and size factors, any one of these strategies can be mimicked by combinations of the others. In other words, the outperformance of the alternative beta passive strategies can be explained by exposure to the common factors. Therefore, by understanding to which factors each strategy is tilted the strategy can be understood and evaluated.

FWI and dividend-weighted indices are essentially value strategies with a value tilt.[186] Minimum variance strategy and non-optimised, ranking-based low volatility strategies are designed to achieve low market beta and low volatility and hence have a negative tilt to the volatility factor. Equally-weighted indices aim to reduce stock specific and concentration risks relative to cap-weighted indices. They tilt the portfolio to the small cap factor.

---

[182] Fama, Eugene and French, Kenneth, 'The Cross-Section of Expected Stock Returns', *Journal of Finance* (1992); and Fama, 'Common Risk Factors in the returns on stocks and bonds'.

[183] Jagadeesh, Narasimhan and Titman, Sheridan, 'Returns to Buying Winners and Selling Losers: Implications for Stock Market Efficiency', *Journal of Finance* 48 (1993); and Carhart, Mark, 'On Persistence in Mutual Fund Performance', *Journal of Finance* 52 (1997).

[184] Haugen, Robert and Baker, Nardin, 'The Efficient Market Inefficiency of Capitalization-Weighted Stock Portfolios', *Journal of Portfolio Management* (1991); Clarke, Roger, Harindra de Silva and Thorley, Steven, 'Minimum-Variance Portfolios in the U.S. Equity Market', *Journal of Portfolio Management* 33 (2006); and Clarke, Roger, de Silva, Harindra and Thorley, Steven, 'Know Your VMS Exposure', *Journal of Portfolio Management* 36 (2010).

[185] Chow, Tzee-man, Hsu, Jason, Kalesnik, Vitali and Little, Bryce, 'A Survey of Alternative Equity Index Strategies', *Financial Analysts Journal* 67 (2011).

[186] Asness, Clifford, 'The Value of Fundamental Indexing', *Institutional Investors* 40 (2006).

Evaluating alternative beta strategies

Analysing to which risk factors each alternative beta strategy is exposed is the first step in evaluating and understanding the strategy. Another important consideration when evaluating alternative beta strategies is *cost of implementation*. Costs are a key consideration when evaluating passive strategies. Implementation costs are a function of portfolio turnover, liquidity and investment capacity.

Other considerations are *simplicity* and *transparency*. These considerations make the strategy more replicable, make the strategy's outcome more clearly defined and easily interpretable, and make it easier to monitor fees.

Risks

The main risks of alternative beta strategies are market risk exposure (e.g. equity risk of an alternative equity beta index) and active risk relative to cap-weighted indices. Investors must accept periods of underperformance of the strategies. However, since the periods of underperformance of the different strategies do not always coincide with each other, combining different alternative beta strategies may potentially reduce the active risks and reduce the absolute risk of the portfolio due to diversification.

Conclusions

The alternative beta indices can be easily accessed through index trackers or ETFs. Alternative betas are not a separate asset class since they repackage existing asset classes such as equities or bonds. However, they do offer investments that have different risk and return characteristics compared to other investments. Their performance does not rely on manager skill since they follow rule-based construction methodologies.

Summary

- The motivation to develop alternative or smart beta strategies is the criticism of market capitalisation-weighted indices. The shortcomings of market cap-weighted indices include concentration in specific sectors, exposure to market sentiment and bubbles, and a tendency to follow trends (buy high and sell low).

- Alternative beta indices follow rules to reweight their constituents.

- The main strategies include diversification strategies (e.g. equal-weighted indices), low volatility strategies and fundamental weighting strategies (FWI).

- The way to evaluate the different alternative beta strategies is to understand to which risk factors they are exposed. The five equity risk factors are market, small cap, value, momentum and volatility.

- An equally weighted index is exposed to the small cap factor. An FWI is exposed to the value factor. The minimum variance strategy has negative exposure to the volatility factor.

- The risk of alternative beta strategies is periods of underperformance relative to cap-weighted indices and relative risk to the cap-weighted indices.

CHAPTER 15: VOLATILITY

Volatility is most commonly measured by standard deviation. Standard deviation has a few shortcomings, such as assuming a normal distribution of returns, while many investments are not truly normally distributed; assuming no serial correlation in returns, while a number of investments do exhibit significant autocorrelation; and equally weighting downside and upside returns relative to the mean, while investors dislike only downside returns. Nevertheless, volatility is a common measure of risk.

Volatility tends to jump when equity markets fall. Figure 4.20 shows the cumulative performance of US equities since January 1940 and the rolling 36-month ex post realised annualised volatility. As can be seen, when equity markets fall, volatility increases. However, during the build-up of the high-tech bubble of the 1990s volatility was high even when equity markets were rising, demonstrating that volatility can increase not only during falling equity markets.

Figure 4.20: Rolling 36-month volatility of US equities and cumulative performance US equities, January 1940 to December 2013

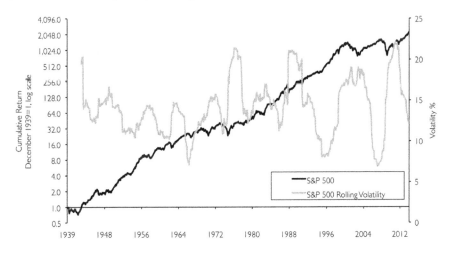

Source: Bloomberg, S&P 500 Index.

Volatility has been traded via the options market since the introduction of exchange traded options in the 1970s.[187] In the early 1990s, volatility swaps appeared and large players, such as hedge funds, started trading volatility through these instruments. It was not until the mid-2000s that the average investor had access to volatility derivatives, namely options and futures on the VIX (Volatility Index). In recent years, with the introduction of ETNs based on VIX derivatives, portfolio hedging using volatility has gained momentum.

The Volatility Index (VIX)

The VIX is the Volatility Index calculated and published by the Chicago Board Options Exchange (CBOE). Its goal is to determine the short-term expected volatility of the market as implied by option prices. It is calculated from the implied volatilities of actively traded options on the S&P 500 Index. The VIX is widely regarded as a proxy for market uncertainty and is appropriately nicknamed the *fear index*.

The VIX has different risk and return characteristics when compared to other assets, and this, in part, explains why volatility is considered to be an asset class of its own. Most importantly, the VIX is not only negatively correlated with the market, but it also bolsters an asymmetric return distribution; it increases, both in magnitude and speed, to a greater extent during crises and slowly decreases when normality returns. This unique property makes it an extremely attractive hedge for the equity investor.

Figure 4.21 shows the prices of the VIX and the S&P 500 Index. As can be seen the VIX tends to increase sharply when equities fall and then drops back again when equities stabilise or move upward.

Figure 4.22 shows the average performance of the S&P 500 Index and the VIX ranked by deciles of the performance of the S&P 500 Index. The chart vividly demonstrates that the VIX performs strongly when equities fall and falls when equities rise.

---

[187] Volatility is one of the factors affecting option prices, according to the Black-Scholes model. Black, 'The Pricing of Options and Corporate Liabilities'.

Figure 4.21: The VIX and US equities, January 1990 to December 2013

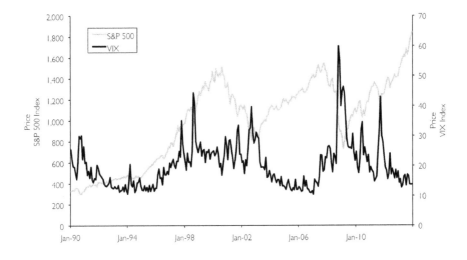

Source: Bloomberg, VIX, S&P 500 Index.

Figure 4.22: The VIX and US equities performance ranked by S&P 500 index deciles, January 1992 to December 2013

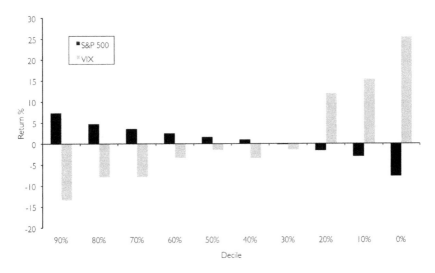

Source: Bloomberg, VIX, S&P 500 Index.

Table 4.6 shows the performance analytics of the VIX and other asset classes. Table 4.7 shows the cross correlation of major asset classes and the VIX. The VIX is highly negatively correlated with the S&P 500 Index and with most other risk asset classes. The VIX is positively correlated with Treasury bonds, which also have protective characteristics (i.e. they tend to increase in value when equities fall).

The performance of the VIX is negative. This means that investments linked to the VIX are expected to lose money over time. Any strategy of investing in investments linked to the VIX must be dynamic, such as maintaining exposure to the VIX and taking profits when the VIX jumps, since it can be expected to fall afterwards.

Table 4.6: VIX return and risk characteristics, February 1990 to December 2013

	VIX	US equities	US Treasuries	US Credit	Global High Yield	Commodities
Start month	Feb-90	Feb-90	Feb-90	Feb-90	Feb-90	Feb-90
Performance (% pa)	-2.5	9.8	6.3	7.4	9.2	4.0
Volatility (%)	63.5	14.8	4.5	5.3	10.0	21.2
Skewness	1.17	-0.62	-0.16	-0.93	-1.33	-0.15
Kurtosis	2.64	1.22	1.01	4.88	7.91	2.11
Sharpe ratio	-0.09	0.45	0.70	0.79	0.60	0.04
Max drawdown (%)	-78.8	-50.9	-5.3	-16.1	-33.6	-67.6

Source: Bloomberg, VIX, S&P 500 Index, Citigroup United States WGBI TR Index, BofA Merrill Lynch U.S. Corporate Master TR Index, Barclays Capital Global High Yield TR Index, S&P GSCI Index.

Table 4.7: Correlation matrix, February 1990 to December 2013

Correlation matrix	VIX	US equities	US Treasuries	US Credit	Global High Yield	Commodities
VIX	1.00	-0.65	0.11	-0.25	-0.50	-0.17
US equities	-0.65	1.00	-0.09	0.29	0.64	0.18
US Treasuries	0.11	-0.09	1.00	0.69	-0.06	-0.09
US Credit	-0.25	0.29	0.69	1.00	0.50	0.12
Global High Yield	-0.50	0.64	-0.06	0.50	1.00	0.18
Commodities	-0.17	0.18	-0.09	0.12	0.18	1.00

Source: Bloomberg, VIX, S&P 500 Index, Citigroup United States WGBI TR Index, BofA Merrill Lynch U.S. Corporate Master TR Index, Barclays Capital Global High Yield TR Index, S&P GSCI Index.

Access

The VIX is not directly tradable and up until 2004 when the first derivatives on the VIX were introduced it was not possible to take advantage of its valuable properties. In 2004, the first futures contracts on the VIX started trading and in 2006 the first options on the VIX began trading. There are also ETNs based on these instruments that have been available since 2009. These instruments allowed retail investors to gain exposure to volatility through VIX derivatives.

It is important to note that these derivatives do not replicate the exact return profile of the VIX, and as such the hedging benefits offered by the VIX are not directly obtainable.

The problem with futures and ETNs based on the VIX is the *roll yield*. When the spot VIX value is low, the expectation is that in the future VIX will mean-revert to its long-term average. As such, the price of the back month VIX futures will be higher than their front-month counterparts. When this occurs, the term structure of VIX futures is upward sloping (contango). Conversely, when the VIX index is high, the market expects VIX to decrease and revert back to its historical mean, so the back month futures trade at lower levels than the front month contracts. This leads to a downward sloping term structure (backwardation).

The VIX exhibits *asymmetric mean reverting* behaviour; it tends to jump abruptly from low levels and slowly revert down to its mean following a sudden rise. When the term structure curve is in contango, the VIX is low and the markets are calm. Anyone buying VIX futures is actually buying insurance against a big jump in the VIX and is poised to profit if the VIX suddenly increases.

Conversely, anyone shorting the futures will essentially be selling "crash insurance" and as such will collect the insurance premium when the markets are calm and will lose when the VIX jumps. A similar situation arises once the VIX has reached elevated levels. Since the VIX is expected to revert downwards to its mean, investors who short the futures when the term structure curve is in backwardation should pay a premium to investors who are willing to take the other side of the trade and go long the futures.

The roll yield of VIX futures is an important issue that prevents futures or ETNs based on these futures from being effective buy-and-hold portfolio hedges. The price that investors must pay to maintain a long position in VIX futures, known as the roll yield, is usually high enough to offset gains made during market crises.

One obvious solution to this problem would be to hedge the portfolio only when the risk of the markets is high. However, due to the way the VIX is calculated, it is usually too late to buy the VIX once a major market move has occurred. You cannot buy fire insurance after your house starts to burn.

Fortunately, different strategies and new instruments based on VIX futures and options may allow investors to effectively hedge their portfolios constantly while minimising or even eliminating the roll yield problem.

Trading strategies

One obvious strategy is trading VIX futures themselves. Investors can take a position based on their views on future changes in the VIX. The investor may buy and hold a constant maturity futures portfolio of VIX futures.

Considering this as a standalone strategy, the mean reversion characteristics of the VIX make this an unattractive approach since if the investment always comes back to its original value, there is no gain in holding the product for the long term. Such a strategy would only make sense for someone who is trying to time the market. If an investor buys these instruments just before a market crash and exits the position after the crash, then they can profit from such a trade. However, market timing is very hard if not impossible to accomplish.

In addition, the roll yield makes this buy-and-hold strategy even more unattractive. A buy-and-hold strategy in constant maturity futures on the VIX does not make sense. As a standalone investment, these instruments should only be used for short-term trading when investors expect sudden increases or decreases in volatility.

Another way to invest in VIX futures is to go long the futures in addition to a traditional portfolio. Here investors aim to take advantage of the negative correlation between the VIX and traditional asset classes. Table 4.8 shows two portfolios that include exposure to the VIX. The first portfolio is made of 90% US equities and 10% VIX. The second portfolio is made of 80% US equities, 10% US Treasuries and 10% VIX. Including an exposure to the VIX in portfolios tends to improve their risk-adjusted performance and reduce their downside risk.

Table 4.8: VIX and portfolios including exposure to VIX return and risk characteristics, February 1990 to December 2013

	VIX	US equities	US Treasuries	90% equities, 10% VIX	80% equities, 10% Treasuries, 10% VIX
Start month	Feb-90	Feb-90	Feb-90	Feb-90	Feb-90
Performance (% pa)	-2.5	9.8	6.3	11.0	10.7
Volatility (%)	63.5	14.8	4.5	10.4	9.1
Skewness	1.17	-0.62	-0.16	-0.26	-0.16
Kurtosis	2.64	1.22	1.01	0.91	0.89
Sharpe ratio	-0.09	0.45	0.70	0.75	0.82
Max drawdown (%)	-78.8	-50.9	-5.3	-37.8	-32.3

Source: Bloomberg, VIX, S&P 500 Index, Citigroup United States WGBI TR Index.

Despite roll yield costs, the addition of the VIX to a traditional portfolio can be extremely beneficial. However, instead of a simple long-only strategy, if investors were to devise a more sophisticated investment approach that utilises the characteristics of VIX futures they could benefit from the general exposure to the VIX while minimising some of the costs associated with such a position.

One such strategy is dynamically changing the exposure to short and mid-term futures based on the shape of the term-structure curve. Since short-term futures suffer the most from the roll yield when the curve is in contango, it is preferable to buy mid-term futures. Although these futures are less sensitive to moves in the spot index – and therefore provide less protection against extreme market events – the amount of protection that investors will receive per unit of roll yield that they pay far exceeds that of short-term futures.

Another strategy employed by some ETNs is shorting a small amount of short-term futures when the curve is in contango to cover the roll yield of a larger amount of long mid-term futures. This strategy aims to achieve free or low cost protection against big upwards moves in volatility.

The nimble and astute investor can construct far more sophisticated trading strategies that can profit in a wide variety of market regimes. As long as the investor understands the dynamics of the futures curve it is possible to devise strategies that provide exposure to volatility while minimising costs associated with such positions. The addition of such strategies to a portfolio is the 'secret sauce' so many seem to be missing in this volatile environment.

Fat-tail hedging

Since the 2008 global financial crisis fat-tail hedging has been on investors' minds. The idea behind it is reducing some of the downside without giving up a lot of the upside of investing in risk assets. While the VIX is helpful in understanding the concept behind volatility and the merits of using it for fat-tail hedging, it is not necessarily the best fat-tail hedging strategy.

The factors to consider when evaluating hedging strategies are defining the hedged event (e.g. a 10% drop in equities, a three standard deviation event), the assets to hedge (e.g. equities), structure of the hedge (e.g. *delta-one* futures – without optionality, options, variance swaps or a combination of different instruments), the horizon of the hedge (i.e. over what time period to hedge) and the costs. Most fat-tail hedging strategies involve a position on volatility.

The costs of the hedge are one of the most important considerations. Cost impacts performance in both up and down markets. Hedging is akin to buying an insurance policy – paying the premium is given but the insurable event occurring is unlikely. Most times the hedge will expire profitless and the hedger is left with the costs. Costs include:

- Timing – the current level of volatility.

- Liquidity – thinner liquidity usually means higher costs.

- Horizon – long maturity is more costly.

- Trade size – trade size can either increase or decrease transaction costs (a larger notional value allows for economies of scale).

- Funded versus unfunded instruments – committing cash, collateral requirements, margins.

- Structure complexity – complexity may mean more instruments to trade (i.e. higher transaction costs) but can also mean using combinations to reduce costs.

Options are a relatively straightforward method for hedging. Simply buying equity index put options is costly, since investors need to pay the premium and on most occasions equity markets rise so the options expire worthless. Hence, normally a structure combining options is used. One hedging strategy is a *put spread collar*. In a collar the hedger buys a put option and finances some of the premium by selling an out-of-the-money call or a put option with the same expiration date and number of contracts as the long put. The downside is limited, but so is the upside.

An example of a put spread collar can explain the concept. Suppose an investor holds 100 stocks that are trading at a price of £53 in March. The investor decides to hedge the downside risk through a collar by writing (selling) an April 55 covered call for £1 while simultaneously purchasing an April 50 put for £2. The cost of the 100 stocks is £5,300, the cost of the put is £200 and the proceeds from selling the call is £100. The cost of the hedge is £100 instead of £200 by buying only a put option. The total investment for the stocks and options is £5,400.

On expiration date at the end of April, the stock price has appreciated to £58. The call option is in the money (stock price £58 > call strike £55) so the call option is exercised and the stocks are sold for £5,500, leaving a profit of £100 (£5,500 – £5,400). The potential upside profit of £500 (£5,800 – £5,300) was reduced to £100. This is one cost of hedging – limiting the upside potential.

Alternatively, on expiration date at the end of April, the stock price has dropped to £48. The investor has on paper lost £500 on the 100 stocks. However, because of the put the stocks are sold for £5,000 instead of £4,800. The net loss is limited to £200 (£4,800 – £5,000). Together with the cost of the collar, the total loss is £300, instead of the potential loss of £500 without the collar. If the trading conditions for the options were better, and the cost of the collar was lower, or perhaps even a zero cost, the situation of the investor could have been better.

Another instrument for hedging is a *variance swap*. It is an OTC derivative making it possible to speculate or hedge risks associated with the magnitude of movement (volatility) of the underlying assets, which can be exchange rate, interest rate or equity index. The two parties to the swap enter the contract on a forward realised variance. At maturity the swap pays the difference between the realised variance and the pre-agreed variance strike. Variance swaps provide pure exposure to the underlying price volatility without the complication of the delta risk of an option.

Conclusions

Volatility is normally associated with risk. However, volatility as an asset class can be the opposite of risk as it can add downside risk protection to portfolios and reduce the risk of the portfolio. However, risk reduction costs money, as does insurance. Investors need to be dynamic and smart when using volatility within their portfolios.

Summary

- Volatility, as measured by standard deviation, tends to jump when equity markets fall.

- Securities linked to the VIX, which measures the implied volatility of the S&P 500 Index from traded options, allow investors to access volatility.

- The VIX has distinctive risk and return characteristics when compared to other asset classes. Most importantly, the VIX is not only negatively correlated with the equity market, but it also bolsters an asymmetric return distribution; it increases, both in magnitude and speed, to a greater extent during crises and slowly decreases when normality returns. This unique property makes it an extremely attractive hedge for the equity investor.

- The primary instruments used to trade the VIX are futures and options.

- The roll yield of VIX futures is an important issue that prevents futures or ETNs based on these futures from being effective buy-and-hold portfolio hedges.

- Considering holding long futures on the VIX as a standalone strategy, the mean reversion characteristics of the VIX Index makes this an unattractive strategy since if the investment always comes back to its mean value there is no value in holding the product for the long term. In addition, the roll yield makes this buy-and-hold strategy even more unattractive.

- When futures on the VIX are combined with other asset classes the benefits of volatility come into play.

- One strategy is to dynamically change the exposure to short and mid-term futures based on the shape of the term-structure curve.

- Fat-tail hedging strategies should consider the definition of the hedged event, hedged assets, structure, horizon and costs.

- Two popular hedging strategies are put spread collar and variance swaps.

CHAPTER 16: ART

Art is the expression or application of human creative skill or imagination, typically in a visual form such as painting or sculpture. The prices of paintings, usually by well-known artists, have increased over time, suggesting that investing in art has the opportunity to generate high returns.

Sotheby's and Christie's, the two art businesses and auction houses, have sold paintings and other jewellery and collectibles for millions. For example, *The Card Players* by Paul Cézanne was sold in 2011 for over $250 million, making it the most expensive painting ever sold. In 1990 Vincent Van Gogh's *Portrait of Dr. Gachet* was sold by Christie's for $82.5 million, making it the most expensive painting ever sold in a public auction until the record was broken in 2012 when Edvard Munch's *The Scream* was sold for $119.9 million. Without a doubt, art investing brings opportunities for handsome returns.

Not so long ago fine art was regarded as an asset class reserved for the rich and super rich but the two economic trends of globalisation and research have changed that perception. The long-term trend of increasing wealth globally, alongside the increasing knowledge about art, has resulted in an increasing number of people being interested in art investing.

These trends, fuelled by rising prices of art and volume of sales, coupled with the increasing challenge of obtaining investment returns and the risks of other investments, inflated the discussions on art as an asset class. This backdrop has stimulated the emergence of new collective investment schemes dedicated to art, as well as other art-related financial products, such as applying securitisation techniques to art. Art has seen remarkable developments, making it more accessible to investors.

In addition to art investment services (facilitating investing in art as an asset class), financial institutions offer other art-related services, such as art advisory (offered by private banks to complement traditional asset management services) and art lending (turning art into a working asset that generates income).

The fine art market has been evolving and expanding across countries and customers. It is estimated that the outstanding value of the painting category of fine art is over $3 trillion, with annual sales of well over $50 billion. The main demographic, social and economic indicators pointing toward continued expansion of the fine art market include:

- *Increasing global wealth.* The global increase in prosperity, in particular in emerging markets, is a major factor supporting the art market. When a nation reaches a certain level of wealth, its citizens begin to purchase art. This has been the trend since the industrial revolution in the 19th century. China, whose wealth has been dramatically increasing over the last two decades, is now ranked third in terms of sales of fine art at auctions after the United States and the United Kingdom. As more countries reach higher wealth levels, there will be an increasing number of people interested in art. The increasing global population with an increasing disposable income means that the demand for fine art will increase.

- *Research and technology.* Art markets are becoming more transparent due to economic research, data dissemination and accessibility. Technological developments (e.g. the internet) have been instrumental in the creation of new market opportunities and business models such as online auction houses, online data transfer, artist websites and new communication channels.

- *The quest for investments.* Investors are looking for assets that retain value over the long term. The expected economic uncertainty, the expected lower returns and increasing volatility of other investments, and the diversification benefits of art, mean that the proportion of portfolios given to fine art is likely to increase. An increasing number of investors recognise art as an asset class as they diversify their portfolios across more investments. The demand for real, tangible assets is increasing because many investors have lost considerable amounts in the last two financial crises (the 2000 high-tech bubble burst and 2008 financial crisis) by investing in financial assets. Many investors now turn to investments that they can understand, touch and store *under the mattress.* You can hang a painting in your living room, store a gold bar in your safe or put a diamond on your finger.

- *Limited supply.* The supply of fine art is limited, in particular art by deceased artists, pushing the price of art upwards.

- *Accessibility.* The vast majority of fine artworks are sold for below $10,000, allowing for relatively small investors to participate in the market. The advent of new ways to access art, such as collective investment schemes, makes art more accessible to an increasing number of investors.

- *Globalisation.* The 21st century is characterised by globalisation of cultural activities. Nations, groups and individuals seek to make a mark and reinforce their identities through purchasing art and building museums, increasing the demand for art.

Fine art can be an expensive and lucrative asset. Works of art are *extraordinary economic goods.*[188] They are both durable consumer goods and store of value assets. They are extremely heterogeneous, with values ranging from a few dollars

---

[188] Stein, John, 'The Monetary Appreciation of Paintings', *Journal of Political Economy* 85 (1977).

to millions of dollars. When hung in museums, they are public goods since everyone can enjoy them. They are speculative goods since demand determines future price appreciation and expected future price appreciation determines demand. They are the archetypal collector good.

Art is a tangible real asset, similar to real estate, commodities and infrastructure. Unlike the other real assets, art is not necessary for the functioning of the economy. It is not used in manufacturing, it is not consumed as are commodities and it is not used by businesses and individuals, as are real estate and infrastructure. This makes art different to other asset classes and so its risks and returns are driven by a different set of risk factors.

Valuing art

It is challenging to value art since it is not a typical financial asset that generates cash flows. The periodic cash flows generated using the rental market can be used as a proxy. However, alongside these cash flows art offers implicit rents to ownership that accrue from the aesthetic benefits of possession (*aesthetic dividends*) and from the status derived from ownership and possession. For example, hanging up a painting in your house and displaying it to guests has value. Frey and Eichenberger[189] discuss whether art is more likely to be a consumption good (with traditional collectors prevailing) or an investment good (with financial speculations prevailing).

Valuing art is one of the most critical points. There is no transparent art pricing mechanism that is commonly accepted. There is no efficient market that determines the price of art and there is no standardised art valuation methodology. The fair price of art is usually based on qualitative assessment by expert appraisers using relative valuation. The ways to value art are by analysing the comparative prices of similar artworks, the aspects of the specific work, the supply relative to demand and by individual perception.

The reasons for investing in art

Since the art market is complex, it allows for informed investors to make substantial gains. Investing in art provides a number of potential financial benefits, beyond the aesthetic dividends:

- *Potential high returns.* Knowledgeable investing has a potential for high returns. Art experts can make very high returns trading fine art.

- *Inflation hedge.* Art offers a hedge against inflation as well as against currency devaluation. The price of art should keep up with inflation. Because of its

---

[189] Frey, Bruno, and Eichenberger, Reiner, 'On the Return of Art Investment Return Analysis', *Journal of Cultural Economics* 19 (1995).

limited supply and not being denominated in any particular currency, art should be immune to expansion of the money supply, which can lead to inflation and currency devaluation, and to the monetary and fiscal policies of any particular government.

- *Limited downside risk.* The risk of losing the principal is relatively small if the artwork is purchased wisely.

- *Tax advantages.* Art enjoys favoured tax treatment in some countries (e.g. favourable inheritance tax under appropriate estate planning).

- *Diversification.* Art can reduce risk in a portfolio because of its diversification benefits.

- *Income source.* Lending artwork opens the possibility for earning revenue. Art as an income source depends on the ability and willingness to let the art for income. This means sharing the aesthetic dividends with the public, for example, when letting the art to a museum.

- *Moveable.* Art has no geographical risk and it is easily transferable.

- *Insurable.* Art can be insured against calamity risk.

Risks

The flipside of the potential return on art investing is its risks. Some of the risks of investing in art include:

- *Volatility.* The standard deviation of returns of investment in art is not observable since art lacks a continuous market pricing. However, prices of art can fluctuate.

- *Taste.* The single largest source of risk for art investing is probably taste. That is the risk that a work of art will fall out of fashion and its price will drop.

- *Illiquidity.* Art is one of the most illiquid asset classes. Similar to real estate, art is not traded on any regular exchange and is sold on a deal by deal basis. However, art is a much more specialised market than is real estate, with a lower number of deals. The positive side of illiquidity is that it is also a source of a liquidity premium.

- *Modelling.* Art lacks a published index that enables easy modelling of the asset class for asset allocation purposes.

- *Information dependence.* Art is a heterogeneous product since each artwork is unique. Substantial time and knowledge are necessary to acquire the specialised knowledge to successfully invest in art.

- *Investment horizon.* Materialising returns on art may require a long investment horizon. Investors with a short horizon should avoid art as an investment.

- *Transaction costs.* High transaction costs should be expected, in particular at the high end of the market.

- *Unregulated market.* The art market is unregulated. Risks of forgery and fraud exist. The unsophisticated investor without expertise or without the ability to hire experts should not invest in art.

- *Valuation.* Art does not pay regular dividends or income to investors. Valuing art is challenging since discounted cash flow models are not applicable.

- *Storage risk.* Art needs to be stored in a safe place and insured. While insurance can minimise the risk of financial loss due to theft or damage, it cannot minimise the emotional and cultural damage of losing a unique artwork. If the Mona Lisa is destroyed by fire, the Musée du Louvre will be financially compensated but Leonardo da Vinci is unavailable to paint another Mona Lisa.

Characteristics of the art market

The art market's inefficiency and illiquidity, the need for the highly specialised know-how and expertise and the uncertainty surrounding tax issues make art investing challenging. The art market is certainly an inefficient market. The drivers of the inefficiency are:

- *Differentiation.* The traded art products are differentiated. Art markets are incomplete and often thin in number, with a small number of available works of art for each specific artist.

- *Low transparency.* The transparency of the art market is low as not all transactions are disclosed.

- *Information asymmetry.* There are potentially large differences in expertise between buyers and sellers.

- *Low liquidity.* Buyers and sellers are often distant in terms of space and time and there is not always an available buyer or seller.

- *Transaction costs.* Transaction costs are high (e.g. auction fees, insurance, handling and storage costs).

- *Psychic benefits.* The psychic benefits of owning art are largely absent in the case of owning financial assets.

Additionally, as William Baumol notes,[190] art markets have a much weaker equilibration process (the process by which market prices tend to the equilibrium price) than other securities. This is because:

- Elasticity of supply is equal to zero for works of deceased artists.

---

[190] Baumol, William, 'Unnatural Value: Or Art Investment as Floating Crap Game', *The American Economic Review* 76 (1986).

- Each individual work of art is unique, while the inventory of a particular stock is made up of a large number of homogeneous securities, all perfect substitutes for one another.

- The owner of a work of art has a monopoly on that specific object, while a given stock is held by many individuals who are potentially independent traders on a near perfectly competitive stock market.

- The purchase and sale of a work of art is an infrequent occurrence and may happen only once in a century.

- The acquisition price of a work of art is not generally public information and is often only known to the parties immediately involved.

- The equilibrium price is unknown, so an objective evaluation (such as a present value of future cash flows) is often impossible.

Successful investment in art requires not only extensive know-how about the artistic quality and authenticity of the object to be acquired, but also an understanding of the peculiarities of the art market. Investors need to establish a scenario of future economic and social developments, also including international factors such as exchange rate movements, special cultural factors and market preferences.

Tax uncertainties add to the difficulty of investing in art. In many countries investment in art is one of the major possibilities of escaping or at least reducing the tax burden.

Access

The traditional way to access art was by purchasing pieces. Depending on the specific item, the price can reach millions, making it difficult to diversify, impossible to access for relatively small portfolios and expensive to maintain (e.g. safe storage, insurance).

Over recent years art investment funds have emerged. The funds pool investors, using their purchasing power to buy art. Such pools are professionally managed and offer diversification. The minimum investment for most funds is still relatively high (about $250,000) so they are not yet accessible to all investors. Most of the art investment funds are still new and as the market matures the minimum investment is likely to fall.

Art return and risk characteristics

In the absence of a widely published index representing the returns of the art market, it is difficult to understand its return and risk characteristics. In place of this, a number of studies focus on analysing and predicting price trends, both for individual artists and for schools of artists.

William Baumol[191] concludes that art prices behave randomly. Further, he shows that large gains and losses occur with shorter holding periods, while the returns on longer holding periods are very close to zero (this is indicative of a random process with a mean of zero).

John Stein[192] treats works of art as a combination of consumer durables, yielding a flow of no pecuniary viewing services, and capital assets, yielding a return from financial appreciation. He divides the rate of return into two components: a return from nominal capital appreciation and a residual return from durable services (the return from viewing services, less insurance and maintenance costs, plus an annualised premium to account for any tax advantages, less an annualised premium to account for the illiquidity of this form of investment).

The results show an estimated annual net return from durable services of 1.6% (i.e. to the investor primarily interested in financial gain and valuing the return from viewing pleasure at only about 1.6% per year, paintings are no more or less attractive than other assets, and yield the going rate for their systematic risk). In comparison, the 10.5% average annual appreciation of paintings in the United States between 1946 and 1968 lends credibility to the assumption that collectors regard paintings as capital assets.

William Goetzmann[193] finds a high correlation between his art index and an index of London Stock Exchange shares. He concludes that, while returns of art investment have exceeded inflation for long time periods, and the returns in the second half of the 20th century rivalled those of the stock market, they are no higher than would be justified by the extraordinary risks they represent. Additionally, he finds that the high correlation with both bonds and stock makes investment in art a poor vehicle for the purposes of diversification.

In a 1995 paper,[194] William Goetzmann uses a simulated portfolio method. This yields different results with median annual returns of 8.24% in nominal terms and 2.42% in real terms, and with standard deviations of 8% and 7.47%, respectively. In his sample of less than 100 paintings there are a few dramatic outliers but the dispersion of annualised returns is surprisingly small, suggesting that, at least for holding periods greater than a decade, the risk is modest. Additionally, this risk not only reflects the risk of the art market as a whole, but it includes the idiosyncratic risk of individual works, to the extent that it is not

[191] Ibid.

[192] Stein, 'The Monetary Appreciation of Paintings'.

[193] Goetzmann, William, 'Accounting for Taste: An Analysis of Art Returns Over Three Centuries', *American Economic Review* 83 (1993).

[194] Goetzmann, William and Spiegel, Matthew, 'Private value components, and the winner's curse in an art index', *European Economic Review* 39 (1995).

diversified away completely through inclusion in a portfolio. These returns clearly beat inflation, bond investment and the capital appreciation of common stocks.

Wieand, Donaldson and Quintero[195] examine the impact of US and Japanese equity markets on art prices, and find a significant relationship. In particular, their analysis shows that art price returns exhibited first-order autocorrelation and heteroskedasticity (i.e. the volatility of returns is not constant). Further, they find that art and stock prices shared a single, common, long-term trend. They believe, though, that investors cannot make above-normal profits through buying and selling art, because the art market is less liquid than stock markets.

Candela and Scorcu[196] study the Italian art market over the 1983 to 1994 period and conclude that art had lower returns than financial assets, explaining this with the aesthetic dividend and ownership effect. They also conclude that in the long run art prices are unrelated to financial asset prices, but they find a positive correlation with real estate prices. Additionally, they show that the correlations are not contemporaneous, due to the different level of liquidity of the assets; equities being the most liquid and real estate being the least liquid.

James Pesando[197] finds a negative correlation of prints with Treasury bills and identifies a minimum variance portfolio with an allocation of 94% to T-bills and 6% to modern prints with a real return of 2.19% and a standard deviation of 3.19%.

The long-term trend in inflation-adjusted art prices follows the general economic trend, with art prices rising above average compared to the prices of other goods. However, most segments of the art market react quickly to a worsening of the economic environment and this is especially true for objects in the lower price category.

Results such as those of Goetzmann have led researchers to conclude that art is an attractive investment only for nearly risk-neutral investors, and then only if the expected returns of art exceed those expected of equities. The high correlation displayed in Goetzmann's studies between art, equity and bond markets clearly makes art a poor investment for the purposes of diversification.

According to an alternative interpretation of these findings, art returns come from two different sources: financial return (change in monetary value) and psychic return (consumption benefit of owning art). Therefore, if there is at least some consumption benefit, the financial rate of return of art objects should in equilibrium be lower than that of other markets with similar risks.

---

[195] Wieand, Kenneth, Donaldson, Jeff and Quintero, Socorro, 'Are Real Assets Priced Internationally? Evidence from the Art Market', *Multinational Published Journal* (1998).

[196] Candela, Guido and Scorcu, Antonello, 'A Price Index for Art Market Auctions – An Application to the Italian Market of Modern and Contemporary Oil Paintings', *Journal of Cultural Economics* 21 (1997).

[197] Pesando, James, 'Art as an Investment: The Market for Modern Prints', *The American Economic Review* 83 (1993).

A study from 2000[198] claims that the long-term trend in inflation adjusted for art prices follows the general economic trend. That is, art prices rise above average compared to the prices of other goods. However, some segments in the art market react quickly to a worsening of the economic environment. An economic downturn leads to a fall in demand and potentially an increase in supply due to forced selling. However, this rarely applies to top range, very expensive artworks since they are typically owned by wealthy individuals who are less affected by economic downturns as they maintain their purchasing power. Therefore, the price sensitivity of different sectors in the art market depends on the distribution of income and level of wealth.

According to a 2009[199] academic study the real return in dollar terms of paintings, drawings and prints was about 4% per annum from 1951 to 2007. The real return from 2002 to 2007 was 11.6% per annum, which suggests that 2002 to 2007 was an art boom period.

Other art

The universe of art can be expanded to include a wide range of physical valuable items such as fine wine, rare coins, stamps, antiques, collectible trading cards, vintage comic books, classic cars and so on. Rare comic books, for example, can surpass a price of $1 million per book. A 1938 edition of Action Comics No. 1, the first comic book featuring Superman, was sold for $2.16 million in 2011. This was the most money ever paid for a single comic book. The original price of the book was just 10 cents.

Wine

Investors can buy and sell many different items that are expected to increase in value over time. Fine wine is such an item. The two main methods for investing in wine are purchasing and reselling individual bottles or cases or investing in a collective investment wine fund.

Directly buying bottles or cases of wine requires expertise. The risk of fraud is material in the unregulated wine market and purchasing should be done only from reliable merchants and with the necessary knowledge. From the tens of thousands of wine producers worldwide it is estimated that only about 250 produce fine wine that should be considered for investment (Investment-Grade Wine or IGW).[200] It is estimated that about 90% of the world's IGW is produced in the Bordeaux region of France.

---

[198] Wilke, Wolfgang, *Investing in Art – the Art of Investing* (Dresdner Bank, 2000).

[199] Renneboog, Luc and Spaenjers, Christophe, 'Buying Beauty: On Prices and Returns in the Art Market', Tilburg University (2009).

[200] Sokolin, David and Bruce, Alexandra, *Investing in Liquid Assets: Uncorking Profits in Today's Global Wine Market* (Simon & Schuster, 2008).

Outstanding vintages from the best vineyards may sell for thousands of dollars per bottle, though the broader term *fine wine* covers bottles typically retailing at about £15 to £30. Investment wines are considered *Veblen goods*; meaning that the demand for them increases instead of decreases as their price rises. The most common wines purchased for investment include those from Bordeaux and Burgundy, cult wines from Europe and elsewhere, and vintage port.

In 1985 publisher Malcolm Forbes paid $160,000 for a bottle of 1787 Chateau Lafite, which was believed to be from the late President Thomas Jefferson's cellar and has the initials ThJ etched in the glass. However, its authenticity has been the subject of speculation, with experts split on the matter.

In 1989, a Chateau Margaux 1787 bottle, also from Thomas Jefferson's collection, was valued at an astronomical $500,000 by its owner, the New York wine merchant William Sokolin. The high price may have been a publicity stunt, but it was never tested. When Sokolin took the wine with him to a dinner, a waiter knocked the bottle over, breaking it. Insurers paid out $225,000.[201]

Wine even has an organised exchange and an index. The London International Vintners Exchange (Liv-ex)[202] is an exchange for IGW based in London and founded in 1999. Liv-ex provides a marketplace where wine merchants trade wine and it publishes two wine price indices based on these transactions.

Conclusions

Art is an illiquid, inefficient and difficult to model market that requires a high level of expertise. Although access to art has become easier over time, it is still challenging. Most investment portfolios do not have exposure to art.

Art can add value to portfolios since it exposes them to a unique set of risk factors. However, art is still appropriate only for a subset of investors who have the expertise or can hire the expertise to tap this market. For some investors art is not an investment but rather a passion.

Summary

In the past fine art was perceived as an asset class reserved only for the rich.

- Globalisation (greater global wealth) and research (increasing knowledge about art), coupled with more challenging returns and higher risks of other investments, have fuelled developments, making art investing more accessible to more investors. The fine art market has been evolving and expanding across countries and customers, and this trend is expected to continue.

---

[201] *Telegraph*. www.telegraph.co.uk.
[202] www.liv-ex.com.

- Works of art are extraordinary economic goods. They are both durable consumer goods and store of value assets.

- It is challenging to value art since it is not a typical financial asset that generates cash flows.

- Valuing art is one of the most critical points. There is no transparent art pricing mechanism, no efficient market that determines the price of art and no standardised art valuation methodology. The fair price of art is usually based on qualitative assessment by expert appraisers using relative valuation.

- The main financial reasons for investing in art (beyond the aesthetic dividends) include: potential high returns; as a hedge against inflation and currency devaluation; a relatively low risk of losing the principal; favoured tax treatment; diversification benefits; as an income source through lending; it is easily transferable; and it is insurable.

- The main risks of art investing include: volatility; changing taste; illiquidity; modelling; information dependence; investment horizon; transaction costs; unregulated market; valuation; and storage risk.

- The art market's inefficiency and illiquidity, the need for the highly specialised expertise and the uncertainty surrounding tax issues make art investing challenging.

- Art remains difficult to access. Purchasing individual works of art may be expensive and lack diversification. Art investing funds have been emerging and they provide diversification and professional management. However, the minimum required investment is still relatively high, making them inaccessible to small portfolios.

- The universe of art can be expanded to include a wide range of physical valuable items such as fine wine, rare coins, stamps, antiques, collectible trading cards, vintage comic books, classic cars and so on.

CHAPTER 17: INSURANCE-LINKED SECURITIES (ILS)

Insurance-linked securities (ILS) are instruments by which insurance risk is transferred via a capital market contract. The idea underlying ILS is *reinsurance*. In 1842 a fire swept through the streets of Hamburg, burning down almost a quarter of the city. Back then such disasters were common because of the narrow streets of wooden houses. However, the city of Hamburg was prepared for such a disaster.

After the infamous Great Fire of London in 1666 and other similar events in towns around Europe, the citizens of Hamburg clubbed together in 1676 and formed the *Hamburger Feuerkasse* (Hamburg Fire Office), the first officially established, publicly owned fire insurance company in the world. In 1817 fire insurance was made mandatory for all citizens.

When the fire devastated the city in 1842 the Hamburg Fire Office was left holding a massive bill to reconstruct the city. Insurers quickly realised that they did not have the capital to cover such disasters and that they needed to transfer some of the insurance risk to third parties. Reinsurance, insurance for insurers, was born. In 1846 *Cologne Re*, the first reinsurance company in the world, was established.

In 1992 *Hurricane Andrew* struck. At the time it was the most expensive hurricanc in the history of the United States. The scale of this and other disasters forced insurance and reinsurance companies to turn to the capital markets for additional risk capital through securing catastrophe risk by issuing ILS.

The demand for catastrophe insurance was boosted after the 2004 and 2005 hurricane season, most notably the August 2005 *Hurricane Katrina* disaster, which overtook Andrew as the most expensive natural disaster in the history of the United States. The death toll was 1,833 and the estimated property damage was over $80 billion; nearly triple the damage caused by Andrew.

The convergence of the reinsurance and capital markets accelerated in the aftermath of Katrina, when rating agencies increased capital requirements for catastrophe-exposed underwriters, causing an increase in demand for reinsurance capacity and a contraction of its supply. Insurers increasingly turned to the capital markets as a supplement to reinsurance for their risk transfer solutions.

Not only has the ILS market grown exponentially since 2004, but also the type of market participants has changed. While in the 1990s most investors in this area were insurance and reinsurance companies with specialised knowledge and expertise in this sector, today the majority of investors are dedicated funds and hedge funds. Sophisticated investors treat ILS as another asset class and invest in it to generate investment returns. Investors are attracted by high spreads and the opportunity to diversify their portfolio by investing in high-yielding ILS that are uncorrelated with economic risks assumed in the financial markets.

Some of the more common forms of ILS include catastrophe bonds, extreme mortality bonds, industry loss warranty derivatives and catastrophe futures contracts.

To date, ILS has been most commonly used by insurance companies to buy supplemental protection for high-severity, low-probability catastrophe risks from the capital markets via catastrophe bonds. These catastrophe bonds often cover risks that are similar to the high layers of a primary insurer's traditional reinsurance programme.

More recently, there has been a blurring of the insurance and capital market industries with some capital market institutions building or acquiring their own internal insurance underwriting expertise, while some reinsurers are taking the route of full convergence and implementing investment banking business models. Others have opted not to participate in the convergence at all, preferring to adhere to their core models.

Catastrophe bonds

Catastrophe bonds (*cat bonds*) are risk-linked securities that transfer a specified set of risks from a sponsor (e.g. insurance company) to investors through a fully collateralised special purpose vehicle (SPV). The SPV issues floating-rate bonds of which the principal is used to pay losses if specified trigger conditions are met. They are typically used by insurers as an alternative to traditional catastrophe reinsurance.

Cat bonds are usually issued with a predefined maturity and deliver a return linked to the premiums paid on the insurance policies. These policies usually cover *peak risk*, which are uncommon but costly events like natural catastrophes. The main insured catastrophe risks are found in areas with developed insurance and reinsurance markets such as United States (hurricanes, earthquakes and tornados), Europe (winter storms) and Japan (earthquakes and typhoons).

Insurance companies are keen to remove these extreme risks from their balance sheets. There are only a limited number of counterparties who are willing and able to assume these risks, so insurers need to offer attractive risk premiums, making it a potentially attractive asset class for skilled investors.

ILS derivatives

Derivatives are increasingly being used in the ILS market to facilitate the transfer of risk among capital market investors. Industry loss warranties (ILWs) are a type of contract through which one party purchases protection based on the loss to the entire insurance industry arising from a particular event, rather than the buyer's losses. These agreements can be documented in either reinsurance or derivative form.

Catastrophe futures contracts now trade on the New York Mercantile Exchange (NYMEX), the Chicago Mercantile Exchange (CME) and the Chicago Climate Futures Exchange (CCFE). The NYMEX and CCFE contracts settle on industry losses and can be used in a manner similar to ILWs. The CME contracts settle based on storm intensity as measured by the *Carvill Hurricane Index*[203] to calculate a storm's destructive potential.

Derivative transactions may settle based on the performance of an existing catastrophe bond, industry losses (i.e. ILWs), a parametric index such as a wind storm making landfall within a certain distance of a given location, or an earthquake of a minimum magnitude within a predetermined distance of an exposure. These structures can be used by customers who may desire a capital market structure, but who do not have enough risk to transfer to make the issuance of a catastrophe bond cost-effective.

The reasons for investing in ILS

Since the returns of ILS are a premium over LIBOR, they offer protection against interest shifts and inflation, making them a potential substitute for bonds. The return drivers of ILS (collection of insurance premium) are different from those of other investments (equity, credit and maturity risk premiums). This indicates diversification benefits, expansion of the investment opportunity set and tapping of an uncorrelated source of risk and return. Low volatility and low correlation with other asset classes adds diversification benefits in portfolio context.

Risks

The main risks of investing in ILS include the difficulty of achieving proper diversification using ILS because of a narrow market. Scale, experience and expertise are extremely important in this asset class. ILS are relatively illiquid investments.

However, the most notable danger is event risk. ILS basically sell insurance for large disasters. When disaster strikes, like the 2005 Hurricane Katrina, the

---

[203] The Carvill Hurricane Index (CHI) describes the potential for damage from Atlantic hurricanes.

potential for losses is substantial. It should be noted that disasters lead to re-pricing of risk, forcing insurers to increase premiums in order to continue to attract risk capital. Investors who continue holding the ILS after a drawdown may be rewarded afterwards with higher returns. *After a hurricane comes a rainbow.*[204] Nevertheless, the material fat-tail risk of ILS requires proper diversification across issues and segments (unless some of the risk is hedged through short positions).

Global warming may be an emerging risk for ILS investors. It may lead to an increase in the number and severity of tropical storms, generating a higher number of claims. However, it has not yet been proven that global warming will indeed have such effects and the timing of such potential effects is unknown. If it does happen, the premium paid on ILS will increase as well, possibly making it a higher risk, higher return investment.

Cat bonds return and risk characteristics

Currently, there is no broad, publicly available benchmark or index for ILS. There are, however, a number of catastrophe bond indices, such as the Swiss Re Cat Bond Total Return Index. ILS tend to pay a fairly consistent and relatively attractive premium over cash (LIBOR) with no correlation with other asset classes.

Figures 4.23, 4.24 and 4.25 compare the cumulative performance of cat bonds (as measured by the Swiss Re Cat Bond Total Return Index), US Treasuries and US investment grade corporate bonds, as well as their correlations and volatilities.

According to the Swiss Re Index, cat bonds exhibit steady returns, with low volatility and drawdowns of between -3% and -4% when natural disasters occur, such as Hurricane Katrina in August 2005, Hurricane Ike in September 2008 and the Tōhoku earthquake and tsunami in March 2011. These disasters struck heavily insured regions (the United States and Japan). When a disaster strikes a region that is not heavily insured, such as the Sichuan earthquake in China in May 2008, the cat bond index does not experience a negative return.

---

[204] Katy Perry, 'Fireworks'.

Figure 4.23: Cumulative performance of cat bonds, US Treasuries and US corporate bonds, February 2002 to December 2013

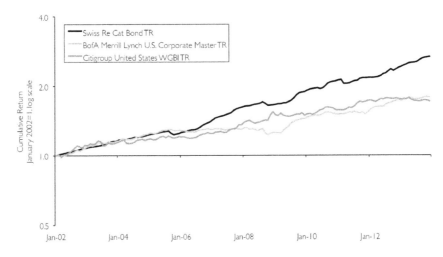

Source: Bloomberg, Swiss Re Cat Bond TR Index, BofA Merrill Lynch U.S. Corporate Master TR Index, Citigroup United States WGBI TR Index.

Figure 4.24: Rolling correlation between cat bonds and US equities and between cat bonds and US Treasuries, February 2005 to December 2013

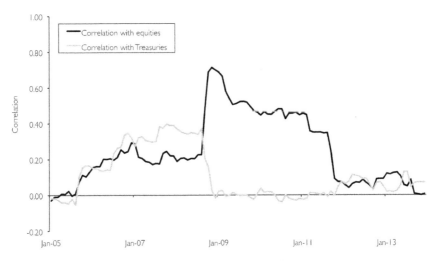

Source: Bloomberg, Swiss Re Cat Bond TR Index, Citigroup United States WGBI TR Index, S&P 500 Index.

Figure 4.25: Rolling volatility of cat bonds, US Treasuries and US corporate bonds, February 2005 to December 2013

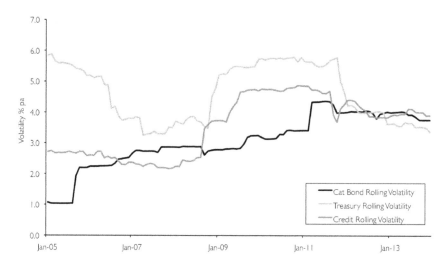

Source: Bloomberg, Swiss Re Cat Bond TR Index, Citigroup United States WGBI TR Index, BofA Merrill Lynch U.S. Corporate Master TR Index.

Table 4.9 shows the performance analytics of cat bonds and other selected asset classes. Table 4.10 is a correlation matrix across the asset classes. Cat bonds delivered higher return with lower volatility compared to other assets over the measurement period. Their Sharpe ratio is impressive and uniquely high. They also offer diversification benefits as their correlations with other assets are low.

Table 4.9: Cat bond return and risk characteristics, February 2002 to December 2013

	Cat Bonds	US equities	US Treasuries	US Credit	US T-Bills
Start month	Feb-02	Feb-02	Feb-02	Feb-02	Feb-02
Performance (% pa)	8.6	6.3	4.6	5.0	1.5
Volatility (%)	3.0	15.2	4.7	3.6	0.5
Skewness	-1.40	-0.75	-0.06	-0.65	0.98
Kurtosis	7.30	1.50	1.55	2.17	-0.43
Sharpe ratio	2.39	0.32	0.65	0.96	-
Max drawdown (%)	-3.9	-50.9	-5.0	-6.8	0.0

Source: Bloomberg, Swiss Re Cat Bond TR Index, BofA Merrill Lynch U.S. Corporate Master TR Index, Citigroup United States WGBI TR Index.

Table 4.10: Cat bond correlation matrix, February 2002 to December 2013

Correlation matrix	Cat bonds	US equities	US Treasuries	US Credit	US T-Bills
Cat bonds	1.00	0.21	0.08	0.24	0.07
US equities	0.21	1.00	-0.34	0.22	-0.02
US Treasuries	0.08	-0.34	1.00	0.31	0.03
US Credit	0.24	0.22	0.31	1.00	-0.17
US T-Bills	0.07	-0.02	0.03	-0.17	1.00

Source: Bloomberg, Swiss Re Cat Bond TR Index, BofA Merrill Lynch U.S. Corporate Master TR Index, Citigroup United States WGBI TR Index.

Life settlements

Life settlements are a relatively new asset class related to life insurance (unlike ILS that are related to general insurance). Life settlement funds acquire interests in life policy investments via life settlements. A *life settlement* is the transfer of the beneficial interest in a life insurance policy from the insured person to a third party (i.e. the fund). The policy owner transfers the policy at a discount to its face value, in return for an immediate cash settlement. The purchaser of the policy is then responsible for premiums payable on the policy and will be entitled to receive the full face value from the insurance company upon maturity (i.e. death of the insured).

Most people acquire life insurance early in their careers as a means of protecting their income and family in the event of the insured person's illness or death. However, over time, changes in people's circumstances often mean that individuals want access to the value locked up in their life insurance policy prior to their death. In the United States people are becoming increasingly aware that their life insurance policy may qualify for a life settlement. These changing circumstances could include the insured having outlived the beneficiaries that the policy was originally intended to protect; premiums may have become unaffordable and unless sold as a life settlement, the insured may have to let the policy lapse; the insured may be financially secure and have no further need for the policy; the insured may wish to make a gift of the monetary value of the policy while still alive; the insured may sell the policy for estate planning purposes; or the insured is considering whether or not to lapse or surrender the policy, for its cash surrender value.

In circumstances where the alternative for the insured is to let the policy lapse and lose a potentially large portion of the premiums that have already been paid on the policy, a life settlement may be an option that is considered.

The returns from life policy investments (through life settlements) are generally not correlated with other investments. Once a policy has been purchased the benefit payable is known; although the timing is unknown and depends on the timing of death of the insured. This means that the performance of the life policies will be based on the characteristics of the pool of the insured lives, and not on the performance of traditional markets, such as the equity and bond markets or on the level of interest rates. Life settlements are exposed to different risk factors compared to other asset classes.

The risk for life settlements is a massive boost to longevity. For example, discovery of a cure for cancer could lengthen the lives of the pool of insurers and delay the cash payment on the life insurance policies.

Conclusions

One of the beauties of the investment management industry is the never-ending innovation and expansion of the investable universe. ILS is yet another relatively new type of investment available for multi-asset investors, exposing a portfolio to a different risk factor or source of return.

Summary

- Insurance-linked securities (ILS) are instruments by which insurance risk is transferred via a capital markets contract.

- Catastrophe bonds (cat bonds) are risk-linked securities that transfer a specified set of risks from a sponsor (e.g. insurance company) to investors. Insurance companies use them to remove the risk of extreme insurable events (e.g. hurricanes, earthquakes) from their balance sheets and pay premiums to investors for assuming the risk.

- ILS derivatives are increasingly being used in the ILS market to facilitate the transfer of risk among capital market investors.

- Since the returns of ILS are a premium over LIBOR, they offer protection against interest shifts and inflation, making them a potential substitute for bonds. Low volatility and low correlation with other asset classes adds diversification benefits in portfolio context.

- The main risks of investing in ILS include event risk, global warming and concentration risk due to a narrow market and illiquidity.

- A life settlement is the sale of an existing life insurance policy to a third party for an immediate cash settlement.

- Life settlement funds invest in a pool of life settlements, delivering a return profile with known cash flow amounts but with unknown timing of cash flows.

- The returns of life settlements are uncorrelated with those of capital market investments (e.g. equities and bonds).

CHAPTER 18: TIMBER

Timber or lumber products are important to our lives in many different ways. Lumber is supplied either rough or finished. Rough lumber is the raw material for making furniture and other items. It is available in many species; usually hardwoods. Pulpwood is used for making wood pulp for paper production. Finished lumber is supplied in standard sizes, mostly for the construction industry; primarily softwood from coniferous species including pine, fir and spruce (collectively known as spruce-pine-fir), cedar and hemlock. Hardwood is used, for example, for high-grade flooring.

An increasing number of investors are discovering timber as an investment. Timber has generally outperformed equities, bonds, real estate and commodities over the long run.

The defining attribute of timber is its steady, long-term biological growth. A tree's wood volume tends to increase by 2% to 8% annually (varying by climate, species and age). Compounding the effect of this biological growth, trees yield price gains when they grow into bigger product classes. For instance, a small tree that is only suitable for paper products may eventually grow into saw timber, where it can fetch dramatically higher prices per ton and be used for products such as plywood or telephone poles. An academic study[205] found that biological growth drives more than 60% of total returns, while timber price changes and land appreciation account for the remainder of the returns of timber investing.

The NCREIF Timberland Index, the standard benchmark for this asset class, has outpaced all the major asset classes, except for small cap equities, over the long term (since the inception of the index in January 1987). After factoring in volatility (as reflected in the Sharpe ratio), timber has exhibited the highest risk-adjusted returns among major asset classes. Timber returns have been particularly high over the past couple of decades.

Timber can also improve a portfolio's risk-adjusted returns by virtue of its fairly low correlation with most asset classes. This low correlation reflects the fact that the primary driver of returns (biological growth) is unaffected by economic cycles. Timber exhibits a moderate correlation to inflation, and research[206]

[205] Caulfield, Jon, 'Timberland Return Drivers and Investing Styles for an Asset that has Come of Age', *Real Estate Finance* 14 (1998).
[206] Washburn, Courtland and Binkley, Clark, 'Do Forest Assets Hedge Inflation?', *Land Economics* (1993).

indicates that timber assets may serve as a good long-term hedge against unanticipated inflation.

Physical risk, such as damage from fire or insects, can inflict significant losses, but not to the extent that many investors fear. Such losses usually erode returns by 0.1% annually for timberland holdings that are well-diversified by geography, age and species. The greatest risks are overpaying for timber assets and the illiquidity of the asset.

Timber has been attracting plenty of capital from large institutions and ultra-high net worth investors. This influx of money is chasing after a limited number of forests. This is particularly the case in the United States. American forest-product conglomerates largely finished divesting millions of acres of forests in the past decade. Thus, investors are increasingly looking overseas for deals. While there are opportunities overseas, they involve political, currency and tax risks. Also, over time institutional ownership of timberland on a global basis will become more prevalent.

Timber is strictly an asset class for long-term investors. Trees generate most of their returns through steady biological growth, and harvesting cycles are typically 15 to 40 years. Also, timber assets are difficult to sell quickly. Some pure-play timber investment vehicles limit the timing or amount of sales by shareholders.

Timber Index

The NCREIF Timberland Index[207] is a quarterly time series composite return measure of the investment performance of a large pool of individual timber properties acquired in the private market for investment purposes only. All properties in the index have been acquired, at least in part, on behalf of tax-exempt institutional investors, the great majority of which being pension funds. As such, all properties are held in a fiduciary environment.

Figure 4.26 compares the cumulative performance of timberland, US equities and commodities. The return of the timberland index is impressive over the measurement period. The return is much higher than that of equities and commodities, with a much lower volatility.

Tables 4.11 and 4.12 show the performance analytics and correlation of timberland. Timberland has outperformed the other asset classes with much lower volatility. With a positive skewness, timberland has not suffered from fat-tail risk during the measurement period. The correlation of timberland with other assets is low, making it a risk diversifier. So timber plays a dual role of a return enhancer and a risk diversifier.

---

[207] www.ncreif.org.

Figure 4.26: Cumulative performance of timberland, US equities and commodities, March 1987 to December 2013. Based on quarterly returns

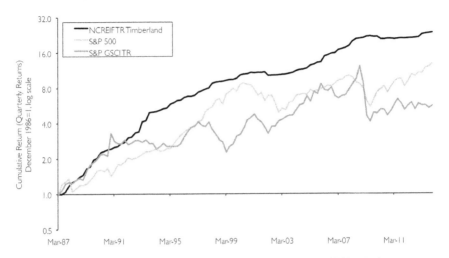

Source: Bloomberg, NCREIF TR Timberland Index, S&P 500 Index, S&P GSCI TR Index.

Table 4.11: Timberland return and risk characteristics, March 1987 to December 2013

	Timberland	US equities	US Treasuries	Commodities
Start month	Mar-87	Mar-87	Mar-87	Mar-87
Performance (% pa)	12.7	10.3	6.4	6.6
Volatility (%)	8.1	16.7	5.2	23.9
Skewness	1.91	-0.68	0.40	0.07
Kurtosis	5.66	0.92	-0.39	5.04

Source: Bloomberg, NCREIF TR Timberland Index, S&P 500 Index, S&P GSCI TR Index.

Table 4.12: Timberland correlation matrix, March 1987 to December 2013

Correlation matrix	Timberland	US equities	US Treasuries	Commodities
Timberland	1.00	0.02	0.16	-0.05
US equities	0.02	1.00	-0.33	0.08
US Treasuries	0.16	-0.33	1.00	-0.27
Commodities	-0.05	0.08	-0.27	1.00

Source: Bloomberg, NCREIF TR Timberland Index, S&P 500 Index, S&P GSCI TR Index.

Conclusions

With financial innovation, investors can expose their portfolios to the biological growth of trees through investing in timber to gain returns and reduce risks through diversification.

Summary

- Investors are increasingly discovering timber as an investment. It has generally outperformed equities, bonds, real estate and commodities over the long run.
- The defining attribute of timber is its steady, long-term biological growth.
- Beyond steady returns, timber offers diversification benefits because of its low correlation with other asset classes.
- The greatest risks of timber investing are overpaying for timber assets and illiquidity (inability to readily sell assets).

Conclusion

The multi-asset investing journey has come to an end. My first book, *Multi-Asset Investing: A modern guide to portfolio management*, covered the basic process and considerations for planning, constructing and managing multi-asset portfolios. *The Investment Assets Handbook* complements the first book by covering each of the available asset classes that can be used as the building blocks of multi-asset portfolios.

One of the fundamental principles of multi-asset investing is that investors need to dynamically combine different sources of risk and return to achieve the highest risk-adjusted returns. Luckily, the ever expanding investment universe, spanning traditional and alternative investments, provides investors with a long list of systematic risks that should be compensated by risk premiums over time.

Equity, maturity and credit are the traditional risk factors. Real estate, commodities and a range of alternative risk factors are available through mainstream alternative investments. Currency, infrastructure, volatility, art, insurance and biological growth of timber are the risk factors of the more uncommon alternatives. In today's financial world investors can expose their portfolios to earthquake risk in Japan, sovereign debt risk in Europe, wine price risk in France, coffee bean price risk in Africa, timberland price risk in Canada and life policy risk in America. The choices are virtually endless. And in a dozen years I have no doubt that I will need to add a number of new chapters to the book, covering new assets and investments.

Beyond the systematic risks on offer, the wide range of asset classes provide ample opportunities for active portfolio management to add value on both the asset allocation level across assets and the security selection models within assets. With a wider array of assets, the breadth of choices expands, allowing active portfolio management to generate higher risk-adjusted returns, subject to the skill to make correct investment decisions. And one of the prerequisites for skill is knowledge.

To manage the ever-expanding universe of choices, investors need to continuously learn to understand how to smartly combine all the investments in a sensible way. As Benjamin Franklin said, "An investment in knowledge pays the best interest."

I hope that the two books have contributed to this learning process and will help you to better manage assets or wealth. I wish you all prosperity and good luck.

Bibliography

Amenc, Noel, Martellini, Lionel, Meyfredi, Jean-Christophe and Ziemann, Volker, 'Performance of Passive Hedge Fund Replication Strategies', EDHEC Risk and Asset Management Research Centre (September 2009).

Ang, Andrew, 'The Four Benchmarks of Sovereign Wealth Funds', Columbia Business School and NBER (September 2010).

Anson, Mark, 'The Beta Continuum: From Classic Beta to Bulk Beta', *The Journal of Portfolio Management* 34 (2008).

Arnott, Robert, Hsu, Jason and Moor, Philip, 'Fundamental Indexation', *Financial Analysts Journal* 61 (2005).

Asness, Clifford, 'The Value of Fundamental Indexing', *Institutional Investor* 40 (2006).

Baca, Sean, Garbe, Brian and Weiss, Richard, 'The Rise of Sector Effects in Major Equity Markets', *Financial Analysts Journal* 56:5 (2000).

Baker, Malcolm, Bradley, Brendan and Wurgler, Jeffrey, 'Benchmarks as Limits to Arbitrage: Understanding the Low Volatility Anomaly', *Financial Analysts Journal* 67 (2011).

Bank of International Settlements, 'The Role of Rating in Structured Finance: Issues and Implications', report submitted by a Working Group established by the Committee on the Global Financial System, **www.bis.org** (January 2005).

Banz, Rolf, 'The Relationship Between Return and Market Value of Common Stocks', *Journal of Financial Economics* 9 (1981).

Barkham, Richard and Geltner, David, 'Price discovery in American and British property markets', *Real Estate Economics* 23 (1995).

Baumol, William, 'Unnatural Value: Or Art Investment as Floating Crap Game', *The American Economic Review* 76 (2004).

Bhansali, Vineer, 'Beyond Risk Parity', *The Journal of Investing* 20 (2011).

Bierman Jr., Harold, 'Convertible Bonds as Investments', *Financial Analysts Journal* 36 (1980).

Black, Fischer, 'The Pricing of Commodity Contracts', *Journal of Financial Economics* 3 (1976).

Black, Fischer and Scholes, Myron, 'The Pricing of Options and Corporate Liabilities', *Journal of Political Economy* 81 (1973).

Booth, David and Fama, Eugene, 'Diversification Returns and Asset Contributions', *Financial Analysts Journal* 48 (1992).

Boyson, Nicole, 'Hedge Fund Performance Persistence: A New Approach', *Financial Analysts Journal* 64 (2008).

Brière, Marie and Signori, Ombretta, 'Do Inflation-Linked Bonds Still Diversify?', *European Financial Management* 15 (2009).

Brown, Gerald and Matysiak, George, 'Using Commercial Property Indices for Measuring Portfolio Performance', *Journal of Property Finance* 6 (1995).

Burrough, Bryan and Helyar, John, *Barbarians at the Gate: The Fall of RJR Nabisco* (Harper & Row, 1989).

Calamos, Nick, *Convertible Arbitrage: Insights and Techniques for Successful Hedging* (John Wiley & Sons, 2003).

Candela, Guido and Scorcu, Antonello, 'A Price Index for Art Market Auctions – An Application to the Italian Market of Modern and Contemporary Oil Paintings', *Journal of Cultural Economics* 21 (1997).

Carhart, Mark, 'On Persistence in Mutual Fund Performance', *Journal of Finance* 52 (1997).

Caulfield, Jon, 'Timberland Return Drivers and Investing Styles for an Asset that has Come of Age', *Real Estate Finance* 14 (1998).

Cavaglia, Stefano, Brightman, Christopher and Akek, Michael, 'The Increasing Importance of Industry Factors', *Financial Analysts Journal* 56 (2000).

Chan, K.C., and Chen, Nai-Fu, 'Structural and Return Characteristics of Small and Large Firms', *Journal of Finance* 46 (1991).

Chow, Tzee-man, Hsu, Jason, Kalesnik, Vitali and Little, Bryce, 'A Survey of Alternative Equity Index Strategies', *Financial Analysts Journal* 67 (2011).

Clarke, Roger, de Silva, Harindra and Thorley, Steven, 'Minimum-Variance Portfolios in the U.S. Equity Market', *Journal of Portfolio Management* 33 (2006).

Clarke, Roger, de Silva, Harindra and Thorley, Steven, 'Know Your VMS Exposure', *Journal of Portfolio Management* 36 (2010).

Cochrane, John, 'The Risk and Return of Venture Capital', *Journal of Financial Economics* 75 (2005).

Collet, David, Lizieri, Colin and Ward, Charles, 'Timing and the Holding Periods of Institutional Real Estate', *Real Estate Economics* 31 (2003).

Cornish, E.A. and Fisher, R.A., 'Moments and Cumulants in the Specification of Distributions', *Review of the International Statistical Institute* (1937).

de Santis, Giorgio and Gerard, Bruno, 'How Big is the Premium for Currency Risk?', *Journal of Financial Economics* 49 (1998).

de Zwart, Garden, Frieser, Brian and van Dijk, Dick, 'Private Equity Recommitment Strategies for Institutional Investors', *Financial Analysts Journal* 68 (2012).

Dumas, Bernard and Solnik, Bruno, 'The World Price of Foreign Exchange Risk', *Journal of Finance* 50 (1995).

Dimson, Elroy, Marsh, Paul and Staunton, Mike, 'Fear of falling', *Credit Suisse Global Investment Returns Yearbook 2011.*

Dimson, Elroy, Marsh, Paul and Staunton, Mike, 'The growth puzzle', *Credit Suisse Global Investment Returns Yearbook 2014.*

Eichholtz, Piet, 'Does International Diversification Work Better for Real Estate than for Stocks and Bonds?', *Financial Analysts Journal* 52 (1996).

Eichholtz, Piet, Hoesli, Martin, MacGregor, Bryan and Nanthakumaran, Nanda, 'Real Estate Portfolio Diversification by Property Type and Region', *Journal of Property Finance* 6 (1995).

Erb, Claude and Campbell, Harvey, 'The Tactical and Strategic Value of Commodity Futures', *Financial Analysts Journal* 62 (2006).

Fama, Eugene, 'Stock Returns, Real Activities, Inflation and Money', *American Economic Review* 71 (1981).

Fama, Eugene and French, Kenneth, 'The Cross-Section of Expected Stock Returns', *Journal of Finance* (1992).

Fama, Eugene and French, Kenneth, 'Common risk factors in the returns on stocks and bonds', *Journal of Financial Economics* 33 (1993).

Fernholz, Robert, Garvy, Robert and Hannon, John, 'Diversity-Weighted Indexing', *Journal of Portfolio Management* 24 (1998).

Fisher, Jeffery, Gatzlaff, Dean, Geltner, David and Haurin, Donald, 'Controlling for the Impact of Variable Liquidity in Commercial Real Estate Price Indices', *Real Estate Economics* 31 (2003).

Forbes, Shawn, Hatem, John and Paul, Chris, 'Yield-to-Maturity and the Reinvestment of Coupon Payments', *Journal of Economics and Finance Education* 7 (2008).

Francis, Jack and Ibbotson, Roger, 'Contrasting Real Estate with Comparable Investments, 1978 to 2008', *The Journal of Portfolio Management* (2009).

Frey, Bruno, and Eichenberger, Reiner, 'On the Return of Art Investment Return Analysis', *Journal of Cultural Economics* 19 (1995).

Fund, William and Hsieh, David, 'Hedge-Fund Benchmarks: Information Content and Biases', *Financial Analysts Journal* (2002).

Fung, William and Hsieh, David, 'Hedge Fund Benchmarks: A Risk Based Approach', *Financial Analysts Journal* 60 (2004).

Geltner, David, 'Smoothing in Appraisal-Based Returns', *Journal of Real Estate Finance and Economics* 4 (1991).

Geltner, David, 'Estimating Market Values from Appraised Values without Assuming an Efficient Market', *Journal of Real Estate Research* 8 (1993).

Geltner, David, Miller, Norman, Clayton, Jim and Eichholtz, Piet, *Commercial Real Estate Analysis and Investments*, 2nd ed. (South-Western Educational Publishing, 2007).

Goetzmann, William, 'Accounting for Taste: An Analysis of Art Returns Over Three Centuries', *American Economic Review* 83 (1993).

Goetzmann, William and Spiegel, Matthew, 'Private value components, and the winner's curse in an art index', *European Economic Review* 39 (1995).

Gordon, Myron, 'Dividends, Earnings and Stock Prices', *Review of Economics and Statistics* (The MIT Press, 1959).

Gorton, Gary and Rouwenhorst, Geert, 'Facts and Fantasies about Commodity Futures', *Financial Analysts Journal* 62 (2006).

Graham, Benjamin, *The Intelligent Investor* (1949).

Graham, Benjamin and Dodd, David, *Security Analysis* (1934).

Greer, Robert, 'What is an Asset Class Anyway?', *The Journal of Portfolio Management* (1997).

Greer, Robert, 'Commodity Indexes for Real Return and Efficient Diversification', *The Handbook of Inflation Hedging Investments* (McGraw-Hill, 2005).

Hasanhodzic, Jasmina and Lo, Andrew, 'Can Hedge-Fund Returns be Replicated?: The Linear Case', *Journal of Investment Management* 5 (2007).

Haugen, Robert and Baker, Nardin, 'The Efficient Market Inefficiency of Capitalization-Weighted Stock Portfolios', *Journal of Portfolio Management* (1991).

Hicks, John, *Value and Capital* (Oxford University Press, 1939).

Hoesli, Martin, Lizieri, Colin and MacGregor, Bryan, 'The Spatial Dimensions of the Investment Performance of UK Commercial Property', *Urban Studies* 34 (1997).

Hoesli, Martin and Serrano, Camilo, 'Securitized Real Estate and its Link with Financial Asset and Real Estate: An International Analysis', *Journal of Real Estate Literature* 15 (2007).

Hoesli, Martin and Oikarinen, Elias, 'Are Reits Real Estate? Evidence from Sector Level Data', ERES Conference 2011.

Huang, Jing-Zhi, and Huang, Ming, 'How Much of Corporate-Treasury Yield Spread Is Due to Credit Risk?: A New Calibration Approach', 14th Annual Conference on Financial Economics and Accounting (FEA), Texas Finance Festival (2003).

Hunter, Delroy and Simon, David, 'Are TIPS the "Real" Deal? A Conditional Assessment of Their Role in a Nominal Portfolio', *Journal of Banking & Finance* 29 (2005).

Ibbotson, Roger, Chen, Peng and Zhu, Kevix, 'The ABCs of Hedge Funds: Alpha, Betas and Costs', *Financial Analysts Journal* 67 (2011).

Ingersoll, Jonathan, 'An Examination of Corporate Call Policies on Corporate Securities', *Journal of Finance* (1977).

Jagadeesh, Narasimhan, and Titman, Sheridan, 'Returns to Buying Winners and Selling Losers: Implications for Stock Market Efficiency', *Journal of Finance* 48 (1993).

Kaldor, Nicholas, 'Speculation and Economic Stability', *Review of Economic Studies* 7 (1939).

Kaplan, Steven and Schoar, Antoinette, 'Private Equity Performance: Returns, Persistence, and Capital Flows', *The Journal of Finance* 60 (2005).

Keynes, John Maynard, *A Treatise on Money, Volume II* (Macmillan & Co, 1930).

Keynes, John Maynard, *The General Theory of Employment, Interest and Money* (Palgrave MacMillan, 1936).

Lerner, Josh, Schoar, Antoinette and Wong, Wan, 'Smart Institutions, Foolish Choices? The Limited Partner Performance Puzzle', *The Journal of Finance* 62 (2007).

Lustig, Hanno and Verdelhan, Adrien, 'The Cross-section of Foreign Currency Risk Premia and Consumption Growth Risk', *American Economic Review* 97 (2007).

Lustig, Yoram, *Multi-Asset Investing: A practical guide to modern portfolio management* (Harriman House, 2013).

Maginn, John, Tuttle, Donald, McLeavey, Dennis and Pinto, Jerlad, *Managing Investment Portfolios, A Dynamic Process*, 3rd ed. (John Wiley & Sons, 2007).

Maillard, Sébastien, Roncalli, Thierry and Teïltche, Jérôme, 'The Properties of

Equally Weighted Risk Contribution Portfolios', *Journal of Portfolio Management* 36 (2010).

Malkiel, Burton, *A Random Walk Down Wall Street* (1973).

Marx, Karl and Engels, Frederick, 'A Contribution to the Critique of Political Economy', *The Collected Works of Karl Marx and Frederick Engels* 29 (1975).

McKinsey Global Institute, 'Global Capital Markets: Entering a New Era', Annual Report (2009).

Mei, Jianping and Lee, Ahyee, 'Is There a Real Estate Factor Premium?', *Journal of Real Estate Finance and Economics* 9 (1994).

Merton, Robert, 'An International Capital Asset Pricing Model', *Econometrica* 4 (1973).

MSCI/Barra, 'Emerging Markets: A 20-year Perspective'.

Naranjo, Andy and Ling, David, 'Economic Risk Factors and Commercial Real Estate Returns', *The Journal of Real Estate Finance and Economics* 14 (1997).

Newell, Graeme and Webb, James, 'Assessing Risk for International Real Estate Investments', *Journal of Real Estate Research* 11 (1996).

Pagliari, Joseph, Scherer, Kevin and Monopoli, Richard, 'Public Versus Private Real Estate Equities: A More Refined, Long-Term Comparison', *Real Estate Economics* 33 (2005).

Persando, James, 'Art as an Investment: The Market for Modern Prints', *The American Economic Review* 83 (1993).

Phalippou, Ludovic and Gottschalg, Oliver, 'The Performance of Private Equity Funds', *Review of Financial Studies* 22 (2009).

Porter, Michael, 'The Five Competitive Forces that Shape Strategy', *Harvard Business Review* (2008).

Pradhuman, Satya Dev, *Small-Cap Dynamics: Insights, Analysis and Models* (Bloomberg Press, 2000).

Quan, Daniel and Titman, Sheridan, 'Commercial Real Estate Prices and Stock Market Returns: An International Analysis', *Financial Analysts Journal* 53 (1997).

Quan, Daniel and Titman, Sheridan, 'Do Real Estate Prices and Stock Prices Move Together? An International Analysis', *Real Estate Economics* 27 (1999).

Rauch, Christian, Umber, Marc and Furth, Sven, 'Private Equity Shareholder Activism', SSRN working paper (2012).

Renneboog, Luc and Spaenjers, Christophe, 'Buying Beauty: On Prices and Returns in the Art Market', Tilburg University (2009).

Roll, Richard, 'A Critique of the Asset Pricing Theory's Tests', *Journal of Financial Economics* 4 (1977).

Roll, Richard, 'Industrial Structure and the Comparative Behavior of International Stock Market Indices', *Journal of Finance* 47 (1992).

Rose, Peter, *Money and Capital Markets* (McGraw-Hill/Irwin, 1999).

Rosen, Lawrence, *The McGraw-Hill Handbook of Interest, Yields, and Returns* (McGraw-Hill, 1995).

Schneeweis, Thomas, Kazemi, Hossein and Spurgin, Richard, 'Momentum in Asset Returns: Are Commodity Returns a Special Case?', *The Journal of Alternative Investments* 10 (2008).

Schneewies, Thomas, 'Dealing with Myths of Managed Futures', *The Journal of Alternative Investments* (1998).

Sharpe, William, 'Imputing Expected Security Returns from Portfolio Composition', *Journal of Financial and Quantitative Analysis* (1974).

Sharpe, William, 'The Arithmetic of Active Management', *The Financial Analysts Journal* 47 (1991).

Siegel, Laurence, 'Alternatives and Liquidity: Will Spending and Capital Calls Eat Your "Modern" Portfolio?', *The Journal of Portfolio Management* 35 (2008).

Sokolin, David and Bruce, Alexandra, *Investing in Liquid Assets: Uncorking Profits in Today's Global Wine Market* (Simon & Schuster, 2008).

Stein, John, 'The Monetary Appreciation of Paintings', *Journal of Political Economy* 85 (1977).

Swensen, David, *Pioneering Portfolio Management: An Unconventional Approach to Institutional Investment* (Free Press, 2000).

Swinkels, Laurens, 'Emerging Market Inflation-Linked Bonds', *Financial Analysts Journal* 68 (2012).

Tobin, James, 'A General Equilibrium Approach to Monetary Theory', *Journal of Money Credit and Banking* 1 (1969).

Washburn, Courtland and Binkley, Clark, 'Do Forest Assets Hedge Inflation?', *Land Economics* (1993).

Wieand, Kenneth, Donaldson, Jeff and Quintero, Socorro, 'Are Real Assets Priced Internationally? Evidence from the Art Market', *Multinational Published Journal* (1998).

Wilke, Wolfgang, *Investing in Art – the Art of Investing* (Dresdner Bank, 2000).

Young, Michael, Lee, Stephen and Devaney, Steven, 'Non-normal Real Estate Return Distributions by Property Type in the UK', *Journal of Property Research* 23 (2006).

Index

MULTI-ASSET INVESTING

A PRACTICAL GUIDE TO MODERN PORTFOLIO MANAGEMENT

By Yoram Lustig

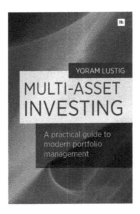

A multi-asset investment management approach provides diversification benefits, enhances risk-adjusted returns and enables a portfolio to be tailored to a wide range of investing objectives, whether these are generating returns or income, or matching liabilities.

This book is divided into four parts that follow the four stages of the multi-asset investment management process:

1. Establishing objectives: Defining the return objectives, risk objectives and investment constraints of a portfolio.

2. Setting an investment strategy: Setting a plan to achieve investment objectives by thinking about long-term strategic asset allocation, combining asset classes and optimisation to derive the most efficient asset allocation.

3. Implementing a solution: Turning the investment strategy into a portfolio using short-term tactical asset allocation, investment selection and risk management. This section includes examples of investment strategies.

4. Reviewing: Evaluating the performance of a portfolio by examining results, risk, portfolio positioning and the economic environment.

By dividing the multi-asset investment process into these well-defined stages, Yoram Lustig guides the reader through the various decisions that have to be made and actions that have to be taken. He builds carefully from defining investment objectives, formulating an investment strategy and the steps of selecting investments, leading to constructing and managing multi-asset portfolios.

'Multi-asset Investing' is an essential handbook for the modern approach to investment portfolio management.